SCIENCE
for Life

SCIENCE for Life

KEITH BISHOP
Kingsfield School, Bristol.

DAVE MADDOCKS
School of Computing, New College, Durham.

BILL SCOTT
Department of Education, University of Bath.

COLLINS EDUCATIONAL

London

© K. Bishop, D. Maddocks and W. Scott 1984

ISBN 0 00 327787-9 (non-net)
ISBN 0 00 197322-3 (net)

First published 1984 by Collins Educational, London.
Reprinted 1985.

Designed, typeset and illustrated by
Parkway Group, London and Abingdon.

Printed in Great Britain by
Hollen Street Press Ltd.

1 2 3 4 5 6 7 8 9 10

British Library Cataloguing in Publication Data

Bishop, Keith
    Science for Life.
    1. Science
    I. Title   II. Maddocks, Dave
    III. Scott, Bill, 19__ _
    500   Q161.2

PREFACE

Science for Life has been written for use by students in science classes in the last two years of compulsory schooling. *Science for Life* consists of this book and photocopy master sets of basic exercises, and practical and other activities. This book contains many hundreds of diagrams, drawings and photographs which are fully integrated into the text. *Science for Life* can be used in the teaching of established science courses up to 16+ or could form the core element of a new course. Its contents cover those nine areas of science and technology which are important aspects of life today: *Earth the Planet*; *Resources*; *The Human Machine*; *Food*; *Health*; *Materials*; *Energy*; *Machines*; *Communications*. These are areas which are central to the human experience of the late twentieth century and *Science for Life* presents information and the ideas, questions and concerns about which young people entering the adult world ought to be aware. The scientific and other ideas dealt with in *Science for Life* are not dealt with in isolation from each other nor as abstractions. Each is firmly rooted in the real world and the attempt has been made to integrate ideas, one with another, throughout the book with human beings as the integrating focus.

The material is arranged as double page layouts, with each one covering one particular area of study. Necessarily, there has to be a sequence of layouts, but this is not prescriptive and there are many different ways of using the material. Each double page layout in this book is complemented by exercises and activities which consolidate and extend the material. These complementary materials are cross-referenced for ease of use.

The thinking behind the production of *Science for Life* mirrors the work currently being done in science curriculum development at 16+ and reflects the anxieties about the inadequacies of the current curriculum. Although designed for integrated courses, *Science for Life* contains material which will be of value to students taking single subject courses in that it will extend their studies and show their relevance to the real world.

Keith Bishop, Dave Maddocks and Bill Scott

CONTENTS

Life on earth — see also notes on plants, Rainbow pp 186–189

Water see also Rainbow pp 194–197

PLANET EARTH

CHAPTER 1

▌ STARS

The *Milky Way* is only one of billions of galaxies that together make up our universe.

It is a faint band of light that can be seen stretching across the night sky, especially when the moon is absent. If it is viewed with a pair of binoculars, millions of faint stars can be seen.

The Milky Way is a galaxy, made up of billions of stars, of which the Sun is but one. If we could step outside our own galaxy and look at it we would see that the Sun sits at the outer edge of a disc that is over 100 000 light years across. A *light year* is the distance that light can travel in a year, at the speed of 300 000 kilometres per second.

The stars in the Milky Way galaxy form a spiral shape. In the centre there is a dense nucleus of old stars.

Side view of the Milky Way

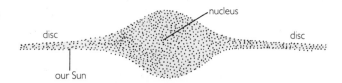

Plan view of the Milky Way

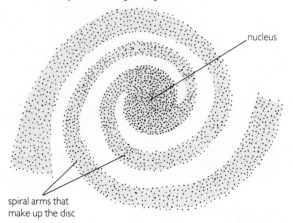

The Sun

The Sun is a 'middle-aged' star. It is about 4600 million years old and is expected to exist for about another 5000 million years.

The Sun is an immense ball of luminous gas that is about 1 400 000 km in diameter, about 1 million times larger than the Earth. It is made largely of hydrogen and helium. At the centre, or core, of the Sun, atoms of hydrogen are crushed together to make atoms of helium. This process is called *nuclear fusion*. The temperature of

the core of the Sun where this reaction takes place is approximately 15 million °C. Each second, over 600 million tonnes of hydrogen is converted to helium. The outer layers of the Sun are heated by the core. The temperature of the Sun's surface is about 6000 °C. Dark patches are frequently seen on the surface of the Sun. These are *sunspots* and they appear dark because they are cooler than the rest of the surface, having a temperature of about 4500 °C. Large amounts of hot gas frequently leave the Sun's surface in the form of jets or *prominences*.

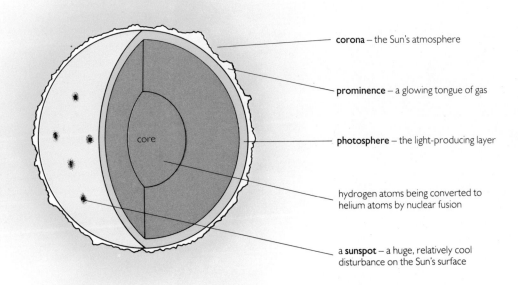

- **corona** – the Sun's atmosphere
- **prominence** – a glowing tongue of gas
- **photosphere** – the light-producing layer
- hydrogen atoms being converted to helium atoms by nuclear fusion
- a **sunspot** – a huge, relatively cool disturbance on the Sun's surface

The Sun is of great importance because it provides our only source of light and heat. Without it there would be no life on our planet. The Sun determines the Earth's climate and weather.

The birth, life, and death of stars

Nebulae are giant clouds of dust and gas (mainly hydrogen) out of which stars may form. There are many nebulae in the Milky Way. A large one can be seen in the constellation Orion, in which stars are being formed today.

The gas cloud in the nebula can break up into smaller parts. These contract because of the inward pull of their own gravity. As they shrink they become smaller and denser causing their internal pressure and temperature to increase. Eventually a nuclear reaction begins and a star is formed. Stars do not usually come into being alone, but in huge clusters which eventually drift apart.

The newly formed star contracts until the production of energy from the nuclear fusion reactions prevents any further shrinking. The star begins to shine. The star is now known as a *main sequence star*. Our Sun is at this stage. If the star is inside a nebula it illuminates the dust cloud making it visible.

Eventually the hydrogen supply at the core runs out because it has been converted to helium. The star then expands and becomes very red. It can expand up to a size about 100 times that of the Sun. At this stage the star is called a *red giant*. This is a relatively short stage in the life of the star, and when it can no longer produce any more nuclear energy it starts to collapse in on itself.

As a result of this collapse the core of the red giant becomes a very small dense object called a *white dwarf*. This would be about the size of the planet Earth, but much denser. An eggcup-full of the material from a white dwarf would have a mass of 20 or 30 tonnes.

Gradually the light of a white dwarf will fade away as all nuclear reactions cease. It will eventually become a dark non-luminous body called a *dark body*.

Not all stars follow this pattern. Some massive stars pass through their life cycle quickly becoming *red supergiants* that eventually explode spectacularly to become *supernovae*. Such an explosion was seen by Chinese astronomers in the year 1054. Occasionally part of the core survives this explosion and will collapse to form a very dense object called a *neutron star*. A thimbleful of the material from a neutron star would have a mass of over a billion tonnes. Some of these neutron stars rotate quickly and give off radio pulses. These stars are called *pulsars*. If the core left after a supernova explosion is large, it may collapse past the neutron star stage and become a *black hole*. These objects are thought to be so dense that their gravity will not even allow light to escape. In effect they become invisible and suck in material from the surrounding space.

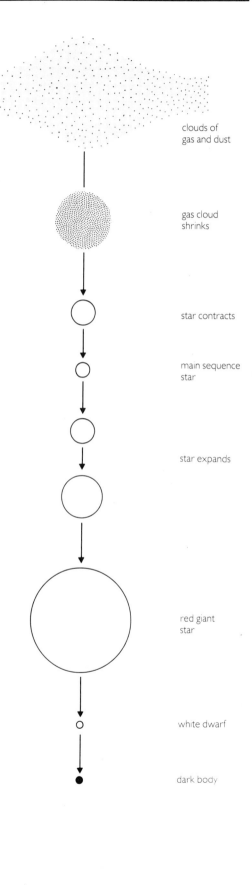

clouds of gas and dust

gas cloud shrinks

star contracts

main sequence star

star expands

red giant star

white dwarf

dark body

Sun

Earth

Mars

This planet can be recognised in the night sky by its slightly red appearance. Because it has a very thin atmosphere we know much more about its surface than that of Venus. Its surface has been mapped by space probes in the Mariner and Viking series, but these have shown there is probably no life there. The atmosphere is mainly carbon dioxide and it has two large polar caps made up of frozen carbon dioxide and ice.

The asteroids

There are thousands of these small bodies orbiting mainly between Mars and Jupiter. The largest is less than 1000 km in diameter.

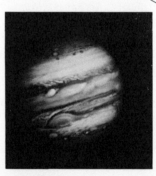

Jupiter

This planet is bigger than all the other eight planets put together, yet is still over 1000 times smaller than the Sun. It is the first of the four giant gas planets (sometimes called gas giants) and is probably made up of a small rocky core surrounded by a large atmosphere of hydrogen and helium. Voyagers 1 and 2 have sent back many details of the planet, showing it has a very small ring system around it. Jupiter has at least 15 satellites, 4 of them larger than our Moon.

Venus

Because this planet reflects about 75% of the light it receives from the Sun, it is a very bright object in the morning and evening. It is sometimes called the 'Evening Star' although it is a planet. It comes closer to the Earth than any other planet, and has been visited by several Mariner, Venera and Pioneer space probes. The rocky surface is hidden below a dense layer of cloud some 70 km thick. The cloud is a thick layer of carbon dioxide. This keeps the heat in and makes the rocky surface very hot.

Mercury

This is the closest planet to the Sun and, therefore, difficult to observe. It is a rocky planet that has a very high surface temperature. In 1974 the space probe Mariner 10 showed that Mercury has a surface covered in craters like the Moon.

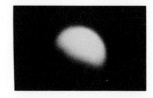

Body	Mean distance from the Sun (millions km)	Diameter (times the diameter of Earth)	Mean surface temperature (°C)
Sun	–	110	6000
Mercury	58	0·4	450
Venus	108	1	500
Earth	150	1	20
Mars	228	0·5	−40
Jupiter	778	11	−150
Saturn	1427	9·4	−160
Uranus	2870	4	−220
Neptune	4497	3·9	−230
Pluto	5900	0·5	−230

The diameters of the planets and their distances from the Sun are drawn to scale.

Saturn

Saturn is instantly recognisable by its large rings. The atmosphere and internal composition of Saturn is very similar to that of Jupiter. The rings are not solid but are made up of millions of separate pieces, some as large as office blocks. These are probably ice crystals, each orbiting the planet like a miniature moon. Their origin is still a matter of doubt even though Voyagers 1 and 2 have observed the planet recently.

Uranus

A gas giant similar to Saturn and Jupiter. Little is known about this planet except that it is very cold and has a small ring system.

Pluto

This is probably an earth-like planet with a rocky body covered with ice. Because it is so far from the Sun it is very hard to study and many of its details are still a mystery. Its orbit sometimes takes it inside that of Neptune.

Neptune

Another gas giant similar to Uranus, and about the same size. Little is known about it.

3 THE ORIGINS OF THE SOLAR SYSTEM

The Sun, its nine planets with their satellites and the many thousands of asteroids that together make up the *Solar System*, were probably all formed at the same time, about 4600 million years ago. Most astronomers agree that the Solar System condensed from the dust and gas that is found all through space. Exactly how this could have happened is difficult to understand.

One theory is that stars start to be formed when a gas cloud starts to break up into smaller parts. A small part of the cloud collapses under the effect of its own *gravity*. As it shrinks, the cloud gets denser and the temperature at the centre rises. When it is hot enough, nuclear reactions start and part of the gas cloud becomes a star. A large amount of gas and dust will be left over. In some cases this will collapse to form a companion star and the two stars together are called a *binary star*.

The Solar System has also been made from the left over gas and dust circling the new star we call the Sun. Specks of dust in this cloud began building up into larger more solid lumps simply by colliding then attracting each other by gravity. This building up process took many millions of years until all the planets were formed. The gas from the cloud formed the early atmosphere of the planets.

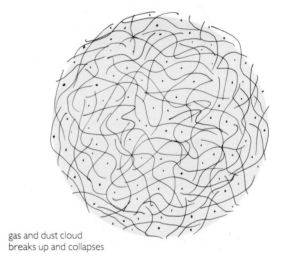

gas and dust cloud
breaks up and collapses

The inner planets

Close to the newly formed Sun it was very hot and most of the gas evaporated leaving only metallic dust grains. These solid grains came together to form the small inner planets: *Mercury, Venus, Earth* and *Mars*. These rocky planets with iron cores are very similar. The new atmospheres of Venus, Earth and Mars were formed when gases produced at the centre of the planet were released through volcanoes.

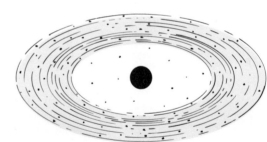
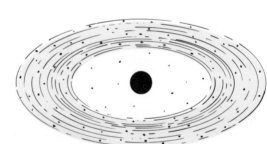

Sun formed surrounded
by dust ring

The outer planets

Away from the new Sun it was very cold, with temperatures near absolute zero ($-273°C$). The gas did not evaporate and crystals of methane, ammonia and water started to clump together, along with the gases helium and hydrogen. As these came together they formed the *gas giants*: the planets *Jupiter, Saturn, Uranus* and *Neptune*. These are all massive planets made up of a small rocky core surrounded by a huge ball of gas.

The planet *Pluto* is the furthest planet from the Sun. It is thought to be a very small rocky planet – possibly a satellite of Neptune, which escaped to move in its own orbit.

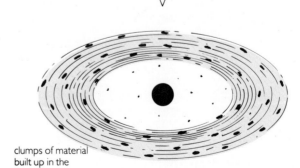

clumps of material
built up in the
dust ring

Movements of the planets

Planetary bodies attract each other with a force that depends on their mass and their distance apart. This force is called gravity. Since the Sun is the largest body in the Solar System, it is found at the centre and all the planets are attracted to it. Each planet is also moving at a great speed. The combination of this forward motion and the force of attraction towards the Sun means that the planets orbit the Sun along an elliptical path, a kind of flattened circle. All the planets revolve around the Sun in the same direction and with the exception of Pluto they lie in much the same plane.

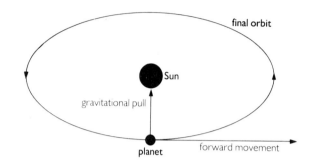

The orbits of the planets

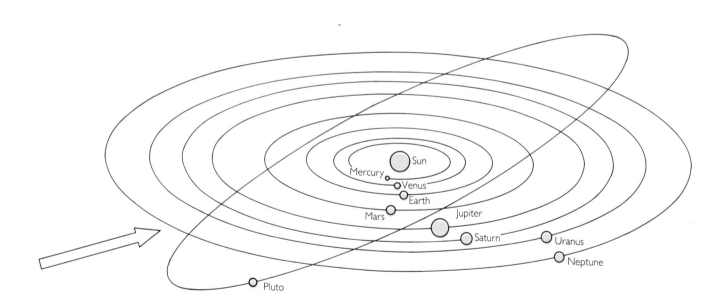

4 ROTATIONS

The Earth

All objects in the universe move and rotate. The Solar System revolves around the Galaxy. The Earth moves around the Sun and also rotates on its north–south axis. It takes almost 24 hours for the Earth to complete one revolution about this axis. The side that faces the Sun has daylight; the side that faces away from the Sun has night because it receives no light.

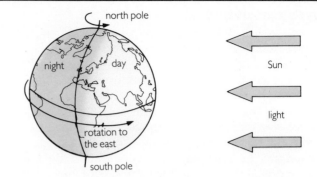

The year

While the Earth spins it also orbits the Sun at 30 km/second (67 000 mph). It takes just over 365 days to complete one orbit around the Sun. The Earth's axis is tilted so we do not get the same amount of sunlight over the whole of the Earth. This means that the climate changes throughout the year.

For some months of the year one half of the Earth is tilted towards the Sun, and this half has its summer. Six months later the Earth has orbited to the other side of the Sun. The other side of the Earth is now tilted towards the Sun and has its summer while the part tilted away from the Sun has its winter. Spring and autumn occur in between summer and winter as the Earth turns.

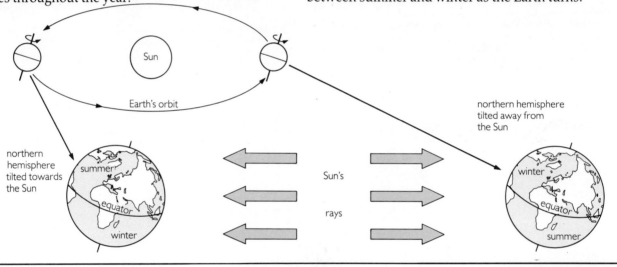

The Moon

The Moon revolves around the Earth once every 28 days. It also rotates once on its axis every 28 days, so the same side of the Moon faces us all the time, and we cannot see the far side from the Earth.

The Moon does not produce its own light. Moonlight is reflected sunlight.

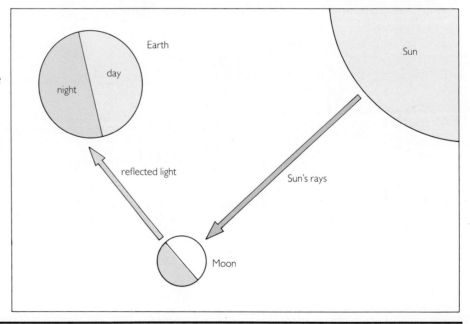

The phases of the Moon

The Moon does not always look the same. Sometimes it cannot be seen, sometimes it looks like a crescent and sometimes like a disc. This is because only the part of the Moon that faces the Sun is illuminated. When the Earth is between the Sun and the Moon, the full face of reflected light can be seen. This is called the *Full Moon.* When the Moon is between the Sun and the Earth it cannot be seen. It is called the *New Moon.* The phase of the Moon depends on the area of reflected light that the observer on the Earth can see.

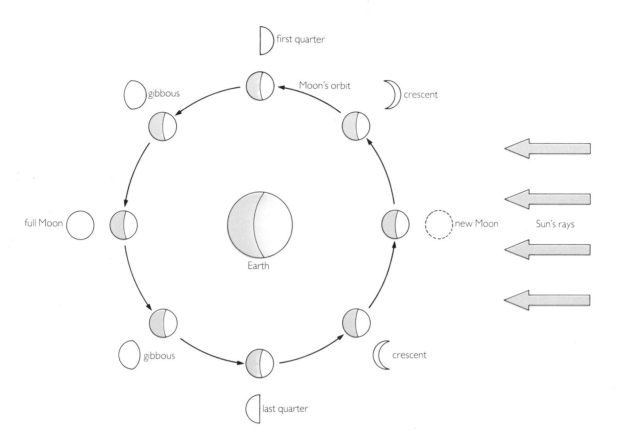

Tides

The Moon's main effect on the Earth is to produce tides because of its gravitational pull. On the side of the Earth nearer the Moon, water is pulled towards the Moon producing a high tide. On the far side of the Earth another high tide occurs at the same time. These high tides occur roughly every 12 hours because of the rotation of the Earth.

The Sun affects the Earth's tides too, but to a lesser extent than the Moon because it is much further away. When the Sun and the Moon are in line, their gravitational effects combine to give very high tides called *spring tides.* When the Sun and Moon are at right angles their pulls partly cancel out, producing weaker tides called *neap tides.* There are usually two spring tides and two neap tides every month.

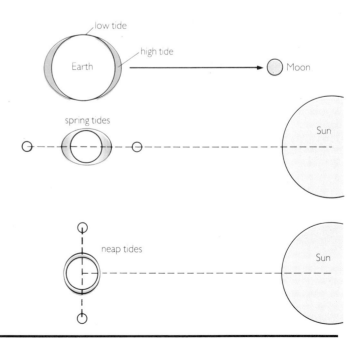

5 THE STRUCTURE OF THE EARTH

The structure of the Earth can be investigated by studying shock waves produced naturally during earthquakes, or by man-made explosions. These shock waves are called *seismic waves*.

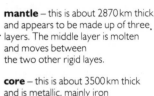

mantle – this is about 2870 km thick and appears to be made up of three layers. The middle layer is molten and moves between the two other rigid layes.

core – this is about 3500 km thick and is metallic, mainly iron and nickel. The inner core is solid while the outer core is liquid.

crust – a relatively thin layer that varies in thickness from about 7 km under the sea to about 40 km under the continents; the top metre forms the soil which is crucial to life on this planet.

The diameter of the Earth around the equator is about 12 800 km.

The continents are part of large *plates* of rock which move slowly on the molten layer of the mantle. About 300 million years ago these continents were grouped together, forming the super-continent called Pangaea. Since then the plates have been moving apart in different directions at different speeds.

When the plates move away from each other, the space between is filled by new molten rock moving up from the mantle. This cools and forms a volcanic crust. This happens at the mid-ocean ridges and produces new ocean crust which spreads out.

Where two plates meet, two things can happen. One of the plates, usually the thinner ocean plate, is forced under the other and eventually melts. The collision of these plates results in volcanoes and new mountains, as in the Andes and Rocky mountains of America.

Sometimes the two plates will collide and crumple forming large mountains such as the Himalayas in Asia. If two plates are sliding past each other rather than colliding, the friction generated will cause earthquakes. This happens in California. Most of the volcanoes and earthquake zones of the world are found in areas where two plates are in contact, or where new crust is being formed.

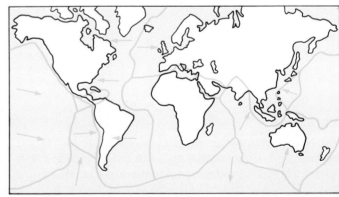

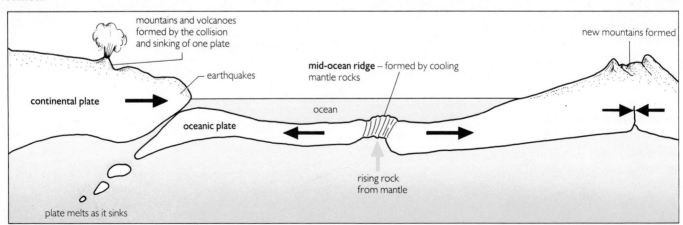

mountains and volcanoes formed by the collision and sinking of one plate

new mountains formed

earthquakes

mid-ocean ridge – formed by cooling mantle rocks

continental plate

ocean

oceanic plate

rising rock from mantle

plate melts as it sinks

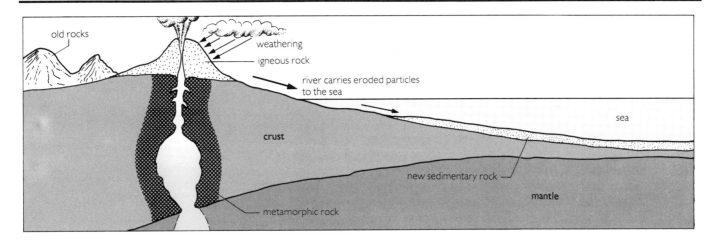

Structure of the crust

There are three main types of rock found in the Earth's crust.

Igneous rocks   These make up over 90% of the crust. Igneous rocks are formed when molten rock (*magma*) cools and solidifies. The molten rock moves up from the mantle and sometimes reaches the surface. This usually happens where plates are either colliding or moving away from each other. The hot molten rock forces its way out through cracks in the crust and forms volcanoes. Igneous rocks are often very rich in minerals. Examples of igneous rocks are granite and basalt.

Sedimentary rocks   Materials such as gravel, sand and mud are produced by the action of frost, wind and rain on the Earth's rocks. These erosion products are transported away by the wind or rivers and are laid down in layers, usually where the river meets the sea. As this layer of sediments gets thicker the lowest layer becomes compressed and hardens into a sedimentary rock. This can also happen to the remains of dead animals and plants. Most of the Earth's crust is covered by a thin layer of sedimentary rock. Examples of sedimentary rocks are limestone and sandstone.

Metamorphic rocks   Sedimentary and igneous rocks can be changed by great heat and pressure into a different form called metamorphic rock. The heat and pressure causing this change can come from hot magma rising into the heart of a volcano, or from the changes that happen when two plates meet. Examples of metamorphic rocks are marble and slate.

The rock cycle

Sedimentary rocks are formed from the broken-down remains of other rocks. Metamorphic rocks are made when sedimentary and igneous rocks are changed by heat and pressure. Over long periods of time the rocky materials of the Earth undergo repeated changes from one type of rock to another. This is called the *rock cycle*.

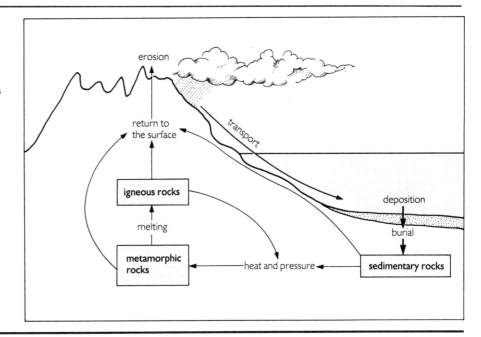

6 LIFE ON EARTH

Earth is the only planet known to have life on it. It is also the only planet in the Solar System to have large quantities of liquid water and oxygen in its atmosphere. This was not always the case. About 3000 million years ago it is thought that the atmosphere was made up of the gases methane, ammonia, hydrogen and water vapour. It was very hot and there were many volcanoes and many violent electrical storms. The thin atmosphere allowed large amounts of ultraviolet (u.v.) radiation from the Sun to reach the Earth's surface. It is thought that under these conditions simple organic molecules were formed from the atmospheric gases and these were brought down to the surface by the heavy rains. Here they collected in seas and lakes to form what has been called the *primeval soup*.

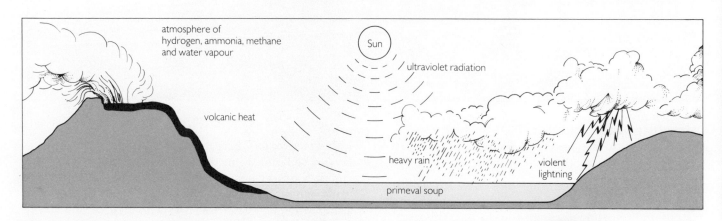

The primeval soup was made up of the organic molecules dissolved in water. It is thought that some of these molecules combined to form the basic building blocks of life – *amino acids* and *nucleic acids*. These combined at random until millions of years later they had become simple forms of life that were capable of reproducing themselves by dividing and growing.

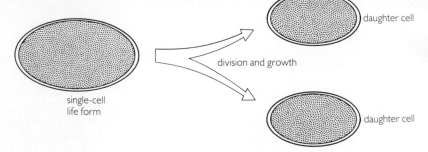

Some of these simple forms of life obtained their energy by using the organic molecules of the soup as a source of food. These were the ancestors of the animals.

Other simple forms of life were able to use the energy of the Sun to make their own food. These were the ancestors of the planets. This process of making food is called *photosynthesis*.

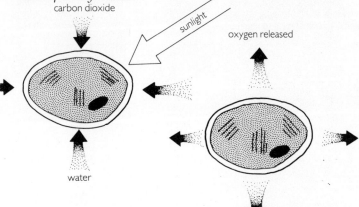

Photosynthesis is a chemical reaction that uses the Sun's light energy to convert carbon dioxide and water into sugar. This sugar is used to provide energy for the living cell. A by-product of photosynthesis is oxygen which is usually released into the atmosphere. The oxygen produced by these simple forms of life gradually changed the methane-rich atmosphere into the oxygen-rich atmosphere we know today.

Evolution

The first recognisable animals were found on the Earth about 600 million years ago. They were extremely simple animals that relied on simple plants as their main food source.

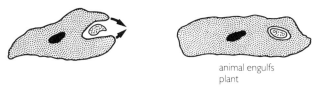

animal engulfs plant

Animals had, by that time, become dependent upon the oxygen which plants produced.

Plants and animals have since changed, or *evolved*, in different ways into the forms we see today. In the last 600 million years many different forms of life have died out (become *extinct*). The best example is the extinction of the dinosaurs. Biologists have drawn up evolutionary trees to show the possible ways in which the animals and plants have changed since life started on this planet.

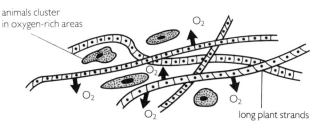

animals cluster in oxygen-rich areas

long plant strands

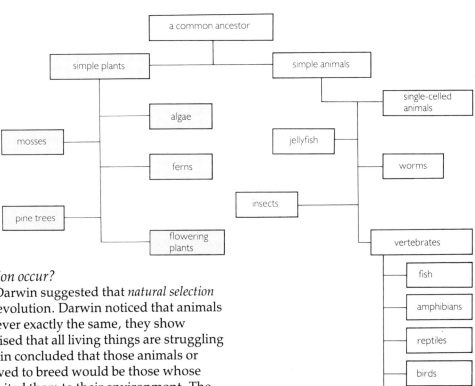

How does evolution occur?

In 1861 Charles Darwin suggested that *natural selection* was the basis of evolution. Darwin noticed that animals and plants are never exactly the same, they show *variation*. He realised that all living things are struggling to survive. Darwin concluded that those animals or plants that survived to breed would be those whose variations best suited them to their environment. The survivors would pass on the successful variations to their offspring. Gradually new types or species of animal and plant would evolve that were better *adapted* to their environment. For example, some plant seeds might be blown on to a spoil heap of a copper mine. The waste metal in the spoil heap would kill off most of the seeds, but some might be able to survive. These would produce plants that were resistant to the copper. If this process was repeated, eventually a new type of plant might be produced.

Whether all evolutionary steps can be explained by this theory is debatable. Many people think that evolution takes place but think that Darwin's theory is incomplete and does not explain all evolutionary change. There are many people who cannot accept evolution and completely reject it as a theory.

The Earth is the only planet in the Solar System that has oxygen in its atmosphere. The composition of the Earth's atmosphere is shown in the table. As you can see, most of the air is nitrogen gas. Although nitrogen is of great importance to living things, the gas is not used by most plants and animals – it must be converted to nitrate ions before it is useful. The amount of carbon dioxide in the air is changeable. For instance, if there are large numbers of people in a closed room, then the carbon dioxide levels will rise.

Gas	Percentage volume of atmosphere
Nitrogen	78.1
Oxygen	20.9
Argon	0.9
Carbon dioxide	0.03
Neon	
Helium	0.02
Ozone	
Hydrogen	

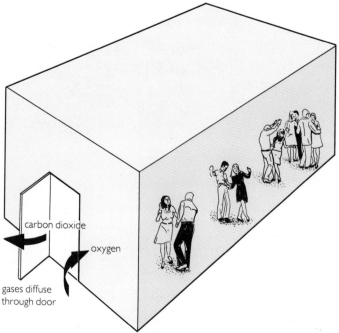

carbon dioxide

oxygen

gases diffuse through door

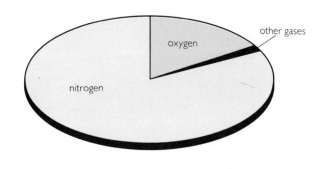

oxygen

other gases

nitrogen

Carbon dioxide is added to the atmosphere by all animals every time they breathe out and by plants at night when they are not photosynthesising. During the day plants photosynthesise and use up carbon dioxide and give out oxygen.

The amount of water that the atmosphere can hold varies according to the conditions.

The water in the atmosphere affects the weather, (see page 18).

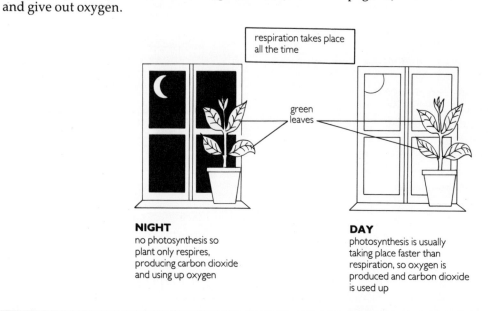

respiration takes place all the time

green leaves

NIGHT
no photosynthesis so plant only respires, producing carbon dioxide and using up oxygen

DAY
photosynthesis is usually taking place faster than respiration, so oxygen is produced and carbon dioxide is used up

The structure of the atmosphere

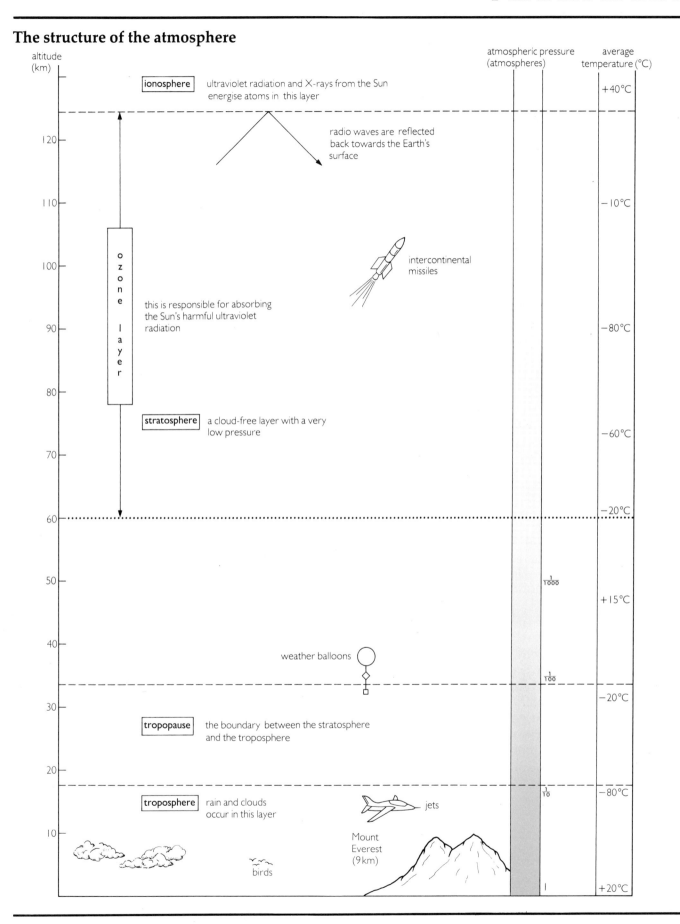

altitude (km)

atmospheric pressure (atmospheres)

average temperature (°C)

ionosphere — ultraviolet radiation and X-rays from the Sun energise atoms in this layer

radio waves are reflected back towards the Earth's surface

ozone layer — this is responsible for absorbing the Sun's harmful ultraviolet radiation

intercontinental missiles

stratosphere — a cloud-free layer with a very low pressure

weather balloons

tropopause — the boundary between the stratosphere and the troposphere

troposphere — rain and clouds occur in this layer

jets

Mount Everest (9km)

birds

+40°C
−10°C
−80°C
−60°C
−20°C
+15°C
−20°C
−80°C
+20°C

$\frac{1}{1000}$
$\frac{1}{100}$
$\frac{1}{10}$
1

8 THE WEATHER

Why does the Earth have weather? If the Earth had no atmosphere then it would be like the Moon and have no weather. If the atmosphere did not move there would be no weather changes. If there was no water vapour in the atmosphere there would be no clouds or rain. The region of the atmosphere responsible for the Earth's weather is the most dense layer – the *troposphere*. This rises 17 km above the equator but only 7 km above the north and south poles. The air in the troposphere is always moving as a result of the Sun's heat and is the main cause of our changing weather. Weather forecasters try to predict the weather by guessing where the air will move and what weather it will bring with it.

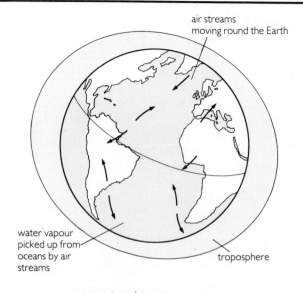

air streams moving round the Earth

water vapour picked up from oceans by air streams

troposphere

The Sun warms up the air at the equator which then rises by convection. If one mass of air rises, another must fall in order to replace it. This is known as the circulation of the air.

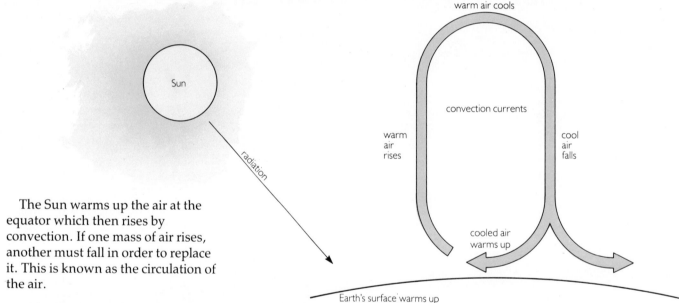

Sun

radiation

warm air cools

convection currents

warm air rises

cool air falls

cooled air warms up

Earth's surface warms up

This simple movement of the air is complicated by the rotation of the Earth which deflects moving air streams towards the west. Surface features, such as hills and mountains, force moving air masses upwards, or cause turbulence which makes the pattern of air streams complicated. The water vapour, or moisture, that is present in the atmosphere produces clouds, rain, snow ice, hail, fog, frost or dew.

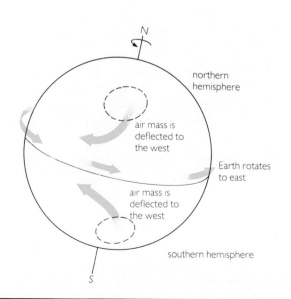

N

northern hemisphere

air mass is deflected to the west

Earth rotates to east

air mass is deflected to the west

southern hemisphere

S

Air movements

Heated air rises above the equator until it reaches the tropopause when it splits, spreading to the north and south. Eventually this heated air falls to the surface of the Earth. Here the air splits again, some returning to the equator and the rest moving to the poles. It meets colder air spreading away from the poles at a region called the *polar front*. In this area the warmer air from the equator is forced over the denser colder air.

In some parts of the world the air remains still for long periods of time allowing it to reach a uniform temperature and humidity. It is then called an *air mass*. Air masses are named according to where they are formed: over the ocean – *maritime*, over land – *continental*, at the poles – *polar*, near the equator – *tropical*.

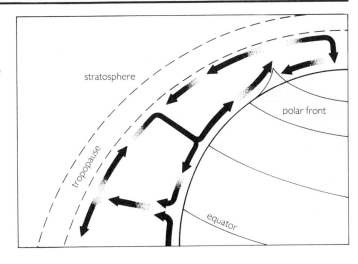

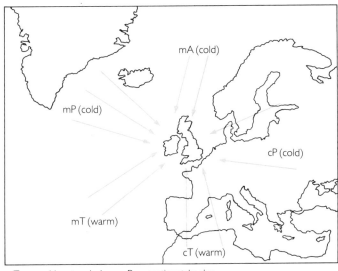

mT = maritime tropical
mP = maritime polar
mA = maritime arctic

cP = continental polar
cT = continental tropical

Air masses can remain still for long periods of time. When they start to move they are called *air streams*. These can keep their temperature and humidity constant for a few days. Air streams themselves bring settled weather but where a cold air stream meets a warm air stream the two will mix very slowly. There will be an area where the temperature and humidity change rapidly from that of one air stream to another. This is called a *front*. Britain is near the polar front and is also in a part of the world affected by five major air streams. This explains why our weather is unpredictable and changeable.

If warm air is being replaced by colder air we say a cold front is developing and if the cold air has been replaced by warmer air we say a warm front has developed. In both types of front the warmer air rises and cools, causing condensation of its water vapour to form clouds which bring periods of rain. When the polar air stream and tropical air stream meet at the polar front they mix irregularly, causing a series of fronts to develop. These are areas of low pressure called *depressions*; a typical depression is shown in cross-section.

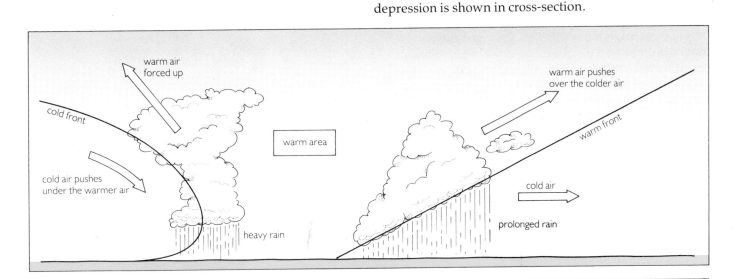

To make a *weather chart* measurements are taken from many weather stations. The instruments used in weather stations are similar to those used in most schools. The most useful instruments measure atmospheric pressure, wind speed and direction, temperature and relative humidity.

Atmospheric pressure

The atmosphere stretches over a hundred kilometres into space and although we are not aware of it, it has mass and so exerts a pressure on the earth's surface. This pressure can be measured by an instrument called a *barometer*. There are two main types.

The mercury barometer

This is a glass tube filled with mercury as shown in the diagram. The mercury in the glass tube is supported by the pressure of the air on the mercury in the bowl. The atmospheric pressure is discovered by measuring the height of the column of mercury. At sea level this height is usually about 760 mm. When the atmospheric pressure changes the height of the column will change. This apparatus is simple but very bulky and awkward to move about.

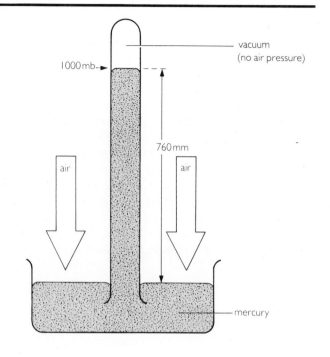

The aneroid barometer

This does not use any liquid and is far more portable than the mercury barometer. The main part of this barometer is a sealed metal box containing air at a very low pressure. Changes in the atmospheric pressure cause the box to expand or contract and these movements of the box are magnified by a system of levers which move a pointer on a scale.

Atmospheric pressure is usually measured in *millibar* (mb), where 1000 mb is the equivalent of 760 mm of mercury as measured by a mercury barometer. At sea level the atmospheric pressure varies between 970 and 1040 mb.

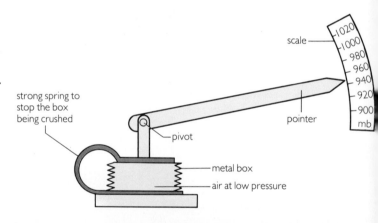

Wind speed and direction

Wind direction is measured by a *wind vane* and wind speed is measured by an *anemometer*. The commonest type of anemometer is shown in the photograph – the wind causes the three cups to rotate and the rate at which they rotate is proportional to the wind speed. It is possible for the wind speed and direction to be recorded electronically from these instruments.

The speed of the wind is normally measured in metres per second, although the Beaufort scale is usually used in gale warnings for sailors.

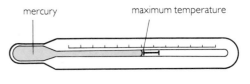

maximum thermometer

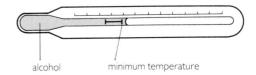

minimum thermometer

Temperature

This is normally measured by *maximum* and *minimum thermometers*. The maximum thermometer contains mercury. When the temperature rises the mercury travels along the capillary tube and pushes a small pointer along. When the temperature falls the mercury travels back along the tube, leaving the pointer at the highest temperature reading. The minimum thermometer contains alcohol. As the temperature falls the alcohol is drawn down the tube, pulling a pointer with it. When the temperature rises, the alcohol moves up the tube, leaving the pointer at the lowest temperature reading. After the readings are taken the steel pointers are reset using a small magnet. Sometimes the two thermometers are combined in a maximum-and-minimum thermometer.

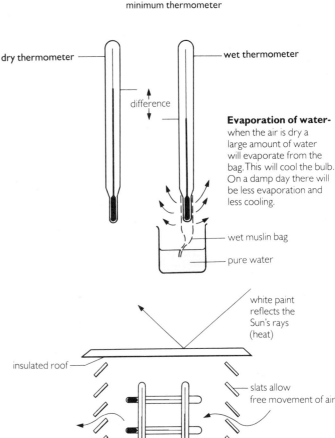

Evaporation of water- when the air is dry a large amount of water will evaporate from the bag. This will cool the bulb. On a damp day there will be less evaporation and less cooling.

Relative humidity

This is an indication of how much water there is in the air. On a dry day the relative humidity is low, on a damp day it is high. Relative humidity is measured using *wet and dry thermometers*. The dry thermometer is of the normal type, while the wet one has a bulb covered by a muslin bag that has one end in a container of pure water. Water evaporates from the bag, cools the bulb and gives a lower reading on this thermometer. The rate of evaporation depends on the amount of water in the air, and the difference between the two thermometers can be used to calculate the relative humidity.

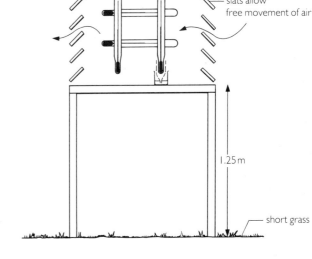

A Stevenson screen

The thermometers which measure temperature and relative humidity are normally kept inside a special box called a *Stevenson screen*. This is painted white and has slotted sides which allow air through while keeping the thermometers shaded from the Sun's rays. This means that the thermometers accurately measure the air's temperature and humidity.

Information about conditions in the upper atmosphere is very useful in making accurate weather forecasts. This information is obtained by attaching instruments for measuring pressure and temperature to a hydrogen-filled balloon. The balloon is released and reaches heights of over 30 km. A small radio transmitter relays information to a receiver on the ground.

Information is collected from weather stations all over the world and then transferred on to weather charts or *synoptic maps*. The curved lines on these maps are called *isobars*. They join places that have the same air pressure at that particular time (like contours on a map that join places that have the same height). Some of the most important features that weather forecasters look for are warm and cold fronts or depressions. These are drawn on the maps using special symbols.

The movement of depressions is very important for weather forecasters, because they bring changes in the weather. Depressions are formed whenever warm and cold air mixes, such as at the polar front.

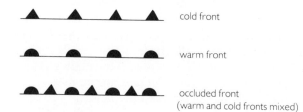

cold front

warm front

occluded front
(warm and cold fronts mixed)

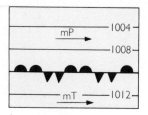

warm tropical air meets cold arctic air at the polar front

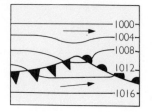

a small wave develops with the warm air pushing into the colder air

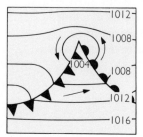

the warm front develops ahead of the cold front and a low pressure area forms where the two fronts meet

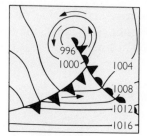

air starts to move anti-clockwise round the low pressure area. The cold front catches up with the warm front. Where they meet they form an occluded front

Warm fronts bring long periods of rain; cold fronts bring heavy rain and sometimes thunderstorms, while occluded fronts bring torrential rain for short periods of time.

These two maps show the weather over Britain and the North Atlantic at 0600 hours and 1200 hours on a winter's day. The symbols used are:

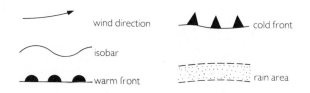

wind direction

isobar

warm front

cold front

rain area

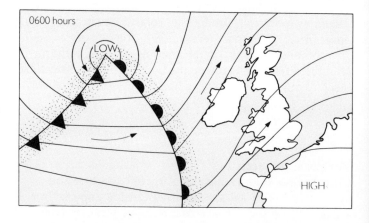

At 0600 hours a depression is moving eastwards from the Atlantic Ocean towards Britain, which is enjoying clear skies and warm temperatures. At 1200 hours the warm front has reached Britain and rain is falling over most of the country. The isobars are close together so a strong south westerly wind is blowing. Once the warm front has passed there will be a short dry spell, then the cold front will reach Britain bringing short periods of heavy rain. Once this has passed there will be a period of settled weather until the next depression reaches the country.

A full synoptic chart contains many other symbols that describe the weather conditions at the major weather stations. These are some of the symbols used:

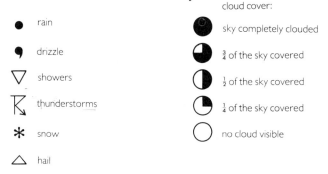

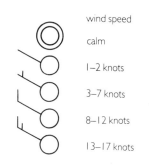

A typical report from a weather station would look like this:

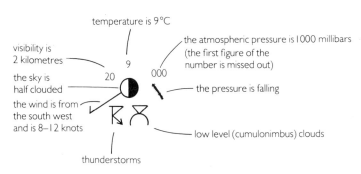

Orbiting weather satellites transmit infrared pictures of the Earth's surface to major weather stations, to show the positions of the major fronts. These are shown up by the positions of various cloud formations. There are two types of satellite used:

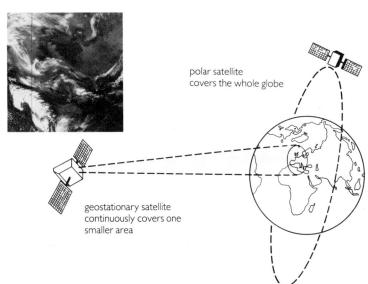

Polar orbiting satellites   These orbit over the poles. Each complete orbit takes about two hours, and it can map the whole globe every 24 hours, from its height of about 1300 km.

Geostationary satellites   These are placed much further out in space. They rotate at the same speed as the Earth, and appear to be stationary in the sky. The satellite rotates with the Earth, staying over the same spot taking pictures every 20 minutes and transmitting them back to Earth.

The weather forecaster decides on a forecast by looking at:
1   the earlier synoptic maps;
2   the position of the fronts on the latest synoptic map;
3   information from the weather balloons in the stratosphere;
4   pictures from the two types of weather satellites.
The forecaster then uses this information together with knowledge and experience of weather patterns to predict what is likely to happen. Many things can interfere with the weather pattern. Only experience can take all these factors into account to produce an accurate forecast.

RESOURCES

CHAPTER 2

NATURAL RESOURCES

All our materials are taken from, or made from the Earth's natural resources.

Non-living resources
All our non-living resources come from the Earth's rocks.

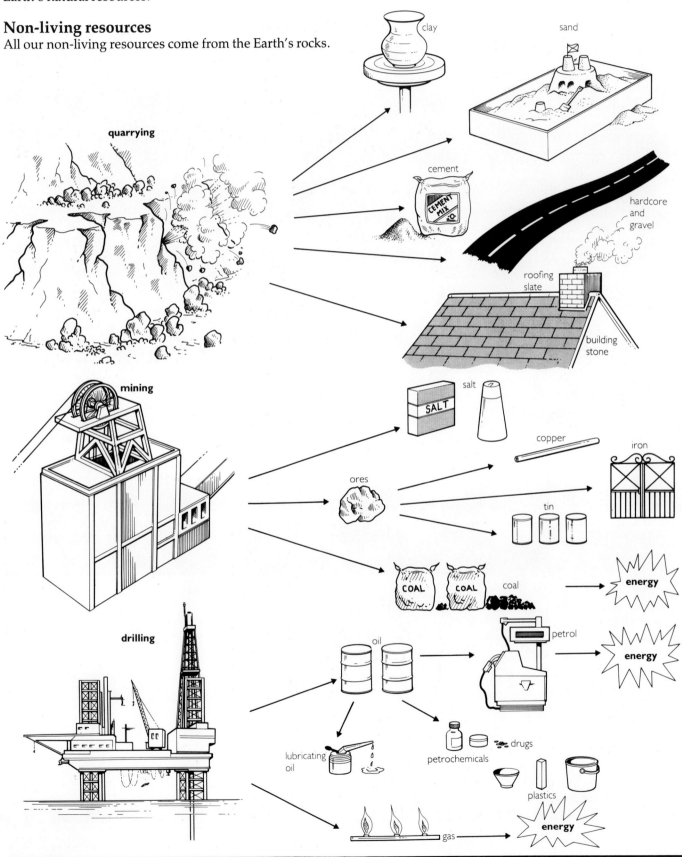

quarrying

clay

sand

cement

hardcore and gravel

roofing slate

building stone

mining

salt

copper

iron

ores

tin

COAL   COAL   coal

energy

drilling

oil

petrol

energy

lubricating oil

petrochemicals

drugs

plastics

gas

energy

Living resources

Plants and animals are our living resources.

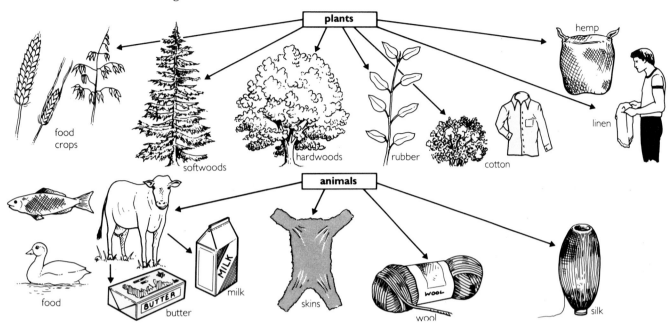

How long will our resources last?

To answer this we must ask four other questions.

How much of the resource is left?
The Earth is abundant in some resources. For example we are not likely to run out of sand in the near future. Other resources are becoming scarce and may run out very soon, e.g. gold.

How fast are we using the resource?
Different resources are used at different rates. Some resources are being used at a faster rate each year, e.g. limestone.

Is the resource renewable?
The time taken for a resource to be replaced naturally is called the **recycling time**. Living resources have short recycling times (measured in years) and are called **renewable**, e.g. wood. Non-living resources have long recycling times (measured in millions of years) and are called **non-renewable**, e.g. coal. Problems will be caused if any resource is used up faster than it can be replaced.

How expensive is it to recover the resource?
Many resources, e.g. some metals, are very expensive to extract. As the metal ore gets scarcer, the market price of the metal increases. Eventually it becomes worthwhile to extract the remaining ore. For instance, abandoned tin mines in Cornwall are being investigated to see if it would be economical to reopen them.

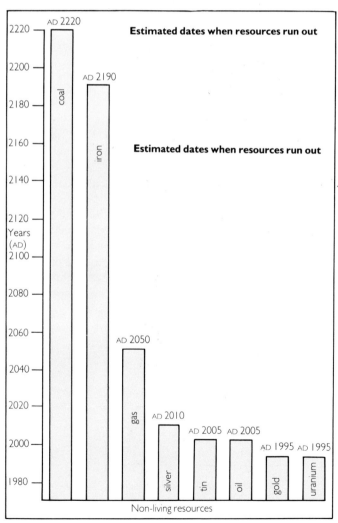

Estimated dates when resources run out

2 CONSUMPTION

What resources are we using? How much of them do we have? Who is using them? What can we do about it?

Abundant non-renewable resources

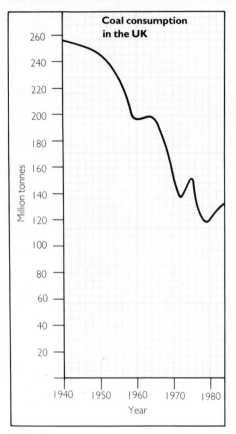

Coal

Coal is still abundant in Great Britain. There is probably still enough coal for another 800 years. However this coal is becoming more difficult to mine and so is more expensive.

Coal production in Great Britain has dropped since 1940 because fewer people use coal in the home (most people have switched to North Sea gas). Coal is still a major source of energy for industrial processes and for generating electricity. The amount of coal mined is likely to increase in the near future.

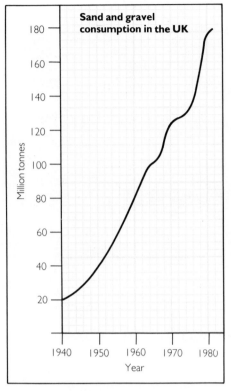

Sand and gravel

Neither of these resources is in short supply in the UK. The main use of sand is in the building industry. It is also used in the manufacture of glass and silicon chips.

Gravel is used in road-building, for making concrete and in house building.

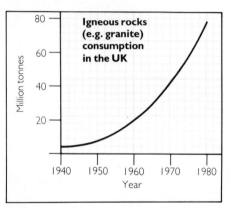

Limestone

This is an important ingredient of cement. In agriculture, it can be spread on the land to neutralise acidic soils. There are many other uses for this important resource.

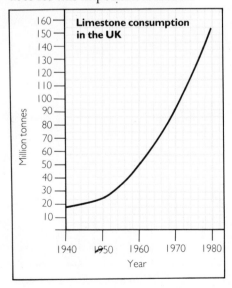

Building stone

Many people prefer the look of natural stone buildings. Building stone is often found in areas of great beauty and its removal can scar the landscape.

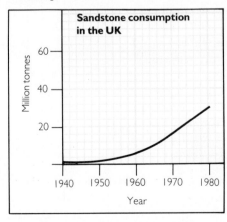

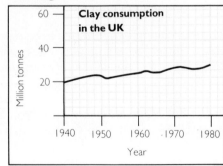

Clay

Clay is made up of very fine particles. There are many different sorts of clay and these can be moulded and baked to make bricks, pottery or sculptures. Some clays may be mixed with limestone to make cement.

Scarce non-renewable resources

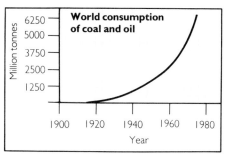

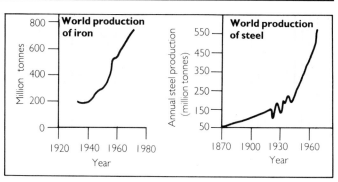

Iron ore
This is the most abundant metal ore in the Earth. Steel is made from iron.

Oil and coal

These make a major contribution to the world's supply of energy. Oil in particular is becoming harder to find. Fewer oil fields are being discovered and the oil is becoming more expensive to extract.

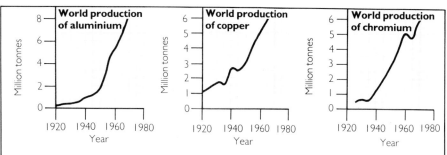

Other metals
These are becoming harder to find. It is likely that the reserves of copper and aluminium will run out soon after AD 2020.

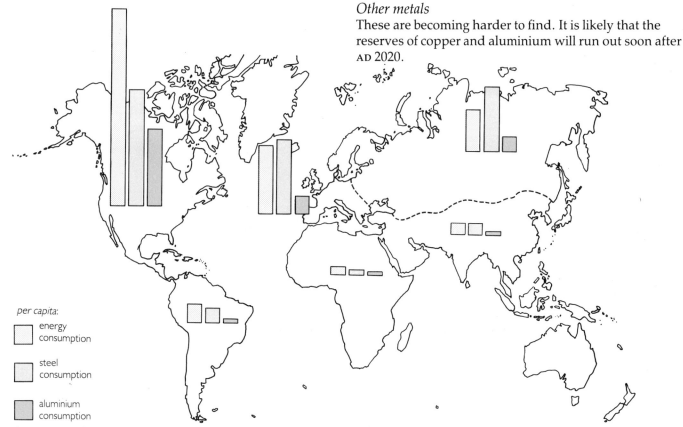

per capita:
- energy consumption
- steel consumption
- aluminium consumption

The pattern of world consumption

A large proportion of the world's natural resources are found in the underdeveloped countries. However, most of these resources are used up by the wealthy developed countries. The amount of resources a country consumes depends on the state of development of the country and its economic performance.

Recycling

This means the re-use of resources. For example, old glass bottles can be melted down and re-used. As resources become scarcer recycling will become more profitable and more common.

3 METALS

Metals are extremely useful and are found in many materials.

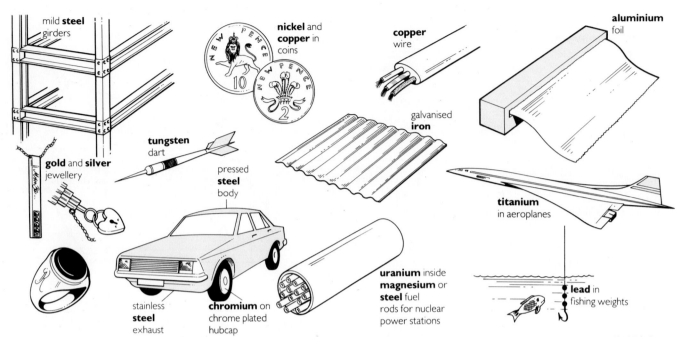

mild **steel** girders

nickel and **copper** in coins

copper wire

galvanised **iron**

aluminium foil

gold and **silver** jewellery

tungsten dart

pressed **steel** body

titanium in aeroplanes

stainless **steel** exhaust

chromium on chrome plated hubcap

uranium inside **magnesium** or **steel** fuel rods for nuclear power stations

lead in fishing weights

Sources

Metals are usually found combined with other elements in rocks. These are called *ores*. A very few metals, such as gold, are found on their own. Prospecting for ores used to be a matter of chance, but now geologists who study the Earth can locate ores more accurately. If these ores are present in large quantities they may be worth mining. As metals become scarcer it becomes more economical to mine poor ore deposits that were passed over in the past.

Mining

Mining takes place on the surface or underground. Surface mining is called *open cast mining*. The surface rock is removed and the ore exposed. This is then blasted free from the rock and moved to a chemical works. Most metal ores are extracted from open cast mines which are often huge, covering many square kilometres. This type of mining destroys the landscape. When most of the ore has been removed, the exhausted open cast mines could be landscaped and allowed to return to a more natural state, although this would take many years. Open cast mine sites may also be filled in and used for building houses or factories.

Underground mining is more expensive and more dangerous. Some mines go down to a depth of 4000 metres in search of a rich ore seam.

An open cast mine before and after reclamation.

Extraction

Once the ore has been mined and purified, the metal must be extracted from the ore. The method of doing this is different for each metal, but each method uses a lot of energy. The process used depends on the type of ore, its purity and its chemical properties. Three examples are shown.

The extraction of iron from its ore, haematite (iron oxide)

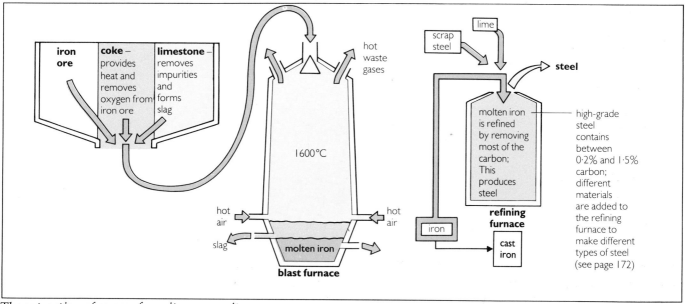

The extraction of copper from its ore, pyrites

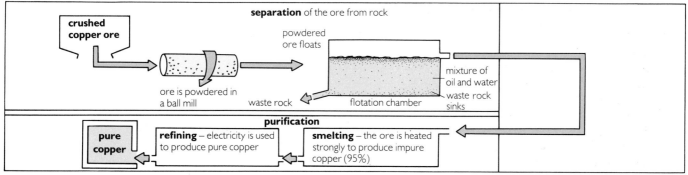

The extraction of aluminium from its ore, bauxite

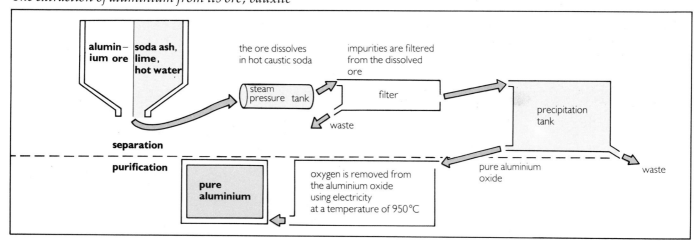

The process for each metal is different because the metals have different properties and the ores differ in purity.

4 CONSTRUCTIONAL

The natural resources that builders use are not in short supply. However, their extraction does create environmental problems. The major building stones used in the UK include limestone, sandstone, granite and slate. These stones are quarried, i.e. removed from the ground by careful blasting which must not shatter the rock. They are then cut to size. Quarries become larger and larger as more and more rock is removed. Some quarries cover huge areas of land – they scar the countryside. Quarrying is now controlled and disused quarries must be restored to a more natural looking state.

Local building stone

Some areas of Britain are famous for their local building stones. Some people think these natural stones are more pleasing than concrete, glass and bricks. Natural building stone is expensive to extract and transport.

Cotswold villages are full of buildings that are made of the local limestone. This has a soft yellow colour that gives the villages a pleasant character.

The local dark granite that is used in Edinburgh's buildings give it a characteristic appearance.

Some rocks are easier to use for building than others. Limestone, for example, is easily cut, but granite is hard and must be sawn into shape. Slate is one of the most long-lasting of all building materials and comes in many colours. It is mainly used in roofing, flooring, and wall cladding on older houses.

Stone quarries

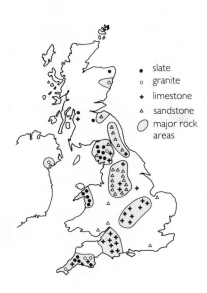

- • slate
- ○ granite
- + limestone
- △ sandstone
- ⬭ major rock areas

Some limestones are famous for use as a building stone, for example Bath stone, Portland stone and Cotswold stone. However, limestone is also used for many other purposes. Limestone from the Peak District and the Pennines is particularly important for producing road stones and cement. They are also used in many other places:

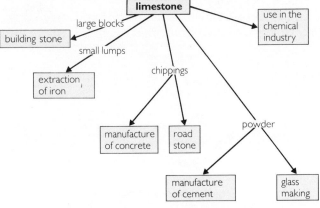

Crushed stone

All kinds of rocks can be pulverised into very small pieces and used to make *reconstituted stone*. There are many types of this 'stone' available to builders. These are often used to copy the more expensive traditional types of building stone. Reconstituted stone is far cheaper because it is often made from small broken bits of expensive stone that would normally be thrown away at the quarry.

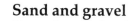

Sand and gravel

Quarrying sand and gravel is simple because they are found either at, or just below, the surface. Sand and gravel differ only in the size of their particles. They are both used mainly as *aggregate* (material that provides bulk and strength) in concrete and road-building. Sand is also used in the manufacture of glass, and silicon chips for computers.

If the quarry takes sand or gravel from beneath the level of water in the ground it is called a wet pit, and becomes flooded. Quarries which are above this water-table are called dry pits. Disused dry pits are often used as refuse tips before being reclaimed. Disused wet pits are often used for recreation such as fishing, sailing and other water sports.

Clay

Clays are usually found where the land is flat. Clay is made up of very fine particles. There are various types of clay, each of which is used for a different purpose. China clay is a white clay found in Cornwall that is used to make fine china. Fuller's Earth is a clay that can be used as an absorbent, to remove colouring.

The main use of clay is for making bricks. At one time the colour of bricks reflected the kind of clay used. Northern clay is red because of a high iron content and produces red bricks. Southern clays are yellower and produce yellow bricks. Nowadays bricks are coloured by adding dyes to the clay. Clay is also used in the manufacture of cement.

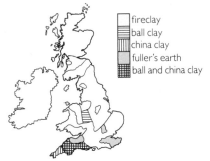

fireclay
ball clay
china clay
fuller's earth
ball and china clay

Environmental issues

Quarries and gravel pits create ugly scars in some of the UK's most beautiful areas. In some cases it is possible to restore and landscape the spoilt areas. In other cases the quarry and its waste is hard to hide. Local people often see the landscape being 'eaten away' in front of their eyes. They also have to cope with the noise and dirt from the quarry. On the other hand, the materials from the quarries are needed. Frequently, these quarries are in or near National Parks such as the Peak District and cause a great deal of argument.

5 TREES

At one time, the British Isles were almost totally covered with forest trees, mainly oak, ash and beech. Now, of course, most of it has been cleared for farming and urban development.

Each year, the United Kingdom uses up an area of forest about the size of Greater London – about 1300 km^2. To be completely self-sufficient in timber we would need over 50 000 km^2 of woodland. In fact only about 15 000 km^2 of the United Kingdom is heavily wooded so we have to import a large amount of wood each year. Most of these imports are softwoods from northern Europe or Canada and the rest is hardwood from the tropics.

Types of trees

Hardwoods are very dense. Examples of native British hardwoods are oak, ash, beech and elm. Common imported hardwoods are teak and mahogany; they grow in tropical areas. Hardwoods take hundreds of years to mature.

Softwoods are usually conifers such as pines and firs. The scots pine is the only native British conifer. The Forestry Commission frequently plants larch, sitka, spruce, norway spruce and corsican pine. Even the fastest-growing conifers take 80 years to mature.

wooded areas

Uses

Wood has three main uses:

Fuel

In the third world this is the major use of wood and is partly responsible for the clearance of forest areas. In the UK, wood which cannot be usefully used any other way is often burnt.

Construction and furniture

Softwoods are used extensively in the building industry for roofing timbers, frames and floorboards. Softwood can also be used to produce *chipboard* (see page 179) – a reconstituted wood made of wood chips pressed and glued together. This is much cheaper than real wood because it can be made from younger trees and there is very little, if any, wasted timber.

Hardwoods are much more attractive and more expensive than softwoods. They are usually much stronger. The main use of hardwood is in the production of expensive furniture or *veneers*. Veneers are very thin slices of attractive hardwood that are used to cover cheaper woods such as chipboards. This gives the cheaper wood the appearance of the more expensive hardwood.

Paper and cardboard products

Softwoods can be chopped into fine chips which can then be pulped to produce wood pulp. This can then be used to produce paper or cardboard. In the UK we use over $2\frac{1}{2}$ million tonnes of pulp every year – a single edition of a national newspaper will use up an area of 5 hectares of forest (over 12 acres).

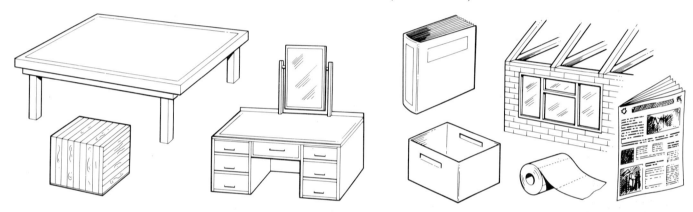

Environmental issues

The rate at which we are using up the world's forests is causing some concern.

Tropical rain forests

These forests remove huge amounts of carbon dioxide from the atmosphere and release oxygen in its place. Tropical forests are being cut down quickly and it is impossible to calculate the effect this will have on the Earth's atmosphere. The main reason for cutting these

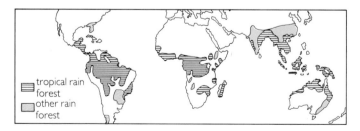

tropical rain forest
other rain forest

forests down is to release land for agriculture. Unfortunately, in South America they have discovered that cleared rain forests are fertile for only one or two years. Farming removes the nutrients from the soil and the Sun then bakes the soil hard. Crops cannot grow successfully in the hard infertile soil.

Acid rain

Sulphur dioxide (SO_2) from industrial areas, is a serious pollutant of the atmosphere. It dissolves in rain to form an acid. Winds carry the SO_2 round the world. If it falls over wooded areas the weak acid severely affects the growth of the trees and may kill them.

Replanting

It is impossible to replace the hardwoods that we have used, in our lifetime. Softwoods grow more quickly and can be usefully cut down after 25 years to make wood pulp. In the UK, the Forestry Commission is responsible for planning tree planting programmes.

Tree farming

In the United Kingdom, many people are concerned about the effect that conifer plantations have on the countryside. This is because, until recently, conifers were planted in straight lines and looked unnatural. Birds and other animals rarely enter these plantations because of the lack of variety of animal and plant life in them.

6 OIL AND GAS

The oil and gas we use today are natural resources that were formed in the Earth over 300 million years ago. The same process is still going on today at a very slow rate. There is a constant worldwide search for oil and gas.

We extract more of these than any other natural resource. Prospecting for oil requires the application of scientific and geological knowledge.

The formation of oil and gas

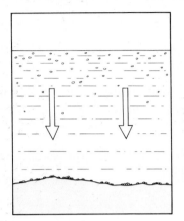

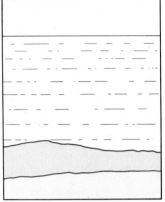

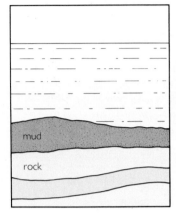

Much of the Earth's surface was covered by seas 300 million years ago. Millions of tiny animals and plants lived near the surface. When they died they sank.

The dead remains of these animals and plants formed a thick layer on the bottom of the sea. This layer became absorbed into a layer of mud sediments.

Over millions of years more layers of mud and silt formed. The layers at the bottom were squeezed and became rock. The animal and plant remains turned to gas and oil.

The gas and oil moved through the permeable rocks until they were trapped under a layer of dense rock. The Earth's movements twisted the rock layers.

Oil bearing rocks

Oil and gas are trapped in rocks that have cracks and pores in them – like water in a sponge. Examples of these *permeable* rocks are sandstone and limestone. The oil and gas can move through these porous rocks and may travel a long way from where they were formed. The gas and oil will continue to move until it meets a layer of *impermeable* rock. This rock is very dense and stops the gas and oil. These rock layers are sometimes called *cap rocks*. Gas and oil can be trapped by cap rocks in several ways.

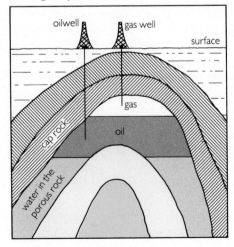

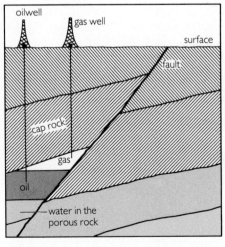

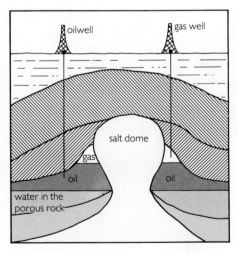

Layers of rock that form an arch are called an *anticline*. If the top layer is impermeable, oil and gas are trapped, e.g. Forties field.

Earth movements can cause faults to develop. If a layer of impermeable rock is moved in front of oil bearing rocks, then the oil and gas is trapped, e.g. Ninian field.

A layer of salt called a *salt dome* can also act as an oil trap if there is impermeable rock present, e.g. West Sole field.

The search for gas and oil

Prospecting for oil, and gas is big business. Finding it – a 'strike' – can be worth thousands of millions of pounds. The only way to find oil is to drill for it, but this is very expensive. A single borehole drilled in the North Sea can cost over three million pounds and there is no guarantee it will make a strike! Oil companies use many methods to increase the chances of successfully finding oil and gas.

Before a test drill is bored the geologist will need a lot of information about the rock beneath the surface. Aerial photographs can reveal a lot about the rocks under the ground, and special instruments such as magnetometers and gravimeters are used. A magnetometer is towed behind the aircraft and measures slight changes in the Earth's magnetism. This tells the geologist what sort of rocks are under the surface. A gravimeter measures slight changes in the Earth's gravity and this also provides information about the rocks beneath. Finally a test drill is bored to see if oil-bearing rocks are present.

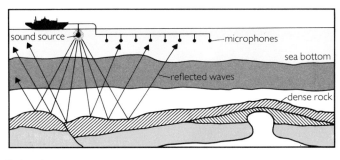

Seismic survey

Shock waves are sent through the sea and down into the layers of rock beneath. The reflected waves are detected by microphones towed behind the ship. A computer converts the recordings from the microphone into a seismic chart. This can tell geologists what rock formations are present and how deep they are.

The North Sea

This is an area that is rich in oil-bearing rocks. Since 1976 oil has been flowing from major oil fields such as Brent, Forties and Ninian.

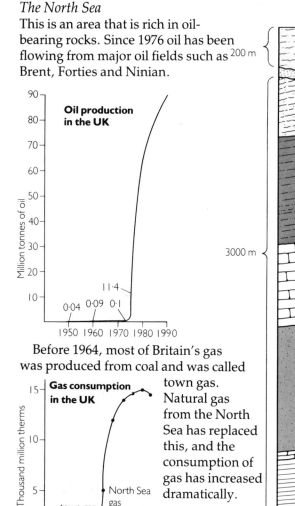

Before 1964, most of Britain's gas was produced from coal and was called town gas. Natural gas from the North Sea has replaced this, and the consumption of gas has increased dramatically.

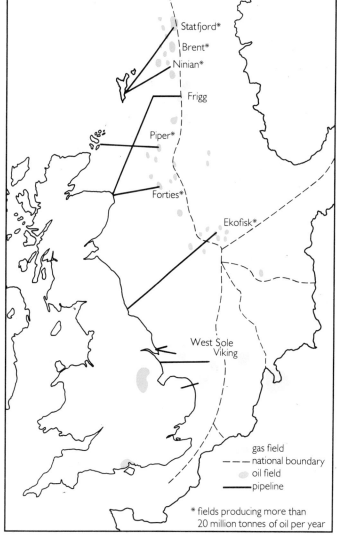

7 COAL

Formation of coal

Coal, like oil, is a fossil fuel. The coal we use today was formed over 300 million years ago from decaying plant matter. The same process is still going on very slowly.

Despite the flow of North Sea oil and gas, coal still provides the UK with about 40% of its energy. Coal will outlast oil by a very long time. At the present rate of consumption there is probably enough coal in the UK to last about 800 years.

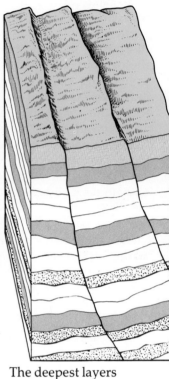

Fern-like trees and giant horsetails formed great forests 300 million years ago. These forests were sometimes found around huge swamps. Dying plants fell into the swamp and sank to the bottom.

As plants sank to the bottom they gradually became covered by silt and mud. The forests disappeared and shallow seas covered the area; new rocks were formed over the remains.

New forests appeared and formed new layers of decaying plant material. The layers sank deeper and deeper and the heat and pressure changed them to coal.

The deepest layers formed the hardest coals while shallow layers formed soft coal. Movements in the Earth's crust broke up the seams, causing problems for miners.

Coal seams

If a coal seam reaches the surface it is said to be *exposed*. If it is buried deep beneath the surface it is called a *concealed seam*. These seams are mined in different ways.

Shaft mining

For underground mining, shafts and tunnels must be driven through the rock to reach the coal. Machines are needed for ventilation, pumping and transport. This is an expensive operation.

Open cast mining

Exposed seams are mined in this way. The soil and rock layers above the coal (the *overburden*) is scraped away by enormous excavators. The coal is then dug out. This is the cheapest way of mining coal. *Drift mining* is a form of open cast mining where one seam is followed. The overburden is used to restore the mined area behind the mine.

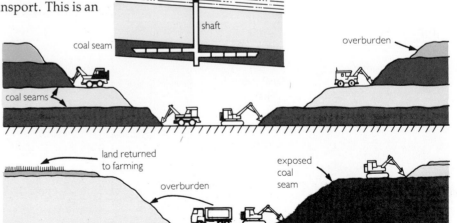

The search

Searching for coal is very expensive. After geologists have found a coal seam, test bores are made to collect samples for analysis. Estimates are made of how much coal is in the seam and how much it would cost to extract it. Geologists and scientists have increased the chances of finding large deposits of coal successfully.

Seismic survey

An explosion on the surface sends sound waves through the rocks. The waves are reflected and picked up by sensitive microphones on the surface. The pattern of sounds gives the geologist information about the rocks.

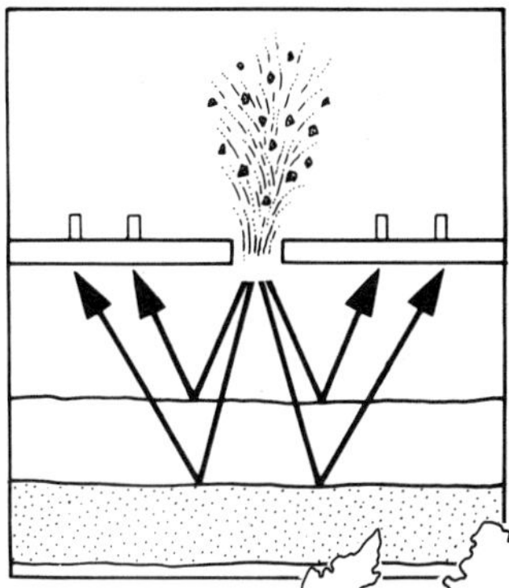

Geological maps

These provide information that give clues to the presence of coal seams.

Test bores

Holes are drilled deep into the rock and a core sample removed. This is then examined and provides direct information about the underlying rocks.

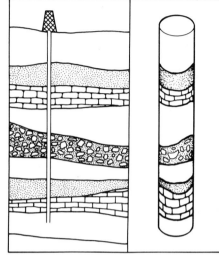

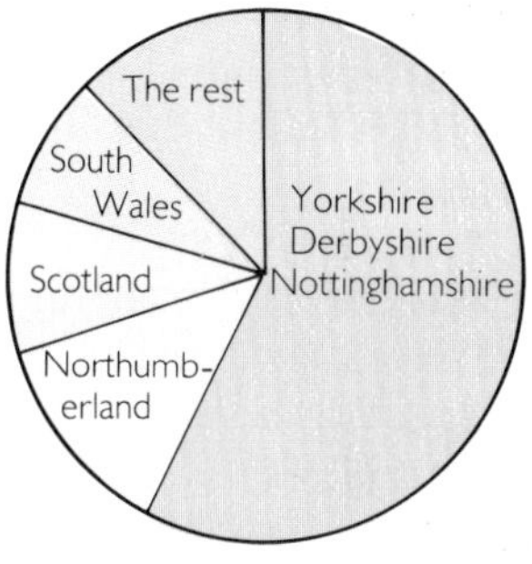

Types of coal

Coal is mainly carbon. The amount of carbon in coal depends on how much it has been compressed or squeezed by other rocks. *Peat* contains about 60% carbon. At shallow depths the peat is turned to a soft brown coal called *lignite* which contains about 70% carbon. At greater depths, house coal or *bituminous coal* is formed. The deepest coal is called *anthracite* and is very hard. This contains over 90% carbon and releases a great deal of heat when it burns.

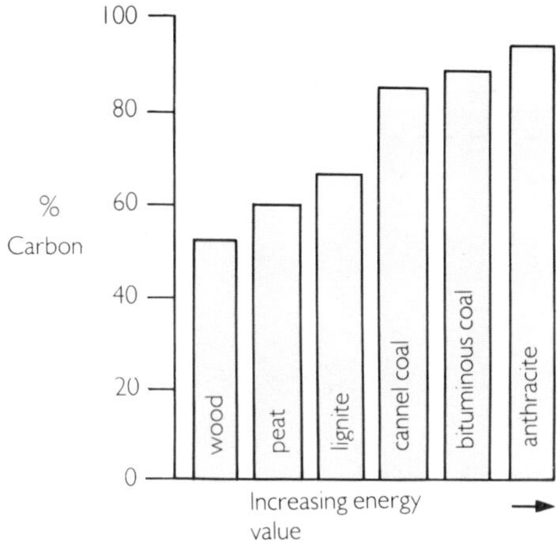

Britain's major coal fields

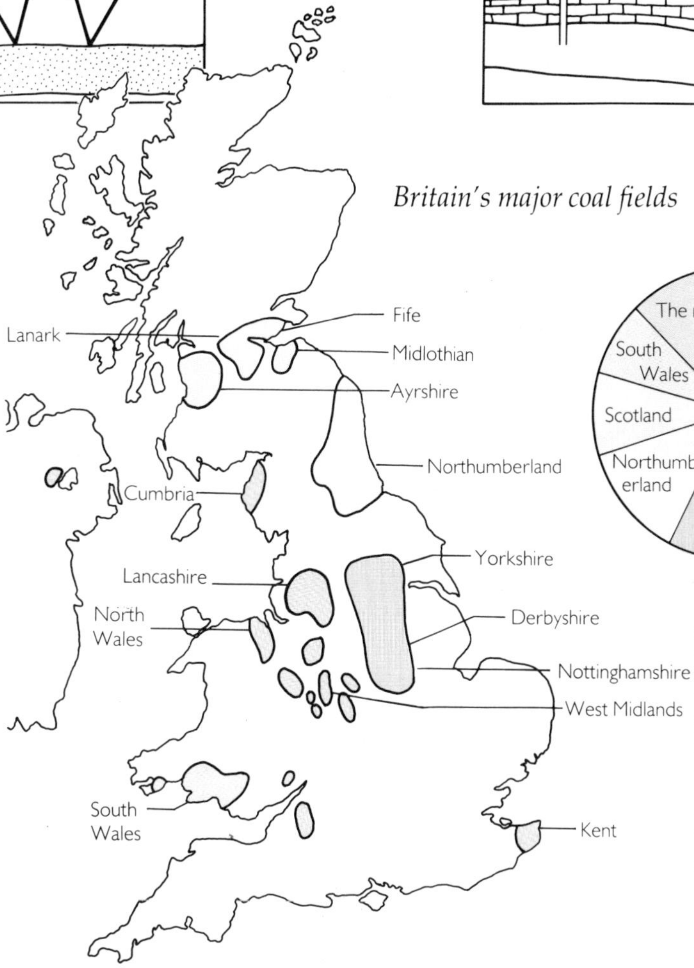

Importance of each coalfield (1980 output)

Pie chart: Yorkshire Derbyshire Nottinghamshire; The rest; South Wales; Scotland; Northumberland

Map labels: Lanark, Fife, Midlothian, Ayrshire, Northumberland, Cumbria, Yorkshire, Lancashire, Derbyshire, North Wales, Nottinghamshire, West Midlands, South Wales, Kent

Bar chart — % Carbon (Increasing energy value →): wood, peat, lignite, cannel coal, bituminous coal, anthracite

Uses of coal

Coal is used mainly as an energy source. It can also be a source of useful chemicals. If coal is heated in the absence of air, *coke*, *coal tar* and *coal gas* are produced. The tar and gas can then be treated to produce useful chemicals. As oil supplies become scarce, coal can be used to provide an artificial crude oil or natural gas. There is a great deal of research going on in the field of technology.

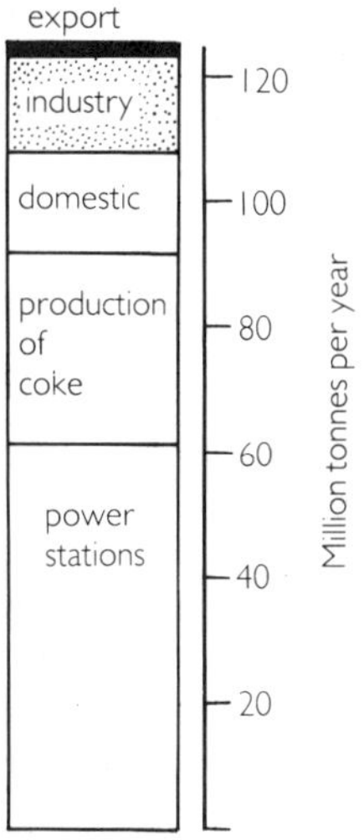

Bar chart (Million tonnes per year, scale 20–120): export, industry, domestic, production of coke, power stations

Uses of coal

8 WATER

Why should we consider water a resource? There is no shortage of it, in fact it has been estimated that there is about 1·5 million million million litres in and on the Earth. Unfortunately over 97% of this is salty and the rest is not always where we want it! We need water for life and for industrial and domestic purposes. The problem of getting the water where we want it usually requires energy and therefore money. Since water is recycled in nature, we can consider it a renewable resource.

Where is the water?

Water is constantly changing state and moving from one place to another. This movement of water is called the *water cycle* (see page 51), and greatly affects our weather. Water is not equally distributed throughout the world and in many places water is a very rare and valuable resource.

The vast majority of the Earth's water is found in the oceans, and only the water in rivers and lakes is freely available for use as a resource.

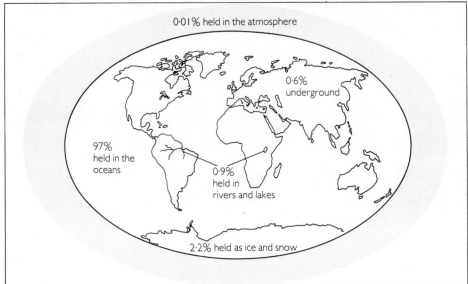

Water in the United Kingdom

We have plenty of water, at least we think so until we get a drought like that of 1976. The average annual rainfall is about 100 cm, but this does not fall evenly over the whole country.

As you might expect, the areas with over 250 cm of rain per year are all areas of high ground, and the areas that have over 100 cm of rain per year are all in the west of the country. This is because the prevailing winds carry large amounts of water from the Atlantic Ocean and this is released over the hills in the west.

About 30% of the water we use in the UK comes from underground rocks. A small amount is taken directly from rivers but most of the rest is taken from reservoirs. These collect the rain which runs off the hills and mountains.

Everything works well as long as the run-off from the hills into the reservoirs continues. Unfortunately this doesn't always happen. In 1976, for example, the demand for water was greater than the amount of water flowing into the reservoirs and a water shortage developed very quickly, especially in the south of the country.

There are two ways of tackling this problem; should we reduce our demand for water or should we increase the number of reservoirs?

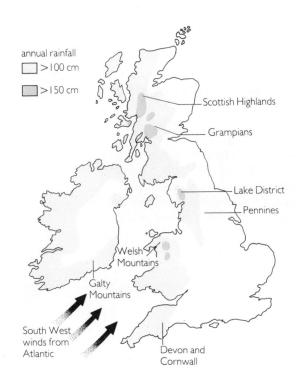

The demand for water

We do not just use water to drink, wash or flush the toilet! Farmers use large amounts of water to produce the food we eat. An average family meal has taken over half a million litres of water to produce. Most industrial processes need vast amounts of water for manufacturing, cooling or heating purposes.

flushing toilet
(50 litres per person per day)

washing
(60 litres per person per day)

agriculture
(150 litres per dairy cow per day)

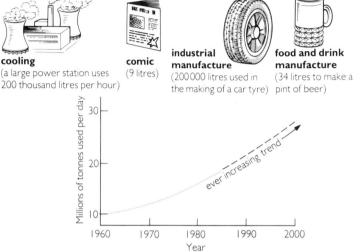

cooling
(a large power station uses 200 thousand litres per hour)

comic
(9 litres)

industrial manufacture
(200 000 litres used in the making of a car tyre)

food and drink manufacture
(34 litres to make a pint of beer)

The demand for water increases every year. This is because as our standard of living increases we use more equipment, such as automatic washing machines and dishwashers, which use large amounts of water. As our industries become more automated, the industrial demand for water increases. Intensive farming – using less land and more machines – needs more water for the plants and animals.

Storing water

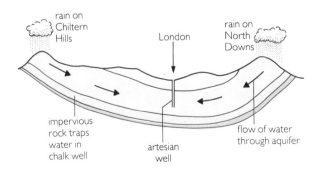

Some water is naturally stored in porous rocks, e.g. chalk, sandstone or limestone, forming *aquifers*. Rain falling on high ground seeps into these rocks and may travel many miles. Wells can be sunk down into these rocks and the water pumped out. In times of high rainfall extra water can be pumped down into the rocks to artificially recharge the aquifer.

rain on Chiltern Hills

London

rain on North Downs

impervious rock traps water in chalk well

artesian well

flow of water through aquifer

London is built over an area of porous rocks in which an aquifer called an artesian basin has formed.

Reservoirs are man-made lakes that have been built to store water. Usually this means flooding valleys and losing valuable agricultural land, areas of natural beauty and people's homes. This occurs most often in areas of high rainfall such as Wales, Scotland and the Lake District. People living there object to their valleys being drowned in order to supply water to people living in big cities many miles away.

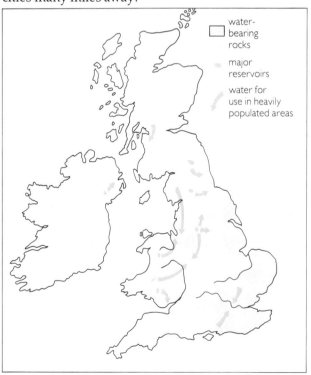

water-bearing rocks

major reservoirs

water for use in heavily populated areas

Solutions

A solution is a mixture of two or more chemicals in which the molecules are completely dispersed or scattered. Chemicals that dissolve are called *solutes* and are said to be *soluble*. The liquid they dissolve in is called the *solvent*. Water is a very good solvent.

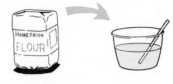

water — solvent

salt (sodium chloride) — solute

mixing/dissolving

some salt has dissolved in the water

not all the salt has dissolved

Suspensions

If a small amount of flour is shaken up in water, a suspension will form.

The tiny particles of flour do not dissolve but become suspended in the water and make it look milky.

Emulsion paint is a suspension of millions of tiny coloured particles suspended in water. When the paint dries on a wall, the water evaporates and the tiny coloured particles are left behind.

Hard & soft water

Tap water can be described as *soft* or *hard*. The 'hardness' of the water depends on the type and amount of salts dissolved in it.

good lather

soft water contains very few dissolved salts and allows soap to produce a good lather easily

layer of scum

hard water contains a high level of dissolved salts which prevent soap from lathering

The dissolved salts stop soap from making a lather or foam. Instead they form a scum. Detergents are not affected by the hardness of water and make a lather easily.

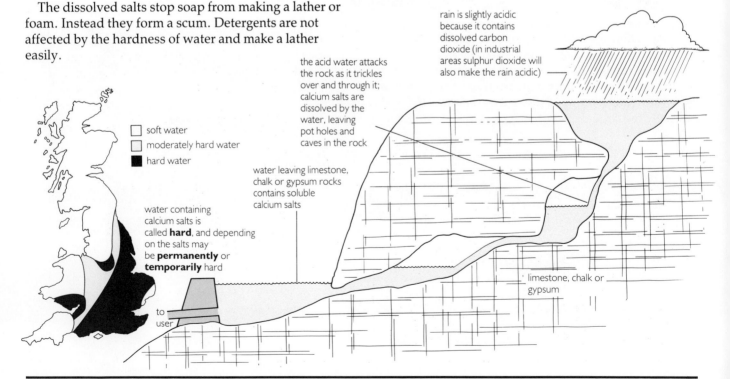

soft water

moderately hard water

hard water

rain is slightly acidic because it contains dissolved carbon dioxide (in industrial areas sulphur dioxide will also make the rain acidic)

the acid water attacks the rock as it trickles over and through it; calcium salts are dissolved by the water, leaving pot holes and caves in the rock

water leaving limestone, chalk or gypsum rocks contains soluble calcium salts

water containing calcium salts is called **hard**, and depending on the salts may be **permanently** or **temporarily** hard

limestone, chalk or gypsum

to user

Temporary hardness

This type of hard water can be softened by boiling. It contains dissolved *calcium hydrogen carbonate* because it has flowed over limestone. When the water is boiled, carbon dioxide is released leaving calcium carbonate which is insoluble and is deposited as scale and so, it does not cause hardness.

Permanent hardness

Permanently hard water cannot be softened by boiling. This water has dissolved *calcium sulphate* as it has flowed over gypsum. Some magnesium salts can also cause permanent hardness. To soften permanently hard water the dissolved calcium and magnesium salts must be removed.

Water softeners

When the water supplied to homes is hard, people sometimes use a water softener. These machines remove calcium and magnesium salts from the water and replace them by sodium salts. These do not make the water hard. There is some evidence to suggest that hard water is better for the human body than very soft water.

Distilled or deionised water

This is water that contains no dissolved impurites. Distilled water is produced by making steam then cooling it back to form pure water.

Some resins, made from petrochemicals, are capable of removing all dissolved chemicals (ions) from water that is passed over them. This is called *deionised* water.

Rainwater

This is usually slightly acidic because it contains dissolved carbon dioxide.

Sea water

This contains many salts dissolved in it. Sixty elements have been discovered in sea water but most are in very low concentrations. Sodium chloride (salt) forms about 3% of sea water.

Drinking water

Water that is fit to drink is called *potable*. It must be free of microbes and any suspended solids, but to taste pleasant it needs traces of other dissolved minerals. Distilled or deionised water has none of these substances and many people find it unpleasant. Most people find hard water is pleasant to drink and it is used by most breweries to make beers.

Spa water

Many places are famous for their water. Some of these are spas which have water that is rich in mineral salts. This water has come from rocks deep in the earth and is usually warm with a slightly unpleasant taste. Many people think that it is healthy to drink and bathe in spa water.

Mineral water

Mineral waters come from springs in rocks. This water contains many minerals and is rich in the trace elements that some people feel are needed in the diet. These waters are usually sold in bottles; they may be still or slightly fizzy. Unlike spa waters, they are usually pleasant to taste.

This is how water reaches your tap:

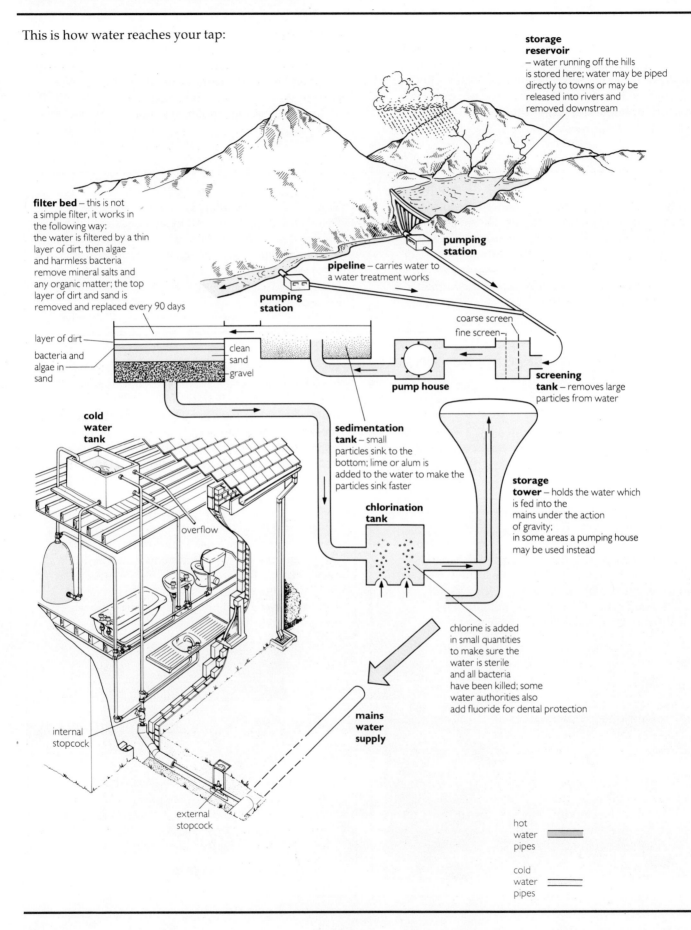

storage reservoir – water running off the hills is stored here; water may be piped directly to towns or may be released into rivers and removed downstream

filter bed – this is not a simple filter, it works in the following way: the water is filtered by a thin layer of dirt, then algae and harmless bacteria remove mineral salts and any organic matter; the top layer of dirt and sand is removed and replaced every 90 days

pumping station

pipeline – carries water to a water treatment works

pumping station

coarse screen
fine screen

layer of dirt

bacteria and algae in sand

clean sand
gravel

pump house

screening tank – removes large particles from water

cold water tank

overflow

sedimentation tank – small particles sink to the bottom; lime or alum is added to the water to make the particles sink faster

storage tower – holds the water which is fed into the mains under the action of gravity; in some areas a pumping house may be used instead

chlorination tank

chlorine is added in small quantities to make sure the water is sterile and all bacteria have been killed; some water authorities also add fluoride for dental protection

internal stopcock

mains water supply

external stopcock

hot water pipes

cold water pipes

Used water

Until the middle of the nineteenth century it was quite common for sewage to flow through open sewers in the streets and straight into rivers. Later it was realised that open sewerage could be linked to diseases such as cholera and typhoid. Human waste is now passed through underground sewers to sewage works where it is treated and made relatively harmless.

In rural areas it would be too expensive to connect isolated houses to sewage farms, so *cesspits* or *septic tanks* are often used.

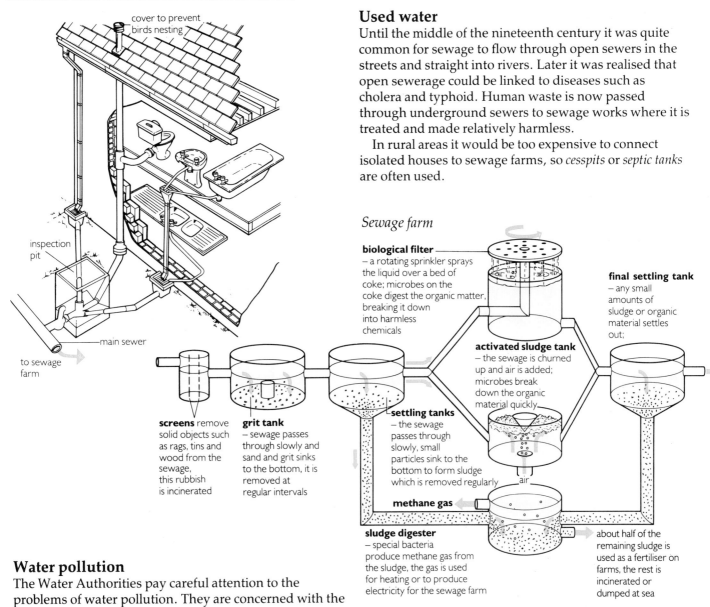

Sewage farm

biological filter – a rotating sprinkler sprays the liquid over a bed of coke; microbes on the coke digest the organic matter, breaking it down into harmless chemicals

final settling tank – any small amounts of sludge or organic material settles out;

activated sludge tank – the sewage is churned up and air is added; microbes break down the organic material quickly

screens remove solid objects such as rags, tins and wood from the sewage, this rubbish is incinerated

grit tank – sewage passes through slowly and sand and grit sinks to the bottom, it is removed at regular intervals

settling tanks – the sewage passes through slowly, small particles sink to the bottom to form sludge which is removed regularly

methane gas

sludge digester – special bacteria produce methane gas from the sludge, the gas is used for heating or to produce electricity for the sewage farm

about half of the remaining sludge is used as a fertiliser on farms, the rest is incinerated or dumped at sea

cover to prevent birds nesting

inspection pit

main sewer

to sewage farm

air

Despite these measures many of our beaches are polluted by sewage. This is because it is much cheaper to pump untreated sewage out to the sea than it is to treat it. Unfortunately tides often return the sewage to the shore.

Water pollution

The Water Authorities pay careful attention to the problems of water pollution. They are concerned with the treatment and disposal of sewage, but they also check the quality of industrial waste water to make sure that laws are not being broken. Industrial waste water should not contain large amounts of chemicals or organic matter.

Recycling and conservation

If we are to treat water as a valuable resource we should try not to waste it. It should be recycled or conserved whenever possible. There are four possible ways of doing this.

1 Water meters – if each house had a meter that measured the amount of water used we would probably not use hosepipes as much, or leave taps running!

2 Domestic water could be recycled. For example bath water and washing up water could be used to flush the toilet.

3 The water that falls on to roofs is sent straight to the sewers. It could be collected and used for washing cars or watering gardens.

4 New laws could be passed to force industries to clean and recycle the water they use.

▮▮ SOIL

Soil has been produced from rocks that have been broken down into small particles. This breaking down has been caused by the weather and chemicals. *Physical weathering* is the disintegration of rock by the action of rain and wind. This form of weathering produces fairly large particles, and anything smaller than sand has been produced by *chemical weathering*. This is the result of acids reacting with the rock. Rainwater is normally a weak acid because it contains dissolved carbon dioxide in it, and rotting plants also produce acids that attack rocks and produce very small particles called *clays*.

acidic rainwater enters cracks in the rocks and begins to break them down into small particles

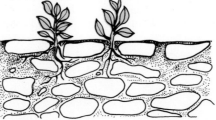

small plants and animals can grow in the cracks and when they die, they decay and produce more acids which attack the rock

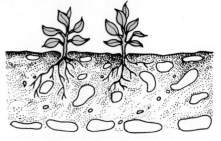

gradually more rock is broken down and a soil starts to develop; dead plants and animals enrich the soil

The different-sized particles that are found in a good agricultural soil can be shown by shaking the soil in a jar of water. After a few hours the soil settles and looks like this:

humus – dead and decaying organic material is recycled by the animals and microbes which live in the soil into a form that plants can take in through their roots and use for growth; humus improves soil structure

suspended clay particles – very small particles which stay suspended in the water for a long time; a soil rich in clay particles holds water very well and may become waterlogged

silt particles – medium-sized particles found in large quantities in good fertile soil

fine sand – fairly large particles which do not hold water; sandy soils drain very easily

coarse sand, gravel and stones – the heaviest particles sink to the bottom rapidly

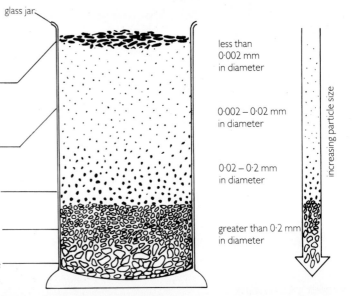

glass jar

less than 0·002 mm in diameter

0·002 – 0·02 mm in diameter

0·02 – 0·2 mm in diameter

greater than 0·2 mm in diameter

increasing particle size

Soil conservation

A good farmer understands the importance of keeping the soil in good condition. The farmers of the mid-western states of the USA paid the penalty for ignoring their soil. They grew the same crop, wheat, year after year, in gigantic fields. This form of farming is called *monoculture*, and rapidly exhausts the soil. In 1934 there was a severe drought and because of the poor soil structure most of the topsoil was blown away by the wind. The area affected became known as the *dust bowl* of America, and covered a vast area of land. Most of this land has been returned to grass and is now used for ranching cattle.

There are a number of ways to reduce soil erosion and increase the fertility of the soil.

Crop rotation

Crops differ in their nutritional needs and will remove different minerals from the soil. By planting different crops each year, the farmer can make sure that the soil does not become exhausted of nutrients. Some crops, such as peas, beans and clover are useful because they add nitrogen to the soil. Grass and clover are often grown to be ploughed in at the end of a season; this increases the amount of humus in the soil. Humus is vital for the formation of a good soil structure.

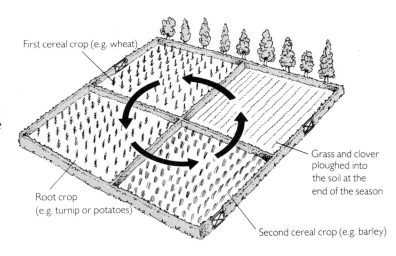

First cereal crop (e.g. wheat)

Root crop
(e.g. turnip or potatoes)

Grass and clover
ploughed into
the soil at the
end of the season

Second cereal crop (e.g. barley)

Organic fertilisers

Man-made fertilizers are very useful for increasing the yield of crops, but they do not help maintain a good soil structure. By spreading manure on his fields the farmer can help provide both the nutrients and structure that maintains a good soil.

Strip farming

Large fields may well improve the efficiency of modern farm machinery but they are less protected from the effects of wind and rain. Hedges and shelter belts of trees increase the yield of crops, as well as providing habitats for many wild flowers and animals.

Land reclamation

Poor agricultural land can often be improved by drainage or irrigation.

Drainage

Land that is too wet or is permanently flooded can be reclaimed by draining it. This is done by digging drainage channels and pumping away the water. The drainage raises the agricultural value of the land but it has a damaging effect on the wildlife that inhabits these wetland areas. Land drainage and reclamation has been practised on a vast scale in northern Holland.

Irrigation

In the south east of England there is a shortage of water for agriculture. The rainfall is only sufficient for crops one year in ten. Farmers in this area have to rely on irrigation to be successful. Many dry countries, especially in Africa, irrigate large areas of land by water supplied by rivers which have been dammed, e.g. Lake Nasser in Egypt.

12 LAND

Less than one-third of the Earth's surface is land, the rest is covered by great oceans. Less than 20% of this land is being cultivated for food.

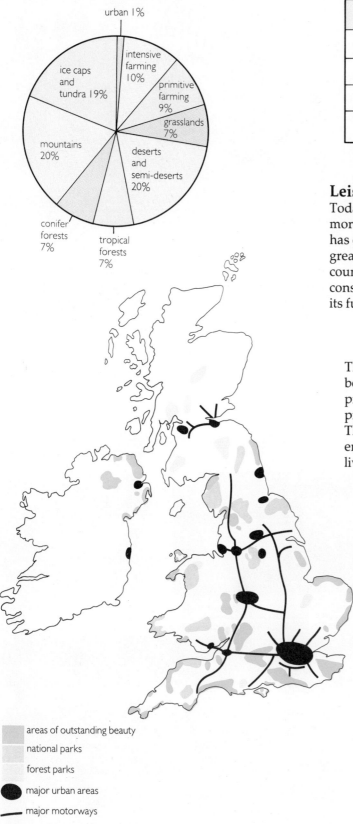

urban 1%
intensive farming 10%
primitive farming 9%
grasslands 7%
deserts and semi-deserts 20%
tropical forests 7%
conifer forests 7%
mountains 20%
ice caps and tundra 19%

Land use in the UK	
Agriculture	80%
Forest and woodland	8%
Urban areas	9%
Other uses	3%

Leisure

Today, more than ever before, people have more income, more leisure time and a much greater mobility. The car has opened up the whole of the countryside, but has put great pressure on the roads and those areas of the country that are used for leisure. We have the problem of conserving our landscape while also trying to provide for its fuller use and enjoyment.

There are ten **National Parks** in England and Wales. They are found mainly in highland areas that have not been altered by man. Most of the land in these Parks is privately owned, but Park authorities have the power to prevent anyone making harmful changes in land-use. The Parks are enjoyed by many tourists, but often their enjoyment conflicts with the interests of the people who live in them.

Areas of outstanding natural beauty are found throughout the United Kingdom. They are preserved like the National Parks and are usually open to the public.

Forest parks are large forests owned by the Forestry Commission which are open to the public. They are all in areas of great natural beauty.

Green belts are areas of land that surround large urban areas. Building is usually not allowed in these areas. They are designed to stop the growth of large towns and to allow open countryside to be in easy reach of people who live in these towns.

areas of outstanding beauty
national parks
forest parks
major urban areas
major motorways

Land – a resource

Land is one of our basic resources –we live on it, work on it and grow our food on it. We should be concerned about how we use it. What are the different pressures on our land?

"That's really superb ... unless the geologist's report is wrong"

Conflict or compromise?

The situations above give you some idea of the problems that may arise over our use of the land. In every conflict there is no 'right' answer, and very often there are more than two sides. Naturally, most solutions are compromises; whether you agree or not will depend on your interests and opinions. Generally speaking it is not possible for people to change the use of their land just as they please. Governments have passed several **Town and Country Planning Acts** to control land-use. Planning proposals must be given to certain authorities before you can change the use of land. These authorities try to consider the views of everyone involved before they approve or refuse the proposed changes.

13 CYCLES OF MATTER

The biosphere

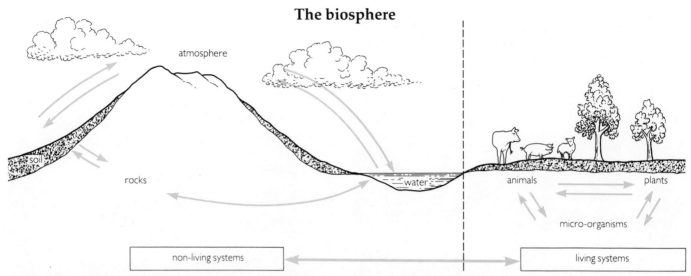

| non-living systems | | living systems |

The biosphere is that part of the Earth that can support life, from the depths of the oceans to the upper limits of the atmosphere. It is made up of two parts, non-living and living. The non-living or physical part is made up of rocks, soil, the atmosphere and the lakes and oceans. The living part consists of all the animals, plants and micro-organisms that live on the Earth. Materials are constantly being moved throughout the biosphere and this is called the *cycling of matter*. **All** matter is cycled, although different materials have different cycling times.

This exchange of materials is vital for the existence of life. Unfortunately, we can easily disturb these cycles, and often do! The consequences of our actions are often difficult to calculate.

The carbon dioxide cycle

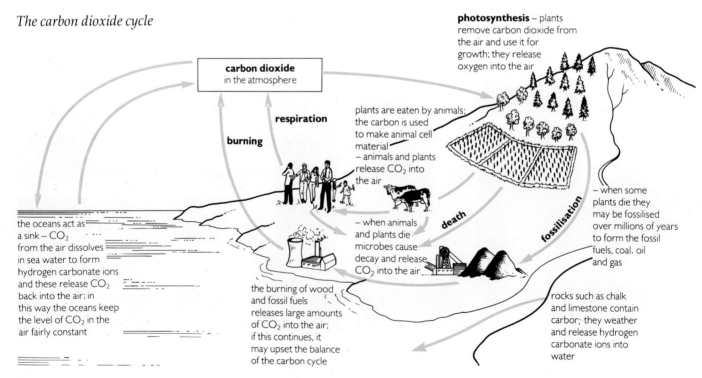

The burning of fossil fuels has increased the concentration of carbon dioxide in the atmosphere. Carbon dioxide allows light from the Sun to pass through the atmosphere to the Earth's surface, where some of it is converted to heat. This heat is reflected but is trapped by the carbon dioxide.

This is called the *greenhouse effect* (see page 212). If the level of carbon dioxide in the atmosphere continues to increase, some people think that the greenhouse effect will cause the temperature of the Earth to increase and cause drastic changes in our climate and weather.

Nitrogen cycle

Agricultural activity interferes with the cycle. Crops remove nitrates from the soil which must be replaced by artificial or natural fertilisers.

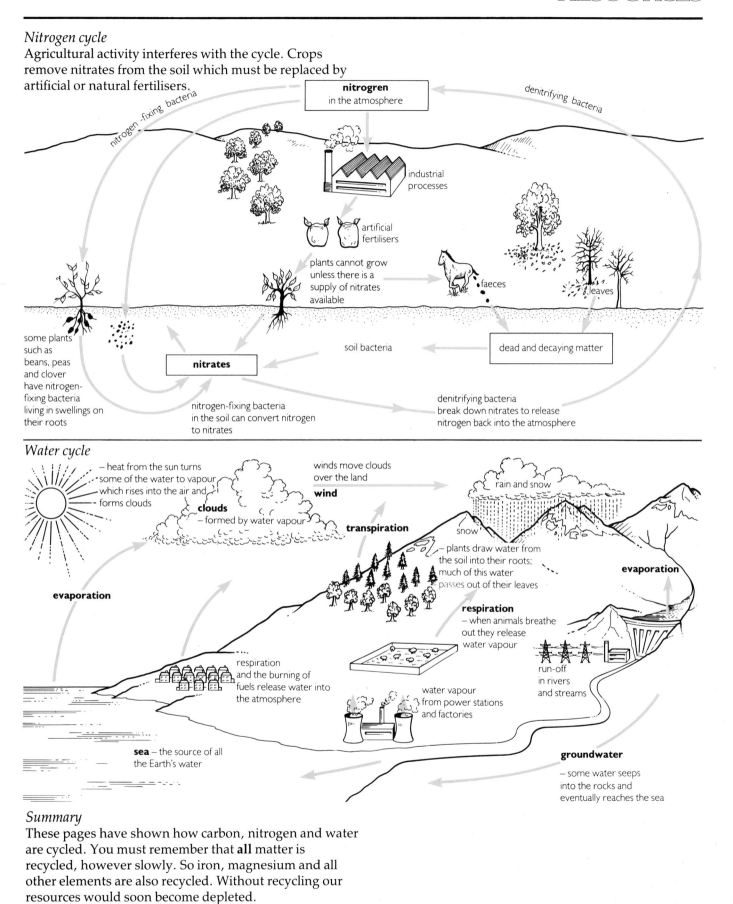

nitrogen-fixing bacteria

nitrogren in the atmosphere

denitrifying bacteria

industrial processes

artificial fertilisers

plants cannot grow unless there is a supply of nitrates available

faeces

leaves

some plants such as beans, peas and clover have nitrogen-fixing bacteria living in swellings on their roots

nitrates

soil bacteria

dead and decaying matter

nitrogen-fixing bacteria in the soil can convert nitrogen to nitrates

denitrifying bacteria break down nitrates to release nitrogen back into the atmosphere

Water cycle

– heat from the sun turns some of the water to vapour which rises into the air and forms clouds

winds move clouds over the land

wind

rain and snow

clouds – formed by water vapour

transpiration

snow

– plants draw water from the soil into their roots; much of this water passes out of their leaves

evaporation

evaporation

respiration – when animals breathe out they release water vapour

respiration and the burning of fuels release water into the atmosphere

water vapour from power stations and factories

run-off in rivers and streams

sea – the source of all the Earth's water

groundwater – some water seeps into the rocks and eventually reaches the sea

Summary

These pages have shown how carbon, nitrogen and water are cycled. You must remember that **all** matter is recycled, however slowly. So iron, magnesium and all other elements are also recycled. Without recycling our resources would soon become depleted.

THE HUMAN MACHINE

CHAPTER 3

ORGANISATION

The human body is a living machine made up of *organ systems*. These organ systems link up and work together to keep us alive. An example of one of our organ systems is the respiratory system – made up of the nose, mouth, windpipe and lungs.

The scheme below shows how various organ systems interact when we move. The relationships are very complicated and not all of them are shown.

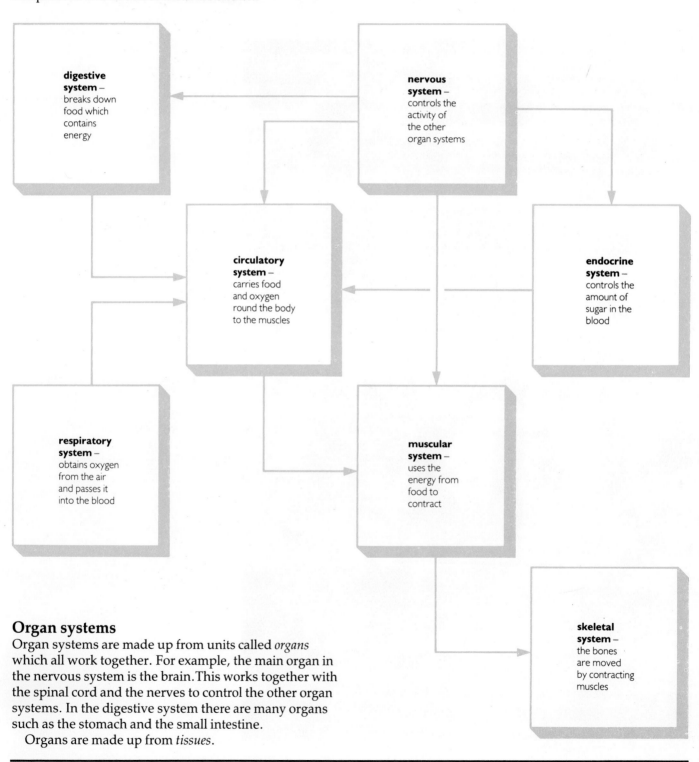

digestive system –
breaks down food which contains energy

nervous system –
controls the activity of the other organ systems

circulatory system –
carries food and oxygen round the body to the muscles

endocrine system –
controls the amount of sugar in the blood

respiratory system –
obtains oxygen from the air and passes it into the blood

muscular system –
uses the energy from food to contract

skeletal system –
the bones are moved by contracting muscles

Organ systems

Organ systems are made up from units called *organs* which all work together. For example, the main organ in the nervous system is the brain. This works together with the spinal cord and the nerves to control the other organ systems. In the digestive system there are many organs such as the stomach and the small intestine.

Organs are made up from *tissues*.

Tissues

An organ is made up of a group of tissues which work together as one unit. The heart is an organ. It is made up of muscle tissue, nerve tissue and connective tissue. Different organs are made up of different types of tissue, depending on the job of that particular organ. Tissues are made up of *cells*.

Cells

Cells are the basic unit of life. There are many different types of cell; each type has a different job to do.

The basic shape of all animal cells is shown in the diagram on the right. Some of the many specialised cells in the human body are shown below.

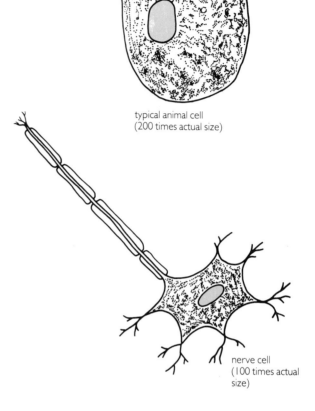

typical animal cell
(200 times actual size)

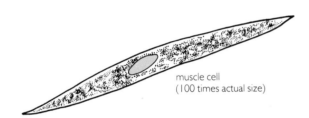

muscle cell
(100 times actual size)

nerve cell
(100 times actual size)

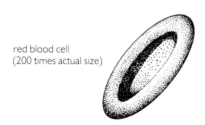

red blood cell
(200 times actual size)

sperm cell
(200 times actual size)

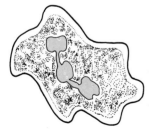

white blood cell
(100 times actual size)

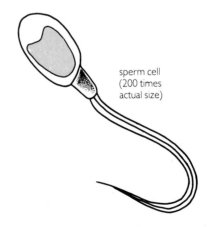

2 ORGAN SYSTEMS

The human body is made up of many organ systems. The diagrams on these two pages show the position of some of these systems.

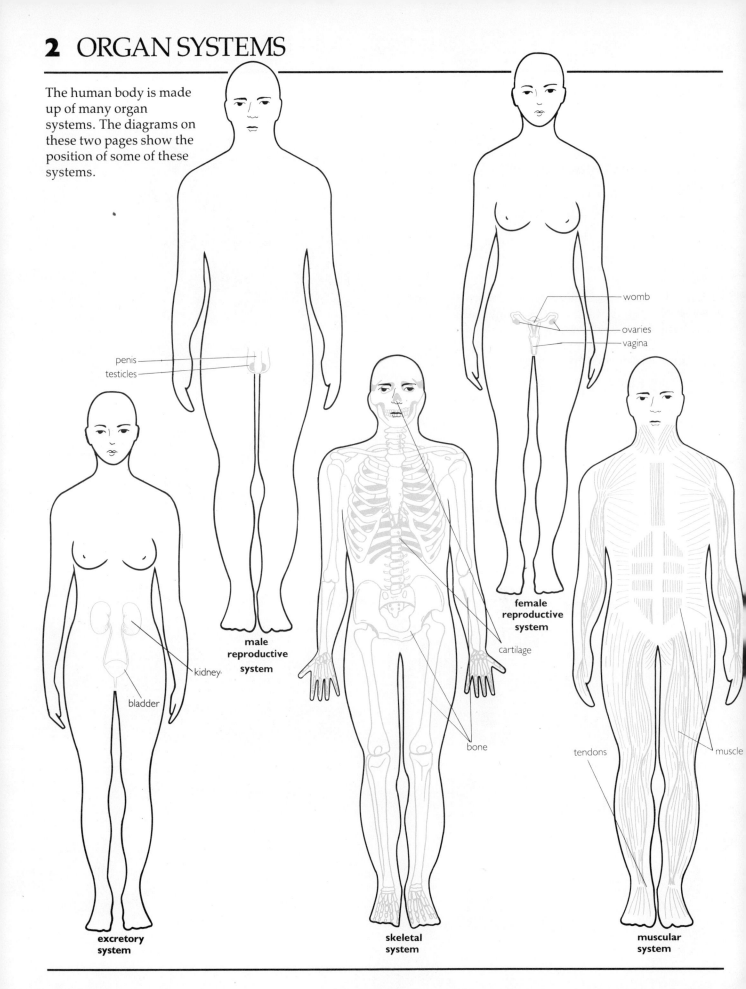

penis
testicles

womb
ovaries
vagina

female
reproductive
system

male
reproductive
system

kidney

cartilage

bladder

bone

tendons

muscle

**excretory
system**

**skeletal
system**

**muscular
system**

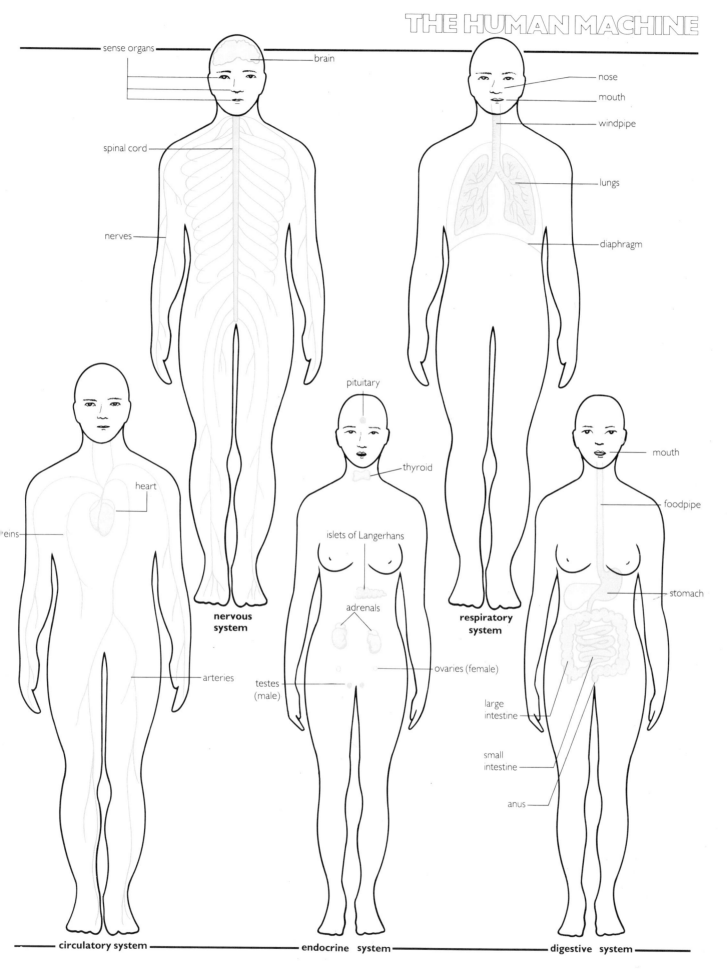

sense organs

brain

nose

mouth

windpipe

spinal cord

lungs

nerves

diaphragm

heart

pituitary

mouth

thyroid

islets of Langerhans

foodpipe

eins

adrenals

stomach

arteries

ovaries (female)

testes
(male)

large
intestine

small
intestine

anus

**nervous
system**

**respiratory
system**

circulatory system

endocrine system

digestive system

3 MUSCLES AND BONES

We are able to move because muscles move our bones. A simple action such as picking up a pencil off the floor involves dozens of muscles; something complicated like riding a bicycle involves hundreds. The nervous system coordinates all the muscles to make the required movements.

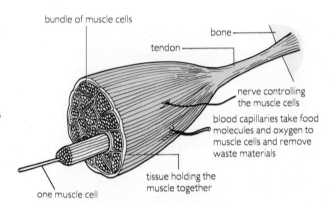

bundle of muscle cells

bone

tendon

nerve controlling the muscle cells

blood capillaries take food molecules and oxygen to muscle cells and remove waste materials

one muscle cell

tissue holding the muscle together

Muscles

About 50% of the human body is muscle. Muscle tissue is made up of *fibres*. These are bundles containing thousands of long thin cells. These cells have the ability to contract (get shorter) when a nerve impulse arrives.

Muscles are joined to bones by *tendons*. When lots of muscle fibres contract they pull on the tendons which in turn pull on the bones.

Muscles need lots of energy so they are well supplied with blood vessels which bring them food molecules and oxygen.

fully relaxed –
all the muscle
cells are
relaxed

half contracted –
some muscle
cells are contracted
while the rest
are relaxed

fully contracted –
all the muscle
cells are
contracted

A muscle cell will contract if it receives a message from a nerve cell. It will be relaxed if no messages are received. Muscle cells cannot expand, they can only contract and relax. This means that muscles can only pull, they cannot push. The amount of contraction that is done by a muscle depends on how many of its muscle cells are contracting. If none of them are contracting the muscle is completely relaxed. If all the cells are contracting, the muscle is fully contracted.

There are three basic types of muscle found in the human body.

involuntary muscle –
this cannot be controlled
consciously; it responds
automatically to stimuli,
e.g. iris muscle in the eye

cardiac muscle –
this contracts regularly
about 70 times a minute;
unlike other muscle it
never gets tired, e.g. heart

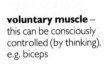

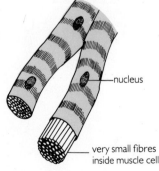

voluntary muscle –
this can be consciously
controlled (by thinking),
e.g. biceps

nucleus

very small fibres
inside muscle cell

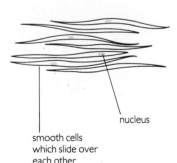

nucleus

smooth cells
which slide over
each other

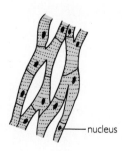

nucleus

Bones

Bone may appear dead, but it is a living tissue. If it was dead it would not mend after being broken.

Bone is made of a network of fibres. A chemical, calcium phosphate, is deposited amongst these fibres. The fibres provide the strength, while the calcium phosphate provides the hardness.

Cartilage

This material provides a smooth, flexible support or protection.

The ends of bones are covered by cartilage which protects them and also reduces friction in the joints. The nose and ears are supported by cartilage.

The skeleton

There are over 200 bones in the human skeleton. They provide the body with *support*, and *protect* some of the internal organs. They also give the muscles something to pull on so the body can *move*.

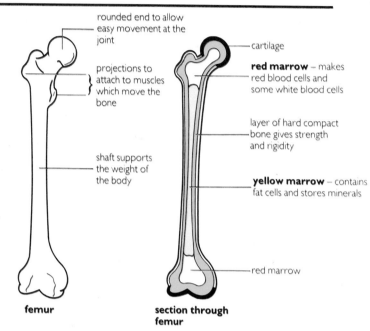

rounded end to allow easy movement at the joint

projections to attach to muscles which move the bone

shaft supports the weight of the body

femur

cartilage

red marrow – makes red blood cells and some white blood cells

layer of hard compact bone gives strength and rigidity

yellow marrow – contains fat cells and stores minerals

red marrow

section through femur

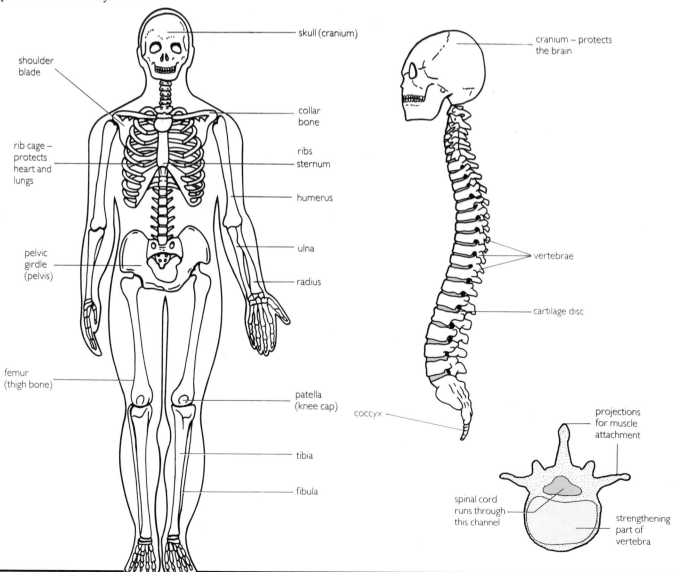

skull (cranium)

shoulder blade

rib cage – protects heart and lungs

pelvic girdle (pelvis)

femur (thigh bone)

collar bone

ribs
sternum

humerus

ulna

radius

patella (knee cap)

tibia

fibula

cranium – protects the brain

vertebrae

cartilage disc

coccyx

projections for muscle attachment

spinal cord runs through this channel

strengthening part of vertebra

MUSCLES AND BONES

Movement

Arms and legs move when a nervous impulse or message from the central nervous system reaches the nerve endings in the muscles. The muscle cells contract, causing the muscles to pull on the bones. The bones move at joints.

Muscles generally work in pairs. They are called *antagonistic pairs* because they oppose one another: when one contracts the other relaxes.

This can be understood by looking at the arrangement of muscles and bones in the arm. The *biceps* and *triceps* are an antagonistic pair. When they contract or relax the arm bones move at the elbow joint.

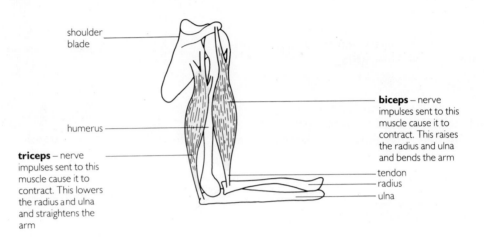

shoulder blade

humerus

triceps – nerve impulses sent to this muscle cause it to contract. This lowers the radius and ulna and straightens the arm

biceps – nerve impulses sent to this muscle cause it to contract. This raises the radius and ulna and bends the arm

tendon
radius
ulna

Joints

These are found wherever two bones meet. There are three main types of joint.

1   Fixed joints: here the bones fit closely and cannot move. The bones of the skull form fixed joints.
2   Slightly movable joints: in these there is a pad of cartilage between the bones. This allows the bones to move slightly. The vertebrae form this type of joint.
3   Freely movable joints: the bones can move easily at these joints. There are three kinds of freely movable joint – *gliding*, *hinge* and *ball and socket*.

fixed joints between skull bones

vertebra

cartilage disc

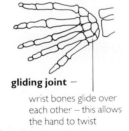

gliding joint –

wrist bones glide over each other – this allows the hand to twist

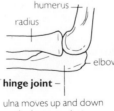

humerus

radius

elbow

hinge joint –

ulna moves up and down on the humerus, just like a door hinge

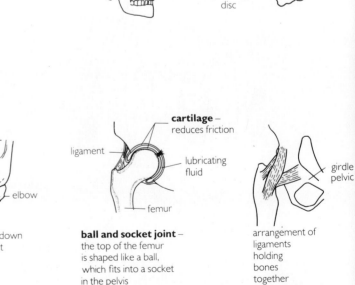

cartilage – reduces friction

ligament

lubricating fluid

femur

ball and socket joint – the top of the femur is shaped like a ball, which fits into a socket in the pelvis

girdle pelvic

arrangement of ligaments holding bones together

Hinge joints and ball and socket joints are lubricated by a fluid. This *synovial fluid* is trapped inside a capsule that forms around the joint.

Disorders

Fractures

A fracture is a broken bone. Healthy bone is very strong and thick bones like the femur rarely break. Thin bones like the collar bone or the fibula can be easily broken if given a sharp blow.

There are four main types of fracture. Some are more serious than others.

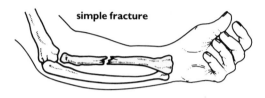

simple fracture

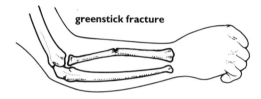

greenstick fracture

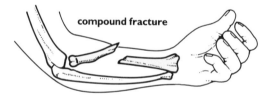

compound fracture

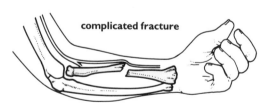

complicated fracture

Treatment   The injured part should not be moved because the broken bone could severely damage muscle, blood vessels or nerves. Medical help should be sought.

X-ray pictures give information about the fracture. The fracture will then be *reduced*. This means the broken ends of the bones will be returned to their normal positions. The bone is then set in position, usually by using a plaster cast. This holds the bone still while it heals naturally. If it is difficult to keep the bones still, for example in the case of a broken femur (thigh bone), *traction* can be used to pull on the bone gently, forcing it and the muscles to be still while healing takes place.

Dislocations

Dislocation occurs when part of a joint is moved out of place. This occurs most often at freely movable joints. A dislocated joint should be carefully supported until a doctor can put the bones back in place.

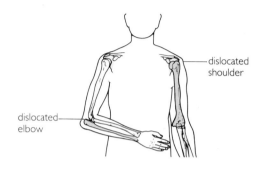

dislocated shoulder

dislocated elbow

Arthritis

The cause of this disorder is not really known. The affected joints become stiff, swollen and painful. The joints of the fingers and wrist are most affected. Old people commonly suffer from this disorder.

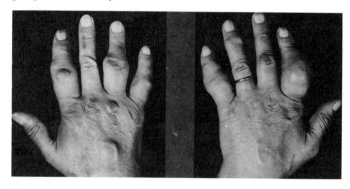

Rheumatism

This is a name given to any painful disorder of the muscles or joints.

Fibrositis

The major symptom of fibrositis is a dull ache in the affected muscle which can increase to become a severe pain. The real cause is unknown although the disorder may be caused by bad posture. It can be corrected by sitting upright, not straining the back and relaxing properly. Drugs can be used in severe cases.

Muscular dystrophy

In this disease the muscle wastes away. The muscle fibres seem to be defective but the cause is not known. It can be a serious disease if important muscles are affected.

4 THE DIGESTIVE SYSTEM

The body needs food to stay alive. When we swallow food, it passes down a long tube called the digestive system. Two important things happen to the food as it passes along the digestive system.

Digestion
Large molecules of food are broken down into smaller molecules.

Absorption
The smaller molecules of digested food pass through the wall of the small intestine into the bloodstream.

The chemical breakdown of food is caused by juices produced in each of the main sections of the digestive system, as shown in the flow chart below.

The active chemicals in all these digestive juices are called *enzymes*. They are produced by living cells. They speed up slow chemical reactions.

Each section of the digestive system produces a juice that contains different enzymes. There are three basic types of digestive enzyme found in the digestive system:

1 carbohydrases (amylases) speed up the breakdown of carbohydrates to simple sugars;
2 lipases speed up the breakdown of fats and oils to fatty acids and glycerol;
3 proteinases speed up the breakdown of proteins to amino acids.

Enzymes work best in the regions where they are produced, because they are very sensitive to the temperature and acidity of their surroundings.

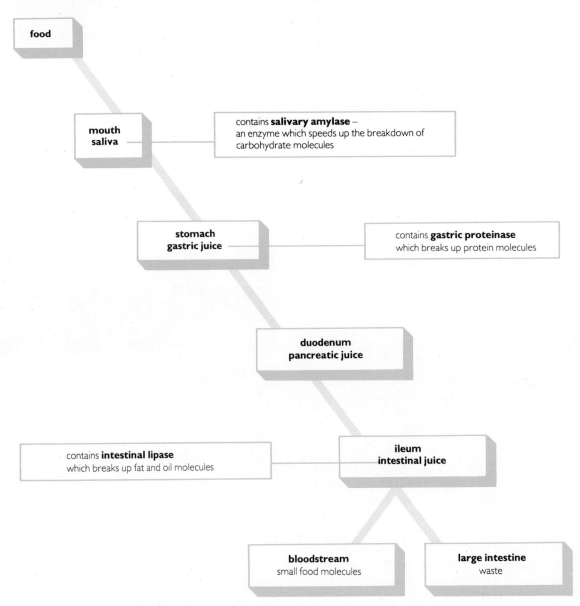

food

mouth
saliva

contains **salivary amylase** – an enzyme which speeds up the breakdown of carbohydrate molecules

stomach
gastric juice

contains **gastric proteinase** which breaks up protein molecules

duodenum
pancreatic juice

contains **intestinal lipase** which breaks up fat and oil molecules

ileum
intestinal juice

bloodstream
small food molecules

large intestine
waste

The design of the digestive system

The digestive system starts at the mouth and ends at the anus.

The mouth

The adult human should have 32 teeth, of four basic types.

Teeth are designed to physically break up our food into smaller pieces.

The tongue is made up of muscle. It is designed to move food around the mouth to meet the different teeth. While the food is in the mouth, it is moistened with *saliva* from three salivary glands. Saliva makes the food easier to swallow; it contains an enzyme, salivary amylase, that starts to breakdown any carbohydrate in the food.

When the food has been chewed sufficiently it is swallowed and passes down the food pipe (oesophagus) to the stomach.

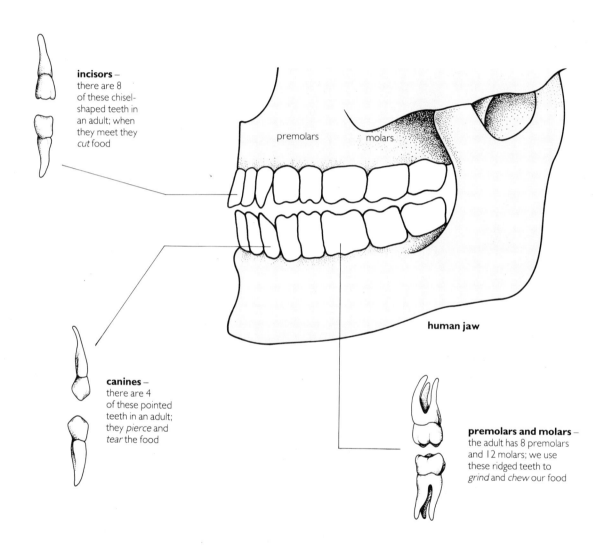

incisors – there are 8 of these chisel-shaped teeth in an adult; when they meet they *cut* food

premolars

molars

human jaw

canines – there are 4 of these pointed teeth in an adult; they *pierce* and *tear* the food

premolars and molars – the adult has 8 premolars and 12 molars; we use these ridged teeth to *grind* and *chew* our food

The stomach

This is a flexible bag of muscle that can enlarge to accept the food that arrives from the oesophagus. Cells in the lining of the stomach wall produce an acid and a digestive liquid called *gastric juice,* which contains enzymes. The stomach wall is protected from these liquids by a slimy layer.

The gastric enzymes continue digestion of the food in the stomach. The food is passed out through a muscle ring into the small intestine.

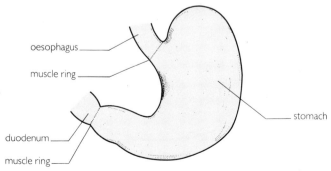

oesophagus

muscle ring

stomach

duodenum

muscle ring

THE DIGESTIVE SYSTEM

The small intestine

This narrow coiled tube is about 6 m long and is divided into two parts. The *duodenum* is the first part; it is only about 30 cm long. The walls of the duodenum produce a digestive juice. The enzymes in the juice help to finish the digestion of carbohydrates, proteins and fats. Digestive juices from the pancreas and the liver enter the duodenum and help with digestion.

The *ileum* is the second and longest part of the small intestine. It also produces a digestive juice but its main job is to allow small molecules of food to pass through its wall into the blood. In order to do this efficiently, the wall of the ileum is folded and is covered with many small hair-like projections called *villi*. These increase the surface area of the ileum wall. They have a rich blood supply to carry away the food molecules to the parts of the body where they are needed.

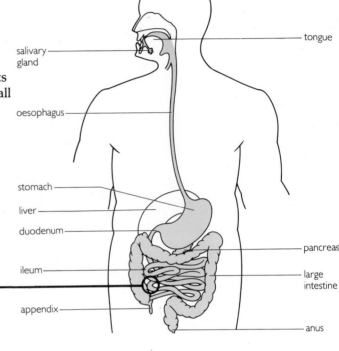

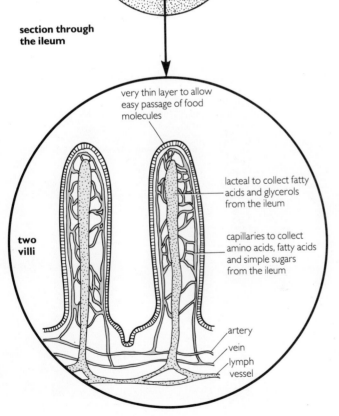

longitudinal muscle

circular muscle

internal wall of ileum

section through the ileum

very thin layer to allow easy passage of food molecules

lacteal to collect fatty acids and glycerols from the ileum

capillaries to collect amino acids, fatty acids and simple sugars from the ileum

two villi

artery
vein
lymph vessel

The large intestine

When the digested food molecules have all been absorbed into the blood all that remains is a watery indigestible waste. This passes out of the ileum into the large intestine.

The large intestine or bowel is much shorter than the small intestine but is much wider. It has two main functions:

1 to remove water from the undigested waste – this water is needed by the body, it is passed through the wall of the large intestine into the blood;
2 to collect the dried waste, now called *faeces*, and store it until it is convenient to pass it out of the body through the anus.

What can go wrong?

A good state of health and a well-balanced diet help the digestive system to work normally. Some common disorders which do occur are given below.

Many people eat refined food that lacks vegetable fibre. There is some evidence to suggest that a lack of fibre in our diet increases the chances of suffering from diseases of the large intestine. In countries where people eat more fibre, fewer people suffer from these diseases. Good sources of fibre are wholemeal bread, brown rice and vegetables.

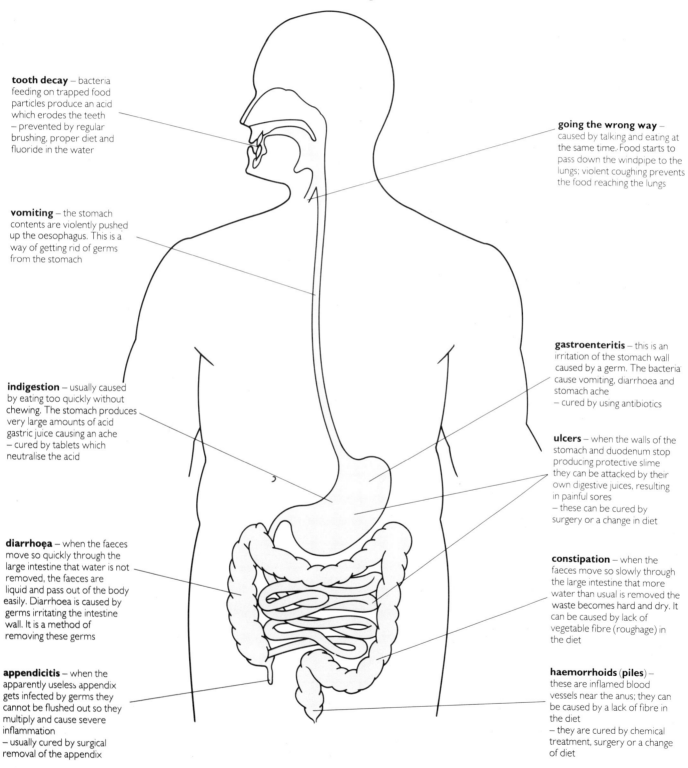

tooth decay – bacteria feeding on trapped food particles produce an acid which erodes the teeth – prevented by regular brushing, proper diet and fluoride in the water

vomiting – the stomach contents are violently pushed up the oesophagus. This is a way of getting rid of germs from the stomach

indigestion – usually caused by eating too quickly without chewing. The stomach produces very large amounts of acid gastric juice causing an ache – cured by tablets which neutralise the acid

diarrhoea – when the faeces move so quickly through the large intestine that water is not removed, the faeces are liquid and pass out of the body easily. Diarrhoea is caused by germs irritating the intestine wall. It is a method of removing these germs

appendicitis – when the apparently useless appendix gets infected by germs they cannot be flushed out so they multiply and cause severe inflammation – usually cured by surgical removal of the appendix

going the wrong way – caused by talking and eating at the same time. Food starts to pass down the windpipe to the lungs; violent coughing prevents the food reaching the lungs

gastroenteritis – this is an irritation of the stomach wall caused by a germ. The bacteria cause vomiting, diarrhoea and stomach ache – cured by using antibiotics

ulcers – when the walls of the stomach and duodenum stop producing protective slime they can be attacked by their own digestive juices, resulting in painful sores – these can be cured by surgery or a change in diet

constipation – when the faeces move so slowly through the large intestine that more water than usual is removed the waste becomes hard and dry. It can be caused by lack of vegetable fibre (roughage) in the diet

haemorrhoids (piles) – these are inflamed blood vessels near the anus; they can be caused by a lack of fibre in the diet – they are cured by chemical treatment, surgery or a change of diet

5 THE CIRCULATORY SYSTEM

The circulatory system is a complicated network of blood vessels (thin tubes) that branch throughout the body. Blood is forced through these blood vessels by the pumping action of the heart. The blood supplies every cell in the body with food and oxygen, and removes waste.

The heart

The heart is a hollow muscular bag that alternately contracts and relaxes (i.e. expands). The space inside the heart is divided into four chambers. The top two have thin walls and collect blood returning to the heart. Each of these chambers is called an *atrium*. The two lower chambers have much thicker walls. They pump the blood through the arteries. These two chambers are called *ventricles*.

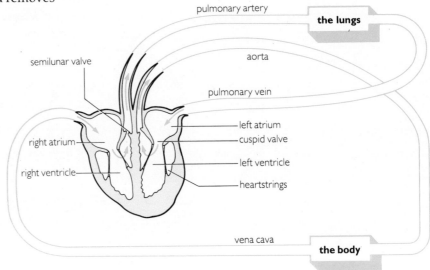

The heart pumps blood to the lungs and the rest of the body at the same time. This means that there are two circulations. Blood is pumped from the heart to the lungs and back again. This is the *pulmonary circulation*. Blood is also pumped from the heart to the body and back and this is called the *systemic circulation*.

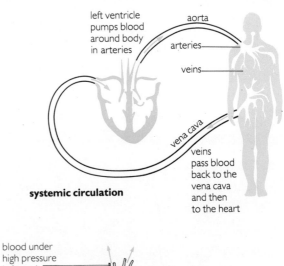

systemic circulation

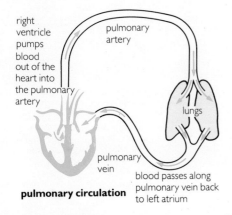

pulmonary circulation

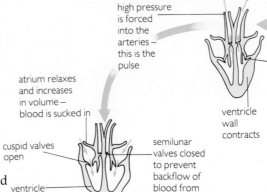

The heart beat
The sound of the heart beat is caused by the slamming shut of the cuspid valves, followed by the closing of the semilunar valves.

Blood vessels

Blood leaves the heart in *arteries* and returns to it in *veins*. Arteries and veins are joined by *capillaries*. These tiny vessels branch and reach every cell.

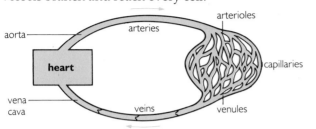

Arteries

These have thick walls containing muscle and elastic fibres to withstand the high pressure of blood.

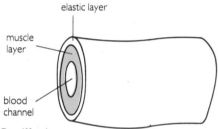

Capillaries

These are very narrow with very thin walls. They connect the arteries and veins together.

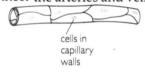

Veins

These are wider than the corresponding arteries. They have thin walls because the blood they carry is at a low pressure.

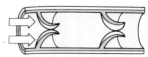

Veins have valves in them to make sure the blood flows in one direction only – back to the heart. When the muscles of the arms and legs are working, they squeeze the veins and force the blood towards the heart. The sucking action of the heart also helps the blood flow.

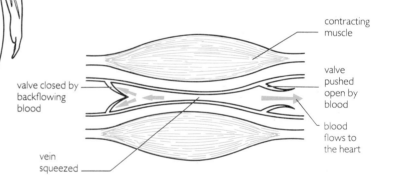

Exchange of materials

Every cell in the body is bathed in a liquid called *tissue fluid*. Blood capillaries pass close to all these cells. Materials such as oxygen, dissolved salts and food molecules diffuse out of the capillaries. They enter the tissue fluid and then the cells. Waste material and carbon dioxide diffuse from the cells and enter the tissue fluid. Some of the fluid is picked up by venules (small veins), but most is collected by small tubes that belong to the lymphatic system. This fluid is called *lymph*.

The lymphatic system

This is a network of thin-walled vessels. Like veins, they have valves in them to maintain a one-way flow. These lymph vessels carry lymph away from the tissue fluid and drain it into the jugular vein at the base of the neck.

Lymph glands are found at various places along the lymphatic system. These contain large numbers of white blood cells. The lymph glands act as filters and prevent germs and their poisons passing into the bloodstream. They may become swollen and painful if large numbers of germs are present.

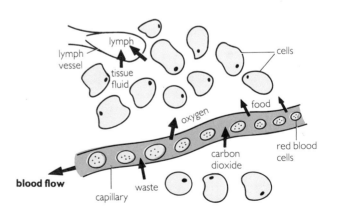

THE CIRCULATORY SYSTEM

Blood

An adult has about 5 litres of blood circulating in the arteries, veins and capillaries that make up the circulatory system.

If a sample of blood is put in a test tube and spun in a centrifuge it will separate into two quite distinct layers. The lower, more dense layer is made up of blood cells while the paler less dense upper layer is made up of blood plasma.

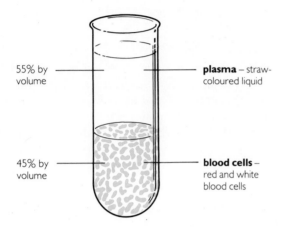

55% by volume   **plasma** – straw-coloured liquid

45% by volume   **blood cells** – red and white blood cells

Red blood cells

Each cubic centimetre of blood contains about 5 thousand million red blood cells. Their job is to carry oxygen from the lungs to the body's cells.

Each red blood cell is packed with a special pigment called *haemoglobin*. Oxygen diffuses into the lung's capillaries and combines with the haemoglobin in the red blood cells to form *oxyhaemoglobin*. The blood is now *oxygenated*. When the red blood cells pass through the body's capillaries, they give up their oxygen and the blood becomes *deoxygenated*.

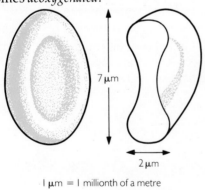

7 μm

2 μm

I μm = I millionth of a metre

(⊢——⊣ is 10 000 μm long)

Mature red blood cells lose their nucleus and take up a shape that is described as a bi-concave disc. This increases its surface area, makes room for more haemoglobin and allows them to pass through very thin capillaries. They have a lifespan of about 4 months. After that time they are replaced by new cells which are made in bone marrow.

White blood cells

These are called *leucocytes*. There are far fewer white than red blood cells – only about one million in every cubic centimetre of blood. Leucocytes are larger than the red blood cells and each one has a nucleus. There are two basic types and both help protect the body against disease.

Phagocytes These are the largest of the white blood cells. They are made in the bone marrow. They can alter their shape and squeeze between the cells in the capillary walls, into the tissue fluid. Here they engulf and destroy bacteria, diseased body cells and any foreign invaders.

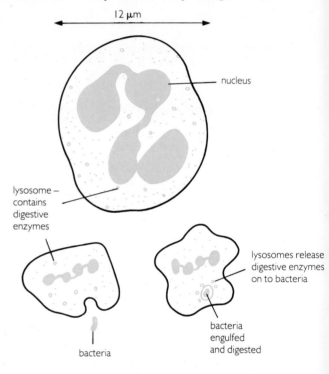

12 μm

nucleus

lysosome – contains digestive enzymes

lysosomes release digestive enzymes on to bacteria

bacteria

bacteria engulfed and digested

Lymphocytes These are smaller than phagocytes and are made in the lymphatic system. They produce special proteins, called *antibodies*. These attack bacteria and viruses. Lymphocytes are mainly concerned with the prevention and cure of long-term infections.

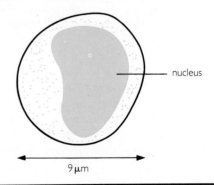

nucleus

9 μm

Changes in the blood

The composition of the blood is changed as it passes around the body.

Lungs

As the blood passes through the fine network of capillaries that surround the air sacs, it picks up oxygen and releases carbon dioxide and water.

carbon dioxide + water

oxygen

blood + water + carbon dioxide in

blood + oxygen out

Intestines

Blood passes through the capillaries in the villi of the small intestine. It picks up small molecules of digested food such as sugars and amino acids. These are transported directly to the liver.

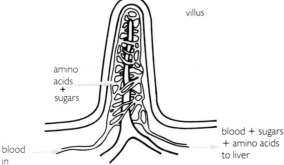

villus

amino acids + sugars

blood + sugars + amino acids to liver

blood in

Liver

As blood passes through the liver several changes take place. The blood sugar level is checked. Sugar is either removed from the blood or added to the blood, depending on the body's needs. Waste proteins are broken down to urea which is carried away in the blood. Poisons, such as alcohol, are made harmless.

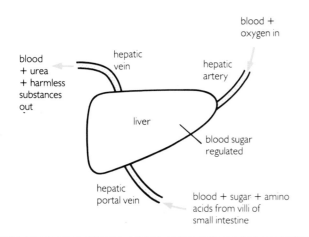

blood + urea + harmless substances out

hepatic vein

blood + oxygen in

hepatic artery

liver

blood sugar regulated

hepatic portal vein

blood + sugar + amino acids from villi of small intestine

Kidneys

As the blood passes through the kidneys, the urea produced in the liver is removed. Poisons and excess salt are also removed. The kidney controls the amount of water in the blood.

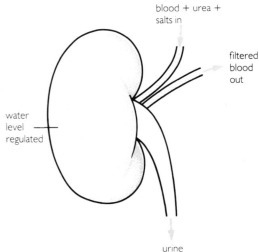

blood + urea + salts in

filtered blood out

water level regulated

urine

Muscles

These tissues need a lot of energy. The blood supplies them with glucose and oxygen for respiration and removes the carbon dioxide and water produced.

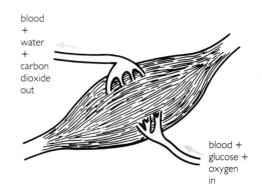

blood + water + carbon dioxide out

blood + glucose + oxygen in

Wounds and cuts

Phagocytes are carried by the blood to the site of infection. They attack any foreign invaders. A soluble protein in the blood, called *fibrinogen*, is converted into threads called *fibrin*. These threads trap red blood cells and form a clot to seal the wound.

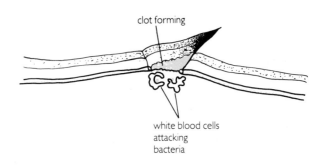

clot forming

white blood cells attacking bacteria

THE CIRCULATORY SYSTEM

Blood transfusions

The first blood transfusions were carried out at the start of the twentieth century. Many were unsuccessful. The blood cells from the *donor's* blood stuck together in the patient's (*recipient's*) blood vessels causing a clot.

A blood transfusion is only successful if the donor's and the patient's blood are similar. They can then mix without clotting or sticking together. This usually means they are the same blood group.

The cell membrane of the red blood cell differs in different people. The chemicals which cause the difference are *antigens*. The blood plasma contains soluble proteins called antibodies. An antibody will react with a special antigen and cause the red blood cells to stick together.

antigens on cell membrane of red blood cells

antibodies in blood plasma

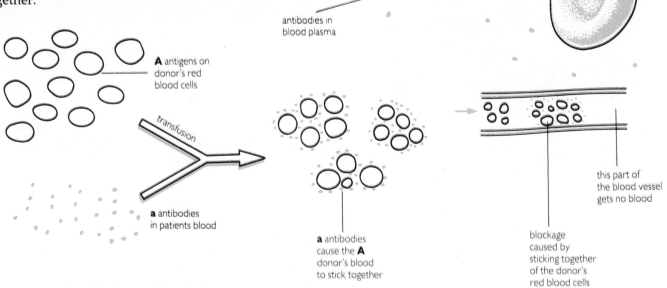

A antigens on donor's red blood cells

transfusion

a antibodies in patients blood

a antibodies cause the **A** donor's blood to stick together

blockage caused by sticking together of the donor's red blood cells

this part of the blood vessel gets no blood

Blood groups

The major blood groups are those of the ABO and Rhesus systems.

Donor blood must not be given to a recipient who has blood with antibodies which correspond to the donor's antigens. For example, antibody b will attack red blood cells that carry antigen B. If you look at the table you will see that a person of blood group O has no antigens. This blood can be transfused safely into anybody. People of blood group O are called *universal donors*. Similarly, people of blood group AB have no antibodies in their blood. They can receive blood from anyone: they are called *universal recipients*. In practice it is best to match the blood as closely as possible.

If a person with Rhesus negative blood is given Rhesus positive blood during a transfusion, very little will happen the first time, but a second transfusion will cause sticking and clotting of the donor's blood. There can be some minor problems during birth if the baby's mother has rhesus negative blood and the father has rhesus positive blood.

Blood group	Antigen on red blood cells	Antibodies in the plasma	%age of UK population
A	A	b	46%
B	B	a	9%
O	None	a & b	42%
AB	A & B	None	3%
Rhesus +ve	Rh	None	85%
Rhesus −ve	None	None	15%

Blood donors

Hospitals store blood in large refrigerators called blood banks. Blood can be stored safely for about 3 weeks. A large supply is needed at all times. Blood donors are aged between 16 and 65. Their blood is tested for certain diseases before it is accepted. During a blood donor session, about 500 cm³ of blood is taken from each donor. The body replaces this in about 24 hours.

Disorders of the circulatory system

Heart disease

The heart has only one function – to pump blood. There are many reasons why the heart may stop doing this.

Greasy material, such as cholesterol, may be deposited on the lining of an artery. This may lead to a thickening and hardening of the artery walls (*atherosclerosis*). If this happens in an artery that takes blood to the heart muscle then a heart attack (*coronary thrombosis*) can occur. This is because the thickened walls have reduced the diameter of the artery and it has become blocked by a blood clot. The heart muscle receives less blood which means less food and oxygen. It eventually stops working.

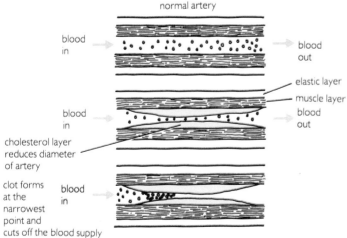

normal artery

blood in → blood out

elastic layer
muscle layer

blood in → blood out

cholesterol layer reduces diameter of artery

clot forms at the narrowest point and cuts off the blood supply
blood in →

It is thought that a high fat diet, smoking, stress and a lack of exercise all increase the chances of having a heart attack. Thrombosis can occur in other arteries. If it affects the blood supply to the legs or arms they may have to be amputated.

Varicose veins

If the valves in the veins do not close completely then blood will collect there. This will make the veins swell and stand out and they become painful. Veins like this are called varicose veins and are usually found in the legs. They are most likely to occur in people who spend a long time standing up or who pick up heavy weights. They can also occur in pregnant women. These people should exercise their legs and not stand in one place for a long time.

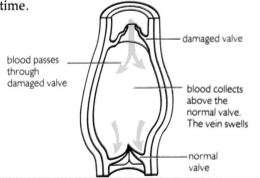

blood passes through damaged valve

damaged valve

blood collects above the normal valve. The vein swells

normal valve

Many disorders are caused by haemorrhage (a loss of blood), as follows.

Shock

This is a state of collapse, or near collapse, of the body. It may follow a serious injury. It is the failure of the blood to circulate properly when the blood pressure becomes too low. This can be serious, especially if the brain does not get enough food and oxygen. Shock may occur after a severe haemorrhage where a large loss of blood causes the blood pressure to drop.

A stroke

This is caused by a haemorrhage of a blood vessel in the brain. The effect of a stroke depends on where the blood vessel is located and how much damage is caused. It can be a slight stroke or it can be fatal. In between these extremes a stroke may cause the loss of control of certain parts of the body or even paralysis.

Haemophilia

In this disorder the blood does not have a vital protein that is needed to make it clot. Without this protein any minor bleeding becomes serious. The disorder is sex-linked. This means that some women are carriers and they can pass the disorder on to their children. Usually it is only men who suffer from haemophilia (*see page 107*). It can be controlled by drugs.

Bruising

A bruise is a sign of internal bleeding. The bruise appears blue because the blood loses its oxygen. The blood is eventually broken down into two green and yellow pigments, and these give a bruise its colour. Medical treatment is rarely needed for bruises.

Anaemia

This is a symptom of the above disorders. It occurs whenever there is a shortage of haemoglobin. This reduces the amount of oxygen available to the body. The commonest causes of anaemia are bleeding, lack of enough iron or a lack of vitamin B_{12}.

Leukaemia

This is the correct name for cancer of the white blood cells. In this disease the white blood cells keep on reproducing and are useless for defending the body against infection, in spite of their vast numbers. The increase in white blood cells also reduces the production of red blood cells causing anaemia.

6 THE RESPIRATORY SYSTEM

The respiratory system is the means by which the body obtains oxygen and removes carbon dioxide.

All living cells need oxygen in order to release energy from food. The waste products of energy production are carbon dioxide and water. The organs that exchange the gases oxygen and carbon dioxide in mammals are called the *lungs*.

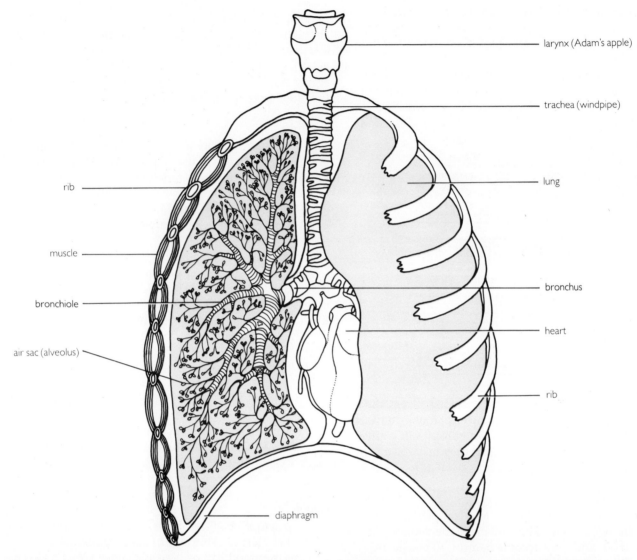

larynx (Adam's apple)

trachea (windpipe)

rib

muscle

lung

bronchiole

bronchus

air sac (alveolus)

heart

rib

diaphragm

The lungs are made up of a branched system of air passages which end in millions of tiny air sacs called *alveoli*. Each air sac, or alveolus, is like a small bag covered in tiny blood capillaries. The air sacs provide a massive surface area for gas exchange, with oxygen diffusing from the inhaled air into the bloodstream, and carbon dioxide diffusing out of the blood and into the air passages of the lungs.

Breathing involves two processes:

VENTILATION

GAS EXCHANGE

The mechanics of breathing

Inspiration (breathing in)
The movement of the ribs and diaphragm increases the volume of the chest cavity and reduces the pressure inside it. Air rich in oxygen is drawn into the lungs.

Gas exchange
Each air passage in the lung ends in a tiny air sac (alveolus). There are millions of these air sacs in each lung. Each one is surrounded by many blood capillaries.

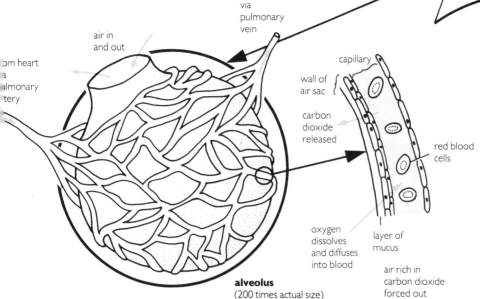

air in and out

to heart via pulmonary vein

from heart a pulmonary tery

capillary

wall of air sac

carbon dioxide released

red blood cells

oxygen dissolves and diffuses into blood

layer of mucus

alveolus
(200 times actual size)

oxygen-rich air drawn in

rib cage rises

diaphragm moves down

As you breathe, feel your rib cage rise. You may be able to feel your diaphragm move down as well. These movements alter the volume and pressure of the air inside each lung. This causes air to move in and out of each lung.

When oxygen reaches an air sac it diffuses through the thin wall of the air sac into the blood in a capillary. Carbon dioxide moves from the blood into the air sac. Each time you breathe you are exchanging oxygen for carbon dioxide. Normally you breathe, without thinking, about 12 times a minute.

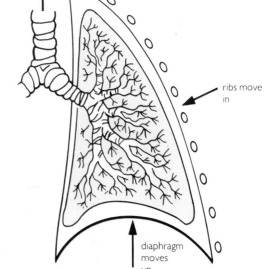

air rich in carbon dioxide forced out

ribs move in

diaphragm moves up

Expiration (breathing out)
The movement of the ribs and diaphragm reduces the volume of the chest cavity. The pressure is increased and the air, now rich in carbon dioxide, is forced out.

THE RESPIRATORY SYSTEM

What can go wrong?

The commonest industrial disease of the lungs is *pneumoconiosis*. It is caused by the continual inhaling of dust into the lungs where it causes constant irritation. There are three common forms:

Silicosis
A disease frequently found in miners. The coal dust causes permanent damage to the lungs and makes it difficult to breathe easily.

Asbestosis
A disease found in people who work in the asbestos industry. Asbestos dust causes permanent damage to the lungs and may also cause lung cancer and even death.

Farmer's lung
A disease found in agricultural workers. It is a result of an allergy to dusts and moulds. The disease is very similar to bronchitis.
    The common non-industrial diseases of the lungs are:

Bronchitis
An inflammation of the air passages in the lungs. This is very common in heavy smokers. Chronic bronchitis causes over 20 000 deaths every year in Britain.
    Continual heavy coughing is common in bronchitis sufferers. This coughing can damage the delicate air sacs and cause a disease called *emphysema.*

Pneumonia
An inflammation of the air sacs which is caused by bacteria or viruses.

Tuberculosis (TB)
A disease caused by bacteria which can spread through the lungs.

Asthma
The muscles surrounding the air passages in the lungs contract at irregular intervals. This leads to severe difficulties in breathing. Asthma attacks can be caused by an allergy, an infection or emotional disturbances.

Smoker's cough
The cells that line the air passages have small hairs which normally pass mucus and dirt out of the lungs. Smoke and tar from cigarettes stops these cells working normally and so large amounts of mucus and dirt collect in the lungs. This increases the risk of getting bronchitis. This mucus and dirt can only be removed by a heavy bout of coughing which is called a *smoker's cough.*

Do you want a cigarette more than you want your baby?

When a pregnant woman smokes she puts her unborn baby's life at risk. Every time she inhales, she poisons her baby's bloodstream with nicotine and carbon monoxide.
    Smoking can restrict your baby's growth inside the womb. It can make him underdeveloped and underweight at birth.
    It can even kill him.
    In just one year, in Britain alone, over 1,000 babies might not have died if their mothers had given up smoking when they were pregnant.
    If you give up smoking when you're pregnant your baby will be as healthy as if you'd never smoked.

The Health Education Council

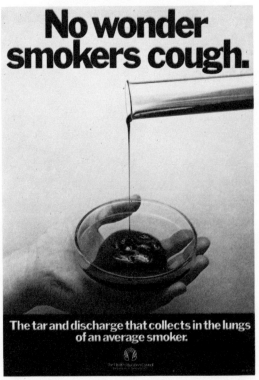

No wonder smokers cough.

The tar and discharge that collects in the lungs of an average smoker.

Smoking

It doesn't matter whether you smoke filter or non-filter cigarettes, roll ups, a pipe or cigars – *all forms of tobacco put your health at risk*.

The following diseases are much more common in smokers than non-smokers – lung cancer; cancer of the mouth, windpipe, gullet and bladder; heart disease and bronchitis.

Tobacco smoke is known to contain over 400 different chemicals. When the smoke is inhaled into the lungs many of these chemicals pass straight through the air sacs into the bloodstream. They are then carried around the body. The liver can make most of them harmless but some of the chemicals are known to cause cancer – they are *carcinogenic*.

The three main chemicals found in cigarette smoke are:

Nicotine

This is the chemical which can make you addicted to cigarettes. It passes straight into the blood and affects the brain. Sometimes nicotine can act as a stimulant and make you feel good. At other times it can act as a depressant and make you feel low. It is not thought to cause cancer but it does have a connection with various types of heart disease.

Tar

The amount of tar contained in cigarettes is marked on the packet. The tar in the cigarette causes the brown stains on smokers' teeth and hands. Tar is made up of many chemicals some of which cause cancer. Tar is trapped in the lungs where it damages the tissues and causes chronic bronchitis and sometimes lung cancer.

Carbon monoxide

This is the gas found in car exhaust fumes. It is also found in cigarette smoke. When smoke is inhaled, carbon monoxide passes straight into the blood where it takes the place of oxygen. It combines with the red blood cells 300 times more easily than oxygen. In heavy smokers this may reduce the efficiency of their blood by over 10% making them very short of breath.

Giving up

The best way to give up is not to start smoking! Someone addicted to smoking is faced with many alternative 'cures'. Unless the smoker has the will to give up and is determined, then it is likely he or she won't be successful. If the smoker really wants to give up then some of the aids might work, e.g. hypnosis, nicotine-flavoured chewing gum or special mouthwashes to make cigarettes taste foul.

Unfortunately the process of giving up smoking can cause severe irritability and lead to the person putting on weight. This increase in weight is caused when the ex-smoker substitutes eating snacks for smoking cigarettes. The benefits of giving up smoking are an increase in fitness and a significant reduction in the risk of lung cancer or heart disease.

7 SENSE AND AWARENESS

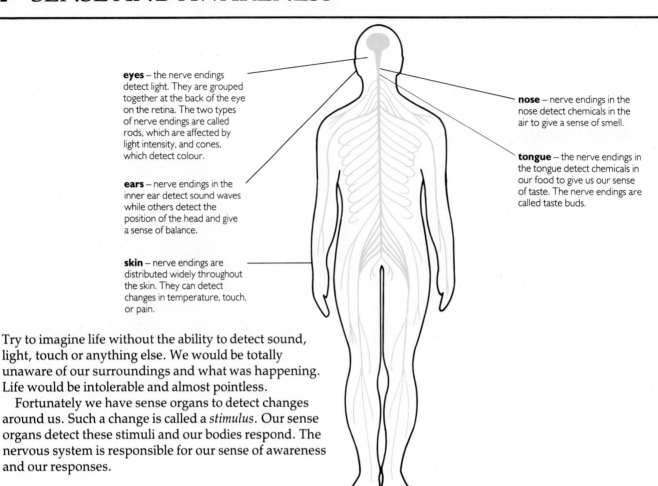

eyes – the nerve endings detect light. They are grouped together at the back of the eye on the retina. The two types of nerve endings are called rods, which are affected by light intensity, and cones, which detect colour.

ears – nerve endings in the inner ear detect sound waves while others detect the position of the head and give a sense of balance.

skin – nerve endings are distributed widely throughout the skin. They can detect changes in temperature, touch, or pain.

nose – nerve endings in the nose detect chemicals in the air to give a sense of smell.

tongue – the nerve endings in the tongue detect chemicals in our food to give us our sense of taste. The nerve endings are called taste buds.

Try to imagine life without the ability to detect sound, light, touch or anything else. We would be totally unaware of our surroundings and what was happening. Life would be intolerable and almost pointless.

Fortunately we have sense organs to detect changes around us. Such a change is called a *stimulus*. Our sense organs detect these stimuli and our bodies respond. The nervous system is responsible for our sense of awareness and our responses.

The nervous system

The brain and spinal cord are called the central nervous system (CNS for short). Nerves form a network which spreads throughout the body. The nerves connect all nerve endings in muscles and glands and sense organs with the central nervous system.

Neurones

These are nerve cells that are responsible for carrying nerve impulses, or messages, around the nervous system. They can be very long, especially if they carry messages to or from the spinal cord to the arms and legs.

There are three main types of nerve cells:

1 *sensory neurones* carry messages to the brain and spinal cord;
2 *motor neurones* carry messages from the brain and spinal cord;
3 *relay neurones* carry messages in the brain and spinal cord.

Nerve impulse

Neurones carry nerve impulses. These are the messages that pass through the nervous system. They are small pulses of electricity that pass along the surface of the neurone at great speed.

Nerves

These are bundles of neurones, rather like the wires in a telephone cable which also transmit information. Each neurone is insulated by a sheath of fat from its neighbours.

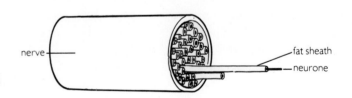

nerve

fat sheath

neurone

Nerve endings

Nerve endings detect stimuli (changes in the environment). They are specialised according to the stimulus they detect. In some cases they are grouped together in special sense organs, while in other cases they are widely distributed, as in the skin.

The synapse

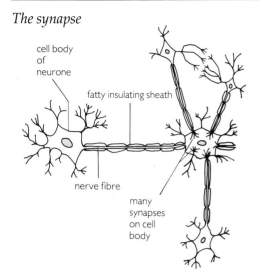

cell body of neurone

fatty insulating sheath

nerve fibre

many synapses on cell body

The junction between two neurones is called a *synapse*. There are millions of these synapses in the nervous system. They act like minature switching stations, where the arrival of one impulse causes the start of another impulse in the next neurone. These synapses form the basis of the mechanism of the nervous system.

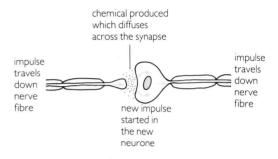

chemical produced which diffuses across the synapse

impulse travels down nerve fibre

impulse travels down nerve fibre

new impulse started in the new neurone

Stimulus and response

Nerve endings detect a stimulus. They send a message along a nerve to the brain or spinal cord. Here the message is interpreted and instructions are sent through nerves to *effectors* (muscles or glands) to act in response to the stimulus.

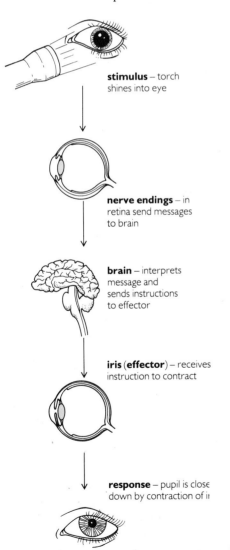

stimulus – torch shines into eye

nerve endings – in retina send messages to brain

brain – interprets message and sends instructions to effector

iris (effector) – receives instruction to contract

response – pupil is close down by contraction of ir

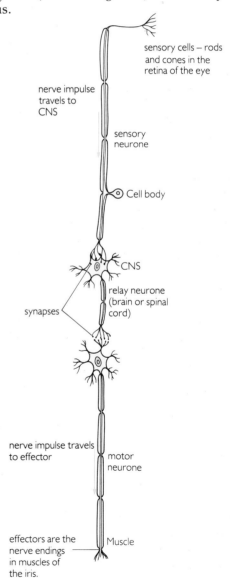

sensory cells – rods and cones in the retina of the eye

nerve impulse travels to CNS

sensory neurone

Cell body

CNS

relay neurone (brain or spinal cord)

synapses

nerve impulse travels to effector

motor neurone

effectors are the nerve endings in muscles of the iris.

Muscle

SENSE AND AWARENESS

Processing the information

The central nervous system (CNS) is made up of the brain and spinal cord. The CNS processes the information that is sent in by the sensory neurones, decides what action is needed and sends instructions by the motor neurones to the effectors.

The brain

The human brain is very large compared to our body size. No other animal has such a well-developed brain. The human brain is made up of three main parts:

1 the cerebrum made up of two cerebral hemispheres;
2 the cerebellum;
3 the medulla oblongata.

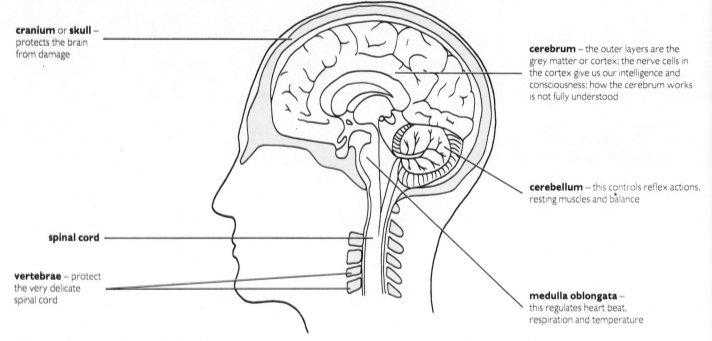

cranium or **skull** – protects the brain from damage

spinal cord

vertebrae = protect the very delicate spinal cord

cerebrum – the outer layers are the grey matter or cortex; the nerve cells in the cortex give us our intelligence and consciousness; how the cerebrum works is not fully understood

cerebellum – this controls reflex actions, resting muscles and balance

medulla oblongata – this regulates heart beat, respiration and temperature

The cerebrum is not just a coordinating centre for processing nerve impulses, it also has the ability to store information in the memory and to reuse this information in order to come to decisions.

The spinal cord

The spinal cord is an extension of the brain. It is protected by the vertebral column. Thirty-one pairs of spinal nerves branch from the spinal cord. These nerves go to all parts of the trunk and limbs.

A cross-section of the spinal cord shows the structure.

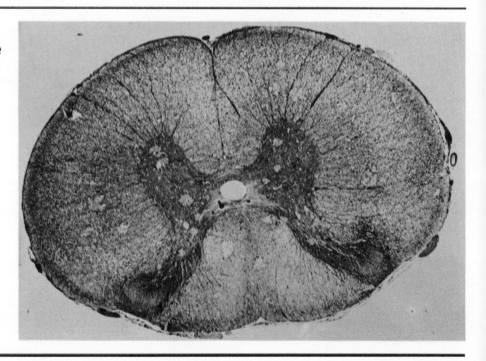

Reflex actions

Coughing, blinking, sneezing and withdrawing from painful stimuli are all examples of simple reflex actions. These are fast actions that you do not have to think about. They are involuntary and are usually safety mechanisms that prevent damage to the body.

Reflex actions usually involve the part of the central nervous system that is nearest the stimulus, either the brain or the spinal cord. A reflex action is carried out by a simple pathway of nerves – the *reflex arc*.

The reflex arc

This is a simple and very fast action. A stimulus causes the nerve endings of a sensory neurone to be stimulated. A message is passed along the sensory neurone to the spinal cord, where a relay neurone passes the message to a motor neurone. The nerve impulse passes down the motor neurone to an effector, which is stimulated causing a response. Sometimes the relay neurone is connected by other relay neurones to the brain which is informed of the action, but only after it has taken place.

Spinal reflexes can be tested by a simple knee jerk.

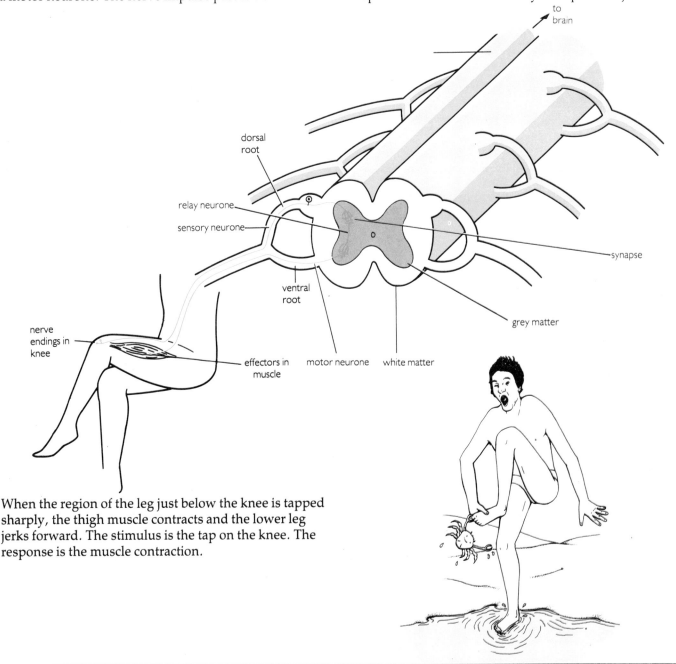

When the region of the leg just below the knee is tapped sharply, the thigh muscle contracts and the lower leg jerks forward. The stimulus is the tap on the knee. The response is the muscle contraction.

SENSE AND AWARENESS

Sense organs

The eyes

Nerve endings that detect light are found in the retina at the back of the eyes. There are two main types of nerve endings in the retina: *rods* which detect light intensity and *cones* which detect colour.

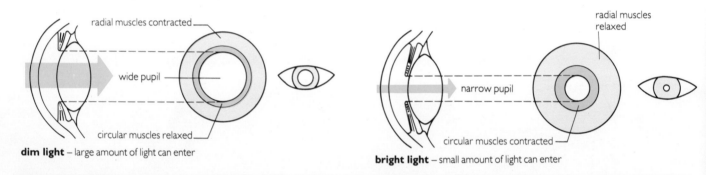

eye muscles – move and swivel the eyeball in its socket

sclera – thick protective outer layer; the white of the eye

iris

pupil

light

cornea

lens – focuses incoming light on to the retina

ciliary muscles – alter the shape of the lens and allow it to focus on near and far objects

suspensory ligaments

yellow spot – when you look straight ahead the light is focused on to this spot which contains many cones for accurate vision

blind spot – the area of the retina where the nerve leaves the eye; there are no rods or cones here and light falling on this spot will not be detected

optic nerve – carries messages from the rods and cones to the brain

retina – responsible for detecting light; composed of many nerve endings

The iris   This is a flat ring of muscle which controls the amount of light that enters the eye. It is made up of two sets of antagonistic muscles, the circular and radial muscles. These surround the pupil and work against each other to change its size.

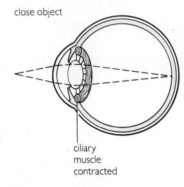

radial muscles contracted

wide pupil

circular muscles relaxed

dim light – large amount of light can enter

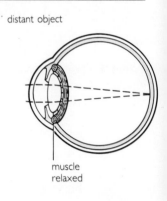

radial muscles relaxed

narrow pupil

circular muscles contracted

bright light – small amount of light can enter

Focusing   When the eye looks at a distant object, the lens is thin. If the eye moves to look at a nearer object, the lens must become fatter, i.e. more convex. The ciliary muscle contracts and distorts the shape of the eye, reducing its diameter. This slackens the suspensory ligaments and the elastic lens becomes more convex.

close object

ciliary muscle contracted

If the eye looks at a far object. again, the ciliary muscle relaxes and the pressure of the fluids in the eye cause the shape of the eye to return to normal. The ligaments become tight and the lens is stretched thin again. This changing of the lens shape in order to focus is called *accommodation*.

distant object

muscle relaxed

The ears

The ear contains two types of nerve endings to detect sound and to assist in balance.

Sound   Sound waves enter the outer ear and hit the eardrum, making it vibrate. The vibrations are picked up and amplified by the three small bones in the middle ear. These bones move a small membrane, called the oval window, which makes the fluid in the inner ear vibrate inside the cochlea. The vibrations stimulate the auditory nerve to send messages to the brain.

Balance   The semicircular canals in the inner ear are full of fluid. When the head moves, fluid in these canals also moves, stimulating nerve endings to send messages to the brain. There are three canals, all at right angles to each other. This means the brain knows the position of the head and, therefore, can control the balance of the body.

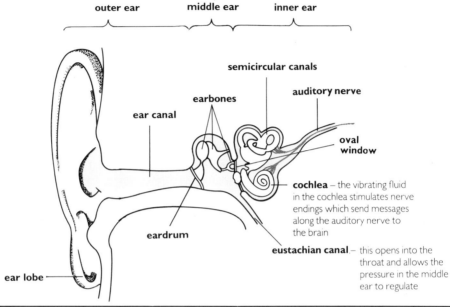

Nose and tongue

Taste and smell are closely linked. Taste is a very weak sense, especially in the absence of smell. If you cannot smell your food it will become almost tasteless.

Smell   When we breathe we draw in gases through our nasal passages and over many nerve endings. These are stimulated and send messages along sensory neurones to the brain.

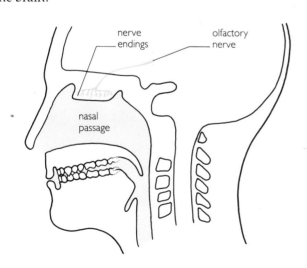

Taste   The tongue is covered by hundreds of *taste buds*. These are small pits which surround a hair-like nerve ending. Different regions of the tongue contain different taste buds which are stimulated by chemicals in our food. The main tastes identified by these different taste buds are: sour, bitter, salt, sweet.

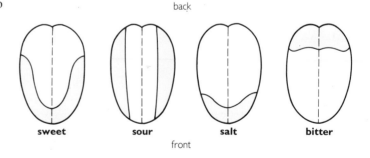

Skin

The skin contains the body's most widely distributed nerve endings. There are different nerve endings for detecting touch, pain, heat and cold (*see p. 89*). The most sensitive areas, such as fingertips, have the most nerve endings.

SENSE AND AWARENESS

Diseases and disorders of the CNS

Damage to the nervous system can affect the whole body and the mind and may have serious consequences. Very often the symptoms of nervous illness are difficult to understand. 'Normal behaviour' is not easily defined. People show all forms of behaviour and the diagnosis of mental illness is very difficult.

Schizophrenia

This disease is very hard to define. The term means that the patient's thoughts are separated from reality. They do not easily recognise the reality of their surroundings. The causes of this disease are largely unknown. Treatment is usually some form of psychiatry. Drugs are not very useful.

Schizophrenics can be difficult to live with but are not usually dangerous.

Cerebral palsy

This is the correct name for some types of brain damage. About 4 babies in every 1 000 are born with brain damage. The result may be paralysis, mental handicap or both.

Depending on the extent of their damage such children may be able to attend normal schools or special schools for the mentally handicapped. People who suffer from this disease are sometimes called spastics. Many spastics are highly intelligent but cannot control their muscles. They frequently have difficulty in speaking clearly.

Paralysis

Severe damage to the CNS can cause paralysis of the muscles. This is caused by the failure of nerve impulses to reach these muscles. Without nerve impulses the muscles cannot contract, and eventually they will wither due to lack of exercise.

Paralysis can be caused by *polio*, a stroke or physical damage to the spinal cord.

Epilepsy

This is a difficult disorder to describe. It is recognised by fits or seizures which are caused by some form of mental disorganisation. At one time people thought these fits were caused by some form of possession by evil spirits that made the patient mad. Even today, many people are suspicious of epileptics. In most cases the problem can be controlled by drugs and most epileptics lead perfectly normal lives.

Encephalitis and meningitis

Encephalitis is an infection of the brain itself, while meningitis is an infection of the membranes that surround the brain. Both are serious diseases that are caused by viruses.

Multiple sclerosis

This is a chronic, long-term disease of the nervous system. Regions of the central nervous system start to degenerate for no obvious reason. The strange thing about this disease is that the symptoms come and go. In many cases the paralysis caused is mild while in others the paralysis is progressive and extreme.

No cure is known to be completely successful although using oxygen under high pressure may help. It may be possible to control the disease by following a special diet.

Disorders of the sense organs

The main disorders of the sense organs are caused by physical factors.

Deafness

Deafness or partial deafness can be caused by a variety of problems. The simplest cause of deafness is a blockage of the ear canal by wax which can be removed easily by syringing.

Damage to the eardrum or to the bones in the middle ear is far more serious, and this is one reason why objects should not be poked into the ear.

As people get older they gradually lose the sensitivity to high-pitched noises. A child that is born deaf may also be dumb. This is because the child finds it difficult to learn to speak.

Anything that affects hearing may also prevent a child from learning to speak. A stroke in an adult can interfere with normal speech.

Poor balance

Infections of the inner ear can damage the cochlea and the semicircular canals. This may interfere with the nerve impulses sent to the brain, causing giddiness and sickness.

Short sight

A short-sighted person can focus clearly on near objects.

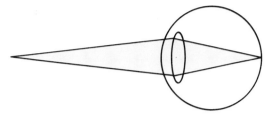

However, the eye cannot focus clearly on distant objects. This is because the eyeball is too long, or the lens is too strong, and the image on the retina is blurred.

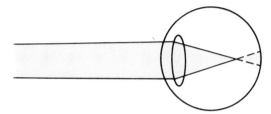

Short sight is corrected by wearing *concave* (diverging) lenses in spectacles or as contact lenses.

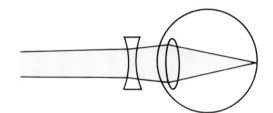

Long sight

A long-sighted person can focus clearly on far objects.

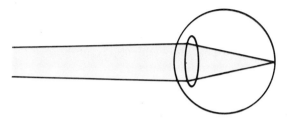

However, the eye cannot focus clearly on near objects. This is because the eyeball is too short or the lens is too weak. The image on the retina is blurred.

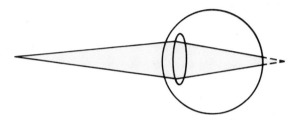

Long sight is corrected by wearing *convex* (converging) lenses in spectacles or as contact lenses.

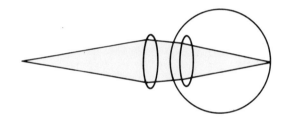

Astigmatism

This is a defect of the cornea which should be perfectly spherical. People with astigmatism have a cornea which is not spherical. This causes their vision to be blurred in certain places on the retina. It is corrected by wearing spectacles with lenses that cancel out the defective areas.

Squints

These are caused when the eye muscles of the two eyes fail to work together. They can be corrected by exercises, special glasses or minor surgery.

Colour blindness

This is when a person is unable to tell the difference between certain colours. The commonest type of colour blindness is where red and green are confused. This is a sex-linked disorder (*see page 107*); many more men than women suffer from colour blindness.

Blindness

Total blindness is uncommon. The term usually means that there is little or no useful sight. This can be caused by many things. Damage to the optic nerve or the optical centres of the brain are obvious reasons. Other causes are:

Cataracts   The lens becomes misty or cloudy which cuts down the amount of light reaching the retina. Cataracts can be removed surgically or the whole lens can be transplanted from a dead donor.

Trachoma   This is an infection causing severe inflammation of the delicate protective layer found at the front of the eye. This reduces the amount of light entering the eye. It can be treated successfully by antibiotics.

Detached retina   Severe blows to the side of the head can cause the retina to detach from the rear surface of the eye. This means that light cannot be focused on to it. This injury is fairly common in boxers. It can be cured by using medical lasers to weld the retina back in place (*see page 234*).

Diabetes   This illness sometimes causes a form of blindness.

8 HORMONES

The nervous system provides us with a very fast form of control that can be very specific and short lived. Hormones provide another control system. They are chemical messengers – chemicals released into the bloodstream, which carries them around the body. Hormones are slower, more widespread and longer lasting in their action than nerves.

The organs that produce and secrete the hormones are called *endocrine glands.* The endocrine glands and the hormones they produce make up the *endocrine system.*

The interactions of the different hormones of the endocrine system is very complicated and not completely understood.

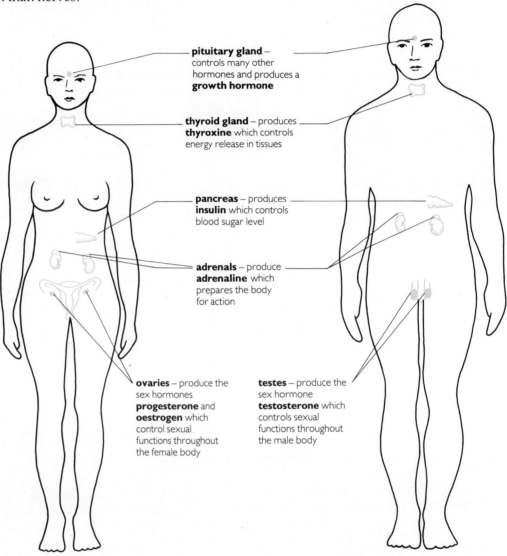

pituitary gland – controls many other hormones and produces a **growth hormone**

thyroid gland – produces **thyroxine** which controls energy release in tissues

pancreas – produces **insulin** which controls blood sugar level

adrenals – produce **adrenaline** which prepares the body for action

ovaries – produce the sex hormones **progesterone** and **oestrogen** which control sexual functions throughout the female body

testes – produce the sex hormone **testosterone** which controls sexual functions throughout the male body

Pituitary gland
This is sometimes called the master gland, because it controls many of the other endocrine glands. It provides a link between the nervous system and the endocrine system. It is situated at the base of the brain. Messages from the *hypothalamus* of the brain control the action of the pituitary. The pituitary also produces a growth hormone which regulates the growth of children.

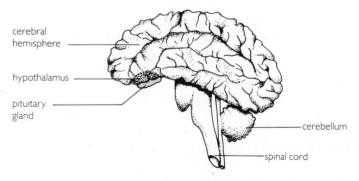

cerebral hemisphere

hypothalamus

pituitary gland

cerebellum

spinal cord

Adrenaline

This hormone is produced by the adrenal glands which are found near the top of each kidney. It is the hormone which prepares the body for sudden action. Adrenaline is produced when you are under stress. It has an extremely complicated effect on the body, causing the following changes:

1 increases heart beat;
2 raises the blood pressure;
3 increases flow of blood to the muscles;
4 increases breathing rate;
5 increases the level of sugar in the blood;
6 stops digestion and excretion.

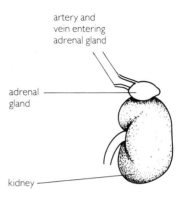

artery and vein entering adrenal gland

adrenal gland

kidney

Disorders of the endocrine system

Pituitary gland

If this gland is underactive during childhood, it will produce too little growth hormone. The child will then grow up to be a dwarf. The height of an adult dwarf can be as little as 60 cm. If the pituitary is overactive during childhood it will produce too much growth hormone and the child will grow up to be a giant. Adult giants can be over 2·7 m tall.

If too much growth hormone is produced in an adult a condition called *acromegaly* occurs. The bones of the feet, hands and head grow out of proportion to the rest of the body.

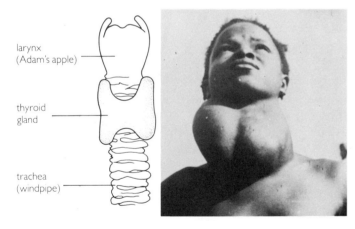

larynx (Adam's apple)

thyroid gland

trachea (windpipe)

Thyroid gland

The thyroid produces an important hormone called *thyroxine*. If the thyroid gland is underactive during childhood it will not produce enough of this hormone. The child will grow up to be a *cretin* – a mentally handicapped dwarf.

An underactive thyroid in an adult causes swelling of the face and hands, and the person becomes very sluggish. An overactive thyroid gland causes a person to become very tense and nervous.

The hormone thyroxine contains iodine. If there is not enough iodine in the diet, the thyroid gland becomes very large. This causes a swelling on the neck, called a *goitre*.

Pancreas

Special cells, called *islets of Langerhans*, produce the hormone *insulin*. If enough insulin is not produced then the result is *diabetes*. Insulin causes the liver cells to take up excess blood sugar. If this hormone is missing or in short supply the sugar remains in the blood and passes out of the body in the urine.

Most diabetics lead perfectly normal lives by injecting themselves with daily doses of insulin. A careful diet that controls the amount of sugar taken in also helps.

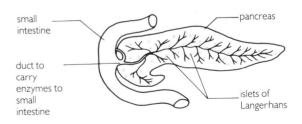

small intestine

duct to carry enzymes to small intestine

pancreas

islets of Langerhans

9 EXCRETION

Waste is removed from our bodies through four organs:

Kidneys – remove urea, salts, water, poisons

Liver – removes bile salts, bile pigments, poisons.

Lungs – remove carbon dioxide, water vapour.

Skin – removes urea, salts, water.

Our bodies are made up of millions upon millions of cells. They all produce waste which passes out into the watery tissue fluid that bathes the cells. This is carried away by the blood to be removed from the body.

The liver

This is an important organ. It has many jobs to do. It:

1 stores digested food;
2 controls the blood sugar level;
3 helps with digestion of fats;
4 produces heat to keep the body warm;
5 removes poisons from the body.

The last job is very important. Most people eat more protein than they need, and this extra protein cannot be stored. Instead the liver breaks it down and gets some energy from it. The rest is turned into ammonia which can poison the body. The liver quickly turns it into a less poisonous chemical called *urea* which is released into the bloodstream. This process is called *deamination*.

If you accidently eat a poison with your food, the liver removes it from the blood. The liver also removes any poisons that are made by the cells in our bodies.

The liver also breaks down dead red blood cells and converts the unwanted parts into *bile pigments* which are passed down the bile duct into the intestine. These pigments give the faeces their brown colour.

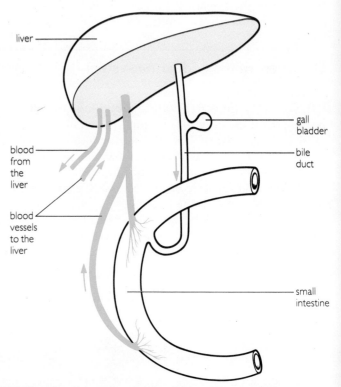

The lungs

All the cells of the body respire. They use oxygen to release the energy from food. In this process water and carbon dioxide are released as waste products.

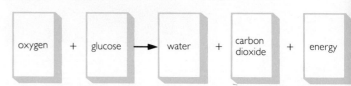

oxygen + glucose → water + carbon dioxide + energy

The water and carbon dioxide pass round the body in the bloodstream. When the blood reaches the lungs, the water and carbon dioxide diffuse from the blood into the air sacs of the lungs. The lungs then excrete these waste products when we breathe out.

The skin

The skin removes urea, salt and water through sweat glands. *See page 88 for more details.*

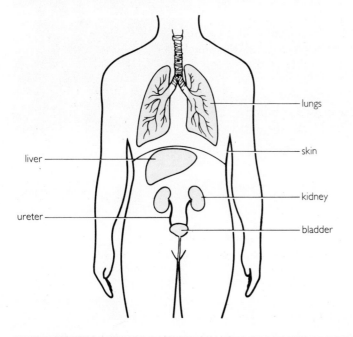

The kidneys

More than half the body's weight is water, kept in by the waterproof skin. The job of the kidneys is to remove waste chemicals and to regulate the amount of water in the body. The kidneys are a pair of dark red-brown organs found on either side of the backbone in the abdomen.

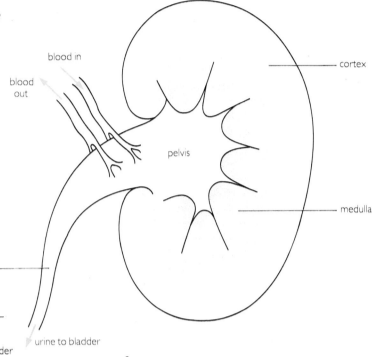

blood in

blood out

pelvis

cortex

medulla

ureter

urine to bladder

kidney
produces
urine

ureter –
carries
urine to
the bladder

bladder –
stores
urine

ring of
muscle –
relaxes
to allow
urine out

urethra –
takes
urine
out of
the body

About 1 000 cm^3 of blood flows through the kidneys every minute. About 120 cm^3 of liquid is filtered from this blood and enters the cortex and medulla. Eventually 99% of this liquid returns to the blood. The remaining 1% contains large amounts of *urea* and salts. This liquid is called *urine* and passes to the kidney's pelvis. Urine trickles down to the bladder where it is stored-until it is convenient to get rid of it. The kidneys, bladder and connecting tubes are called the *urinary system*.

Disorders of the urinary system

Kidney failure   Kidneys can fail to work for various reasons. If one fails, the remaining kidney can cope, but if both fail there are only two possible treatments.

1 An *artificial kidney machine* or *dialysis machine* – the patient spends 2 or 3 nights each week connected to the machine. Blood is passed from the body to the machine which filters it and then returns it to a blood vessel.

2 *Kidney transplant* – a kidney can be removed from a person who has just died in an accident. If the kidney matches the patient's body it can be transplanted successfully to replace a diseased kidney. Many people carry Kidney Donor cards to give permission for the removal of their kidneys after death.

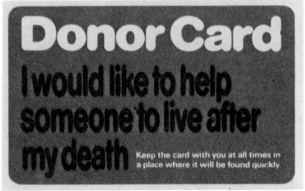

Donor Card
I would like to help someone to live after my death   Keep the card with you at all times in a place where it will be found quickly

Cystitis   This is a bacterial infection of the bladder. It is more common in women. Its symptoms are the frequent, painful passage of urine. It is treated by antibiotics.

Sexually transmitted diseases   Infections can pass from the reproductive system into the lower parts of the urinary system. These can be extremely painful. They are usually more easily detected in men because the urethra forms part of both systems, while in women it only forms part of the urinary system.

10 SKIN

The skin has many jobs to do. It:

1 is a major sense organ;
2 acts to regulate the temperature of the body;
3 is an excretory organ, removing urea in the sweat;
4 determines our physical appearance;
5 is waterproof and prevents the uncontrolled loss of water;
6 acts as a barrier to disease-causing organisms;
7 produces hair and an oil called sebum.

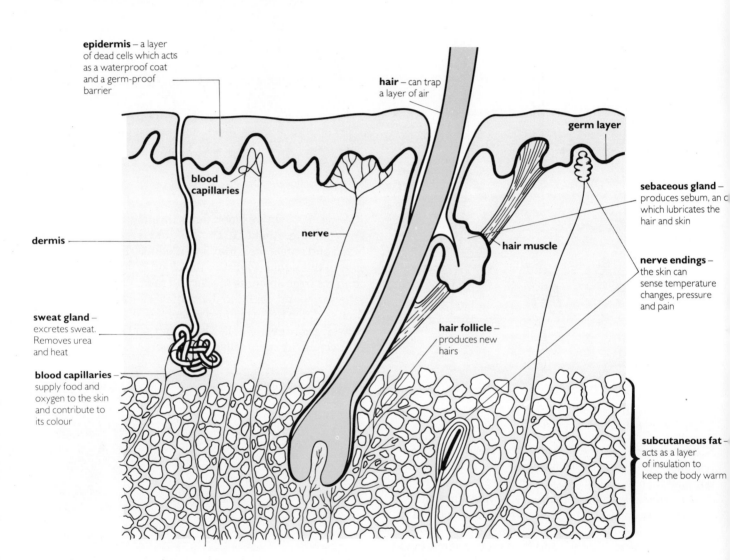

epidermis – a layer of dead cells which acts as a waterproof coat and a germ-proof barrier

hair – can trap a layer of air

germ layer

blood capillaries

dermis

nerve

sebaceous gland – produces sebum, an o which lubricates the hair and skin

hair muscle

nerve endings – the skin can sense temperature changes, pressure and pain

sweat gland – excretes sweat. Removes urea and heat

hair follicle – produces new hairs

blood capillaries – supply food and oxygen to the skin and contribute to its colour

subcutaneous fat – acts as a layer of insulation to keep the body warm

The structure of the skin
The skin is made up of two layers, the dermis and epidermis, plus an underlying layer of fat.

Epidermis   This is made up of dead cells which are being constantly worn away. These cells are replaced by new cells made in the germ layer. The surface of the skin has to be dead to be completely waterproof and microbe-proof.

Dermis   This is a thicker tissue containing the sweat glands, hairs, blood capillaries and nerve endings.

Subcutaneous fat   This layer varies in thickness from person to person. It acts as a heat insulator. The fat can be broken down and used as a food source in emergencies. This layer tends to be thicker in women than men.

Skin as a sense organ

There are thousands of nerve endings buried in the dermis. They react to changes in our environment and relay information to the brain. There are nerve endings that detect touch, pressure, pain and changes in temperature. Many nerve endings are concentrated in small areas of skin such as the fingertips. These areas are very sensitive to any change in our surroundings.

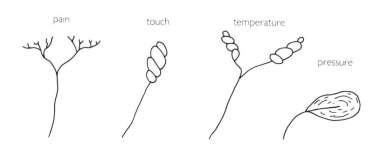

Skin as a temperature regulator

One of the most important functions of the skin is to help keep the body temperature constant at about 37°C. The nerve endings in the skin can detect changes in the temperature and this can lead to changes in our behaviour, e.g. putting on or removing clothes, finding shade, etc. However, the skin can directly affect the amount of heat lost from the body in the following ways.

Altering the flow of blood in the skin capillaries

On a hot day the diameter of the skin capillaries increases and more blood passes through them. This means that more heat is carried to the skin and is lost to the outside by radiation. On cold days the diameter of the capillaries decreases and they carry less blood. A shunt blood vessel opens to divert the blood away from the skin's surface. This means that less heat is lost from the skin by radiation.

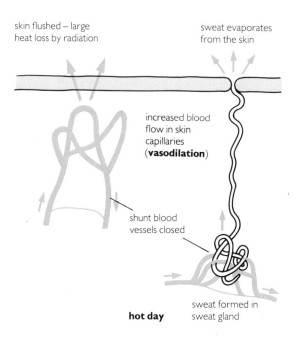

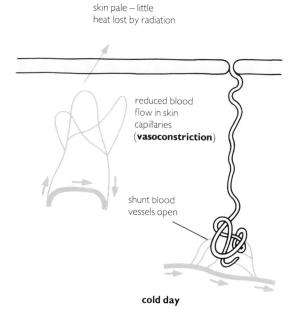

Sweating

Embedded in the skin are millions of sweat glands. Blood capillaries pass through the base of these glands. Water, salts and small amounts of urea pass out of the blood and into the sweat gland. This liquid moves up to the sweat pore on the surface of the skin. As the sweat evaporates it takes heat away from the surface. This cools the skin and the blood that passes through it.

On a hot day the sweat glands may produce as much as 10 litres of sweat and about 30 g of salt. The loss of so much salt can lead to heatstroke. On cold days a shunt blood vessel opens to divert blood away from the sweat glands, so far less sweat is produced.

Goose pimples

These appear on cold days. They are caused by tiny muscles contracting and making the hairs in the skin stand on end. In furry animals this is useful because it traps a layer of air next to the skin. This layer insulates the body by slowing down heat loss. It is of little use in humans because we do not have enough hair.

SKIN

Health and hygiene

Appearance

Skin colour is determined by a pigment called *melanin*. The amount of melanin in the skin is controlled by heredity and the amount of sunlight the skin receives. Skin colour is also affected by the blood flow in the dermis. Blushing, a healthy 'glow' or other forms of redness are caused by an increased flow of blood to the skin. The colour of the skin can be a clue to the state of our health.

Texture

This depends on age and health. Healthy skin should be clear, smooth and supple. The production of sebum from the sebaceous glands prevents dry skin, but over-production of this oil can lead to greasy skin and acne.

Body odour

If the skin is not kept clean, germs or microbes can thrive in the mixture of sweat, sebum and dirt that collects there. These microbes can produce an unpleasant smell that is called body odour. Sweat is heaviest in the groin, under the armpits, on the soles of the feet and the palms of the hands where most sweat glands are found. These are the regions most likely to develop body odour if not cleaned regularly.

Acne

This condition often occurs during puberty when the numbers of sebaceous glands on the face, neck and shoulders increase and become active. These glands often become over-active. The glands may become blocked by dried sebum which forms a blackhead. This plug of dried sebum may force more sebum into the layers of the skin around the gland which then becomes infected forming red lumps. Picking or squeezing these spots may make the acne worse by spreading the infection. Careful and thorough washing of the infected area helps control acne.

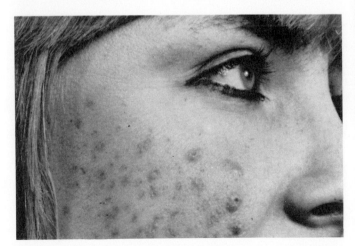

Boils

A boil is a small abscess that forms in a sebaceous gland or a sweat gland. They are very painful for a few days but they soon heal. They must not be picked or they could become infected by germs.

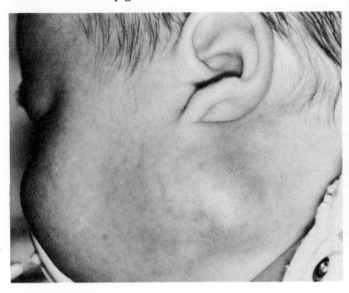

Ringworm

This is a common infection of the skin. It is caused by a fungus. Ringworm is found on the scalp and forms a small disc but it can occur on the foot, in-between the toes, when it is called *athlete's foot*. It can be cured easily by applying a fungicide.

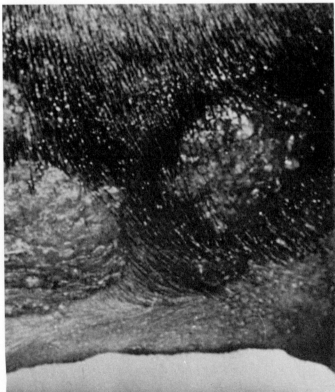

Warts

These are small skin tumours that are caused by a virus. They usually appear and disappear of their own accord. Warts that appear on the sole of the foot are forced to grow inwards. These are called *verrucas* and can be painful. All warts are infectious, although it is possible to become immune to them.

Psoriasis

This condition appears as red blotches on the skin. The blotches are very dry. It is due to the abnormal production of new skin cells in the dermis. Its cause is not fully understood, but it may be connected with emotional upset. It runs in families so it is likely that there is a hereditary factor involved.

Dermatitis and eczema

Dermatitis is an inflammation of the skin, and eczema is a form of dermatitis. Both appear to be allergies but their cause is unknown. The symptoms are dry flaking and cracked skin which may itch considerably.

Ectoparasites

These are parasites which live on the surface of the skin or on hair. They either eat the skin cells or drink blood from the skin capillaries. They are more likely to be found in areas of poor housing and overcrowding. These parasites are easily passed on to other people, even you!

Lice   All lice have curved claws to give a good grip on the skin or hair. Lice lay eggs on the hairs of the body. These eggs are called *nits*.

Fleas   A flea has piercing mouthparts which allow it to suck blood from the skin capillaries.

Mites   The scabies mite burrows under the skin and causes severe itchiness.

Treatment   Most of these ectoparasites can be treated with an insecticide cream. Careful examination of schoolchildren can also help to prevent the spread of these parasites.

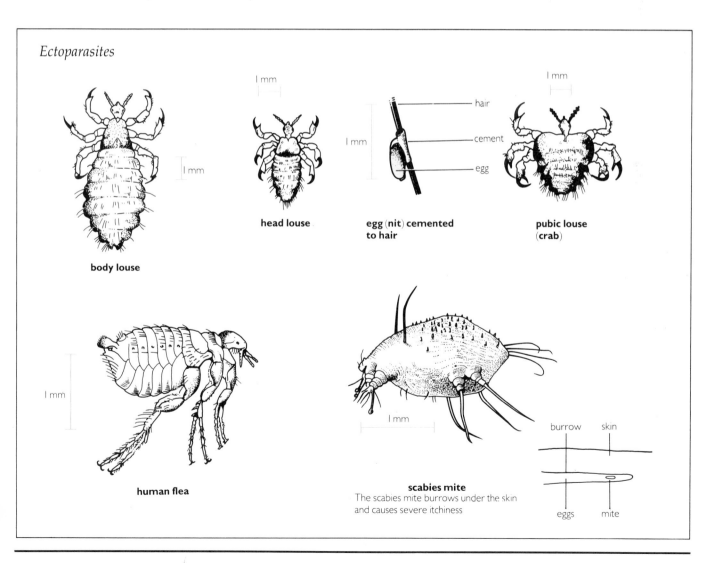

Ectoparasites

1 mm

1 mm

body louse

head louse

hair
cement
egg

egg (nit) cemented to hair

1 mm

pubic louse (crab)

1 mm

human flea

1 mm

scabies mite
The scabies mite burrows under the skin and causes severe itchiness

burrow   skin

eggs   mite

▌▌ REPRODUCTION

Infant to adult

The main function of the adult reproductive or sexual
organs is to create new life.

Infancy to childhood: age 0 – 12
At birth the sexual organs in both sexes are immature.
The only visible difference is the small penis of the boy
and two flaps of skin called the vulva of the little girl.
Gradually during childhood, the sexual organs begin to
mature.

Puberty: age 12 – 16
Puberty is the age at which sexual maturity advances very
rapidly. The secondary sex characteristics start to appear,
under the influence of the sex hormones released by the
testes of the male or the ovaries of the female. The male
starts to make *semen*, a creamy fluid that contains the
sperms. The female starts to menstruate and releases an
egg or *ovum* once a month.

Secondary sex characteristics

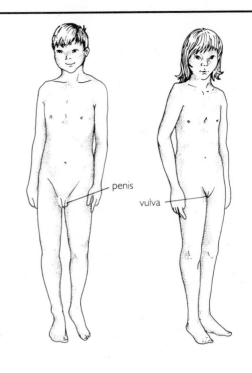

penis

vulva

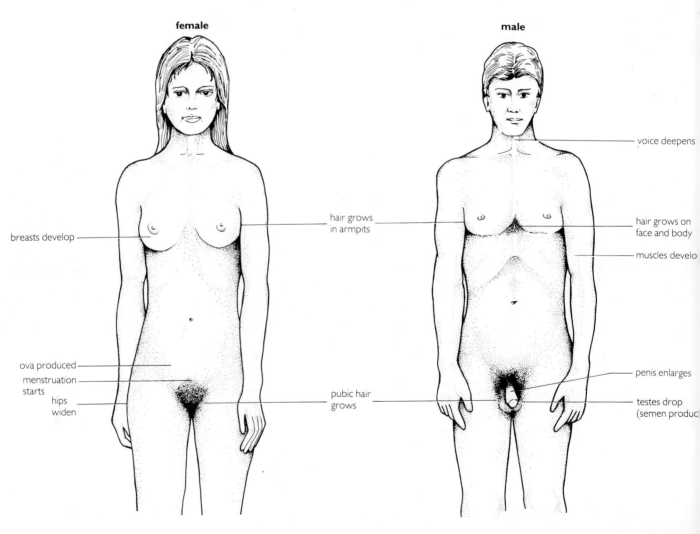

female

male

breasts develop

hair grows
in armpits

voice deepens

hair grows on
face and body

muscles develo

ova produced
menstruation
starts
hips
widen

pubic hair
grows

penis enlarges

testes drop
(semen produc

Adulthood: age 16 +
Sexual maturity is reached soon after puberty. A period called *adolescence* follows, and during this period the body is adapting and the person is becoming emotionally mature. Adulthood is reached in the late 'teens or early twenties, although this varies from one person to another.

Male reproductive organs (side view)

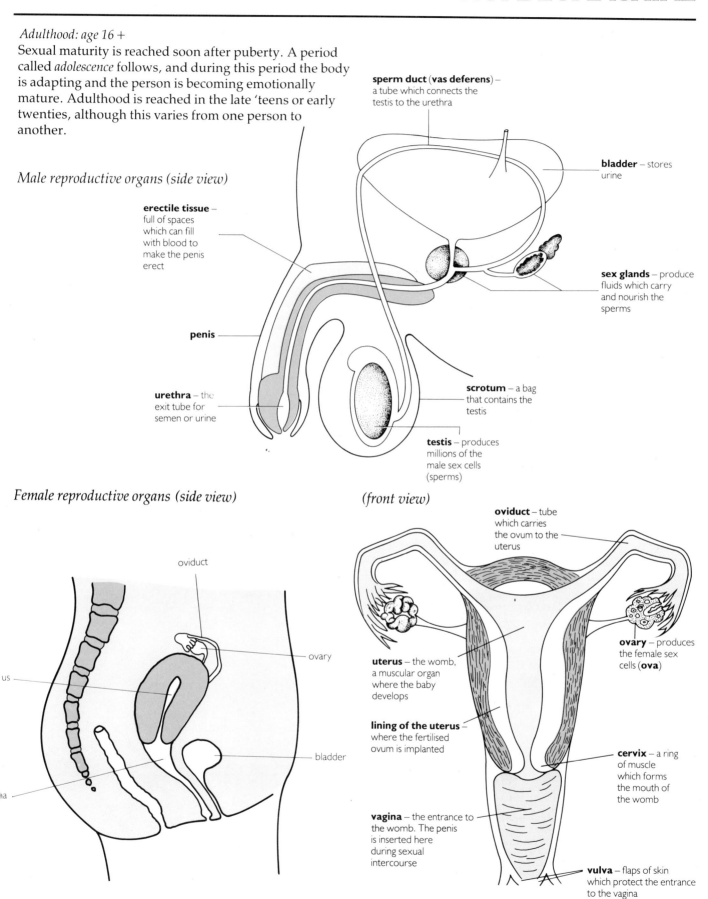

sperm duct (vas deferens) – a tube which connects the testis to the urethra

bladder – stores urine

erectile tissue – full of spaces which can fill with blood to make the penis erect

sex glands – produce fluids which carry and nourish the sperms

penis

urethra – the exit tube for semen or urine

scrotum – a bag that contains the testis

testis – produces millions of the male sex cells (sperms)

Female reproductive organs (side view)

(front view)

oviduct

ovary

us

bladder

a

oviduct – tube which carries the ovum to the uterus

ovary – produces the female sex cells (**ova**)

uterus – the womb, a muscular organ where the baby develops

lining of the uterus – where the fertilised ovum is implanted

cervix – a ring of muscle which forms the mouth of the womb

vagina – the entrance to the womb. The penis is inserted here during sexual intercourse

vulva – flaps of skin which protect the entrance to the vagina

REPRODUCTION

Mental and physical development

Girls

The most obvious physical changes that occur in young girls are the development of the breasts and the start of menstruation. These changes may start at any time between the ages of 10 to 17.

Breasts   The function of the breasts is to make milk after a baby has been born. The correct term for the breasts is the *mammary glands*. The size of the breasts does not affect their ability to produce milk. Small breasts will feed twins just as well as larger breasts.

It is unfortunate that the size of a woman's breasts can cause her anxiety. Some women are embarrassed by the fact that their breasts seem too large, while others are worried by the smallness of their breasts. Both feel that they affect their physical attractiveness. Drastic cosmetic surgery is expensive and rarely completely successful. More women are now learning to accept themselves as they are, rather than try to conform to some 'ideal' set up by society.

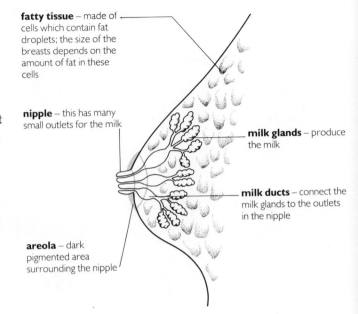

fatty tissue – made of cells which contain fat droplets; the size of the breasts depends on the amount of fat in these cells

nipple – this has many small outlets for the milk

milk glands – produce the milk

milk ducts – connect the milk glands to the outlets in the nipple

areola – dark pigmented area surrounding the nipple

Boys

The change that most boys will be aware of is the development of the penis and testicles, and the ability to have an erection. An erection is caused by blood filling spaces in the penis which then becomes hard, large and erect. The usual reason for having an erection is sexual excitement, but it is quite normal to have an erection for no apparent reason.

The size and shape of the penis sometimes causes anxiety, but this is groundless. An erection will always make the penis large enough for sexual intercourse to be possible.

The most sensitive part of the penis is the tip. This is normally protected by the foreskin. Stimulation of the tip will cause an erection and will give sexual pleasure. The foreskin should slide back easily over the tip, and this is helped by a lubricant called *smegma*. The tip of the penis should be washed regularly, or the smegma will become trapped under the foreskin and will become the breeding ground for germs. Some parents have their sons *circumcised*. This means that the foreskin is cut and removed when the boy is very young. This is done for hygienic or religious reasons.

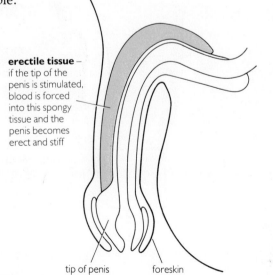

erectile tissue – if the tip of the penis is stimulated, blood is forced into this spongy tissue and the penis becomes erect and stiff

tip of penis   foreskin

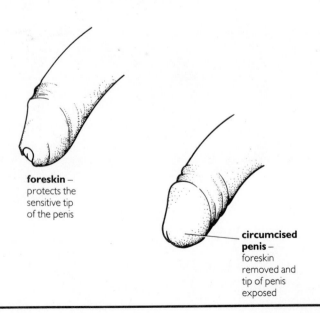

foreskin – protects the sensitive tip of the penis

circumcised penis – foreskin removed and tip of penis exposed

Menstrual cycle

This cycle is related to the monthly release of an ovum from one or both of the ovaries.

Menstruation is sometimes painful because hormone changes, extra fluid in the tissues, and muscle spasms can cause back pains. The menstrual cycle can have an emotional, as well as a physical effect on women. Women can become tired, depressed and moody at times before the start of menstruation.

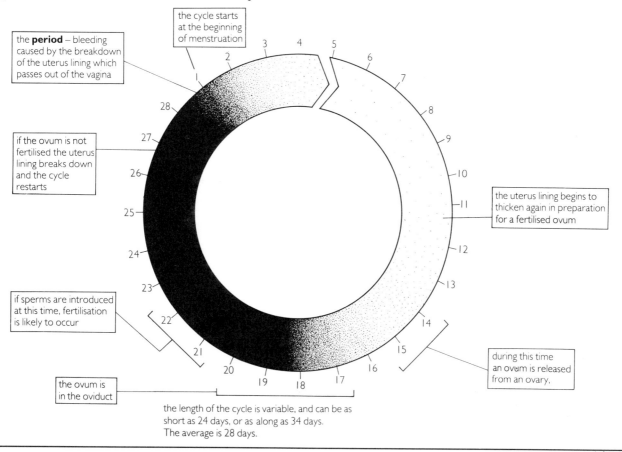

the cycle starts at the beginning of menstruation

the **period** – bleeding caused by the breakdown of the uterus lining which passes out of the vagina

if the ovum is not fertilised the uterus lining breaks down and the cycle restarts

the uterus lining begins to thicken again in preparation for a fertilised ovum

if sperms are introduced at this time, fertilisation is likely to occur

during this time an ovum is released from an ovary,

the ovum is in the oviduct

the length of the cycle is variable, and can be as short as 24 days, or as along as 34 days. The average is 28 days.

Sexual tension

Men and women experience sexual tension. This is sometimes called the sex drive, and is perfectly normal. Married couples usually release this tension by having sexual intercourse. This usually finishes with a climax or orgasm. In men, the climax comes when the sperm are ejaculated from the penis. In women, the orgasm is harder to describe, and some women never have one. This is quite normal and sexual intercourse can be just as satisfying without an orgasm.

Stimulating one's own sexual organs to release tension and give sexual pleasure is called *masturbation*. At one time this was thought to be abnormal and unhealthy. It was often thought to bring about madness or other illnesses. It is now known to be quite harmless and is a normal method of relieving sexual tension for both men and women.

In women, the most sensitive part of the sexual organs is the *clitoris*. This is small lump of tissue that is buried between the folds of skin that form the lips around the vagina.

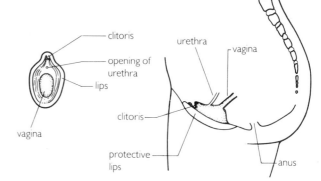

Stimulation of the clitoris, either by masturbation or sexual intercourse gives sexual pleasure, and can produce an orgasm.

In men, the tip of the penis is the most sensitive area of the sexual organs. If this is stimulated by rubbing, the penis will become erect. Further stimulation, during masturbation or sexual intercourse, will lead to the ejaculation of sperms and the male orgasm.

Ejaculation can occur during sleep without the person realising. This is called a *wet dream* and is quite normal.

REPRODUCTION

Conception

If a new life is to be created, an ovum must be fertilised by a sperm. To reach the ovum the sperms are released into the female's body during sexual intercourse.

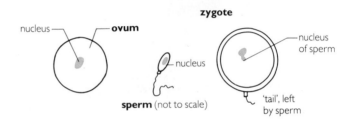

penis is firm and erect because blood has filled spaces in the erectile tissue

if an ovum is in one of the oviducts, then fertilisation will occur

stimulation of the tip of the penis causes semen to be ejaculated from the penis into the vagina; the semen contains millions of sperms

the sperms swim through the cervix into the uterus and then enter the oviducts

Fertilisation

Fertilisation occurs in the oviducts. The sperm use their long tails to swim through the uterus to reach the oviducts.

The sperm nucleus penetrates the ovum and fuses with the egg nucleus. The result is a fertilised egg or *zygote*.

nucleus — **ovum**

zygote

nucleus

sperm (not to scale)

nucleus of sperm

'tail', left by sperm

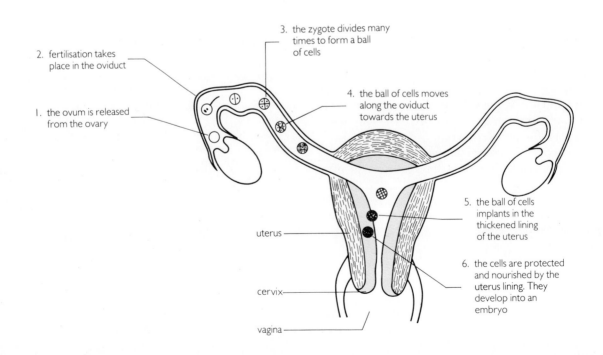

2. fertilisation takes place in the oviduct

3. the zygote divides many times to form a ball of cells

1. the ovum is released from the ovary

4. the ball of cells moves along the oviduct towards the uterus

5. the ball of cells implants in the thickened lining of the uterus

uterus

6. the cells are protected and nourished by the uterus lining. They develop into an embryo

cervix

vagina

Contraception

The aim of contraception is to prevent pregnancy. There are natural and artificial methods. The artificial methods are generally more reliable.

Natural methods

Withdrawal   The man withdraws or removes his penis from the woman's vagina before he ejaculates his semen. This method is very unreliable because sperms may leak out of the penis into the vagina without the man realising. It is also difficult for a man to guess when he is about to ejaculate.

Rhythm method   This relies on the idea that there are safe times before and after ovulation during the menstrual cycle. These are when the ovum is not in the oviduct. Intercourse is confined to these safe periods. This method is unreliable because it is difficult to calculate the date of ovulation. Sperms can also survive inside the woman for a few days.

Artifical methods

These are either barrier methods which prevent the sperms meeting the ovum, chemical methods which prevent ovulation or methods which stop the development of the embryo in the uterus.

The sheath   Often called a condom, rubber or French letter, it is made from a very thin rubbery material which is rolled over the penis before any contact with the vagina. It is important that the sheath is carefully removed after intercourse. If used properly it is very safe.

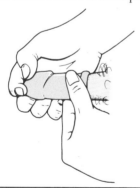

The cap   Sometimes called a diaphragm, it is placed over the cervix before intercourse, and must remain in the vagina for 8 hours after intercourse has finished. It prevents sperms getting into the uterus. It is very safe if fitted properly. A spermicide cream is usually used to kill sperms.

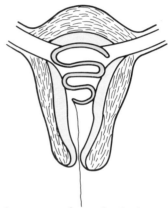

The IUD   This is an intrauterine device – a small plastic coil or loop that prevents a fertilised egg from implanting in the wall of the womb.

The pill   This is a very safe method of contraception because it prevents ovulation. It copies the hormone pattern of a pregnant woman and stops the ovaries releasing more eggs. As long as the pill is taken regularly it is safe, although some women suffer side effects such as headaches and nausea, or more serious conditions. A new development is the post-coital pill that is taken after sexual intercouse. It is supposed to prevent the implantation of the fertilised egg, but it is still being tested. Injections of hormones and long-term implantation methods of contraception are also being tested.

Sterilisation   This method is the safest of all, but can only be used if no more children are wanted. It is almost irreversible because it involves a surgical operation. In the man, the sperm tubes are cut and tied. This is called a *vasectomy*, and prevents sperms entering the semen. In the woman the oviducts are cut and tied.

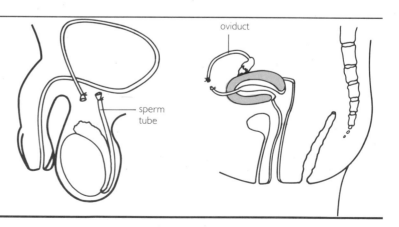

REPRODUCTION

New life

When a woman becomes pregnant her menstrual cycle stops. The thickened lining of the uterus protects and nourishes the implanted zygote. At this stage the zygote becomes the *embryo*. On average the process of pregnancy, from the time of the mother's last period to the time of the birth, will last about 40 weeks. Throughout this time the mother's womb provides the developing child with food, oxygen and warmth, and removes its waste. It is a constant sheltered environment.

Ante-natal care

This is care given to the mother during pregnancy. During this time the health of the mother and developing child are checked regularly by the health services. The mother will be advised about her diet to make sure she knows how to provide food for both herself and the child. She may be given extra vitamins and iron tablets. She may also be taught how to relax and control the muscles used during childbirth.

The course of pregnancy

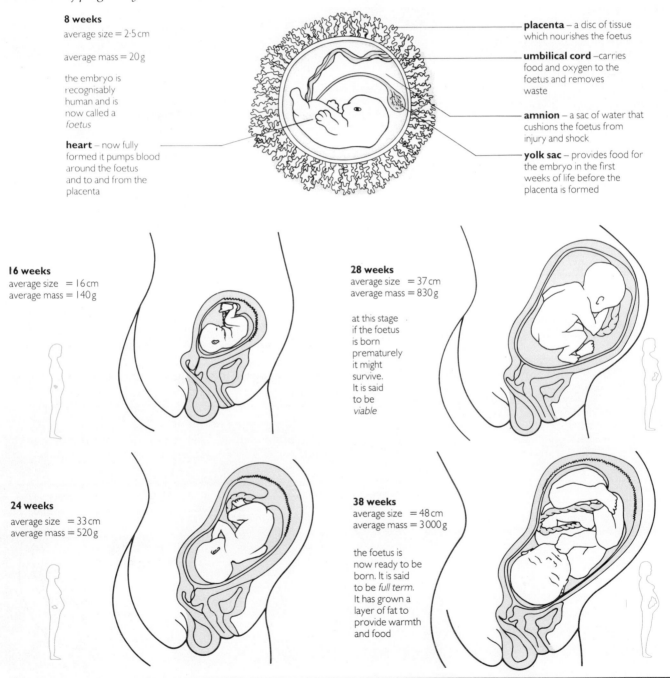

8 weeks

average size = 2·5 cm

average mass = 20 g

the embryo is recognisably human and is now called a *foetus*

heart – now fully formed it pumps blood around the foetus and to and from the placenta

placenta – a disc of tissue which nourishes the foetus

umbilical cord –carries food and oxygen to the foetus and removes waste

amnion – a sac of water that cushions the foetus from injury and shock

yolk sac – provides food for the embryo in the first weeks of life before the placenta is formed

16 weeks
average size = 16 cm
average mass = 140 g

24 weeks
average size = 33 cm
average mass = 520 g

28 weeks
average size = 37 cm
average mass = 830 g

at this stage if the foetus is born prematurely it might survive. It is said to be *viable*

38 weeks
average size = 48 cm
average mass = 3 000 g

the foetus is now ready to be born. It is said to be *full term*. It has grown a layer of fat to provide warmth and food

Birth

There are three stages which occur when a new human is brought into the world.

Stage 1 – labour

Just before birth the muscles of the uterus start to contract. This is the start of labour, and this stage may last from a few minutes to as long as a whole day. At first the muscles contract at intervals of about half an hour or so, but gradually they become more frequent and stronger.

The contracting muscles are forcing the baby down towards the base of the womb, and are causing the cervix to be stretched, ready to allow the baby through. Eventually the *amnion* bursts releasing the protective liquid that surrounded the baby. This is known as the 'breaking of the waters' and heralds the start of the next stage.

Stage 2 – birth

The contractions become very strong and the baby's head is pressed hard against the cervix. The head is forced past the cervix into the vagina and then through the gap in the pelvic bones. This stage may last up to an hour.

Sometimes the baby's legs or buttocks are pushed through first. This is a *breech birth* and can sometimes lead to serious complications.

The baby suddenly experiences a completely new world. It must now obtain its own oxygen by taking its first breath. The layers of fat under the baby's skin, and the mother's embrace will keep it warm.

Stage 3 – afterbirth

After the birth the umbilical cord is tied in two places and then cut. A few more powerful contractions and the placenta is expelled. The placenta is a dense mass of tissue about 30 cm across and has an average mass of about 500 g. It leaves the uterus as a tight knot of muscle and is commonly called the *afterbirth*.

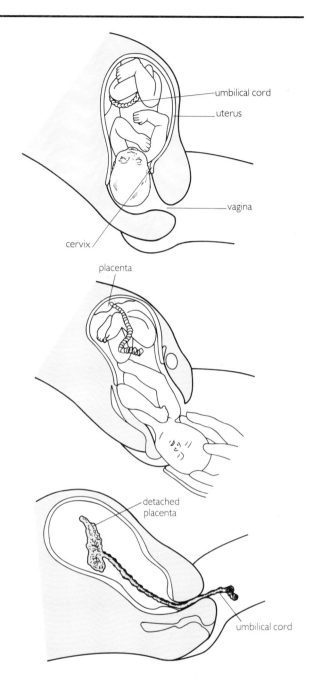

Breast feeding

During pregnancy the mother's breasts get bigger in preparation for supplying milk to the baby. Immediately after the birth the breasts produce a yellow fluid called *colostrum*. Later, the composition of the milk changes.

Human milk is ideal for babies. It is a balanced food designed for their needs. It also contains antibodies which increase the baby's resistance to disease. Breast feeding is also said to encourage a warm and loving relationship between mother and baby.

Bottle feeding

The use of bottle-fed artificial milk is sensible if the mother cannot produce sufficient milk of her own or if breast feeding is inconvenient. Artificial milk can provide a balanced diet for the baby but lacks antibodies.

	Colostrum	Milk
Protein	2.0%	8.0%
Lactose	8.0%	3.5%
Fats	4.0%	2.5%
Minerals	0.05%	0.05%
Vitamins	0.05%	0.05%
Water	85.9%	85.9%

REPRODUCTION

What can go wrong?

Miscarriage and abortion

If the baby dies during pregnancy the uterus will expel it automatically. This is a *miscarriage*; it is caused by abnormal development of the baby or an injury or illness of the mother. Most miscarriages occur in the third or fourth month of pregnancy.

An *abortion* is a deliberate miscarriage. There are many reasons for having an abortion, some of which are considered acceptable and others which are not. Abortion is relatively easy in the first 3 months, but becomes more difficult later on in the pregnancy. It is illegal in Britain to abort a foetus of more than 28 weeks.

Caesarean and forceps birth

Sometimes the child cannot be delivered in the normal way. It may be positioned incorrectly or the muscles of the womb may be too weak. In this case it can be delivered by caesarean section. The abdomen wall and uterus wall are cut and the surgeon slides a hand under the baby's head and lifts it out.

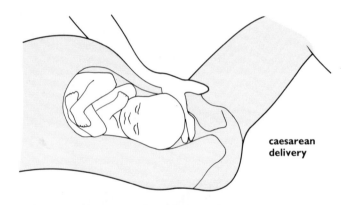

caesarean delivery

A forceps delivery is used to aid the mother's own muscles. The two halves of the forceps are inserted into the vagina on either side of the baby's head. The head is then firmly but gently pulled and the child is drawn out of the womb.

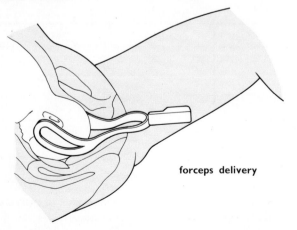

forceps delivery

Congenital defects

If the baby is born with a physical or mental disorder it is said to have a congenital defect. There is about a 1 in 50 chance of a baby being born with such a defect although some high-risk parents are much more likely to have such babies.

Congenital defect	Cause and effect
Inherited	
Down's Syndrome	The baby is born with 47 chromosomes instead of the normal 46. The effect is mental retardation and a characteristic appearance. In the past, this was called 'mongolism'.
Cystic Fibrosis	Many of the glands fail to function properly.
Spina Bifida	One or more of the backbones are fused (joined) together. If not treated it can cause paralysis.
Haemophilia	The blood clots very slowly or not at all. This is a sex linked disorder because the males suffer from the disease while females carry it.
Non-inherited	
Thalidomide	Between 1958 and 1961 some pregnant mothers were given a sedative drug called Thalidomide. It caused serious disorders and deformities in their children. All drugs are now thoroughly tested on pregnant mice before being released.
German Measles (Rubella)	The Rubella virus that causes german measles also causes the internal organs of babies to develop abnormally, especially in the third month of pregnancy. Women should check that they have had german measles or have been vaccinated against it before becoming pregnant.

Cancer

Breast cancer and cancer of the womb are the commonest forms of cancer to affect women. If detected early, both these cancers can be controlled or removed. Cancer of the sex glands of the male can also be removed easily if detected early enough.

Sterility and infertility

This is the inability to produce live eggs or sperm. If this is caused by blocked tubes it may be possible to correct by a surgical operation.

Fertility drugs can be given to a woman to make her ovaries produce eggs. However, if successful, it often causes the ovaries to release more than one egg and the woman may produce twins, triplets or even quadruplets.

It is sometimes possible for the doctor to remove an egg from the ovary and then fertilise it with sperms from the father while it is outside the body. After a few days when the doctor is sure the zygote is healthy, it is transferred back to the mother's womb where it is implanted. These babies are called test-tube babies (although test-tubes are not used!). This operation is used when the mother's oviduct is severely damaged.

blocked oviduct

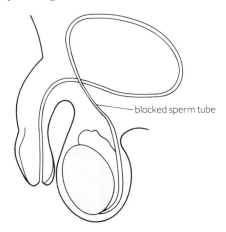

blocked sperm tube

Sexually transmitted diseases

Two of the more serious sexually transmitted diseases are syphilis and gonorrhoea. These are sometimes called veneral diseases or VD.

Disease	Cause	Transmission	Symptoms	Treatment
SYPHILIS	Spiral bacteria	During sexual contact	1–12 weeks after infection a small hard lump appears at the site of entry of the bacteria. This quickly disappears and is replaced by a rash. Eventually this also disappears. After a dormant period the final stage of the disease appears, which causes severe damage to organs and the nervous system and possibly death.	Antibiotics – such as penicillin. This can stop the disease but cannot repair the permanent damage caused to organs.
GONORRHOEA	Bacteria	During sexual contact	The first sign is a smelly yellow discharge – this is difficult to see in women, but obvious in men. In men, it hurts to urinate. If not treated early it can lead to sterility in men and women.	Antibiotics – usually penicillin.
NON-SPECIFIC URETHRITIS (NSU)	Unknown bacteria	Usually during sexual contact	The symptoms are not obvious in women. In men, the first sign is a smelly discharge from the penis, which is followed by a swelling of the testes.	Antibiotics – usually penicillin or tetracycline.
THRUSH	Fungus (Candida)	Possibly a normal inhabitant of the body	The woman's vagina may be infected. A characteristic white patch forms where the infection started.	Antibiotics.

12 GENETICS

Different people have different mental and physical characteristics. This makes everyone an individual. Everyone inherits their characteristics from their parents. The passing on of characteristics from parents to children is called *heredity*. The study of how they are passed on is called *genetics*.

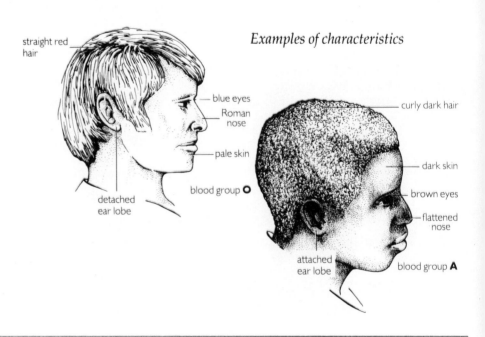

Examples of characteristics

straight red hair
blue eyes
Roman nose
pale skin
blood group **O**
detached ear lobe

curly dark hair
dark skin
brown eyes
flattened nose
attached ear lobe
blood group **A**

Each of us arose as a result of fertilisation: mother's ovum by father's sperm. The ovum and sperm must, therefore, contain the information that determines our characteristics. This information is carried in the nucleus of the sperm and ovum.

Chromosomes

The information is carried in the nucleus by very long, thread-like structures called *chromosomes*. For every chromosome in the sperm nucleus, there is a similar one in the ovum nucleus. Altogether there are *23 pairs* of chromosomes in the fertilised egg – a total of 46.

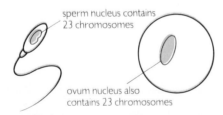

sperm nucleus contains 23 chromosomes

ovum nucleus also contains 23 chromosomes

Each chromosome is made up of protein and a long thin molecule called *DNA*. Each pair of chromosomes is divided up into thousands of sections called *genes*. At the same point on each pair similar genes are found. Combinations of genes determine each characteristic.

Chromosome behaviour in body cells
The fertilised ovum has 23 pairs of chromosomes. In order to grow it must divide into two cells, then four, eight and so on. This process of cell division is called *mitosis*. It makes sure that all subsequent cells also have 23 chromosomes.

During mitosis, each chromosome makes an exact duplicate of itself. The original chromosome goes to one of the new cells and the duplicate goes to the other new cell.

In this way, every cell of the body will have 23 pairs of chromosomes, each set being an exact copy of the original chromosome pairs in the fertilised ovum. Mitosis occurs millions upon millions of times during growth, and continues throughout life as cells are replaced.

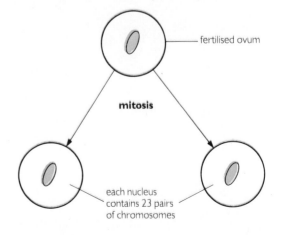

fertilised ovum

mitosis

each nucleus contains 23 pairs of chromosomes

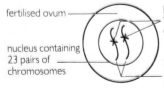

fertilised ovum

nucleus containing 23 pairs of chromosomes

position of a pair of genes that determine **one** characteristic, e.g. hair colour

one pair of chromosomes – one from the mother's ovum, and one from the father's sperm

Development of the sex cells

There is an exception to the rule that all cells in the human body contain 23 pairs of chromosomes. The sex cells have 23 single chromosomes. If they had 46 then after the fertilisation of the ovum by the sperm, the fertilised egg would have 92 chromosomes. This does not happen because of a special type of cell division called *meiosis*. Meiosis only occurs in the ovaries and testes of the human during production of the sex cells. This type of cell division halves the number of chromosomes in the sperm and ova to 23.

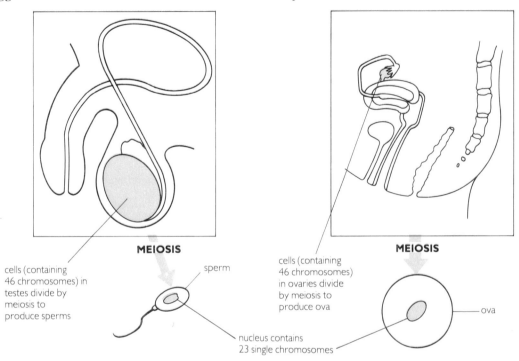

MEIOSIS

MEIOSIS

cells (containing 46 chromosomes) in testes divide by meiosis to produce sperms

sperm

nucleus contains 23 single chromosomes

cells (containing 46 chromosomes) in ovaries divide by meiosis to produce ova

ova

Only one pair of chromosomes actually carry the genes that determine sex. These are called the *sex chromosomes*. The genes are called the X and Y genes. A female has a pair of X genes on her sex chromosomes, while a male has an X and a Y gene. During meiosis the sex chromosomes separate. A female can only produce ova that have an X gene, but males can produce sperm that carry either the X gene or the Y gene. The Y gene is the male gene and about 50% of the sperms will carry it. This is why about half of the babies born are male.

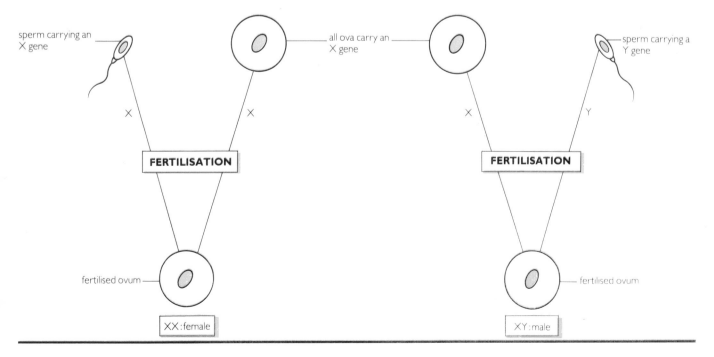

sperm carrying an X gene

all ova carry an X gene

sperm carrying a Y gene

X

X

X

Y

FERTILISATION

FERTILISATION

fertilised ovum

fertilised ovum

XX : female

XY : male

GENETICS

Inheritance

Characteristics are determined by pairs of genes. These become separated during meiosis and are then passed on to the children via the sex cells. The pair of genes which determine the characteristic is the *genotype*. The characteristic itself is called the *phenotype*.

In the case of sex determination, the genotypes are XX and XY, while the phenotyopes are female and male.

Genotype	Phenotype
XY	
XX	

Inheritance of blood groups

There are four blood groups in the ABO system. This means there are four phenotypes. However, there are six genotypes, as shown in the diagram. There are two alternative genotypes for both group A and group B. For instance, in group A, if both genes are A then the blood group is A. If one of the pair is an O and the other an A then the blood group is still A. This is because gene A is a strong or *dominant* gene. Gene O is a weak or *recessive* gene. In a similar way, gene B is dominant over gene O. The genes are the same in group O, but in the case of group AB the two genes are equally strong or *codominant*, so both are expressed, or shown in the phenotype. These differences in the genotypes can cause problems in blood transfusions.

Phenotype	Genotype
A	AA or AO
B	BB or BO
O	OO
AB	AB

Consider two parents who are both blood group A.

Before meiosis   The circle represents a cell in the sex organs, before it has divided by meiosis to give the sex cells. Inside is shown one of the 23 pairs of chromosomes. They contain two genes which control blood groups, gene A and gene O.

After meiosis   There is an equal chance of the mother releasing an ovum that will carry either gene. About 50% of the father's sperm will carry gene A, and 50% gene O.

After fertilisation   Although, in this case, both parents had blood group A, it does not mean they cannot produce children with another blood group. In this case there is a 1 in 4, or 25%, chance that they will have a child of blood group O. There is a 75% chance their child will have blood group A.

Blood groups can be used to establish who is the father of a child.

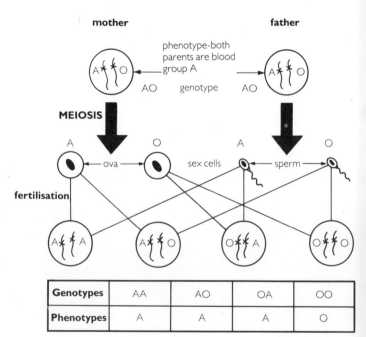

Genotypes	AA	AO	OA	OO
Phenotypes	A	A	A	O

Tongue rolling

The ability to roll your tongue into a U shape is inherited. It is controlled by a single pair of genes on one pair of chromosomes.

The gene that allows rolling can be called R, and it is dominant to the gene that doesn't allow rolling, which can be called r.

The rolling gene is *dominant*. Gene r is *recessive*.

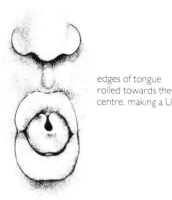

edges of tongue rolled towards the centre, making a U

Consider a woman who can roll her tongue and a man who cannot. The phenotype of the two people is easy to work out, but the genotype is more difficult. The father must have two recessive genes (rr) because one R gene would make him a roller. The mother could be RR or Rr because the rolling gene is dominant and could mask the r gene if it were there. If the man and woman marry and have children we might be able to find out which genotype the mother had by looking at the children's ability to roll their tongues.

PARENT	MOTHER	FATHER
PHENOTYPE	ROLLER	NON-ROLLER
GENOTYPE	RR or Rr	rr

If the mother has the genotype RR, she will always provide a dominant gene in her ova. This is because these are the only ones she has. This means that all her children will receive an R gene, so all her children will be able to roll their tongues.

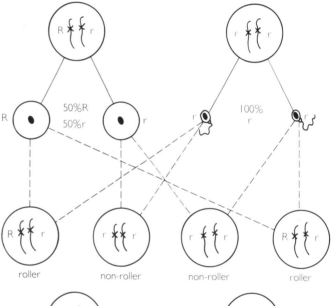

If the mother has the genotype Rr, the genes will separate during meiosis. There will be an even chance that any ovum will carry an R or r gene. This father's sperm can only have r genes because he is a non-roller. After fertilisation the possible genotypes of the children will be Rr or rr. There is a 50:50 chance that any particular child will be able to roll its tongue. In this way it is possible to calculate the genotype of the roller mother by looking at the children. This principle is used a great deal in genetics, especially in the search for new and better varieties of plants and animals for farmers.

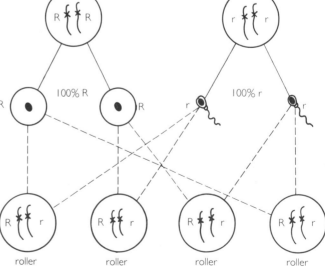

GENETICS

Genetic disorders

All genetic disorders are inherited. Anything that interferes with the process of meiosis, or affects the cells of the testes or ovary, will increase the chances of a genetic defect being passed on to the children.

Down's syndrome

During the process of meiosis, it is possible for an error to create an ovum that contains 24 single chromosomes instead of the normal 23. If this egg is fertilised, the zygote will contain 47 chromosomes, one too many. A child developing from this fertilised ovum could suffer from Down's syndrome, which is sometimes called mongolism. The chance of an error occurring during meiosis increases with age so older parents are a higher risk.

The 46 chromosomes found in the body cells of a normal adult are shown in the photograph. They can be rearranged into 23 pairs. A person suffering from Down's syndrome has an extra chromosome.

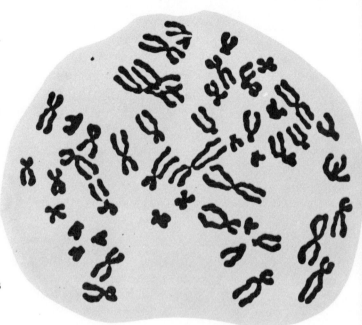

Mutations

Certain types of radiation and some chemicals can cause *mutations*. Possible sources of such radiation are nuclear explosions, leakage from nuclear power stations and X-rays. Mutations are changes in the DNA of the chromosomes. Many mutations are harmful since they can give rise to abnormal genes.

Abnormal genes

These are inherited and are usually recessive. If one is passed to a child by one parent the chances are that the other parent will supply a normal dominant gene. The abnormal gene will not then be expressed by the child. Problems arise if both parents possess the abnormal gene, and by chance they both supply it to their child. In this case there is a double recessive gene, i.e. there is no dominant gene to mask the abnormal one. *Cystic fibrosis*, an uncommon hereditary defect of the glands is an example of this.

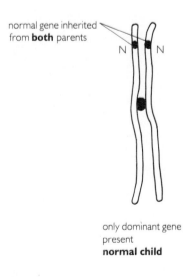

normal gene inherited from **both** parents

N   N

only dominant gene present
normal child

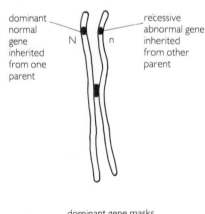

dominant normal gene inherited from one parent

recessive abnormal gene inherited from other parent

N   n

dominant gene masks the recessive gene
normal child

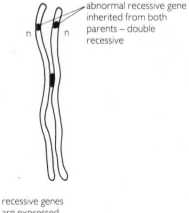

abnormal recessive gene inherited from both parents – double recessive

n   n

recessive genes are expressed
child with abnormal characteristics

Sex-linked abnormalities

The sex chromosomes are the only paired chromosomes that have different shapes. The chromosome that carries the Y gene is smaller than the chromosome that carries the X gene. Because of this genes on the X chromosome may not have partners on the Y chromosome.

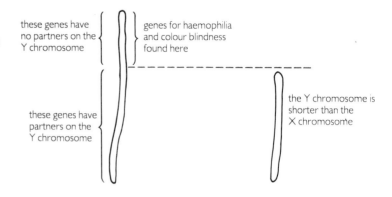

Haemophilia   People who have haemophilia have blood which will not clot normally. The disorder is caused by an abnormal gene on the X carrying chromosome. This is why it is called a sex-linked disease – it is linked to the X chromosomes. In the following diagrams only the sex chromosomes are drawn.

The normal gene is written as H. The abnormal gene is written as h. H is a dominant gene while h is recessive.

In this female the normal H gene is dominant and masks the h gene. Unfortunately, this female can pass on the abnormal gene to some of her children, so she is called a *carrier*.

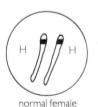 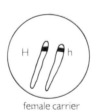

This male only has the abnormal h gene. He will have haemophilia, and is said to be a *haemophiliac*. There is no H gene on his Y chromosome that could mask the abnormal gene on his X chromosome.

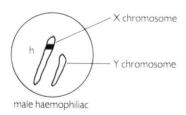

Colour blindness   This is a disorder of the eyes. In its commonest form the colour blind person confuses the colours red and green. It is a sex-linked disorder. Most colour blind people are males, while women can be carriers.

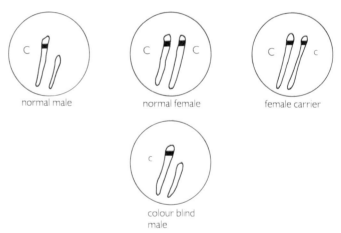

It is possible for a woman to be colour blind. This could happen if a female carrier married a colour blind male. However, this is an unlikely event because colour blindness is relatively rare.

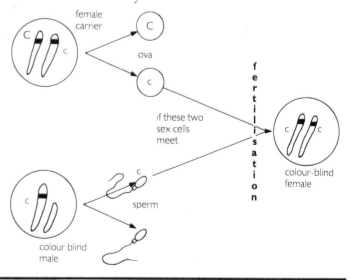

FOOD

CHAPTER 4

MAKING FOOD

Green plants are living things that can directly use the energy from the Sun to make food. The heat and light energy they absorb is stored as food.

Green plants make their own food by a process called *photosynthesis*. During photosynthesis the plant produces oxygen that is released into the air. Animals need this oxygen in order to live.

Sun

carbon dioxide

light

oxygen

water

The raw materials that plants use to make food are:
energy from the sun,
carbon dioxide from the air,
water and minerals from the soil.

Leaves have a large surface area which can trap large amounts of sunlight. This is where the green plant makes most of its food. Most plants make glucose, and some plants then change this to *starch* and store it until it is needed.

Some plants store large amounts of food in order to survive the winter, or to produce seeds. These plants are cultivated by farmers.

wheat   maize (sweetcorn)   potato   carrot   onion

Some plants are grown for animal feed. For example, farmers grow grass, maize and turnips for sheep, cows and pigs.

These animals can be eaten, or used to produce animal products for humans to eat.

cattle   sheep   pigs   poultry

beef   milk   cheese   lamb and mutton   bacon   pork and ham   eggs   chicken

dairy products

Food chains

The transfer of energy from the Sun to plants and then to animals is often shown in a food chain. The Sun is always at the start of a food chain.

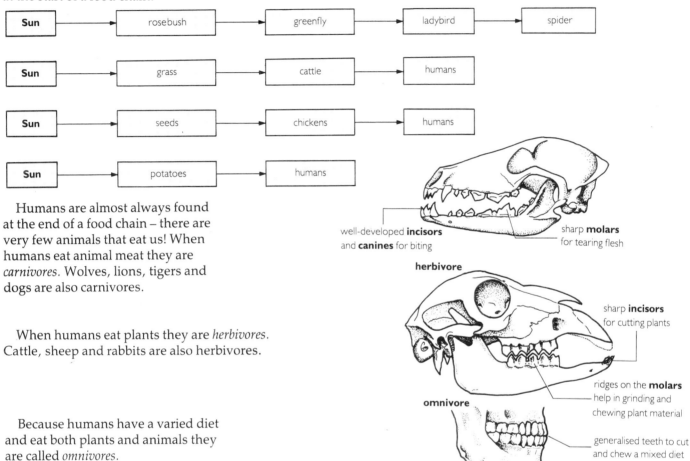

| Sun | → | rosebush | → | greenfly | → | ladybird | → | spider |

| Sun | → | grass | → | cattle | → | humans |

| Sun | → | seeds | → | chickens | → | humans |

| Sun | → | potatoes | → | humans |

Humans are almost always found at the end of a food chain – there are very few animals that eat us! When humans eat animal meat they are *carnivores*. Wolves, lions, tigers and dogs are also carnivores.

When humans eat plants they are *herbivores*. Cattle, sheep and rabbits are also herbivores.

Because humans have a varied diet and eat both plants and animals they are called *omnivores*.

well-developed **incisors** and **canines** for biting

sharp **molars** for tearing flesh

herbivore

sharp **incisors** for cutting plants

ridges on the **molars** help in grinding and chewing plant material

omnivore

generalised teeth to cut and chew a mixed diet

Losses in food chains

Useful energy is lost at every link in a food chain. The energy passed on to the next stage gets less each time. The lost energy has been used for respiration and excretion and is not available for the next stage. This goes some way towards explaining why plant products, such as potatoes or bread, are much cheaper than animal products, such as meat.

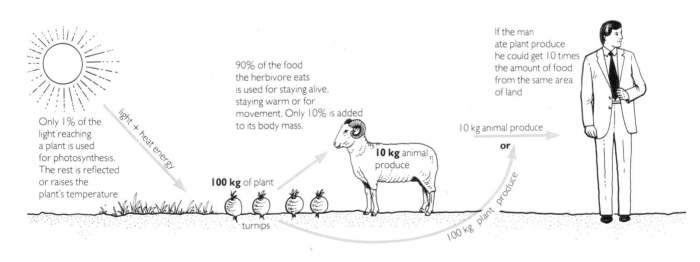

Only 1% of the light reaching a plant is used for photosynthesis. The rest is reflected or raises the plant's temperature

light + heat energy

90% of the food the herbivore eats is used for staying alive, staying warm or for movement. Only 10% is added to its body mass.

100 kg of plant

turnips

10 kg animal produce

10 kg animal produce

or

100 kg plant produce

If the man ate plant produce he could get 10 times the amount of food from the same area of land

2 GROWING FOOD

Agriculture is the name given to using land to grow food on a large scale. It includes raising livestock and growing crops.

Agriculture in Great Britain

The type of agriculture practised in a particular area depends upon a variety of factors.

Altitude Lowlands and highlands are suited for quite different types of agriculture.

Soil fertility This affects the type of crops that can be grown.

Climate The effect of temperature and rainfall are important.

Economics The cash value of the crop is important to the farmer.

Consumers The needs of the consumer must be considered.

Highland and moorland
This land is useful for grazing sheep which can survive bad weather. Crops cannot be easily grown here.

Lowlands
This land is best used for growing a variety of crops and for raising livestock.

Wetlands
These have often been drained to improve the pasture for cattle and crops.

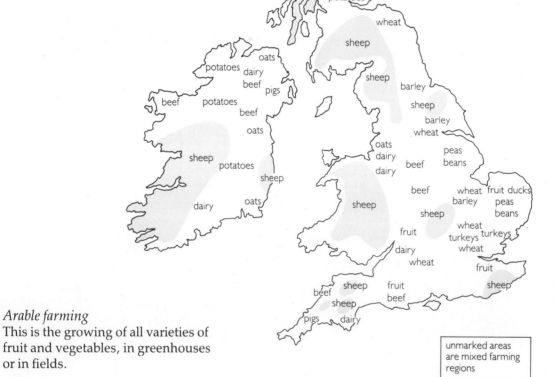

unmarked areas are mixed farming regions

Arable farming
This is the growing of all varieties of fruit and vegetables, in greenhouses or in fields.

Crops
These include:
   cereals, e.g. barley, wheat, oats, rye, maize;
   grass for pasture, straw, hay or silage;
   sugar beet;
   oil seed rape;
   root crops such as turnips;
   market garden produce such as fruit and vegetables.

Making the choice

Sheep are raised in hilly countryside where crops would be hard to grow. Dairy and beef cattle are raised where there is good pasture. Crops are grown where the soil is fertile and agricultural machinery can be easily used. The availability of fertilisers, pesticides and agricultural machinery will affect the farmer's choice of what to grow. The possibility of improving or altering the land by drainage or removing hedges will also be considerations.

Paying for the choice

Any improvements that the farmer makes has to be paid for in one way or another.

Fertilisers   If fertilisers are not used, the farmer must use *crop rotation*. This means planting a different crop each year in a field. This prevents the removal of the same nutrients from the soil every year. If fertilisers are used crop rotation is not necessary. The fertiliser replaces the nutrients that are being used up by each year's crop. Fertilisers are expensive chemicals which can pollute the water supply if they are washed off the land into rivers and streams. They do not keep the soil structure in good condition. They do allow a high crop yield on poor soil.

Pesticides   The use of pesticides has increased as *monoculture* has become more common. This is the growing of a single crop on a large farm. Pesticides are needed to protect the crop and to prevent the rapid spread of diseases. Pesticides are expensive and are often indiscriminate, killing useful organisms as well as the harmful ones. Some pesticides can linger in the soil for many years without breaking down into harmless chemicals.

Agricultural machinery   Machinery is labour and time saving. However, it is usually expensive, and has to be maintained, repaired, fuelled and eventually replaced.

Land drainage   Draining water from wetlands increases the amount of good agricultural land available. Unfortunately it also reduces the range and diversity of the animal and plant life in the country. Conservationists are concerned about the rapidly decreasing amount of wetland in the country.

Removal of hedges   If hedges are removed the number of fields is reduced, but each new field is, of course, much larger. This makes it more economical to use the larger farm machines. Unfortunately hedges are the habitat of a wide range of animals and plants. Hedge removal also changes the character of the countryside, usually for the worse.

The energy balance

The highly intensive method of farming that is practised over much of Great Britain has a high energy cost, but it produces very high yields.

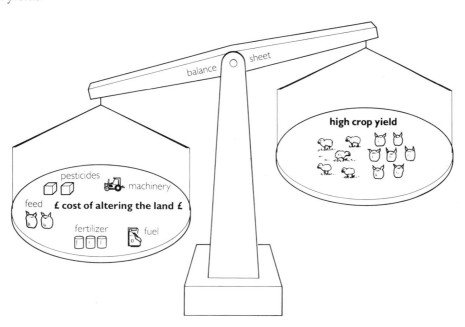

3 FOOD AROUND THE WORLD

Most of the world's agriculture is devoted to producing starchy foods. The high proportion of carbohydrate in these foods make them energy-rich. They are the staple foods which form the main part of the diet for the majority of the world's people. The two main types of starch-rich foods are *cereals (grain)* and *tubers*. Cereals and tubers provide over 80% of the energy the people of the world get from food. For a healthy diet, these carbohydrates must be supplemented with protein.

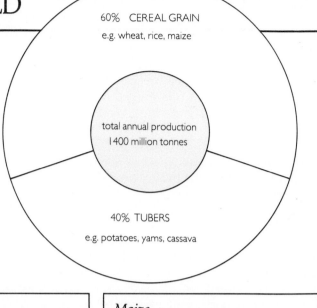

60% CEREAL GRAIN
e.g. wheat, rice, maize

total annual production
1400 million tonnes

40% TUBERS
e.g. potatoes, yams, cassava

Cereals
Cereals are grown for their seeds, which is the part we eat. These seeds are rich in starch, but low in protein. The husk of the seed is rich in vitamin B.

The main types of cereal are:

Wheat This is grown in the cooler parts of the world. The seeds are ground and milled to make flour.	*Rice* This is the main cereal crop of the world's warmer regions. It is the staple food of all the Asian countries where 90% of the world's rice is grown.	*Maize* This is called corn-on-the-cob or sweetcorn. Most of it is grown in North America, where it is often used as cattle food.

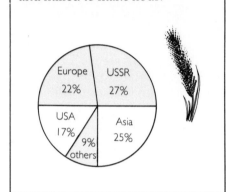

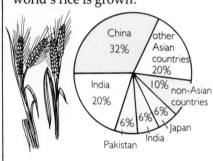

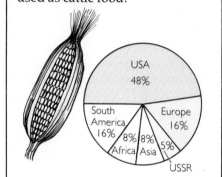

Tubers
Tubers are grown for their underground food storage organs. These are rich in starch.

Potatoes These are the main tuber crop of Europe and the USSR.	*Yams* These tubers are grown in warmer countries. Most are grown in Asia, but they are an important crop in Africa where they form a large part of the diet.	*Cassava* Cassava is poisonous until is has been ground into a flour and washed. This removes the cyanide that is found in the tuber. It forms a large part of the African and South American diet.

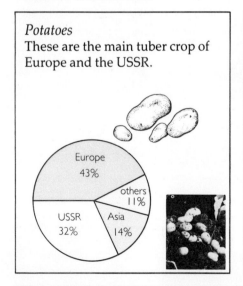

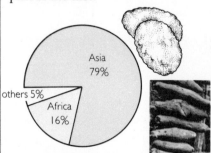

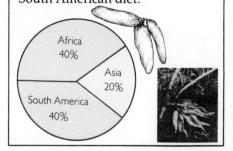

Food and population

The present population of the world is over 4000 million. Almost 60% of the world's people live in Asia. Most of these people, plus Africans, Central Americans and South Americans make up the *third world*. Life for people living in the third world is very difficult; they are the 'hungry world'. Britons are among 500 million people who live in the 'satisfied world', made up of the *first* and *second worlds*. The first world is western Europe, North America and other developed countries. The second world is the USSR, eastern Europe and parts of southern Europe.

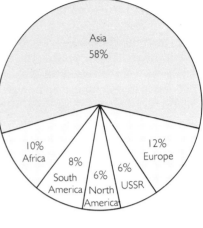

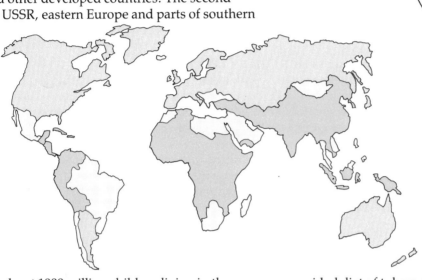

average food intake is sufficient

average food intake is 10–25% *less* than is required

average food intake is over 20% *more* than is required

There are about 1000 million children living in the world today. About 60% of them will never celebrate their 14th birthday. They will die of malnutrition and its side effects. A large proportion of mankind survives on a one-sided diet of tubers or cereal. This provides them with energy but little protein, and so they suffer from *protein deficiency*.

Protein deficiency

Shortage of protein is much more common than shortage of carbohydrate. First-class animal protein (meat) is expensive to produce. It requires an extra stage in the food chain and needs more land than crop farming (see page 111). Protein deficiency is the most important factor in the world's hunger crisis. It paves the way for all kinds of diseases. Protein can be obtained from animals or plants.

Animal protein   This contains all the amino acids the human body needs. Meat and animal products are usually rich in protein.

Plant protein   No plant contains all the amino acids we need. People who eat only plant protein must eat a variety of types of plant to get all the essential amino acids.

Over two-thirds of the world's production of meat is eaten by only a quarter of the world's population. The satisfied world gets far more than its fair share of animal protein.

The growing population

By the year AD 2000 the population of our planet may have reached 7000 million people. If most of today's population are already hungry, what of the future? The satisfied world countries are providing aid to the third world, but many people argue that the impact of this aid is negligible. Much of the suffering of the third world is caused by the greed of the satisfied world.

Animal protein	Satisfied world eats	Hungry world eats
Beef	75%	25%
Pork	62%	38%
Poultry	70%	30%
Eggs	60%	40%
Total of all animal protein	67%	33%

4 WHAT'S IN FOOD?

Food is made up from the chemicals that we need in order to live and grow. Our digestive system is designed to extract the chemicals we need from the food, and to get rid of the remaining waste. The useful chemicals, or *nutrients,* are then used for growth, repair or energy.

Food is mainly made up of water, which is not surprising since your body is 75% water! We need between two and three litres of water a day. About half of this is obtained in our food and the rest we drink. This intake of water, balances the loss of water from urination, defaecation, breathing and sweating. If we do not get enough water we become *dehydrated.* Dehydration is very serious – the body can survive for far longer without food than without water. If we removed the water from the food we eat, the dry matter left behind would contain the chemicals our bodies need. These chemicals can be divided into five groups: **protein, carbohydrate, fats, minerals and vitamins.**

Protein

Protein is required for growth, the replacement of worn out or damaged cells and the repair of damaged tissues. Protein deficiency is serious because it weakens the body and leads to many illnesses. The amount of protein a human body needs every day is about 1 g of protein for every 1 kg of body mass. Extra protein cannot be stored by the body. It is broken down by the liver to provide carbohydrates and heat.

Protein is made up of chains of *amino acids.* There are 22 different amino acids. Animal protein contains all 22, but plant proteins do not. Ten of the amino acids are essential to the normal working of the human body. All animal protein has these essential amino acids, so animal proteins are called *first class protein.* No single plant protein contains all the essential amino acids although they can be obtained by eating a range of plant proteins. For this reason, plant protein is often referred to as *second class protein.*

During digestion protein is broken down and the amino acids are separated. They then enter the bloodstream and are taken first to the liver and then to the rest of the body.

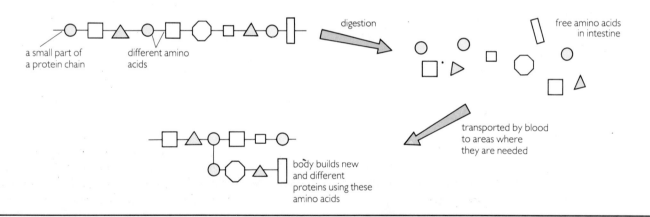

a small part of a protein chain

different amino acids

digestion

free amino acids in intestine

transported by blood to areas where they are needed

body builds new and different proteins using these amino acids

Fats

Fat is the nutrient which contains most energy. Fat is made up of a combination of *fatty acids* and glycerol. There are three fatty acids that are essential to the normal working of the human body. Meat and animal products contain more fat than food that has come from plants. During digestion the fat is broken down into fatty acids and glycerol. These then pass into the lymphatic system and pass around the body until they enter the bloodstream.

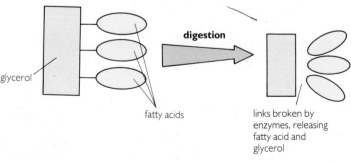

glycerol

digestion

fatty acids

links broken by enzymes, releasing fatty acid and glycerol

Some fatty acids are called *saturated* and others are called *unsaturated.* Both types are found in our bodies and our food. Unsaturated fats are thought by some to be healthier than saturated fats. They are found in plant foods. Some people believe it is better to fry food in vegetable oil and eat unsaturated margarines rather than butter.

Carbohydrates

Sugar, starch and fibre are all forms of carbohydrate. Sugars and starches are used as a source of energy. All carbohydrates are made up of chains of simple sugars linked together. During digestion the links are broken and the simple sugars become separated and pass into the bloodstream. Fibre (or roughage) is made up of *cellulose*, which is a very long chain of sugars. Humans cannot digest cellulose, so fibre passes through the digestive system and out in the faeces. Fibre is important in our diet because it absorbs water and gives bulk to the digested food. Fibre allows the muscles of the digestive system to grip the food. People who have a high amount of fibre in their diet seem to be less likely to suffer from diseases of the digestive system.

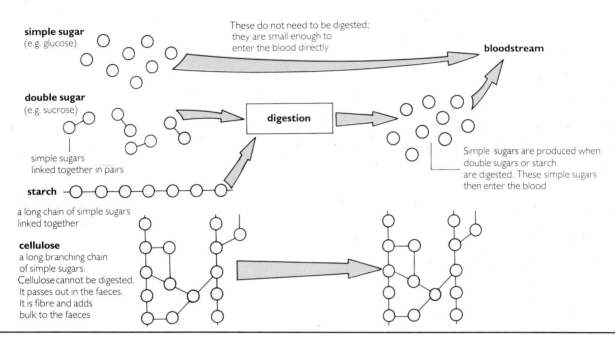

Vitamins and minerals

Vitamins and minerals are only needed in small amounts, but they are essential to maintain a healthy body. Vitamins are chemicals needed for all kinds of biochemical processes. If missing from the diet, illnesses called *vitamin deficiency diseases* can develop.

Humans need about 15 different minerals in their diet. Each mineral is needed by different parts of the body. If we eat too many vitamins or minerals they pass out in the faeces; they cannot be stored. In some cases eating too much of a mineral or vitamin can be harmful. Vitamins and minerals do **not** provide the body with any energy. Different foods contain different vitamins and minerals so a mixed diet is important.

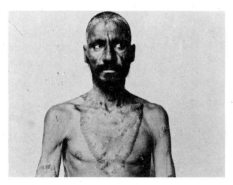

Pellagra – lack of Vitamin B$_2$

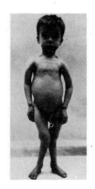

Rickets – lack of Vitamin D

A balanced diet

Different foods contain different proportions of proteins, carbohydrates, fats, minerals and vitamins. So long as we eat a variety of foods which contain the right proportions of these five groups for our individual needs, we will be getting a healthy balanced diet (see page 120).

5 SOURCES AND DEFICIENCES

A balanced diet must contain all of these in the correct proportion.

Food	Sources	Needed for	Deficiency disease
Protein 1st class (animal origin) 2nd class (plant origin)	beef, fish, liver, lamb, eggs, kidney, poultry, milk, legumes (pulses), e.g. broad beans, butter beans, haricot beans, soya beans groundnut e.g peanuts peas bread	Protein is vital for growth, the making of new cells and the repair and replacement of old cells. Body builders and athletes need a larger proportion of protein to make more muscle tissue	**Kwashiorkor** – this is the name given to protein deficiency in growing children. They become listless, miserable and weak; this is common in tropical Africa
Carbohydrate	bread, potato, cake, sugar breakfast cereals, beer, biscuits,	Carbohydrates are needed for energy, a small amount is needed to make cells. Fat cannot be used as a source of energy unless some sugar is present	Lack of energy from carbohydrates leads to starvation and malnutrition
Fat	cheese, margarine, cream, dripping, milk, lard, meat, vegetable oil, butter	Fat is needed for the energy it contains. Some fat is used to line the body and act as an insulating layer	Very rare and is only found in people who are suffering from malnutrition
Minerals Calcium	milk, cheese, green vegetables	Both are needed for the formation of healthy bones and teeth	**Rickets** – the lack of enough calcium and phosphorus leads to abnormal bone formation. The bones are soft because they lack calcium phosphate
Phosphorus	milk, cheese, green vegetables		
Iron	liver, cereals, meat, vegetables, eggs	Iron is needed to make haemoglobin for red blood cells	**Anaemia** – a disease caused by the shortage of haemoglobin
Iodine	Found in drinking water and most sea foods; added to table salt	Iodine is used by the thyroid gland to make a hormone (see page 85)	**Goitre** – a swelling of the thyroid gland in the neck; rare (see page 85)
Fluoride	drinking water	Fluoride is needed for strong healthy teeth	**Dental caries** – tooth decay is more common where fluoride is deficient; some authorities add it to water
Sodium	table salt (sodium chloride)	Sodium is needed to maintain the composition of the blood	Extremely rare
Potassium	fruit, green vegetables	Too much or too little interferes with the heart action. Potassium is needed inside cells	Extremely rare

Food	Sources	Needed for	Deficiency disease
Vitamins A	milk, butter, liver, green vegetables, fatty fish, e.g. herrings sardines,	Needed for proper resistance against disease	Skin becomes dry and scaly. Severe cases can cause night-blindness
B₁ (thiamine)	liver, egg yolk, brown rice, breakfast cereal, wholemeal bread, yeast extract	Needed for the general maintenance of health	**Beri-beri** – loss of appetite and weight, swelling of the feet and legs. This is common in the Far East
B₂ (riboflavin and niacin)	milk, meat, cheese, green vegetables, yeast extract	Needed for general health	**Pellagra** – loss of weight, skin disease and eventually mental disorders
C (ascorbic acid)	potatoes, green vegetables, blackcurrants, pineapples, tomatoes, citrus fruits, e.g. lemon lime orange	Needed for healthy skin, mouth and gums. Vitamin C is thought to increase the body's resistance to disease	**Scurvy** – wounds do not heal easily; skin cracks; mouth and gums bleed; joints become stiff
D	milk fish	Needed to allow the bones to form properly	**Rickets** – vitamin D aids the absorption of the calcium needed for normal bone growth; Vitamin D is made by the skin when exposed to sunlight
E (tocopherol)	wholemeal bread, butter, green vegetables	It is thought that this vitamin is used in the ovaries and testes	Rarely deficient
K	cabbage, peas, spinach	Vital for normal clotting of blood	Rarely deficient
Fibre (roughage)	cereals, wholemeal bread, bran, celery, green vegetables most plant foods (it is not found in animal products)	Helps in the digestion of other foods. It absorbs and holds water and speeds up the removal of waste by providing bulk for the muscles of the digestive system to push against	Countries with a diet rich in fibre have few people suffering from diseases of the digestive system. In the western world we eat a lot of refined (purified) food that is low in fibre. We have high rates of incidence of constipation, gallstones, bowel cancer and diabetes

6 A BALANCED DIET

Your diet is what you eat. It may be a good diet or it may be a bad diet. A good diet will be a balanced diet because it will provide all the energy and nutrients that you need.

A balanced diet for one person is not necessarily a good diet for someone else. What makes a balanced diet for you depends on five factors.

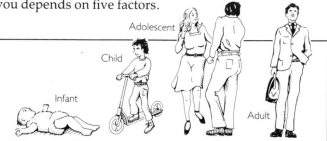

Age
During growth the proportion of protein in the diet should be greater than in an adult. Growing children also need extra minerals such as calcium and phosphorus, for making teeth and bones, and iron for making red blood cells.

Size
The bigger your build is, the more food you will need to stay healthy.

Slight small person

Large tall person

Sex
Men and women have slightly different dietary needs. As a general rule, men usually require more energy-rich foods than women.

Occupation and recreation
The more active you are at work and play, the more energy-rich foods you will need. You will also need slightly more protein if you are an active person. Eating too much fat or carbohydrate for your needs will lead to obesity (extreme fatness).

Light work and play

Medium work and play

Heavy work and play

Special needs
Pregnant women must provide protein and minerals for their developing baby.

A mother breastfeeding her baby must make milk for her baby. She will need more protein and energy-rich food.

Illness puts extra stress on the body. Extra protein is needed for replacement of damaged tissue.

The energy needed in a balanced diet

Fats, carbohydrates and protein all provide the body with energy. To maintain a constant body mass the intake of these must match the body's demand for energy. The amount of energy that the body can obtain from a food is called the food's energy value. This is measured in kilojoules (kJ) per unit mass. Some people, however, still use Calories to measure the energy value. One Calorie is the same as 4.2 kJ.

Fats are the most concentrated source of energy. Weight for weight fats provide more than twice as much energy as carbohydrate or protein.

The average energy requirement for an adult in the UK is about 12500 kJ (3000 Cal). Most of this is likely to be supplied in the form of carbohydrate, but any fat or excess protein will provide energy as well.

Many factors will affect the energy requirement of a balanced diet for adults, but one of the most important is the occupation of the person concerned.

Food	Energy value (per gram of food)
Fat	39 kJ (9 Cal)
Carbohydrate	17 kJ (4 Cal)
Protein	17 kJ (4 Cal)
Minerals	0
Vitamins	0

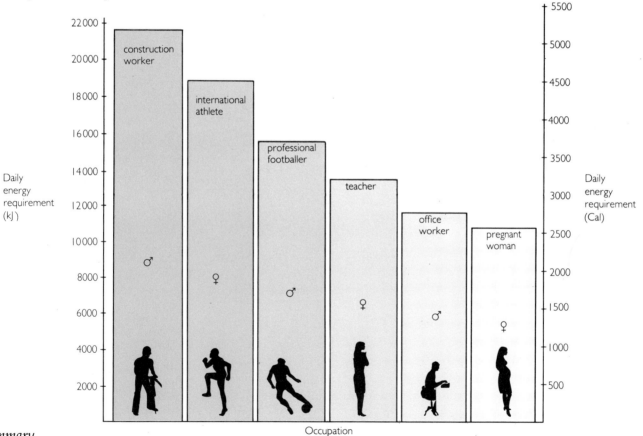

Summary

Taking all the above factors and special needs into account, a balanced diet is one that provides:
1 an adequate, but not excessive energy content;
2 a protein content that is sufficient for growth, repair and replacement;
3 a fat content that is sufficient to provide the essential fatty acids, but not so much that it might lead to obesity;
4 a mixture of different foods that provide all the necessary minerals and vitamins.

A balanced diet provides no more and no less than the requirements of the body.

121

7 FOOD PREPARATION

Food should be prepared hygienically and in a way that keeps its nutritional value.

Food hygiene

It is very easy to infect food with micro-organisms (microbes). Our skin is normally covered in microbes and there are many different types floating in the air around us. If harmful microbes infect the food and breed then there is a danger of disease.

Food shops

People who work in food shops must follow rules of food hygiene and should understand the cycles of microbes.

Shop assistants have to handle food. Microbes are bound to be transferred onto the food

Harmful microbes can reach the hands after visiting the toilet or after touching the nose or mouth

If everyone uses the same towel microbes can easily be transferred from one person to another.

Dirty bandages can easily carry microbes which can get onto food

Accepting cash from customers also transfers microbes. Ideally cashiers should not handle fresh food or cooked meats

At home

The same rules should apply at home. However, most people do not understand what microbes are or what they can do to food once it is infected.

Microbes on the hands   These are usually harmless. Washing the hands makes sure that most of them are removed. This is especially important after visiting the toilet. Remember that microbes can pass through toilet paper on to the hands – particularly if soft toilet paper is used.

Microbes in the air   Coughs and sneezes release thousands of microbes into the air. A handkerchief should be used to reduce this and the hands washed afterwards. Airborne microbes will eventually land, so you should cover food that is not going to be cooked again.

Microbes on cooking utensils   The same knife should never be used to cut raw meat and cooked meat. It might transfer harmful microbes from the raw meat to the cooked meat. They will not be visible but they could easily breed in the cooked meat.

Food nutrition

The art of cooking food is to maintain the full nutritional value of the food. Raw foods will give the best value, but most foods are more palatable and digestible if they are cooked before being eaten.

Meat and fish

All meat and fish provide us with first class protein and many minerals and vitamins. Very little of the nutritional value will be lost during cooking, especially if any juices are used to make sauces or gravy.

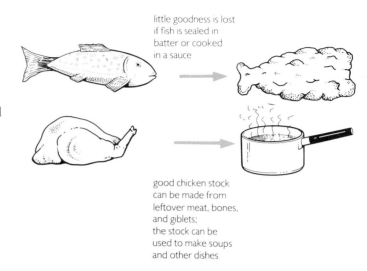

little goodness is lost if fish is sealed in batter or cooked in a sauce

good chicken stock can be made from leftover meat, bones, and giblets; the stock can be used to make soups and other dishes

juices from roast meats make excellent gravy

Vegetables

Nutrients are easily lost during the cooking of vegetables. This is because vegetables are often boiled and the minerals and vitamins can dissolve easily in the cooking water. Overcooking of vegetables can destroy vitamins, especially vitamin C which is found in most green vegetables.

These guidelines will reduce nutritional losses during cooking:

1 Prepare the vegetables only when you are ready to use them. Vitamins can be broken down if they are exposed to the air for long periods.

2 Put the vegetables straight into boiling water. This destroys any enzymes that break down vitamins. It also reduces cooking time.

air breaks down enzymes on the exposed surface

cover peeled vegetables with water until ready

cold water

vegetables

vegetables

boiling water

3 Boil the vegetables in the smallest amount of water possible. Many minerals and vitamins will dissolve in this water. The cooking water should be used to make a gravy or sauce. If you throw it away you also throw away these vitamins and minerals.

4 Do not overcook the vegetables. Long periods of cooking can destroy vitamins, especially vitamin C and will leave a pan-full of stringy cellulose with no nutritional value.

too much water

too long

short cooking time

Fruit

This is best eaten raw, but if it is to be cooked you should follow the guidelines given for cooking vegetables.

8 FOOD POISONING

Most food poisoning is caused by microbes called *bacteria*.
There are four major types, of which *Salmonella* is the
most common. It is not possible to tell if food is infected
by bacteria just by looking at it.

Bacteria	How poisoning is caused	Symptoms of poisoning
Salmonella These bacteria are commonly found in poultry Some people are carriers – they are infected with *Salmonella*, but do not become ill. Carriers can infect food and other people	Food becomes infected. The *Salmonella* breed rapidly and vast numbers are produced in the food. When the food is eaten, the body reacts strongly to the millions of bacteria in the digestive system	Symptoms appear between 12 and 36 hours after eating the infected food – severe muscular pains, diarrhoea and sometimes vomiting. The symptoms last for 1 to 8 days. Salmonella poisoning is rarely fatal
Clostridium welchii These bacteria are sometimes found in meat	If these bacteria get into food they release a chemical called a toxin. This toxin causes the body to react strongly. The toxin is only destroyed by boiling for 30 minutes	Symptoms appear 6 to 12 hours after eating the infected food. Pain is felt in the digestive system and diarrhoea may occur. The symptoms last for between 12 and 24 hours and it is never fatal
Staphylococci These bacteria are common in the human mouth, throat and nose	If these bacteria get into food they release a chemical or toxin which causes the body to react strongly. The toxin is only destroyed by boiling for 30 minutes	Symptoms develop after 2 to 6 hours; diarrhoea, vomiting and severe pains are quite likely. These symptoms last for between 6 and 24 hours and recovery is rapid
Clostridium botulinum These cause the disease botulism. It is very rare but these microbes are common in the soil	These bacteria can only grow well in the absence of oxygen. If they are found in canned food, the bacteria grow rapidly and release a toxin in the infected food. The toxin is destroyed by heating	The symptoms appear after 6 to 36 hours. The toxin attacks the nervous system; and paralysis of the respiratory system is very common. This type of food poisoning is fatal in over 50% of cases. If the patient survives then recovery may take as long as 6 to 8 months

There are other bacteria which can cause food
poisoning, but the four in the table are the most common
causes.

Why food poisoning occurs

There are two causes of food poisoning – ignorance and carelessness. In order to avoid food poisoning you must know what conditions are best for the growth of microbes.

Bacteria like **warmth**. They will survive and breed in temperatures between 10°C and 50°C. Low temperatures will stop them breeding, but will not destroy them. High temperatures kill bacteria and other microbes, and can destroy toxins they may release.

Bacteria need **food** and **water** to grow and breed successfully. They cannot breed if water is missing.

Bacteria need **time** to breed. In ideal conditions, with moisture, food and warmth they will breed extremely rapidly. One bacterium can divide and produce 2 million bacteria in 7 hours, and 7000 million after 12 hours.

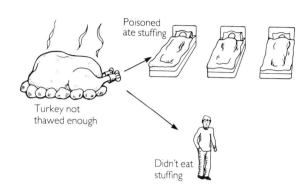

Turkey not thawed enough

Poisoned ate stuffing

Didn't eat stuffing

Situations which might lead to food poisoning
Leftover food not covered. Airborne microbes can fall into the food.

A hot-dog salesman fails to keep the temperature of the sausages high enough. He infects the food after visiting the toilet and not washing his hands.

Cross-contamination – a knife used to slice raw meat is then used to cut a pork pie. The knife could transfer the bacteria from the raw meat to the cooked meat.

A large frozen turkey is thawed out overnight. It is prepared, stuffed and cooked in the oven; 12 hours after eating, all but one of the family have food poisoning. The odd one out did not eat any stuffing. All the meat had been cooked thoroughly, but the inside of the turkey had not thawed properly. This kept the stuffing cool and bacteria bred rapidly in the warm moist conditions. Food must be thawed thoroughly before cooking.

Cakes or meat handled by someone with harmful bacteria on their hands. Food is put in a picnic box and left in a warm car for a few hours.

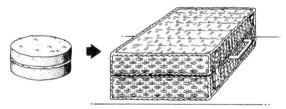

Cross-contamination – blood from a thawing chicken falls on a cooked ham. The blood contains *Salmonella*. The ham is left in a warm place for a few hours.

Blood

A faulty thermostat in a warming cabinet keeps pies at a warm temperature rather than at a safe hotter temperature.

9 FOOD PRESERVATION

Supermarkets and grocers contain a wide variety of foods. Many of these have a long shelf life. They do not start to 'go off'. They have been *preserved*. Food goes off because of the action of microbes, enzymes and oxygen.

Microbes   Some microbes cause food poisoning. Other less dangerous microbes give food an unpleasant taste and release gases.

Enzymes   These chemicals are present in all plants and animals. When an animal or plant dies its own enzymes start to break down the tissues. Freshly killed meat, poultry and game are hung (left) for a while to let their enzymes make them more tender. Eventually the tissues start to decompose and unpleasant flavours and smells are formed.

Oxygen   Oxygen can cause fats to turn sour or rancid. This is called oxidation.

Ways of preserving food

Heat   High temperatures can destroy enzymes and kill bacteria.

Freezing   Low temperatures can prevent bacteria breeding and stop enzymes working. When the temperature rises the bacteria will start to breed and the enzymes will become active. Vegetables must be blanched (put in boiling water for a short time) before freezing. This blanching destroys the enzymes that would make the vegetables too soft.

Dehydration   Microbes cannot grow or breed if water is missing. Enzymes need water to work.

Preservatives   These chemicals can be used to kill or stop bacteria from breeding.

Antioxidants   These chemicals are used to prevent the oxidation of any fat in the food. This stops the fat going rancid and giving the food an unpleasant flavour.

The refrigerator
The use of the refrigerator has made keeping food much easier and safer. The refrigerator usually keeps its contents at a temperature of about 4°C. Food will still deteriorate at this temperature, but much slower than at room temperature. Milk will still sour after a few days, and cheese will still go mouldy.

The freezer
Most freezers keep their contents at about −20°C. At this temperature bacteria and enzymes are inactive. Food will keep for long periods, but the flavour may well alter if it is kept for very long periods. Once the food is thawed any bacteria in it will start to breed.

   Some foods, such as strawberries, are damaged by the ice crystals that form inside them when they are frozen. This damage can be reduced by freezing these foods as quickly as possible. Freezing firms do this by plunging fruit into liquid nitrogen (−196°C). When food is frozen in this way the ice crystals inside are very tiny and the food is not damaged.

Milk
Fresh milk, straight from a cow, cannot be kept for very long because it goes sour. If the milk is boiled, most of the bacteria in it are destroyed and the milk is *sterilised*. This milk can be kept for a few weeks before it goes sour, but the strong heat has destroyed some vitamins and altered

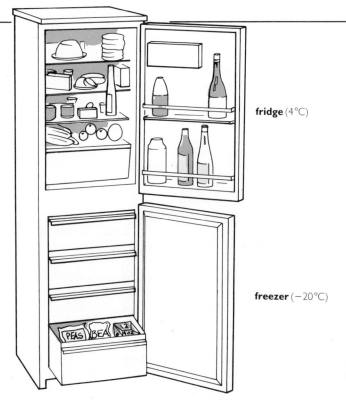

fridge (4°C)

freezer (−20°C)

its taste. If fresh milk is heated to 72°C for fifteen seconds then cooled quickly, most of the bacteria are killed and the taste is not altered. This type of milk is called *pasteurised*; it is the normal milk that is delivered to your door.

A survey of preserved foods

Frozen foods

As home freezers and refrigerators have become commonplace, the frozen food industry has grown. Food stored at −20°C is safe and will not deteriorate. Food must be eaten or cooked soon after thawing because any microbes in it will start to breed as soon as the temperature rises. The range of frozen foods on the market is enormous.

Canned foods

Most canned foods are cooked in giant pressure cookers. The high temperature kills all the microbes and destroys any enzymes in the food. While the food is still hot it is put into sterilised cans. These are heated and the steam produced forces out any air. The can is then sealed. Canned foods are very safe. Foods such as rhubarb, which are acidic, do not need to be heated. Their natural acids destroy any bacteria. Some canned meats also contain a chemical preservative, usually sodium nitrite.

Dried foods

This is the oldest method of food preservation. Grapes are dried to form raisins, sultanas or currants. Microbes in the food cannot multiply without water. Some foods are dried by gentle heat, but this can alter the flavour and destroy vitamins. Some food is dried in a vacuum, e.g. coffee granules. This is called *vacuum freeze drying* and does not affect the flavour or the vitamins. Dried soups, curries, stuffing and cake mixes often contain an antioxidant to prevent the fat going rancid and affecting the taste.

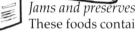

Pickled foods

These are placed in vinegar which is a weak acid. Microbes cannot grow in it.

Smoked foods

Foods such as kippers and smoked bacon are hung in a smoke-filled room. Wood smoke contains chemicals which kill microbes.

Salted foods

This is an old method that is often used for fish or meat. The salt draws water out of the food and this kills the microbes. Salted butter lasts longer than unsalted.

Cooked meats

Cooking the meat kills any microbes in it. They are then vacuum-packed and kept in cold conditions. This slows down microbe growth. They are also injected with sodium nitrite, as a preservative.

Jams and preserves

These foods contain a high sugar concentration. The sugar draws water out of the food and the microbes cannot breed. Jam jars must be sealed while they are still hot if they are to be effective in preserving food.

Vacuum packing

The food is placed in a plastic coat, and all the oxygen is removed. The plastic is then sealed. This method prevents the oxidation of the food. This method is usually used with another form of preservation, e.g. with chemical preservatives or dehydrated foods.

Some microbes can be useful. The oldest known process that uses microbes to make food is *fermentation*. This uses a microscopic fungus called *yeast*.

If yeast is placed in warm water and given a food such as sugar, it will start to grow and multiply. It uses the sugar as a source of energy and produces alcohol and carbon dioxide as waste products.

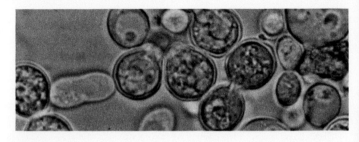

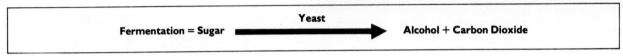

Fermentation = Sugar ──── **Yeast** ───▶ **Alcohol + Carbon Dioxide**

Yeast can be used in a number of useful ways:

Making bread
Bakers use the fermentation of sugar to make the bread rise. The yeast produces a small amount of alcohol, but it is the carbon dioxide that the baker wants. This gas makes the holes or bubbles in bread. Most of the alcohol evaporates during baking.

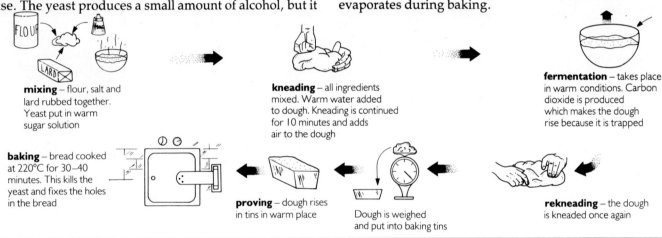

mixing – flour, salt and lard rubbed together. Yeast put in warm sugar solution

kneading – all ingredients mixed. Warm water added to dough. Kneading is continued for 10 minutes and adds air to the dough

fermentation – takes place in warm conditions. Carbon dioxide is produced which makes the dough rise because it is trapped

baking – bread cooked at 220°C for 30–40 minutes. This kills the yeast and fixes the holes in the bread

proving – dough rises in tins in warm place

Dough is weighed and put into baking tins

rekneading – the dough is kneaded once again

Winemaking
Most commercial wines are made from grape juice, but homemade wines often use other fruit juices. The type of wine produced will depend on the variety of fruit, the time of picking and the type of fermentation used. The yeast is used to ferment the sugars in the grape or fruit juice. This produces carbon dioxide and alcohol. The carbon dioxide is usually allowed to escape. Some sparkling wines use the carbon dioxide produced for 'fizz'.

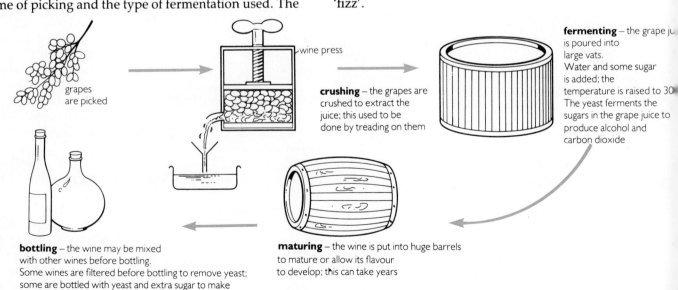

grapes are picked

wine press

crushing – the grapes are crushed to extract the juice; this used to be done by treading on them

fermenting – the grape ju[...] is poured into large vats. Water and some sugar is added; the temperature is raised to 30[...] The yeast ferments the sugars in the grape juice to produce alcohol and carbon dioxide

maturing – the wine is put into huge barrels to mature or allow its flavour to develop; this can take years

bottling – the wine may be mixed with other wines before bottling. Some wines are filtered before bottling to remove yeast; some are bottled with yeast and extra sugar to make a sparkling wine

Beermaking

Beer is made from barley seeds. These are roasted (malted) – to destroy the enzymes inside them; this also alters the flavour. The different types of beer are produced by using different types of malted barleys, hops and yeasts.

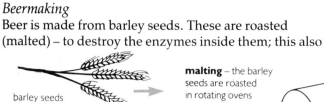

barley seeds

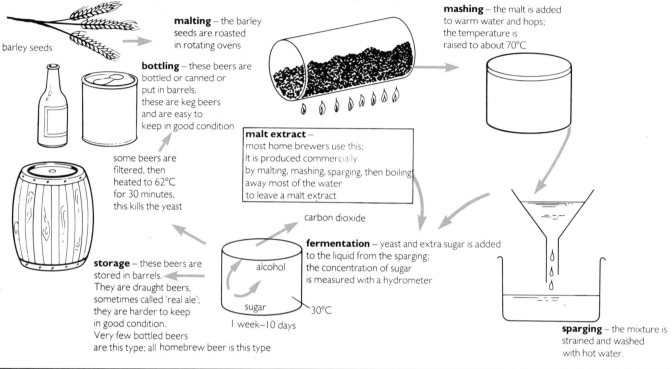

malting – the barley seeds are roasted in rotating ovens

mashing – the malt is added to warm water and hops; the temperature is raised to about 70°C

bottling – these beers are bottled or canned or put in barrels, these are keg beers and are easy to keep in good condition

some beers are filtered, then heated to 62°C for 30 minutes, this kills the yeast

malt extract –
most home brewers use this;
It is produced commercially
by malting, mashing, sparging, then boiling
away most of the water
to leave a malt extract

carbon dioxide

alcohol

sugar 30°C

1 week–10 days

fermentation – yeast and extra sugar is added to the liquid from the sparging; the concentration of sugar is measured with a hydrometer

storage – these beers are stored in barrels. They are draught beers, sometimes called 'real ale'; they are harder to keep in good condition. Very few bottled beers are this type; all homebrew beer is this type

sparging – the mixture is strained and washed with hot water.

Dairy products

Microbes are used to produce cheeses and yoghurts from milk.

Yoghurt

Fresh milk contains millions of bacteria called *lactobacilli*. If they are allowed to grow they multiply rapidly and produce *lactic acid.* This acid makes the milk clot and forms yoghurt. This is a rather hit and miss affair, so to make consistent yoghurt the milk is sterilised to kill all the natural bacteria. A known strain of lactobacilli, called a *starter culture*, is then added to the cooled milk.

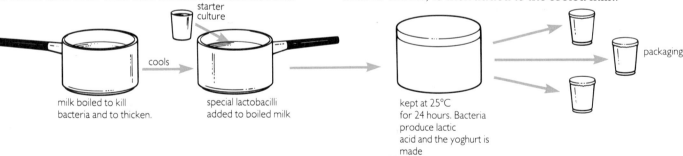

starter culture

cools

packaging

milk boiled to kill bacteria and to thicken.

special lactobacilli added to boiled milk

kept at 25°C for 24 hours. Bacteria produce lactic acid and the yoghurt is made

Cheesemaking

Fresh milk is allowed to go sour. The liquid is then removed leaving the more solid *curd.* This is left and naturally occuring microbes break the curd down, softening it and changing its flavour. Some microbes may also be added to the curd at this stage. Eventually the curd changes to cheese. Each type of cheese is produced by different microbes. Some microbes may be visible as blue threads in cheeses like stilton or gorgonzola. Other types may release gases that form holes in the cheese such as gruyere.

Food law

The most important law concerning food is the *Food and Drugs Act* of 1955. Its aims are to

1 prevent the sale of contaminated, impure or low quality food;
2 safeguard against poor standards of hygiene in premises where food is handled;
3 stop manufacturers making false claims on labels and in adverts;
4 stop food being sold short-weight.

In addition, food manufacturers must obey codes of practice agreed with the Ministry of Agriculture, Fisheries and Food and the Food Standards Committee. The *Trades Description Act* of 1968 also applies to the sale of food. The Weights and Measures department of the local authority is responsible for preventing false descriptions being used. Public Health Inspectors and Public Analysts are people who make sure that manufacturers and retailers obey the law.

Food labelling

By law, a food label must show the following:

1 the name and address of the packer;
2 a correct description of the contents;
3 the amount of food in the package or container;
4 all the ingredients, listed in descending order of mass.

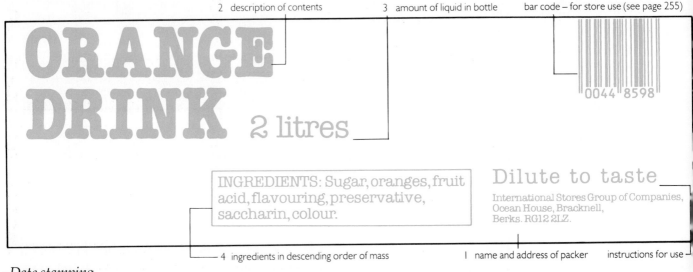

Date stamping

Perishable goods such as pre-packed meats, fish, poultry and dairy foods must also carry a date stamp. After that date the food should not be sold.

Unit pricing

The unit price is the price per pound or kilogram. Pre-packed foods such as meat or cheese should be priced with the total mass of the pack, and the unit price shown.

Food additives

Additives are chemicals that are put into the food by the manufacturer. They improve the flavour, appearance or keeping properties of the food. The safety of these chemicals is tested by feeding experiments on animals. They are usually fed to these animals in concentrations at least one hundred times greater than are likely to occur in a human diet. If the additive causes any disease in the animals it will be banned. Many additives have been banned in the past because they have increased the risk of cancer.

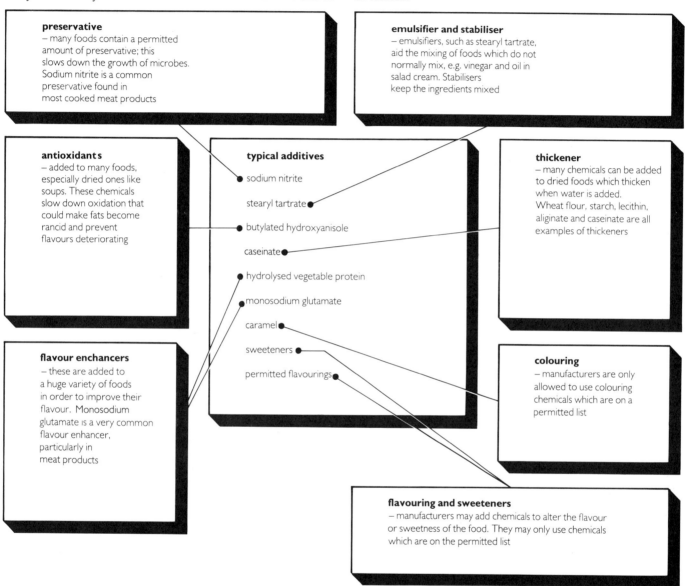

preservative
– many foods contain a permitted amount of preservative; this slows down the growth of microbes. Sodium nitrite is a common preservative found in most cooked meat products

emulsifier and stabiliser
– emulsifiers, such as stearyl tartrate, aid the mixing of foods which do not normally mix, e.g. vinegar and oil in salad cream. Stabilisers keep the ingredients mixed

antioxidants
– added to many foods, especially dried ones like soups. These chemicals slow down oxidation that could make fats become rancid and prevent flavours deteriorating

typical additives
- sodium nitrite
- stearyl tartrate
- butylated hydroxyanisole
- caseinate
- hydrolysed vegetable protein
- monosodium glutamate
- caramel
- sweeteners
- permitted flavourings

thickener
– many chemicals can be added to dried foods which thicken when water is added. Wheat flour, starch, lecithin, aliginate and caseinate are all examples of thickeners

flavour enchancers
– these are added to a huge variety of foods in order to improve their flavour. Monosodium glutamate is a very common flavour enhancer, particularly in meat products

colouring
– manufacturers are only allowed to use colouring chemicals which are on a permitted list

flavouring and sweeteners
– manufacturers may add chemicals to alter the flavour or sweetness of the food. They may only use chemicals which are on the permitted list

Meat products

Many meat products must contain a minimum amount of meat. It is against the law to sell sausages, beefburgers, pies or other similar meat products which contain less than the stated amount of meat.

Product	Percentage of meat (by mass)	
	cooked	uncooked
Pork sausage	—	65%
Beef sausage	—	50%
Beefburger	—	80%
Meat pies	25%	21%
Sausage roll	12·5%	10·5%

HEALTH

"He's tried to give up smoking before, but I think he's serious this time."

CHAPTER 5

THE HEALTH SERVICES

The United Kingdom is called a welfare state because the government provides many basic services free of charge.

Health care is provided by the National Health Service (NHS) and some departments of the social services.

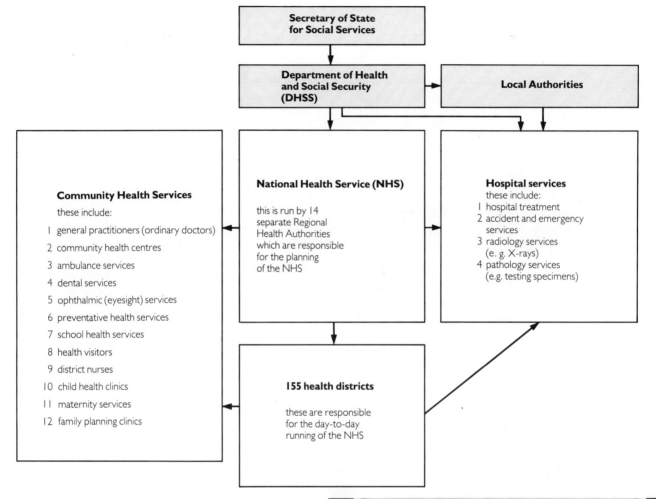

Secretary of State for Social Services

Department of Health and Social Security (DHSS)

Local Authorities

Community Health Services

these include:

1 general practitioners (ordinary doctors)
2 community health centres
3 ambulance services
4 dental services
5 ophthalmic (eyesight) services
6 preventative health services
7 school health services
8 health visitors
9 district nurses
10 child health clinics
11 maternity services
12 family planning clinics

National Health Service (NHS)

this is run by 14 separate Regional Health Authorities which are responsible for the planning of the NHS

Hospital services

these include:

1 hospital treatment
2 accident and emergency services
3 radiology services (e. g. X-rays)
4 pathology services (e.g. testing specimens)

155 health districts

these are responsible for the day-to-day running of the NHS

The general practitioner (GP)

GPs may work single handed or in a partnership. A large number of GPs may come together and form a group practice. The GP is the central figure of the NHS. Ninety % of all enquiries about health are dealt with by the GP; other patients will be sent to a specialist or will be admitted into hospital for treatment.

Health centres

More and more doctors are forming group practices. When they are large and offer specialist services, they are called health centres.

Some services which are offered by a health centre are: nursing services; immunisation and vaccination; ante- and post-natal care; midwifery services; health visitors; health education.

WEST ESSEX HEALTH AUTHORITY
DUNMOW CLINIC
TEL : DUNMOW 2346—2619
CHILD HEALTH CLINIC — MOTHERHOOD AND RELAXATION CLASSES
CHIROPODY · · SPEECH THERAPY SESSIONS
CYTOLOGY · · SCHOOL CHILDRENS CLINIC
DENTAL · ·
FOR DETAILS OF TIMES AND APPOINTMENTS PLEASE APPLY TO CLINIC RECEPTION

Many people are not aware of the variety of services provided by the NHS. Let's look at some examples and see how many points of contact can be made with the NHS.

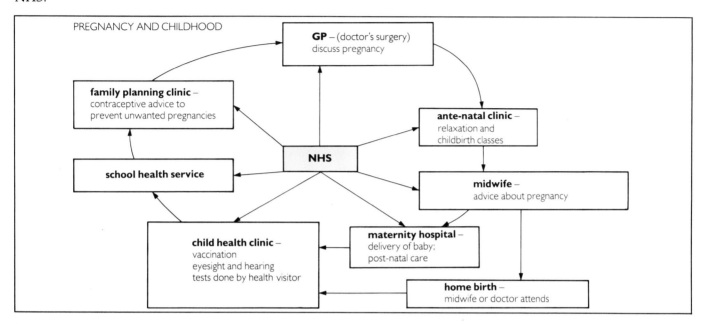

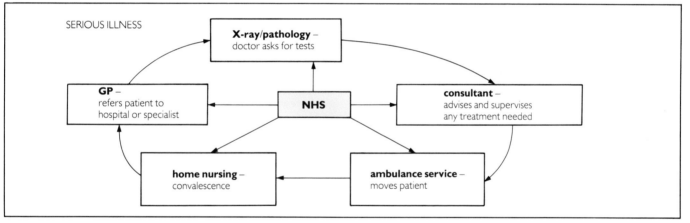

School health service

This is run by the NHS and the Local Education Authority. It has these aims:

1 to make sure that children are as fit as possible;
2 to make routine inspections for head lice, scabies and other parasites;
3 to carry out eyesight and hearing tests;
4 to carry out dental inspections;
5 to organise the education of handicapped children;
6 to provide school nurses in many districts.

Accident and emergency departments

These departments are found in most large hospitals. They were once called *casualty* departments. Staff are on 24-hour call and there is usually a full medical and surgical team available to treat serious injuries or diseases.

The social services

These are run by the local authorities. They provide a variety of services concerned with the health of deprived, elderly, disabled or handicapped people. Help is given, either by providing residential care or by sending out social workers. Many voluntary bodies, such as Dr Barnardos, Age Concern, Help the Aged or family service units may be called upon.

2 OBESITY AND DIET

Obesity

An obese person has too much body fat. This is not always the same as being overweight because an athlete or a body-builder can be said to be overweight with muscle. Obesity can be caused by glands which are not working properly, but this is not very common. Usually obesity is simply the result of eating too much of the wrong foods. If more food is being eaten than is required to provide energy, then the extra will be converted into fat.

It has been estimated that half the population of the 'satisfied' western world is obese. Poor people in the western world are often obese because they eat a fattening carbohydrate-rich diet (because protein is expensive). Such people are also often under-nourished. Things are made worse by the old belief that fat, bouncing babies are healthy babies. Unfortunately, fat babies tend to grow into fat children and fat adults. The picture shows an extreme case of obesity. This 38 year old man weighs over 215 kg (33 stones).

It is significant that many diseases are more common among fat people than thinner people. Life Insurance companies provide statistics that calculate the life

expectancy of people. These are called actuarial tables, and they show that, on average, fat people tend to live shorter lives than thinner people. Diseases which are linked to obesity include diabetes, diseases of the heart, arteries and kidneys.

Use these charts to compare your weight with recommended weights.

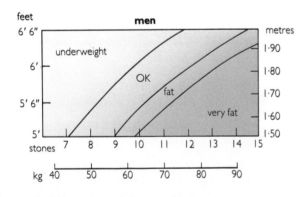

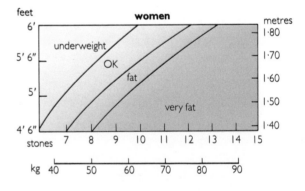

Slimming and dieting

To lose weight the amount of energy used by the body must be greater than the amount of energy in the food that is eaten. The body will then have to make up the difference by using up its own fat store. In other words:

> **eat less and use more energy through exercise**

Unfortunately it isn't as simple as this! If you increase the amount of exercise you do, you also increase your appetite. A little food cancels out a lot of exercise.

The graph shows the relative amounts of energy needed to carry out various activities for an hour. As you can see, an hour's running will use up about 3000 kJ (720 Calories) of energy. You only need to drink two pints of milk and any weight you have lost by running will be cancelled out.

The only way to reduce weight is to eat less. This is best done in a properly controlled diet, which reduces the appetite.

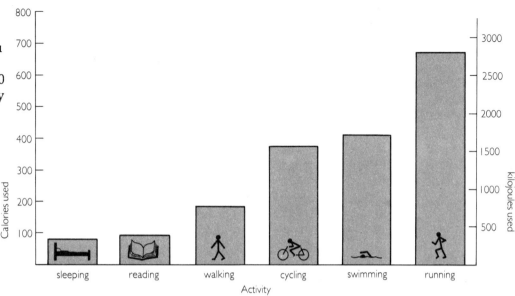

Reducing the appetite

A proper diet should reduce the appetite but still be balanced. Carbohydrates and fat-rich foods should be avoided.

The high fibre and protein diet   This is a good example of a properly controlled diet. A high fibre diet is filling. Green vegetables and wholemeal bread are rich in fibre which is indigestible. It cannot be turned into fat by the body. The proportion of protein in the diet is increased, while the amount of fat and carbohydrate is reduced. This means that the total energy value of the food will be much less. Any extra protein taken in will be converted to energy and not to fat. Some foods that are allowed in this diet are:

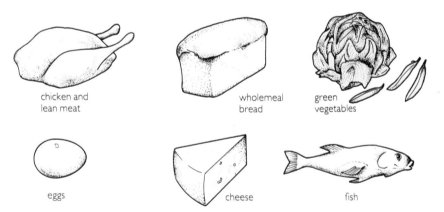

chicken and lean meat

wholemeal bread

green vegetables

eggs

cheese

fish

If this diet is combined with an exercise programme, the chances of slimming successfully are improved. Before an overweight person starts a diet a doctor's advice should be taken. Many of the slimming foods and drugs that are available are expensive and not proven to be effective. Many people who want to slim are not, in fact, overweight. They are influenced by society's expectations of a 'correct' size or shape.

Anorexia

When a person carries slimming to extremes, they may suffer from anorexia. There are two forms of this disease.

Anorexia nervosa   This is when slimming becomes such an obsession that severe undernourishment results. The sufferers lose all appetite but are convinced that they are still eating well. They become so concerned with their appearance, seeing themselves as overweight, that they try to eat even less. A vicious circle develops. This type of anorexia is found most often in adolescent girls and is easily treated.

Bulimia nervosa   In this condition the sufferer appears to eat well, but later, in private, vomits the food. The symptoms are similar to anorexia nervosa.

3 MICROBIOLOGY

Microbiology is the study of micro-organisms or *microbes*. These are organisms that are so small you need a microscope to see them. There are four main types of microbe.

Viruses
These are the smallest microbes of all. They can only be seen clearly through a very powerful microscope. Different viruses have different protein coats and genetic material.

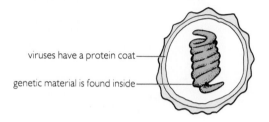

viruses have a protein coat

genetic material is found inside

If viruses invade living tissue they take over control of the cells. They then use the cell to manufacture millions of copies of themselves. Viruses can only grow and breed in living tissues.

Viruses vary in size from $\frac{1}{100\,000}$ mm to $\frac{1}{2000}$ mm.

Between 2000 and 100 000 would fit on a full stop.

Bacteria
Bacteria are found everywhere. Most are harmless, but some can cause disease. They vary greatly in shape and size. They are only visible through a powerful microscope.

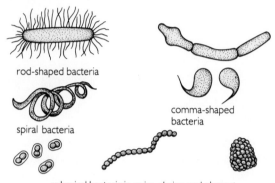

rod-shaped bacteria

comma-shaped bacteria

spiral bacteria

spherical bacteria in pairs, chains and clumps

The size of bacteria varies from $\frac{1}{1000}$ mm to $\frac{1}{20}$ mm.

Between 20 and 1000 would fit on a full stop.

Protozoans
These are very simple single-celled animals. The largest can just be seen as specks by the naked eye. A microscope is needed to see them clearly.

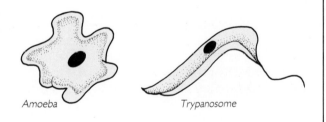

Amoeba

Trypanosome

They exist in a variety of shapes. Most protozoans are harmless, but some are human parasites and can cause serious diseases.

Protozoans vary in size from $\frac{1}{10}$ mm to 2 mm.

Fungi
Fungi are very simple plants. Some are microscopic, like yeast, but others are much more noticeable because of their large fruiting bodies, such as mushrooms and toadstools.

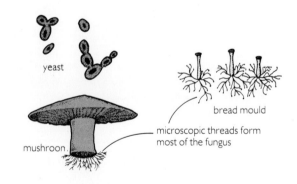

yeast

bread mould

microscopic threads form most of the fungus

mushroon

Some of the microscopic fungi can infect humans and cause disease.

Fungi vary in size from $\frac{1}{200}$ mm to 50 cm.

Disease

Microbes which cause disease are called *pathogenic microbes* or *pathogens*. These can infect us and cause harm by multiplying rapidly to produce vast numbers, or by releasing poisons called *toxins* into our bodies.

The human body has internal defence forces which enable us to recover from infection. Some microbes can cause permanent disabilities or death, e.g. polio or rabies.

Viruses	Bacteria	Protozoans	Fungi
colds influenza mumps shingles yellow fever German measles chickenpox smallpox polio cold sores rabies viral pneumonia	food poisoning whooping cough scarlet fever tetanus diphtheria typhoid cholera bacterial pneumonia gonorrhoea syphilis sore throats tuberculosis bubonic plague	malaria sleeping sickness amoebic dysentry	ringworm thrush athletes foot

Transmission of microbes

There are many ways in which microbes can be passed on, and some are very simple. A *contagious* disease, for example, is one that is passed on from person to person. Infectious microbes may be passed on in many ways.

Transmission in the air Coughing and sneezing releases millions of microbes into the air. This is called *droplet infection*. Tiny droplets of water in the cough or sneeze contain the microbes, some of which may be pathogenic. Examples of disease passed on in this way are colds, 'flu', tuberculosis (TB) and whooping cough.

Transmission in water Poor sanitation is the quickest way to infect water with harmful microbes. Untreated drinking water that is polluted with sewage might be carrying microbes that cause cholera, typhoid or dysentery.

Transmission in food If food is kept in unhygienic conditions (see pages 122 and 125) bacteria can breed quickly. Typhoid, TB and food poisoning can be caused this way.

Transmission by vectors A vector is an animal that can pass on a disease. Houseflies, mosquitoes, cockroaches and rats can all act as vectors. They may transmit the microbes directly, or they may be a link in a chain. Malaria and plague are examples of diseases transmitted in this way.

Transmission by contact The venereal or sexually transmitted diseases, gonorrhoea and syphilis, are examples of highly contagious diseases that are transmitted by physical contact.

Transmission by carriers Occasionally people can harbour pathogenic microbes but show no symptoms of the disease. They are called *carriers* because they carry the disease and may pass it on to others. Typhoid and *salmonella* food poisoning can be passed on in this way.

Entry of microbes

Most microbes are harmless; they live in the soil or on plants and animals. Our own body surfaces are covered in bacteria. Infection occurs when these microbes pass through the skin or inner linings and grow and multiply.

Entry through the skin

The skin acts as a barrier to microbes. If it is broken by an animal bite, graze, cut or wound then microbes can enter.

Entry through the inner linings

The inner linings are called *mucous membranes*. They line the inside of many parts of the body, including the mouth, nose, throat, digestive system and sex organs. Many microbes pass through these mucous membranes and cause no trouble. However, some microbes are harmful. Typhoid and food poisoning microbes enter through the lining of the intestine. Whooping cough microbes enter through the lining of the air passages, while venereal disease bacteria enter through the linings of the sex organs.

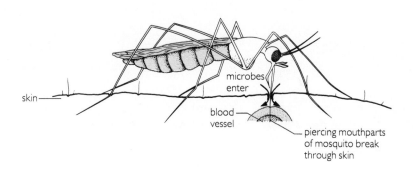

skin

microbes enter

blood vessel

piercing mouthparts of mosquito break through skin

Infection

Infection of the body occurs after a period of *incubation*. This is the time when the microbes are establishing themselves by growing and multiplying rapidly. The length of this period of incubation varies according to the microbes and the person infected. The body's reaction to the invading microbes causes the symptoms of the disease.

Virus diseases	Incubation period in weeks (1–5)
common cold	
influenza	
measles	
smallpox	
chickenpox	
polio	
German measles	
mumps	
hepatitis	

Bacterial diseases	Incubation period in weeks (1–3)
food poisoning	
cholera	
gonorrhoea	
scarlet fever	
diphtheria	
tetanus	
whooping cough	
typhoid	

Symptoms

The commonest symptom of infection by microbes is *fever*. The other symptoms of infection will depend on the type of microbe that has invaded the body. These other symptoms and effects give doctors clues as to the possible type of infection.

Fever There are two stages during fever. These are *pyrexia* and *rigor*. Pyrexia is the first to occur. The body detects the invading microbes and its temperature is raised. This may help the body to fight the microbes. The turning point, or crisis of the fever occurs when rigor sets in. This is the stage where the patient starts to sweat profusely and shiver.

Temperature charts

The temperature chart shows the temperature of someone who has been infected with a disease. The temperature has been taken twice daily. The incubation period is short, lasting only three days. The fever is also short-lived and the recovery from the disease is complete after six days. In many infections the stages are much longer. In malaria, there may be repeated bouts of fever following periods of apparent recovery.

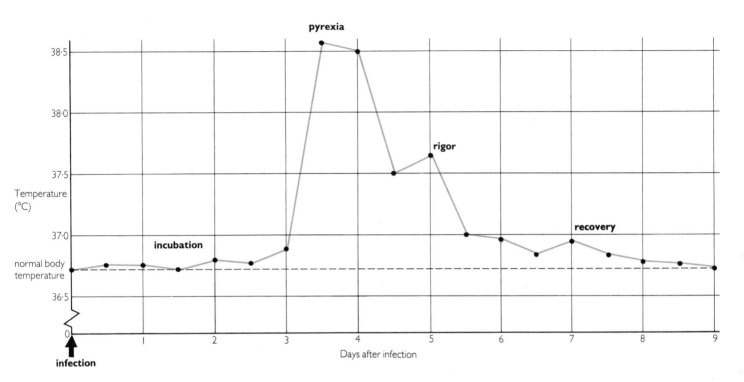

Treatment

The doctor's diagnosis of an infectious disease is determined by the symptoms observed and the results of any tests carried out. The doctor must then decide on a course of treatment for both the symptoms and the infection. In some diseases the symptoms may cause severe pain.

Analgesics

These are drugs such as aspirin and paracetamol which are mild pain killers. They can also help to reduce the body temperature. If the pain is severe there are stronger analgesics available. Analgesics are useful for treating the **symptoms** of disease.

Antibiotics

Antibiotics are used against bacteria and fungi but are useless against viruses. The search for effective drugs against viruses has so far been unsuccessful. Protozoan infections are treated using other drugs. Antibiotics are useful for treating the **infection**.

Some people are allergic to some antibiotics, but other alternatives can be prescribed.

Penicillin This is a very safe antibiotic. It is a naturally occuring antibiotic that can now be manufactured. There are many different types and they have different properties. They are used against a wide range of bacteria, e.g. streptococcal and staphylococcal infections, syphilis, gonorrhoea, and pneumonia.

Streptomycin This is another very safe antibiotic that also occurs naturally. It is used to combat tuberculosis and other diseases.

Some antibiotic drugs are produced in laboratories, e.g. chloramphenicol – used to combat typhoid; tetracycline – used against a wide range of diseases; sulphonamides – used against pneumonia, dysentery, meningitis, gonnorhoea, trachoma and cystitis.

5 DEFENCE AGAINST DISEASE

The human body has three main defences against microbe infection.

The skin

The skin is a microbe-proof barrier unless it is cut, grazed or broken in any other way. The slightest pin prick will allow infection.

If the skin is cut, blood will clot in order to seal it and prevent the further entry of microbes. Many of the body's fluids are mild antiseptics. Sweat, tears, blood, urine and digestive fluids all contain substances that are harmful to microbes.

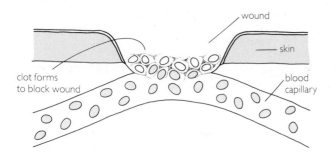

wound

skin

clot forms to block wound

blood capillary

White blood cells

Should microbes get through the skin, then large white blood cells move quickly to the site of infection.

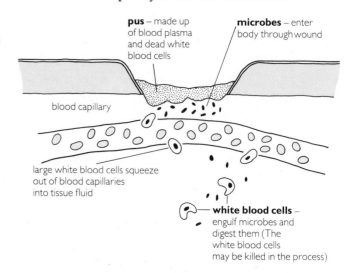

pus – made up of blood plasma and dead white blood cells

microbes – enter body through wound

blood capillary

large white blood cells squeeze out of blood capillaries into tissue fluid

white blood cells – engulf microbes and digest them (The white blood cells may be killed in the process)

The immune response

The immune response is a complicated line of defence which lasts a long time. An invading microbe, or any foreign material, is recognised by the body as an invader. In response the body makes proteins called *antibodies*. These attack a part of the invader called an *antigen*. The type of antibody that is made depends entirely on the type of antigen that is present. This production of antibodies in response to the presence of antigens is called the *immune response*.

It usually takes several days to form a large number of antibodies, but once that particular type of antibody has been made, the process can be repeated without delay. This explains why it takes time to recover from measles, but once you have had the disease you are unlikely to have it again. The second time around some antibodies are already there and more can be made quickly. This gives the microbe no time to grow and multiply.

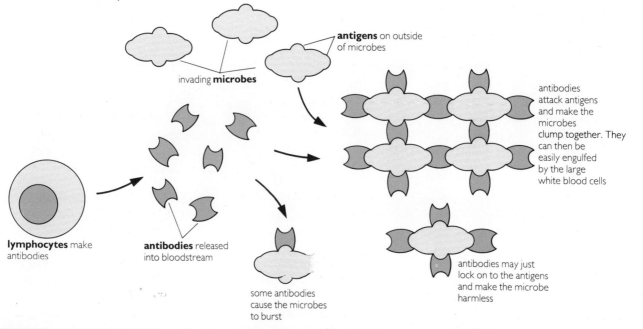

antigens on outside of microbes

invading **microbes**

antibodies attack antigens and make the microbes clump together. They can then be easily engulfed by the large white blood cells

lymphocytes make antibodies

antibodies released into bloodstream

some antibodies cause the microbes to burst

antibodies may just lock on to the antigens and make the microbe harmless

Immunity

If someone has a natural resistance to an infecting microbe, they are immune, or have a *natural immunity*. This means they can easily form, without delay, vast numbers of antibodies that attack the type of microbe which has infected them. The microbe has no chance to multiply.

Immunisation

The purpose of immunisation is to give immunity against a particular disease. There are two ways of becoming immune in this way.

Vaccine   A vaccine is used to encourage the body to make its **own** antibodies. This is done before a person gets a disease. The effect is long lasting.

Example:
Anti-tetanus vaccine encourages the body to make antibodies. These antibodies will be used to attack the poisons that the tetanus bacteria release. This vaccine is usually given in the first year of life. If, at a later date, tetanus bacteria enter the body, it is already prepared and starts to manufacture large numbers of the tetanus antibodies without delay.

There are three types of vaccine, as shown below. Each is designed to make the body think it has been infected by a real disease, without putting the person at risk.

In each case the body is encouraged to make antibodies against the antigens carried or produced by the invading microbe. Once the body has made a particular antibody it can store the information and produce the same antibody rapidly at a future date.

Some vaccines need booster injections. Immunity against tetanus needs boosting about once every five years, while cholera needs a booster twice a year.

Serum   A serum contains antibodies. This is injected into the blood after a person gets a disease, or as an emergency measure if someone is thought to be at risk. The effect is only temporary.

Example:
Anti-tetanus serum contains antibodies that act against the tetanus poison. The serum is injected into a person who is thought to have been infected. It protects the body until it can produce its own antibodies.

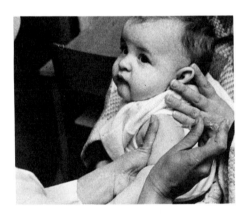

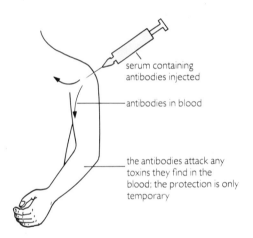

serum containing antibodies injected

antibodies in blood

the antibodies attack any toxins they find in the blood; the protection is only temporary

---

Modified microbes   This vaccine contains microbes that have been altered and made harmless. However, they still carry antigens, and the body produces antibodies to deal with them.

This type of vaccine is used against: smallpox, tuberculosis, rabies and polio.

Killed microbes   This vaccine contains microbes that have been killed. Because they are dead, they cannot cause disease, but they still carry antigens. The body reacts and produces antibodies, in the same way as it would if they were alive.

This vaccine is used against: cholera, typhoid, influenza, rabies, polio and whooping cough.

Modified toxins   Some microbes are dangerous because of the poisonous toxins they release. This vaccine contains toxins that have been altered to be harmless. The body recognises the antigens in these toxins and produces antibodies against them.

This vaccine is used against: diphtheria and tetanus.

Life expectancy has increased not only in the more affluent western world, but also in many parts of the third world. This is due to the availability of modern drugs which can cure disease and to programmes of immunisation which prevent disease. The raising of living standards in certain parts of the world has also increased life expectancy.

Immunisation

Immunisation and health education form the basis of *preventative medicine*. The object of immunisation is to protect the individual, but the immunisation of many protects the whole community. It is generally agreed that about 75% immunisation of a community against a disease will cause that disease to die out.

Immunisation in Britain

Diseases such as smallpox, polio, diphtheria and tuberculosis were once common in Britain. Now, organised programmes of immunisation start from infancy and the incidence of these diseases is low. Smallpox has been wiped out in this country and in most of the world.

Programme of immunisation in the United Kingdom

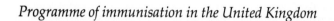

Approximate age	Immunisation
5–6 months	Dose 1: diphtheria, tetanus, whooping cough Dose 1: polio
7–8 months	Dose 2: diphtheria, tetanus, whooping cough Dose 2: polio
12–14 months	Dose 3: diphtheria, tetanus, whooping cough Dose 3: polio
3 years	Measles
5 years	Diphtheria and tetanus booster, polio booster
10–13 years	BCG against tuberculosis (if not naturally immune) German measles (rubella) for girls

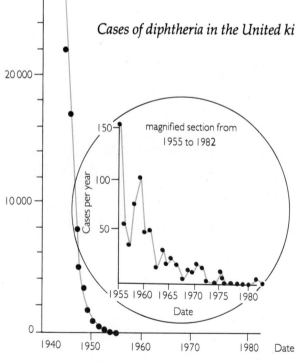

Cases of diphtheria in the United kingdom, 1940 – 1982

In the United Kingdom the risk of catching diphtheria is extremely small. Before the First World War the disease was commonplace and 5000 children died in 1911 alone.

Immunisation against the disease started before the Second World War, and in 1941 there were nearly 50 000 cases and 2624 deaths. As more and more people were immunised after the Second World War, the number of reported cases also fell. In 1980 there were only 5 reported cases of diphtheria. Many diseases have shown this tremendous fall in reported cases and deaths since widespread immunisation was started.

Unfortunately, this is not the case for all diseases. Some vaccines used are not as successful as the diphtheria vaccine, and some parents choose not to have their children vaccinated.

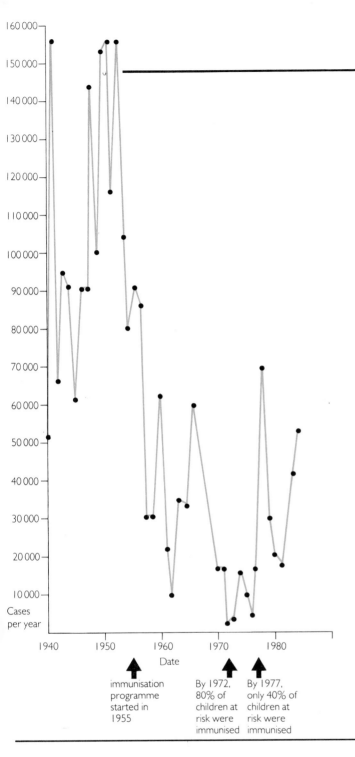

160 000
150 000
140 000
130 000
120 000
110 000
100 000
90 000
80 000
70 000
60 000
50 000
40 000
30 000
20 000
10 000
Cases
per year

1940   1950   1960   1970   1980
Date

immunisation
programme
started in
1955

By 1972,
80% of
children at
risk were
immunised

By 1977,
only 40% of
children at
risk were
immunised

Whooping cough   During the 1940s and the early 1950s, whooping cough was a very common disease and there were over 150 000 cases in 1941, 1948, 1950, 1951 and 1953. Immunisation against whooping cough was started in 1955 and there was an immediate and dramatic drop in the number of cases. By 1976 over 80% of children were immunised against the disease and there were relatively few cases. Some doctors then discovered that the vaccine caused brain damage in a small number of children. Because of this, and because the disease was then quite rare, many people decided not to have their children immunised. By 1981 only 40% of children had been immunised. In 1982 over 50 000 cases were reported.

Notifiable diseases

In order to prevent any possibility of epidemics breaking out, some of the more infectious diseases are notifiable. This means they must be reported to the community doctor.

Notifiable diseases include:

cholera	diphtheria
polio	food poisoning
smallpox	lassa fever
tetanus	tuberculosis
measles	whooping cough
typhoid	yellow fever
malaria	scarlet fever

Travelling abroad

If you intend travelling abroad you must be immunised against the diseases that are found in the countries you are visiting. You should be immunised against cholera, typhoid and smallpox.

Other preventative methods

Many infectious diseases which were once common in this country have declined, because we now understand how diseases are transmitted. A variety of safeguards ensure that epidemics are unlikely to occur.

Housing   Building regulations now ensure that houses are properly lit and ventilated. Sunlight kills many microbes, and ventilation allows the healthy circulation of air. The regulations also insist on proper sewage disposal by connection to a main sewer or by the use of a septic tank. Either way, raw sewage is prevented from contaminating water supplies (see page 45).

Water   All domestic water is treated by the local water authority. It has chlorine added to kill any microbes in it. Sewage is also treated by the water authority at sewage works. Microbes are killed and only safe water is released into streams and rivers.

Refuse   The local authority has a responsibility to collect and dispose of refuse. Uncollected refuse is a breeding ground for all kinds of harmful microbes.

Health education   The Health Education Council and other bodies advise and give information about prevention of disease.

7 DRUGS

The word *drug* has come to mean an addictive substance or a narcotic. To a doctor, a drug is any substance that is taken to relieve symptoms or to aid recovery from sickness.

Analgesics

These are valuable drugs that are designed to relieve pain. The commonest are *aspirin* and *paracetamol*. They act on the brain and nervous system to relieve pain and lower the body temperature.

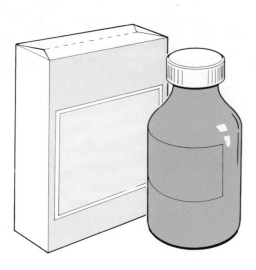

Antibiotics

These drugs are able to kill bacteria. The most famous antibiotic is *penicillin*. It is important that a course of antibiotics is completed, even if the patient feels better before all the tablets have been taken. This makes sure that all the bacteria are killed.

Tranquillisers

This is a group of drugs which can calm people without causing sleepiness. They help to control tension and anxiety. *Valium* is such a drug. Unfortunately, sometimes they are prescribed without finding out the cause of the anxiety.

Sedatives

These drugs cause sleep. They are often called 'sleeping pills'. The commonest drugs in this group are the *barbiturates*. They can be habit-forming.

Anti-depressants

Depression is an illness where people become miserable for long periods. Anti-depressant drugs can brighten up the patient but they do not help to find the cause of the depression.

Narcotics

These are drugs which relieve pain and sedate people. They are drugs that cause *narcosis*, a dulling of the consciousness. *Morphine* is the most common and well-known of the narcotics. It relieves extreme pain but can be addictive.

Anaesthetics

These drugs cause sleep or numbness. A *general anaesthetic* is used to put you to sleep, for example during a serious operation. A local *anaesthetic* is used to make part of your body numb so you won't feel pain – for example, the dentist may give you an injection of a local anaesthetic before having fillings.

Side-effects Many drugs have side-effects. For instance, drugs such as anti-histamine can reduce sensitivity to pollen and are used by asthma sufferers. Unfortunately they also cause drowsiness. The doctor's prescription and the instructions on the packet or bottle must always be carefully followed if the side-effects of drugs are to be avoided.

Drug abuse

Alcohol

Alcohol is widely used as a drug, especially in the western world. Beer, wine and spirits all contain alcohol, which is an anaesthetic. It slows down body reactions and upsets muscular coordination. It only appears to be a stimulant because it relieves anxiety and shyness. Regular drinkers may appear quite sober when every 100 ml of their blood contains 80 mg of alcohol – but they aren't. Their reactions will be very slow and it would be illegal if they drove a car.

Alcoholic poisoning   If the level of alcohol goes above 250 mg per 100 ml of blood, poisoning will occur. The liver will be seriously damaged and death may occur.

Alcoholism   Dependence on alcohol can creep up unknowingly. Quite often alcoholics are unaware of their dependence until it is too late. They require alcohol more and more often.

Tobacco

Tobacco smoke contains nicotine, tar and carbon monoxide. The nicotine produces a soothing effect and a sense of well-being. The nicotine is probably the addictive chemical that makes smoking habit-forming. Smoking is a difficult habit to break.

Heroin

Heroin is a drug that is seriously abused. It was originally made to replace morphine, but was found to be even more habit forming. Heroin, sometimes known as 'H', is injected directly into the bloodstream, usually into a vein in the arm. This is known as 'mainlining'. It can also be heated and the fumes given off inhaled.

Heroin induces a feeling of euphoria, a sense of great well-being and heightened sensitivity. The addict craves for the drug when this effect wears off. Eventually the body needs more and more of the drug to experience the same effect. This is drug addiction at its worst, and can lead to death. Withdrawal from this drug is extremely painful.

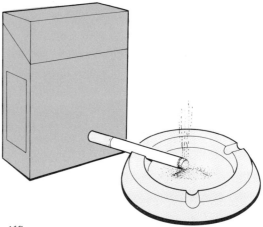

Glue-sniffing

Some glues contain a chemical solvent. If the fumes of the solvent are inhaled a sense of well-being is produced. Glue sniffing is extremely dangerous and can become addictive. Addicts are often incoherent after a period of sniffing. The fumes can cause brain damage or even death.

Hallucinogens

These are drugs that cause the taker to experience unusual dreams. Cannabis and LSD are typical examples.

LSD   These initials stand for *lysergic acid diethylamide*. It is sometimes called 'acid'. It can cause serious mental derangement. The drug is taken for the hallucinations or 'trips' it causes. It does not appear to be physically addictive but it can cause abnormal behaviour in regular takers. There is evidence that it is a harmful drug.

Cannabis   This is also known as dope, grass, hemp, hashish, grass or pot. It is the leaves or resin from the plant *Cannabis indica*. It is smoked or eaten for the feeling of well-being and hallucinations it produces. There is some evidence to show that it is addictive and may cause mental deterioration in some people.

8 HANDICAPPED PEOPLE

If you are fit and healthy try to imagine what it must be like to be handicapped or disabled. Do you ever think about the problems that disabled people face in their everyday lives?

People may be disabled throughout their lives, or become disabled at some time during their lifetime. For the latter there must be a period of adjustment, of coming to terms with the handicap. This is a difficult period during which peoples' attitudes to the person change.

Handicapped or disabled

Physically handicapped

Mentally handicapped

People may be handicapped or disabled in different ways. Some people are physically handicapped, perhaps through the loss of a leg or arm. Others may be mentally handicapped, perhaps by brain damage at birth. Some unfortunate people are both mentally and physically handicapped.

In our welfare state it is the duty of society to care and help for those people who cannot help themselves.

How do people become handicapped?

1   At birth
Handicaps may occur as a result of inheritance or because of events during the pregnancy. However they occur, these handicaps that are present at birth are termed *congenital defects.*

Inherited handicaps:

Down's syndrome   This disorder is caused by an extra chromosome (see page 106). The child is normally mentally retarded, and has a distinctive appearance.

Cystic fibrosis   This is a serious physical handicap. The respiratory and digestive systems are affected.

Congenital deformation of the hip (CDH).   This purely physical handicap can be treated by surgery. The hip is slightly deformed and the leg bone can move out of its socket.

Handicaps caused during pregnancy:

Spastics   A lack of oxygen during the last stages of pregnancy can damage the brain cells. This may lead to difficulties in controlling the voluntary muscles. Some, but by no means all, spastics also suffer from mental handicaps.

Rubella   If the mother catches German measles during pregnancy, the normal growth of the baby may be affected and a disabled child will be born. The child may be blind, deaf or have missing or deformed limbs.

Drugs   Some drugs may be given to pregnant women to relieve pain or sickness. They must be carefully tested. Sometimes mistakes happen and the drug affects the baby. This happened with the drug thalidomide. Babies were born with missing or deformed limbs. Alcohol and smoking also affect the growth of the baby during pregnancy.

2 Injuries

Disablement can be caused by accidents at work, home or on the roads. These injuries may cause physical or mental disablement, or both.

3 Disease

There are many diseases which can cause disablement. The most notable are polio, multiple sclerosis, heart attacks or strokes.

4 Immunisation

There is a very tiny percentage of children who have been handicapped as a result of being immunised. In most cases the risk of such damage is much smaller than the risk of damage caused by the illness itself. Doctors do not immunise people who are thought to be at risk. Immunisation can cause physical and mental damage.

5 Age

As we get older we become more infirm. Some people may become senile. There is a gradual loss of hearing and eyesight in many old people. Bones become much more brittle, and are more likely to break as we get older. Cuts take much longer to heal.

Handicaps and disabilities

Physically handicapped

The physically handicapped have problems moving. Many buildings make no allowances for people in wheelchairs. Steps and narrow doors often prevent access.

The NHS provides help for the physically handicapped. It supplies wheelchairs, artificial limbs and aids. The social services provide a mobility allowance to make it easier for them to travel.

Mentally handicapped

Severe mental handicaps in young children can cause great problems for parents. In many cases the social services provide help, but residential care may be necessary in extreme cases.

Mentally handicapped adults can have the mental age of a young child. These adults cause great problems in a caring society. There is often no chance of recovery.

Deaf or hard of hearing

People may be born deaf or may become deaf during their lives. Children are normally tested regularly from birth to check for any signs of deafness.

The NHS provides hearing aids and specialist teachers for deaf children. The social services provide special facilities, and voluntary bodies such as the Royal National Institute for the Deaf help with lipreading and sign languages.

Blind or partially sighted

People may be born blind or partially sighted, or may become so during their lives. The NHS provides treatment and aids for the partially sighted through the hospitals.

Social services can provide help and advice, training in Braille and help with transport. The Royal National Institute for the Blind can help by providing employment. Libraries can supply large print books or 'talking books'. These are tape recordings of volunteers reading the book or magazine aloud.

9 SEVEN AGES OF MAN

A character in Shakespeare's play *As You Like It* begins a famous speech with the words 'All the world's a stage, and all the men and women are merely players'. He then goes on to describe the life of a man as seven stages. The speech is called the seven ages of man. Each of these diagrams represents one of those stages together with part of the text of the speech.

The names of the seven stages are those in use today.

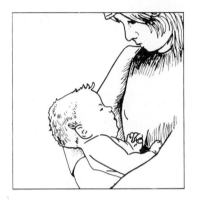

1   Childhood
'At first the infant, mewling and puking in the nurses' arms.'

2   Adolescence
'Then the whining schoolboy . . . . . creeping like snail unwillingly to school.'

3   Young adult
'Then the lover . . . . with a woeful ballad made to his mistress' eyebrow'.

4   Parenthood
'Then a soldier . . . . . bearded like the pard.'

5   Forties
'In fair round belly . . . . . full of wise saws and modern instances.'

6   Middle Age
'The sixth age shifts . . . . . with spectacles on nose and pouch on side.'

7   Retirement
'Last scene of all . . . . is second childishness and mere oblivion; sans teeth, sans eyes, sans taste, sans every thing.'

Try to imagine how people in different stages of their lives see one another. What will it be like to be old? What was it like being very young? How much do we misunderstand one another because we cannot see things from another age's viewpoint?

The opposite page raises lots of these points for you to think about – things like growing up, having children, growing old and eventually dying.

Childhood

Adults do not have clear memories of being children. They only remember scattered incidents. Children find it difficult to explain what its like! Perhaps this is why there are so many misunderstandings. Childhood is an age of development and it is important that parents find time to talk to and play with their children.

Adolescence

Adolescence is the period of time from the start of puberty to about the age of majority (18). It varies in length from person to person. This is the age of sexuality when you become aware of your body and of the opposite sex. It is supposed to be the age of awkwardness, rebellion and the 'generation gap', but much of this is pure fairy tale. It is the age of education and deciding whether to continue education or to leave school and seek employment.

Young adults

This period lasts between the late teens and the mid-twenties – a time of wondering if you have finally grown up and whether it is time to leave home or not. This is when you make long-term friends, when you start to talk about yourselves and when you fall in and out of love and think about marriage and settling down.

Parenthood

Ninety percent of the people in the United Kingdom get married. A large number of them also get divorced! Is this then the time of real adulthood? It is a time of financial responsibility and restrictions as children are born. Perhaps the romance of marriage is over and the couple have to learn to live with each other as well as loving one another. It is a time of disappearing youth, the milestone of turning 30 and the thought of growing old.

Over forty

Is there such a thing as a mid-life crisis? People in this fifth age, the forties, may worry about their appearance. They worry about their health and growing old. Other

people think of this as a period of responsibility, maturity and confidence. Parents of this age often have teenage children and this may increase their worries.

Middle age

This is the sixth age of man, and lasts from about 50 till the age of retirement. In women this is also likely to be the time of the menopause when they stop producing ova. Any children may have left home and even started

their own families. This is a time of wisdom and experience, but also a period of freedom from parental responsibility. Couples have time to get to know one another once more. This is a time for nostalgia, but also a time for looking forwards.

Retirement

This affects different people in different ways. The problem is often that of free time. Many people welcome it, while others don't know how to handle it. Some people choose not to retire until as late as possible while others choose to retire early. This is the age of grandparents who have the fun of children without the worry or responsibility. Their own children may reject their advice and this is often difficult to accept. The conclusion of the seventh age is never in doubt!

MATERIALS

CHAPTER 6

■ ATOMS

'What are things made of?' is a natural question. If we look around we can see many materials that have all kinds of different properties. They look as though they are made of different things, but are they? What would we see if we could take them apart?

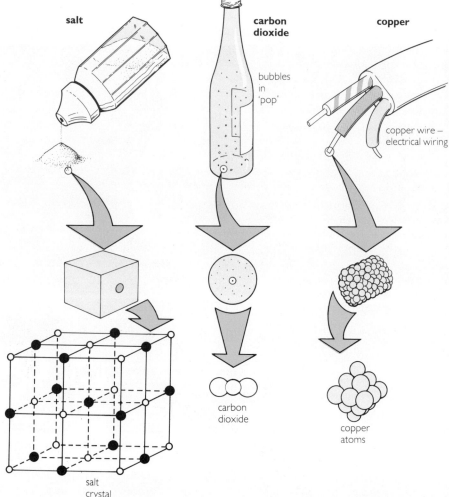

salt

carbon dioxide

copper

bubbles in 'pop'

copper wire – electrical wiring

Common salt, carbon dioxide and copper are three familiar materials. Imagine that we had a sample of each that we could repeatedly cut in half. Eventually the amounts would get so small that we would not be able to see them under the most powerful microscope.

Suppose we had a super-microscope that could show us the smallest amounts of these materials, what would we see? If this was possible we would see many round shapes of varying sizes. These small particles, too small to be ever seen, are called *atoms*. This theory, that all things are made up of atoms, is called the *atomic theory*.

A material that is made up of only one type of atom is called an *element*. There are 105 elements discovered so far. Some of these are vary rare, while other elements, like copper, sodium and chlorine are common.

carbon dioxide

copper atoms

salt crystal

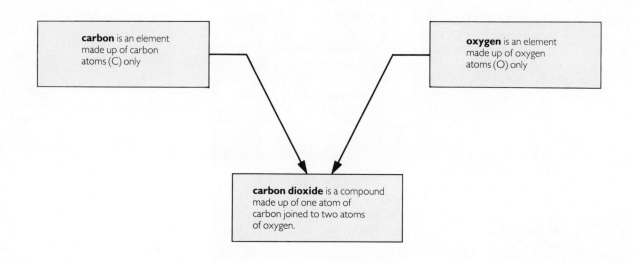

carbon is an element made up of carbon atoms (C) only

oxygen is an element made up of oxygen atoms (O) only

carbon dioxide is a compound made up of one atom of carbon joined to two atoms of oxygen.

Inside the atom

What makes atoms different? If we could pull an atom apart, what would we see? There are three important particles that make up atoms. These are called:

 protons neutrons electrons

Atoms are made up of these particles. Atoms differ from one another because they are made up of different combinations of these three particles.

Every atom contains a **nucleus which is made** up of protons and neutrons. Electrons move rapidly around the nucleus.

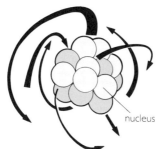

nucleus

If an atom was enlarged to the size of a football pitch, the nucleus would be the size of a pinhead on the centre spot.

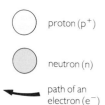

proton (p^+)

neutron (n)

path of an electron (e^-)

Protons and neutrons are about the same mass but electrons are much lighter. Protons and electrons both carry a small electrical charge. The proton has a positive (+) charge while the electron has an equal but negative (−) charge. Neutrons are neutral, they carry no charge at all. An atom that has equal numbers of protons and electrons is electrically neutral.

The smallest atom of all is *hydrogen*. This has only one proton and one electron. The largest naturally occurring atom that we know much about is *uranium*. This has 92 protons and 92 electrons. It is the number of protons that makes the difference between the atoms. This number is called the **atomic number**. Each element has a different atomic number.

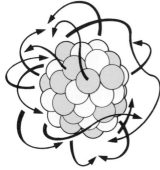

hydrogen atom
atomic number = 1
1 proton
1 electron
0 neutrons

oxygen atom
atomic number = 8
8 protons
8 electrons
8 neutrons

aluminium atom
atomic number = 13
13 protons
13 electrons
14 neutrons

The atomic number also tells us the number of **electrons** an atom has. The arrangement of electrons around the nucleus determines the chemical properties of the atom and, therefore, the properties of any materials of which it might be part.

2 ISOTOPES

The number of protons in any particular type of atom is always the same. The number of neutrons can vary. For example, a carbon atom **always** has 6 protons, but the number of neutrons can be 6, 7 or 8. Neutrons do not affect the chemical properties, so all carbon atoms have the same chemical properties.

6 protons
6 neutrons
6 electrons
carbon—12

6 protons
7 neutrons
6 electrons
carbon—13

6 protons
8 neutrons
6 electrons
carbon —14

Atoms which have a different number of neutrons but the same number of protons are called *isotopes*. Protons and neutrons have the same mass (about 2000 times larger than the mass of an electron), so the mass of an atom is concentrated in its nucleus. The *mass number* of an atom is the number of protons and neutrons in that atom. Isotopes are called by their mass number, e.g. carbon-12 has a mass number of 12.

Radioactivity

Most atoms are stable but a few are not. Unstable atoms break up into smaller, more stable atoms. As they break up, radiation is released. Unstable atoms are *radioactive* and we call them *radioisotopes*. There are three types of radioactivity:

Alpha particles (α)   These are the nuclei of helium atoms with no electrons. They are the largest and slowest moving of the three kinds of radioactivity. They can be absorbed by one or two sheets of paper.

Beta particles (β)   These are very fast-moving electrons. They can be stopped by a few millimetres of metal foil. They are released when a neutron breaks up, forming a proton (p^+) and an electron (e^-).

Gamma rays (γ)   These are like X-rays (see page 239). They are the fastest and most dangerous kind of radioactivity. They can pass through up to 15 cm of lead.

Radioactivity can harm the human body. The more the body is exposed the more damage will be done. Gamma rays in particular are dangerous, and exposure can lead to burns, cancers, birth defects and death.

Radioactive decay

Some radioisotopes release radiation more quickly than others. The length of time it would take for 2 g of an isotope to break down (decay) into 1 g is called the *half-life*. In the case of carbon-14, the half-life is about 5600 years.

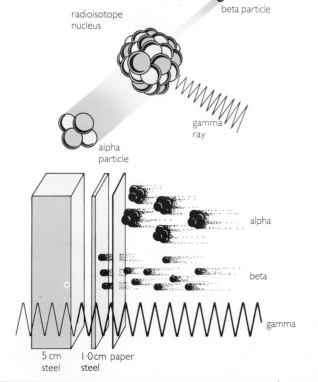

Radioisotope	Half-life
Lawrencium – 257	8 seconds
Sodium – 24	15 hours
Sulphur – 35	87 days
Hydrogen – 3	12 years
Carbon – 14	5 600 years
Plutonium – 239	24 360 years
Chlorine – 36	300 000 years
Uranium – 235	713 000 000 years
Potassium – 40	1 300 000 000 years

Uses of radioisotopes

Atomic energy

The energy from the breakdown of some radioisotopes can be used. The atom is bombarded with neutrons and breaks down, producing nuclear or atomic energy. The radioisotope most commonly used is uranium-235.

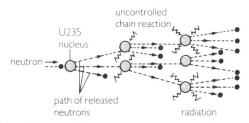

Each collision releases energy. In a nuclear weapon this energy is released all at once and causes great destruction. In a nuclear power station the chain reaction is controlled. The energy is released slowly as heat which turns water to steam. The steam is used to turn a turbine connected to a generator which produces electricity (see page 190). Some nuclear power stations use an artificial radioisotope, *plutonium-239*, instead of uranium.

Nuclear batteries

Each time a radioisotope decays naturally it releases a small amount of energy. This can be used in a nuclear battery to produce a small electrical current. Nuclear batteries have a long life and can be very small. They can be used by people with certain heart diseases. The battery is placed inside the chest and delivers a small shock to the heart to keep it beating. These machines are called *pacemakers*.

Medical uses

Tiny amounts of radioisotopes can be injected into or swallowed by a patient. The path the isotope takes inside the body can then be traced and displayed on a television screen. The activity of organs can be studied in this way. For example, the digestive system can be checked using a barium radioisotope. The patient swallows a barium meal and its passage can be followed. Strong sources of gamma rays can be used to destroy cancer cells inside the body without using surgery. Many medical instruments can be sterilised using gamma rays.

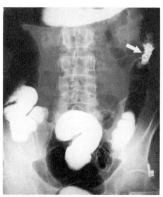

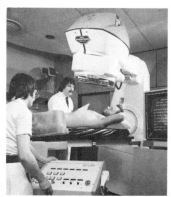

Industrial uses

Radioisotopes are often used in industry. Gamma rays can penetrate metals easily. They can be used to check for cracks and faults inside metal objects. Gamma rays can also be used to sterilise containers and check that they are properly filled. Thick sheets of material allow less radioactivity to pass through than thinner sheets. Therefore radioisotopes can be used to check and control the thickness of materials produced.

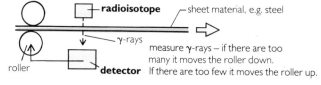

Dating

Carbon-14 (^{14}C) is a naturally occurring radioisotope that is being produced all the time in the upper atmosphere. Living things take in ^{14}C from the air they breathe and the food they eat. The amount taken in each day equals the amount that decays so living things contain a known proportion of ^{14}C. Once they die, the ^{14}C that decays is not replaced. If the amount of ^{14}C in dead objects is measured, their age can be calculated because we know the half-life of this radioisotope.

Rocks can be dated fairly accurately in a similar way if a radioisotope with a long half-life is used, e.g. potassium-40.

3 JOINING ATOMS

Atoms can be held together by forces which act between them. We think of these forces as *bonds*. Most solid materials are made up of regular arrangements of atoms held together by these bonds. Crystals are a good example.

The regular arrangement of the atoms gives the crystal a definite shape:

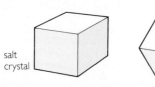 atoms in lattice

Regular patterns of atoms are called *lattices*. All solid elements and compounds have a lattice structure. There are three main types of bond that join atoms together.

salt crystal
diamond crystal

Ionic bonding

An *ion* is an atom that has gained or lost electrons. If it has gained electrons it is a *negative ion* because it has more negatively-charged electrons than positively-charged protons. If it has lost electrons it is a *positive ion* because it has more protons than electrons.

Salts and metal ores are common materials in which the atoms are held together by ionic bonds. The attraction of the electrically charged ions forms the ionic bonds.

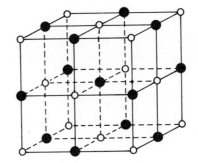

negatively charged **chloride ion** formed when a chlorine atom gains an electron

positively charged **sodium ion** formed when a sodium atom loses an electron

attraction of oppositely-charged ions holds the lattice together

Metallic bonding

The atoms in a metallic lattice are held together by moving electrons. The electrons form the metallic bond because they are free to move around the lattice. They form a 'sea' of electrons around the metal ions. All metals and alloys are held together by this type of bonding.

Because electrons are free to move in the lattice, metals are good conductors of electricity and heat. The electrons form a strong bond which allows metals to be hammered or bent into shape.

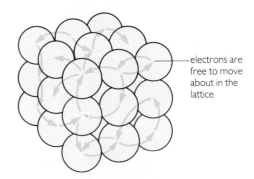 electrons are free to move about in the lattice

Covalent bonding

Covalent bonds are formed when electrons are *shared* between atoms. These bonds hold together the atoms of a vast number of materials. Most of the chemicals found in living things are linked by covalent bonds. When atoms are joined together by covalent bonds, **molecules** are

formed. Molecules can contain a fairly small number of atoms e.g. carbon dioxide CO_2 (3), glucose $C_6H_{12}O_6$(24), or a **very** large number of atoms as polythene and polystyrene. Some elements exist as molecules e.g. oxygen gas is made up of a molecule formed from two atoms O_2.

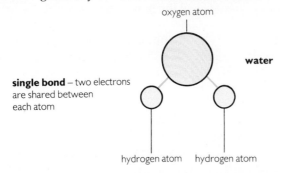
oxygen atom

water

single bond – two electrons are shared between each atom

hydrogen atom   hydrogen atom

double bond – pairs of electrons are shared between each oxygen atom and the carbon atom

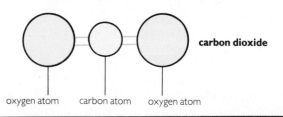

carbon dioxide

oxygen atom   carbon atom   oxygen atom

Properties of materials

The properties and characteristics of the materials that we use depend on the kinds of atoms they are made from and the way these atoms are joined together. We can separate materials into three groups: elements, compounds and mixtures.

Elements

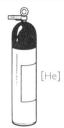

Helium gas (He) only contains atoms of helium.

Aluminium (Al) window frames are often used in new double-glazed windows. They only contain aluminium atoms.

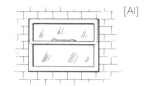

The mercury (Hg) in a thermometer only contains atoms of mercury.

Every element is made up of atoms, *all* of the *same* type. Every element, and so far 105 have been discovered, is given a chemical symbol (shown in brackets).

The inside of cans are coated with a thin layer of tin (Sn).

The diamond in an engagement ring is made up of carbon (C) atoms – nothing else.

Compounds

A polythene bucket is made up of millions of carbon and hydrogen atoms all joined together by covalent bonds. These atoms form very long chains.

Blackboard chalk is made from a compound of calcium, sulphur and oxygen. The atoms are held together by ionic and covalent bonds. This compound is called calcium sulphate and has the formula $CaSO_4$.

True chalk and limestone is a compound of calcium, carbon and oxygen. Its chemical name is calcium carbonate, $CaCO_3$.

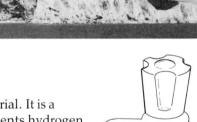

A compound is a combination of atoms of different elements joined together by bonds. Materials made up of compounds are far more common than pure elements. A compound can be given a chemical formula.

Water is a vital material. It is a compound of the elements hydrogen and oxygen. Two atoms of hydrogen are joined to one atom of oxygen by covalent bonds (H_2O).

Mixtures

Wood is a very complicated mixture of many kinds of compounds.

Concrete is a mixture of sand, cement and gravel. These are compounds or mixtures of compounds.

Glass is a mixture of materials. Sand and limestone are two compounds used to make this mixture.

Metals are usually mixed to form alloys. Stainless steel is a mixture of iron, carbon and chromium. It is a mixture of elements.

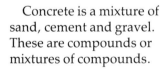

Mixtures are much harder to describe chemically than elements or compounds, yet they are much more common. You cannot give a mixture a chemical formula. Mixtures are nearly always complicated materials with unusual structures.

4 STATES OF MATTER

The behaviour of the atoms in a material depends on the temperature of the material.

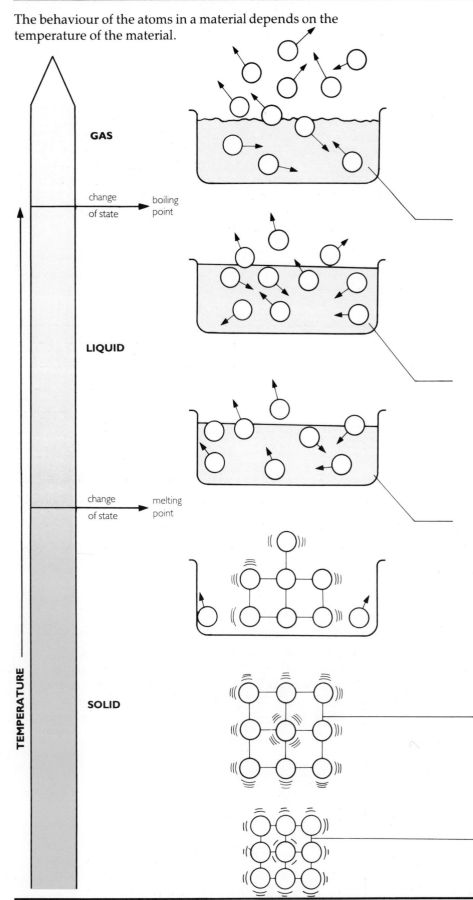

GAS

change of state → boiling point

LIQUID

change of state → melting point

SOLID

TEMPERATURE

The particles are fast moving and are widely spaced. They are not attracted to each other at all.

The particles now have so much energy that the forces of attraction are overcome. *The particles start to leave the surface of the liquid.*

The liquid expands as the temperature increases.

The increased heat energy makes the particles move about more quickly. The liquid becomes 'runnier' and the faster particles escape from the surface.

The particles begin to move freely but are attracted to each other. *The liquid takes on the shape of its container.*

The heat energy has made the particles vibrate strongly. The lattice structure of the solid breaks down. *The solid melts.*

Heat energy causes the particles to vibrate more. *The solid expands.*

The particles are packed closely together; they are held by strong forces. *The solid has a fixed shape of its own.*

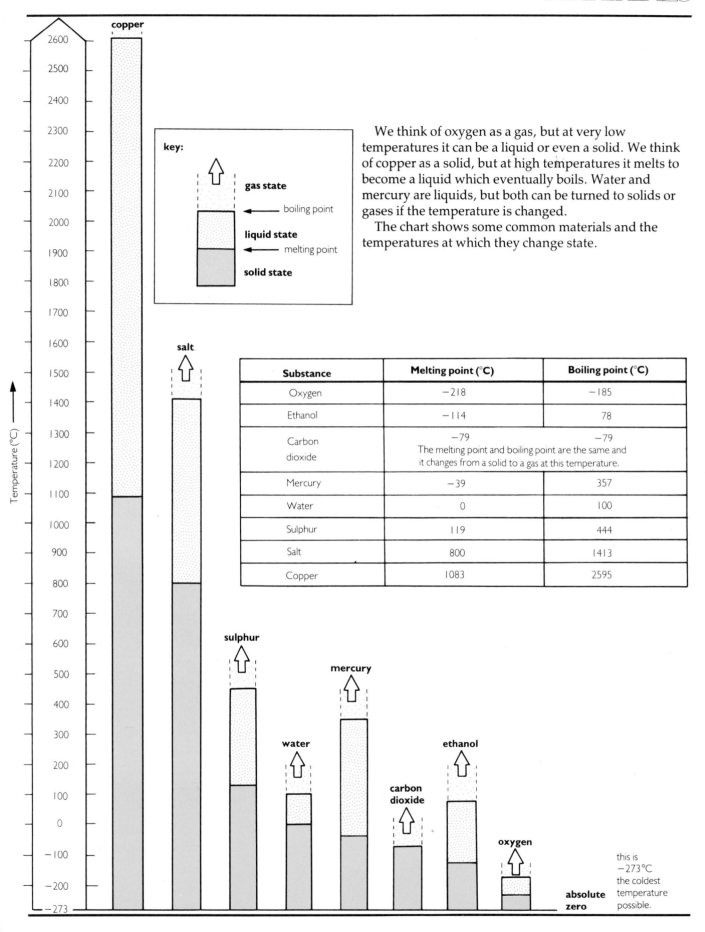

Temperature (°C)

We think of oxygen as a gas, but at very low temperatures it can be a liquid or even a solid. We think of copper as a solid, but at high temperatures it melts to become a liquid which eventually boils. Water and mercury are liquids, but both can be turned to solids or gases if the temperature is changed.

The chart shows some common materials and the temperatures at which they change state.

key:

gas state
← boiling point
liquid state
← melting point
solid state

Substance	Melting point (°C)	Boiling point (°C)
Oxygen	−218	−185
Ethanol	−114	78
Carbon dioxide	−79	−79
	The melting point and boiling point are the same and it changes from a solid to a gas at this temperature.	
Mercury	−39	357
Water	0	100
Sulphur	119	444
Salt	800	1413
Copper	1083	2595

copper

salt

sulphur

mercury

water

carbon dioxide

ethanol

oxygen

absolute zero

this is −273°C the coldest temperature possible.

5 MATERIALS FROM OIL

Crude oil is a complicated mixture of thousands of different chemicals. The identity of some of them is still not known. Because it is so complicated, crude oil does not have a fixed boiling point – different chemicals in the mixture boil at different temperatures. This difference in boiling points allows us to separate crude oil into various parts called *fractions*. The process of separating the oil into its fractions is called *fractional distillation*.

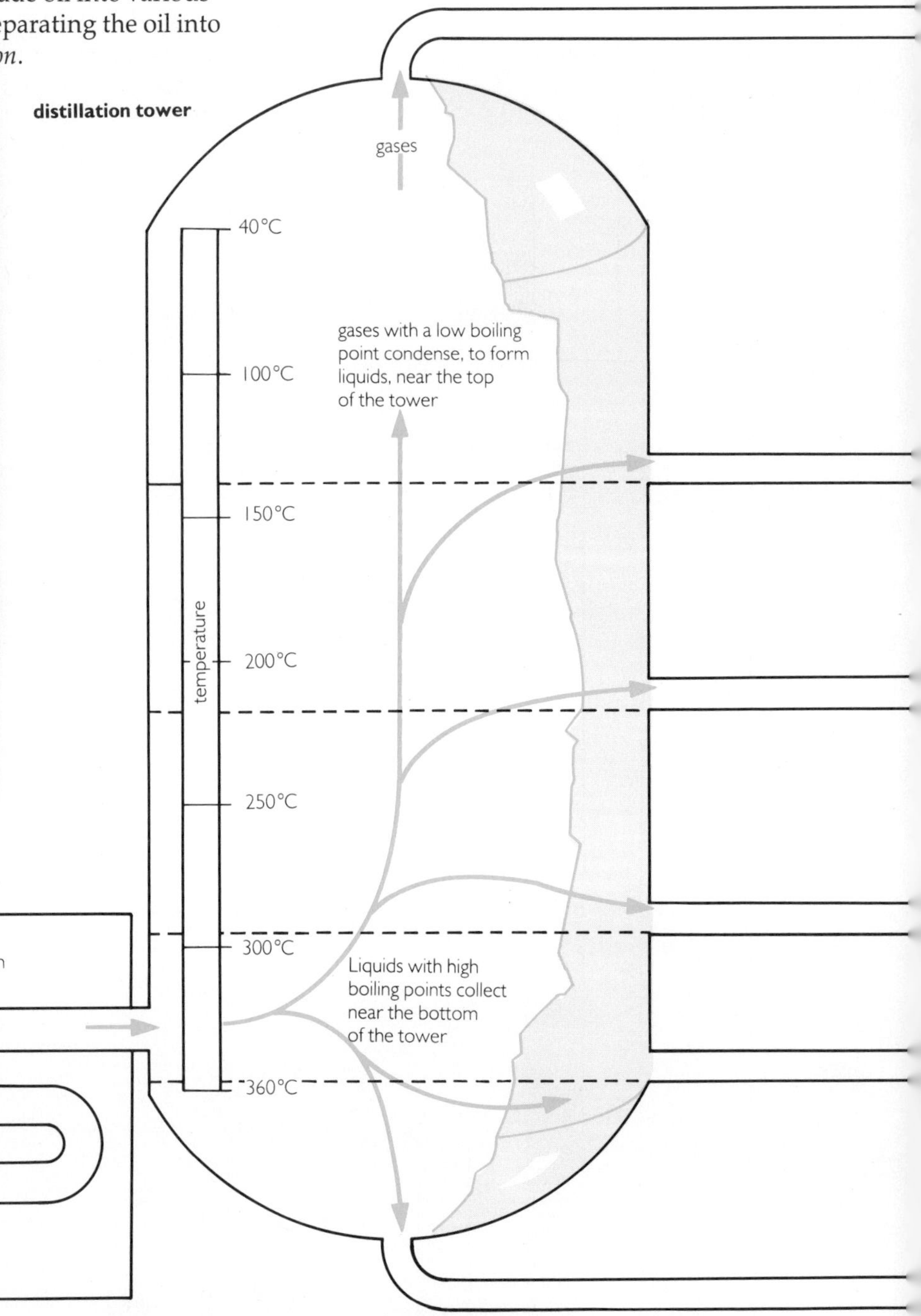

distillation tower

gases

40°C

100°C

gases with a low boiling point condense, to form liquids, near the top of the tower

150°C

temperature

200°C

250°C

the crude oil is heated to about 350°C to turn most of it into a gas

300°C

Liquids with high boiling points collect near the bottom of the tower

360°C

crude oil →

heater

What happens to the crude oil?

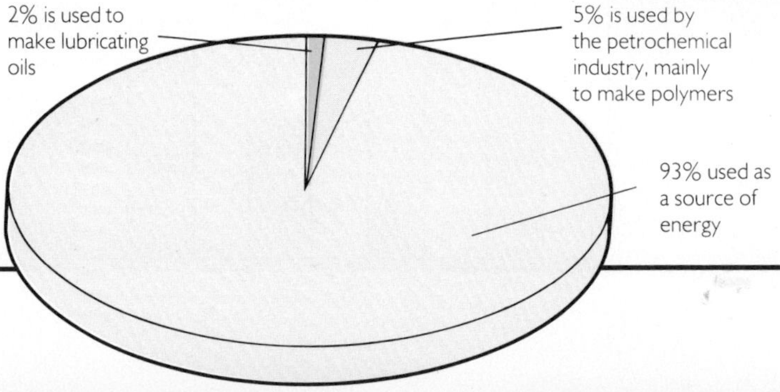

2% is used to make lubricating oils

5% is used by the petrochemical industry, mainly to make polymers

93% used as a source of energy

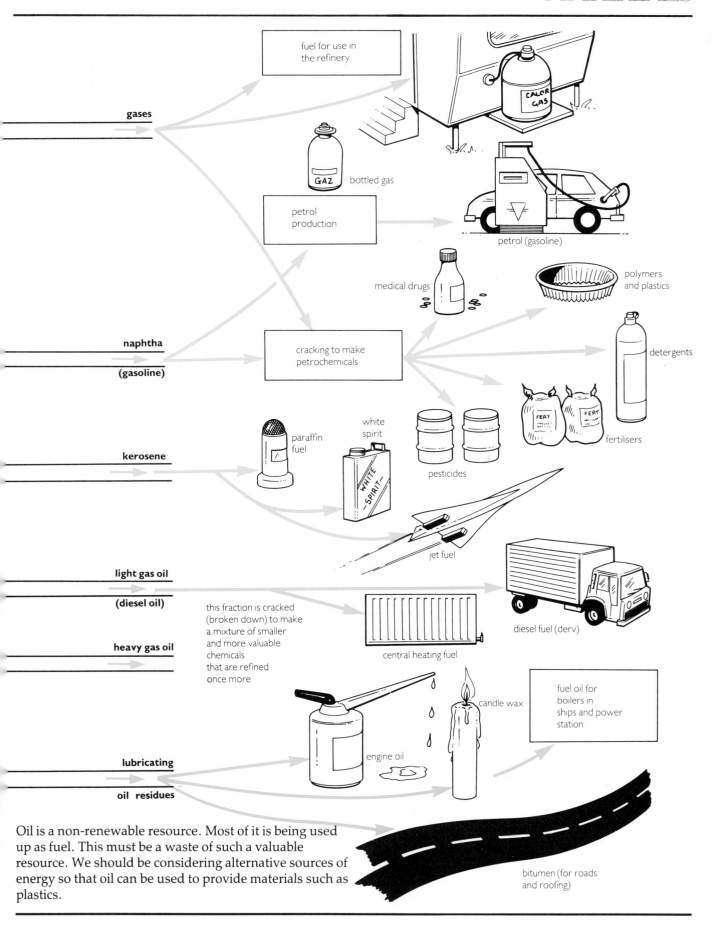

fuel for use in the refinery

gases

CALOR GAS

bottled gas
GAZ

petrol production

petrol (gasoline)

naphtha

(gasoline)

cracking to make petrochemicals

medical drugs

polymers and plastics

detergents

FERT   FERT

fertilisers

kerosene

paraffin fuel

white spirit

WHITE SPIRIT

pesticides

jet fuel

light gas oil

(diesel oil)

this fraction is cracked (broken down) to make a mixture of smaller and more valuable chemicals that are refined once more

central heating fuel

diesel fuel (derv)

heavy gas oil

candle wax

fuel oil for boilers in ships and power station

engine oil

lubricating

oil residues

Oil is a non-renewable resource. Most of it is being used up as fuel. This must be a waste of such a valuable resource. We should be considering alternative sources of energy so that oil can be used to provide materials such as plastics.

bitumen (for roads and roofing)

6 POLYMERS

Polymers are large molecules that are made up of many smaller repeating molecules linked together to form a chain. These polymers can be natural or *synthetic* (man-made).

Natural polymers

Living organisms contain many large molecules and lots of these are polymers.

Cotton A soft white fibre produced by cotton plants. It is almost 100 % pure cellulose.

Silk A natural fibre produced by a silkworm to make its cocoon.

Rubber A natural polymer produced by rubber trees.

Wool Produced from the short hairs of a sheep.

Some natural polymers can be converted into synthetic polymers. The natural polymer cellulose (which is found in cotton, wood and all plants) can be treated to produce long thin threads of *rayon*, a synthetic polymer which can be woven into fabric.

Synthetic polymers

The majority of our synthetic polymers are made from crude oil and these are very important materials in our society. You only have to look around your own kitchen to see their many uses in the home. Often they replace natural polymers such as cotton, wool or rubber. In fact, production of some natural polymers cannot keep up with demand.

The properties of synthetic polymers differ from those of natural polymers. Sometimes new uses are thought of to take advantage of these properties. For example, non-stick frying pans were developed to take advantage of Teflon (PTFE).

Artificial football pitches and modern running tracks have been developed from these new materials.

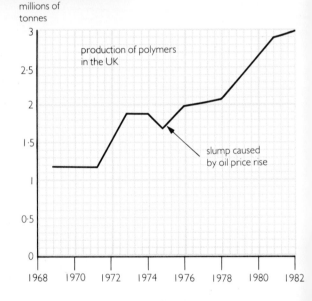

millions of tonnes

production of polymers in the UK

slump caused by oil price rise

world fibre production 1960–1980

1960 — 11 million tonnes
1970 — 21.5 million tonnes
1980 — 29.5 million tonnes

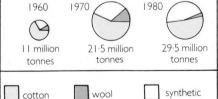

☐ cotton   ■ wool   ☐ synthetic

Advantages

Synthetic polymers are often cheaper than natural polymers.

They are often better than natural polymers, e.g. harder or more durable.

They can be designed to have different properties.

Disadvantages

Many people prefer the look and feel of natural polymers such as wool.

When thrown away they take a very long time to rot and so can cause great litter problems.

They are made from a non-renewable resource – oil.

Synthetic polymers can be divided into three groups:

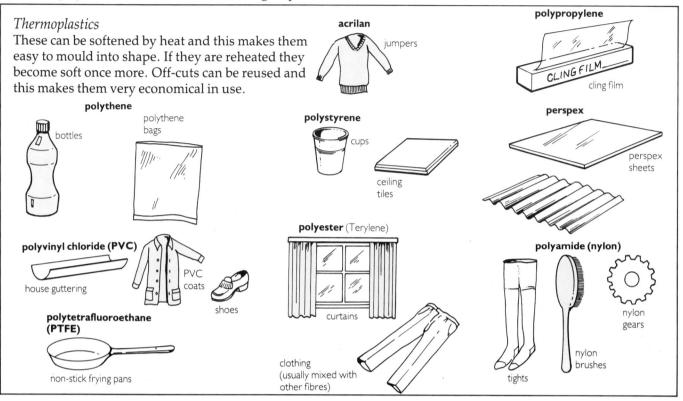

Thermoplastics

These can be softened by heat and this makes them easy to mould into shape. If they are reheated they become soft once more. Off-cuts can be reused and this makes them very economical in use.

acrilan — jumpers

polypropylene — cling film

polythene — bottles, polythene bags

polystyrene — cups, ceiling tiles

perspex — perspex sheets

polyvinyl chloride (PVC) — house guttering, PVC coats, shoes

polyester (Terylene) — curtains, clothing (usually mixed with other fibres)

polyamide (nylon) — tights, nylon brushes, nylon gears

polytetrafluoroethane (PTFE) — non-stick frying pans

Thermosets

These can be moulded when first made, but cannot be remoulded when reheated. They are much more rigid than thermoplastics and are good at withstanding heat and acting as insulators.

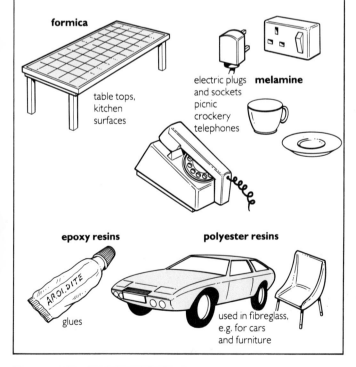

formica — table tops, kitchen surfaces

melamine — electric plugs and sockets, picnic crockery telephones

epoxy resins — glues

polyester resins — used in fibreglass, e.g. for cars and furniture

Elastomers

These are materials that stretch and then return to their natural or original shape. Rubber is an example of a natural elastomer.

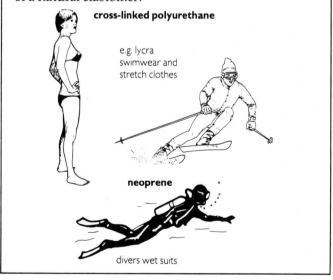

cross-linked polyurethane — e.g. lycra swimwear and stretch clothes

neoprene — divers wet suits

Synthetic polymers are sometimes called *plastics*. A plastic substance is one that can have its shape changed. Strictly speaking not all synthetic polymers are plastics. However, the word plastic is in common use as in 'plastic bag', 'plastic teaspoon' or 'plastic ruler'.

7 STRUCTURE OF POLYMERS

All polymers, whether synthetic or natural, are made up of repeating units called *monomers*. The monomers are joined together to form the very long molecules of polymers. There are three main types of polymer:

Thermoplastic polymers
When these are heated they become more flexible, but they become hard again when cooled.

The molecules are long unlinked chains that are intertwined. There are no cross-links and the molecules can slide over each other.
Examples: polythene and polystyrene.

Thermosetting polymers
These do not soften if they are heated.

cross-links

The molecules are long chains that become cross-linked when the polymer is produced.
Examples: melamine and formica.

Elastomers
These polymers can be stretched, but will return to their original shape.

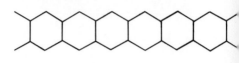

The molecules are long chains which are folded.
Examples: rubber and lycra.

Making polymers
Making polymers is called *polymerisation*. Most monomers are produced from petrochemicals. There are two main methods of polymerisation.

Addition polymerisation
Addition polymers, such as polythene are formed by adding similar monomers to each other. If the monomer is *ethene*, it will make the polymer poly(ethene) – usually known as *polythene*.

Ethene is a reactive molecule because of the double covalent bond. Two of the electrons can form bonds with other monomers.

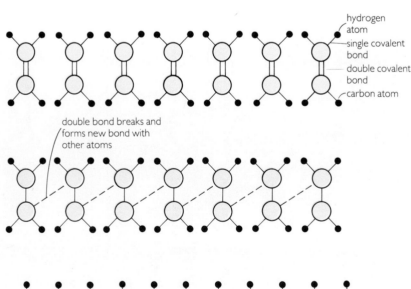

hydrogen atom
single covalent bond
double covalent bond
carbon atom

double bond breaks and forms new bond with other atoms

The double bond breaks and forms new bonds with other atoms.

When lots of ethene monomers join up a polymer is formed – polythene.

rest of polythene molecule

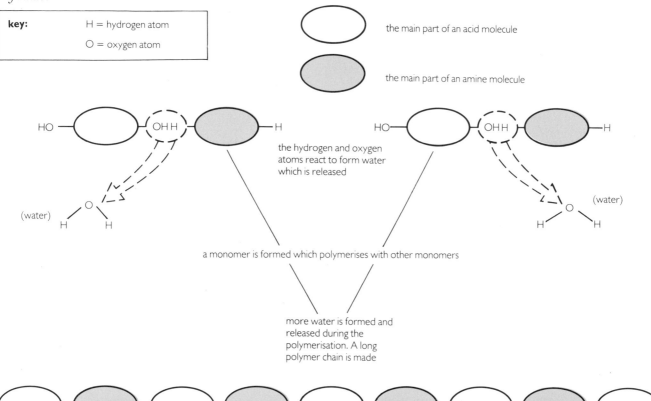

Condensation polymers

Condensation polymers such as nylon are formed by reacting two different monomers together. When these monomers react together they produce a molecule of water, hence the name 'condensation'.

Nylon is a condensation polymer that is made from an acid and a chemical called an amine. Nylon is called a *polyamide*.

key: H = hydrogen atom
O = oxygen atom

the main part of an acid molecule

the main part of an amine molecule

the hydrogen and oxygen atoms react to form water which is released

(water)

(water)

a monomer is formed which polymerises with other monomers

more water is formed and released during the polymerisation. A long polymer chain is made

Terylene is a condensation polymer that is formed from an acid and an alcohol. Terylene is called a *polyester*. Both these polymers can be formed into long strong fibres that can be easily woven into clothes.

Copolymers

If two or more different monomers are polymerised together then a copolymer is formed. These have special properties and can be developed for special purposes, e.g. making nylon fibres more elastic.

It is also possible to mix different types of polymer together to form polymer *blends*. In this way materials with special properties can be designed. Examples are polyester/cotton blends for blouses, shirts and night clothes, and terylene/wool blends for suits.

different monomers

8 MAKING PRODUCTS FROM POLYMERS

Chemical companies produce polymers in the form of powders or granules. To make them into a recognisable product they must be heated until they become very flexible or 'plastic'. They are then put through one of the following processes.

Injection moulding

Injection moulding is an efficient way of making plastic goods. This process can be used to mould thermosetting and thermoplastic polymers.

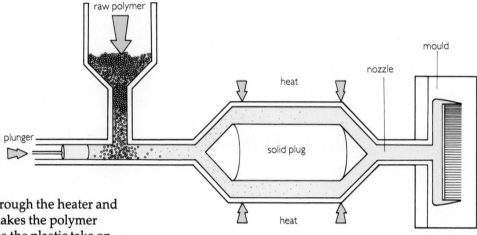

The plunger forces the polymer through the heater and nozzle into the mould. The heat makes the polymer become a plastic. The mould makes the plastic take on a particular shape. Moulds are expensive because they have to take high pressures.

Compression moulding

This process is usually used for thermosetting plastics which form a rigid structure in the mould. The time taken to make the object is quite long to allow cross-links to form.

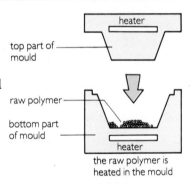

the raw polymer is heated in the mould

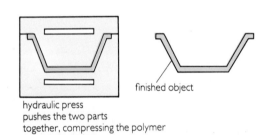

hydraulic press pushes the two parts together, compressing the polymer

finished object

Slush moulding

The polymer is heated and becomes a liquid plastic. It is then placed inside a hollow mould which is then spun round. The inside of the mould becomes covered in plastic which hardens. When the plastic has hardened the mould is opened and the object removed. Cheap plastic footballs are made in this way.

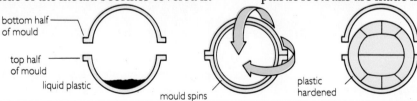

Altering polymers
Colour Polymers can be easily coloured to produce bright materials.

Fillers Additives can be put into polymers to affect their properties. If mica is added to some polymers they become more heat-resistant.

Extrusion moulding

This is a continuous process. The material is forced out (extruded) as a continuous length. This is similar to the way toothpaste is forced out of its tube. The finished material can be easily cut to length. The shape of the die can be altered to produce different sections. Extrusion moulding is the commonest way of producing plastic products.

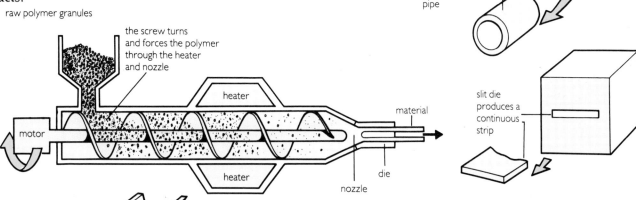

annular die produces a continuous pipe

slit die produces a continuous strip

raw polymer granules

the screw turns and forces the polymer through the heater and nozzle

heater

heater

motor

material

die

nozzle

Calendering

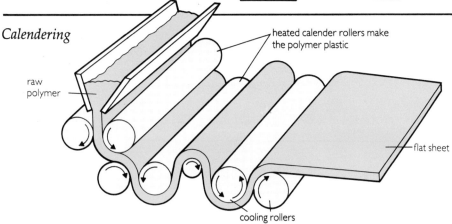

heated calender rollers make the polymer plastic

raw polymer

flat sheet

cooling rollers

Calendering is a way of producing a flat sheet of material. The rollers squeeze the thermoplastic material into flat sheets that can be cut to length.

Vacuum forming

This is the cheapest way of producing plastic goods. There is no need for high pressures so the moulds are very cheap.

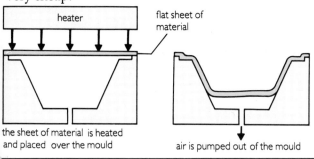

heater

flat sheet of material

the sheet of material is heated and placed over the mould

air is pumped out of the mould

the plastic is pulled down to take on the shape of the mould

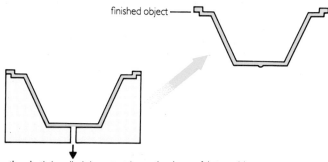

finished object

Altering polymers

Plasticised polymers   Oils can be added to a polymer to plasticise them. The chains will then slide over each other more easily.

Expanded polymers   Expanded polystyrene is made by blowing a gas (such as carbon dioxide) into the liquid polymer. These expanded polymers are very good for insulation and shock absorption.

9 TEXTILES

Textiles are made from fibres: *natural* fibres come directly from animals or plants, while *man-made* fibres are called synthetic fibres.

Natural fibres

Cotton and *flax* are the commonest plant fibres while *wool* and *silk* are the most important animal fibres.

Usually fibres which absorb water are comfortable to wear.

Other examples of natural fibres are *jute* and *hemp* which come from plants, and *camel hair* and *angora* goat hair (*mohair*).

Most natural fibres are short and are called *staple fibres*. Cotton and wool fibres are rarely longer than 10 cm, while flax is the longest staple fibre, reaching a length of up to 1 metre. Silk is the only natural fibre that is produced in a long continuous thread or *filament*.

Some minerals e.g. *Asbestos* also occur naturally in the form of fibres. Asbestos fibres can be used to form a cloth that does not burn. Asbestos was very useful but it is now known to be a cause of lung disease and cancer.

Wool is a protein. Under the microscope the fibres are crinkled and look scaly. Because they are crinkled the fibres are elastic. They trap air which makes woolen clothes warm. Wool absorbs water.

Silk is also a protein. The individual fibres are very fine and flexible. Silk is shiny, soft and strong. It is a hard wearing material but it is very expensive.

Flax is made of cellulose fibres. Under the microscope the fibres look coarse and stiff. Flax is used to make linen which is very strong and hard wearing. Linen looks shiny and absorbs water.

Cotton is made of cellulose fibres. Under the microscope the fibres look twisted and flattened. Cotton is strong and hard wearing. It will absorb water.

Synthetic fibres

Under the microscope, all synthetic fibres look like very smooth continuous fibres. Most of these fibres are made from petrochemicals, or from coal and belong to three main groups, polyamides, polyesters and acrylics.

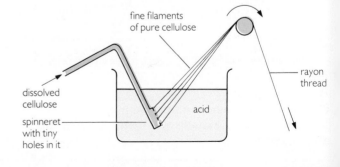

Polyamides

These are very strong, elastic, hard-wearing and rot resistant. *Nylon* is a trade name of one type of polyamide. These fibres are used in all sorts of clothing and in many carpets.

Acrylics

Acrylic fibres are very light, soft and warm. *Acrilan, courtelle* and *orlon* are all trade names of acrylics. These fibres are used in all sorts of clothes and carpets. They are often used to make warm linings for anoraks.

Polyesters

These do not stretch like polyamides but they are strong and hard-wearing. *Terylene* and *dacron* are trade names of some polyesters. These fibres keep their shape well so are used in all sorts of clothing. Net curtains are often made of polyester.

Rayon

This is a synthetic fibre that is made from wood pulp. The pulp is treated with chemicals to dissolve the cellulose fibres. The cellulose solution is then forced through small holes into an acid. The acid makes the solution turn back into threads of pure cellulose known as rayon. This is a widely used fibre, and *tricel* is a trade name of one type.

Synthetic fibres are usually much stronger than natural fibres. They are also water-resistant so can 'drip dry', or be used for protective clothing such as anoraks or cagoules.

fine filaments of pure cellulose

dissolved cellulose

spinneret with tiny holes in it

acid

rayon thread

Fabrics

Many of today's fabrics are mixtures of natural and synthetic fibres. This mixing allows the different properties to be combined and also produces a cheaper fabric than pure natural fibres.

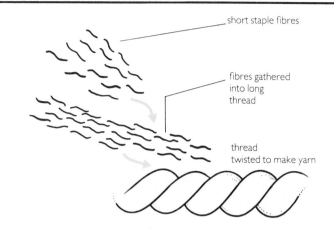

short staple fibres

fibres gathered into long thread

thread twisted to make yarn

Spinning

All natural fibres, with the exception of silk, form short staple fibres. These are too short and weak to be used to make textiles. The fibres must be gathered together, drawn into a long thread then twisted together to make *yarn*. This process is called spinning. Synthetic fibres are often cut short then spun into a yarn in order to give them the feel of natural fibres. Yarn or continuous filaments are generally either woven or knitted to make a fabric. Cloth and carpets are normally woven, while clothing which needs to stretch is usually knitted.

Weaving is the interlacing of two sets of threads, which is done on a loom. One set of threads is passed under and over a set of lengthwise threads.

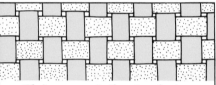

Plain weave is the simplest weave where the thread goes over a thread, under the next and over the next. Many materials are woven in this weave.

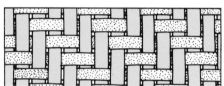

Twill weave is where the thread goes under two threads, then over the next two threads. This weave is often used to make materials for suits, blankets and denims.

Satin weave is where the thread goes over one thread then under the next four threads. This weave is often used for linings because it produces a very smooth finish.

Knitting   One thread is formed into rows of loops. Each row of loops hangs from the row above. Knitted fabrics stretch and 'give' much more than woven fabrics because the loops allow more movement. This is why underwear, socks and tights are always knitted. If one loop breaks, the loop hanging below it also drops and a run or ladder results. This often happens in women's tights which are knitted from a very fine thread.

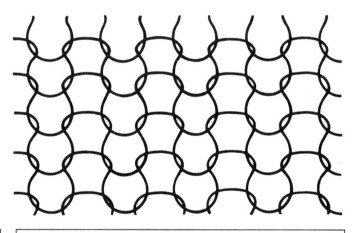

Dyeing and printing

Most of the fabrics we buy are coloured by dyeing or printing. Natural fibres are usually off-white or brown, while synthetic fibres are usually colourless.

Dyeing   This may be done at any stage from the fibre to the finished article. Natural fibres are easy to dye because they absorb water. Synthetic fibres are usually dyed by adding coloured pigments to the polymer before it is drawn out into fibres. Dyes must not fade after washing or when exposed to the light. Dyes that retain their colour are called *fast*. Dyeing a fabric colours it throughout in the same colour.

Printing   This is the main method of colouring fabrics. Most of the attractive designs you see on fabrics will have been printed. This process uses dyes that are applied to the surface of the material as a paste. If you turn a printed fabric over you will see that the colours are much fainter. Printing allows more than one colour to be applied to a piece of material. This is done by printing each single colour separately.

The study of metals is called *metallurgy*. Metallurgists study the properties of metals and *alloys* which are mixtures of metals.

With a few exceptions, such as copper wire, metals are rarely used in their pure state.

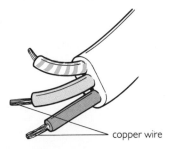

copper wire

Most pure metals are weak and soft, but if other metals are added in small amounts the resulting alloy can be much harder and stronger.

Aluminium bronze

Copper is a soft weak metal. If aluminium is added to it its strength increases.

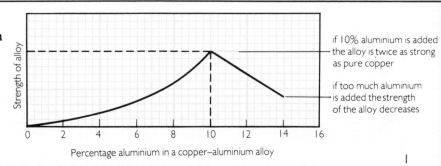

if 10% aluminium is added the alloy is twice as strong as pure copper

if too much aluminium is added the strength of the alloy decreases

Strength of alloy

Percentage aluminium in a copper–aluminium alloy

Steel

Steel is an unusual alloy because it is formed from a metal, iron, and a non-metal, carbon. Only tiny amounts of carbon are needed to strengthen and harden steel. Once again, if too much carbon is added the strength of the alloy decreases. Cast iron is quite strong but is very brittle – a sharp knock can shatter it.

The atoms of a metal are arranged in a lattice. These lattices are rarely perfect and have areas of weakness callled *slip planes*.

In an alloy these areas of weakness are strengthened by the addition of a few different atoms. Adding too many will weaken the alloy.

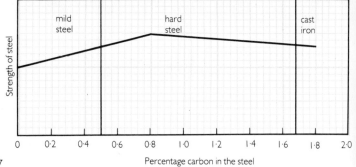

Strength of steel

mild steel

hard steel

cast iron

Percentage carbon in the steel

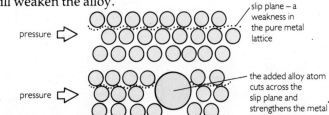

pressure

slip plane – a weakness in the pure metal lattice

pressure

the added alloy atom cuts across the slip plane and strengthens the metal

movement of atoms in the lattice above the slip plane

no movement along the slip plane because the added atom blocks it

Heat treatment

Some alloys, particularly steel, can be made much harder if they are heat treated.

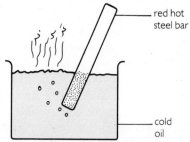

red hot steel bar

cold oil

Quenching

The alloy is heated until it is red-hot (over 700 °C for steel). It is then plunged into cold oil. The alloy becomes very hard but is also very brittle.

Tempering

The quenched alloy is reheated (to 200 °C for steel). It is then allowed to cool slowly. Tempering takes away the brittleness but leaves the metal hard.

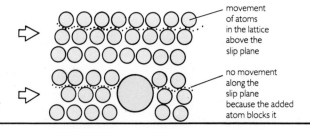

reheating

slow cooling

Heat treatment causes changes to the metal lattice that increases the strength.

Properties and uses of alloys

The engineering and construction industries need materials that have all kinds of properties. Much research goes into the development of new alloys. This page shows some properties and uses of different alloys.

Cupro-nickel
Alloy of copper and nickel.

 coins propeller shaft

Properties: cheap, light, hard and corrosion resistant.

Aluminium bronze
Alloy of copper, aluminium, and tin.

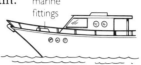 marine fittings

Properties: strong, light and corrosion resistant.

Brass
Alloy of copper and zinc.

ornaments

door fittings

terminals on electric plugs

Properties: shiny, attractive, strong, corrosion resistant and takes a polish.

Nichrome
Alloy of nickel and chromium.

 heating coil on electric fires

Properties: high melting point, resists corrosion.

Duralumin
Alloy of aluminium and copper.

aircraft bodies

Properties: light, strong, resists corrosion, has a high melting point.

Bronze
Alloy of copper and tin.

ships propellers

statues

Properties: resists corrosion, attractive and takes a good polish.

Solder
Alloy of tin and lead.

 solder

Properties: low melting point, good electrical conductor.

Magnesium alloy
Alloy of magnesium and aluminium.

sports car engines

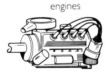

Properties: high melting point, hard, light and easily cast.

Osmiridium
Alloy of osmium and iridium.

fountain pen nibs

Properties: very hard.

Steel alloys

Mild steel
Alloy of iron and carbon.

car bodies

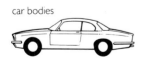

Properties: can be rolled into thin sheets, cheap.

Stainless steel
Alloy of steel, chromium and nickel.

cutlery

some car exhausts

sink tops

Properties: corrosion free, shiny strong and hard.

Tungsten/manganese steel
Alloy of steel and tungsten or manganese.

high speed drills

Properties: very, very hard and resistant to wear.

Shaping metals

Some metal products, such as engine blocks, are cast into moulds, but most metal is not cast directly. It is either rolled or squeezed continuously into the desired shape. Rolling has the added advantage that it increases the strength of the metal. The sheet is then cut into smaller sheets called slabs, or rectangles called blooms.

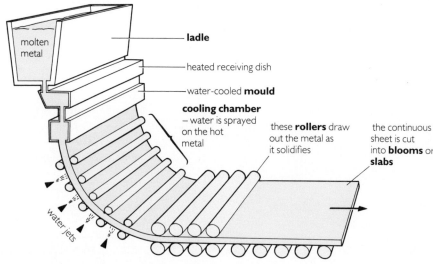

Slabs are reheated for rolling.

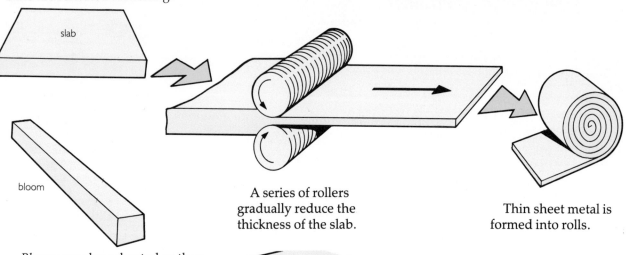

A series of rollers gradually reduce the thickness of the slab.

Thin sheet metal is formed into rolls.

Blooms are also reheated so they can be squeezed, like toothpaste, through moulds to produce various shapes.

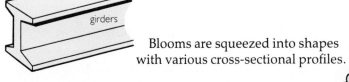

Blooms are squeezed into shapes with various cross-sectional profiles.

There are three basic methods of producing direct casts of objects.

Sand moulding
A shape the same as the object is made in special sand. The molten metal is poured directly into the mould.

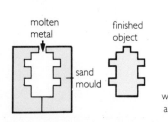

Wafer moulding
Instead of sand, the mould is made of steel coated in a resin and a thin layer of sand. This method has largely replaced sand moulding.

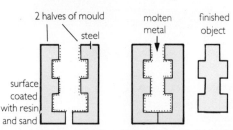

Die casting
A mould is made of hollow steel. Light alloy components can be made to a high degree of accuracy using this method.

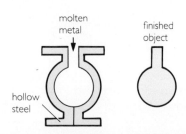

Other methods of working with metals

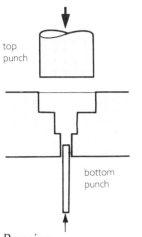

Sintering
An exact amount of powdered metal is put in a die cavity.

All kinds of small mechanical components are made this way. The points in a car are sintered from tungsten, cobalt and copper.

The powder is pressed between two punches.

Drawing

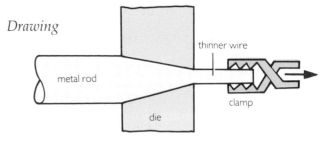

Cold metal rods are drawn into wire by pulling them through dies made of tungsten carbide.

Pressing
Car body sections are made by pressing cold rolled steel into moulds.

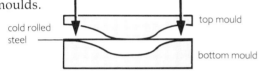

Stamping
Coins, and many other objects are formed by using a punch to stamp them out of cold rolled metal.

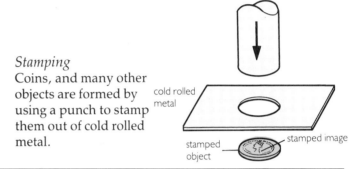

Joining metals
It is obviously not always possible to make objects in one piece. Sometimes metals must be joined together. This can be done in various ways.

Riveting
This method is widely used in the construction industry. The rivet is simply a small metal plug.

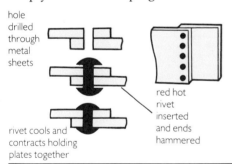

Welding
The edges of the metal are heated red hot. They melt together along with the molten metal from a filler rod.

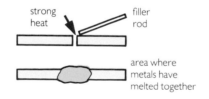

The joint has a continuous structure inside that makes it very strong.

Soldering and brazing
Solder is an alloy of tin and lead. It has a low melting point (about 200°C). The solder is applied to the join and heated.

The solder cools and holds the metals together in a weak joint. Molten brass is used in the same way in brazing.

Corrosion
Metals are attacked by air, moisture, sulphur dioxide and other chemicals. This attack is called *corrosion*. *Rusting* is a form of corrosion that affects iron and steel. Metals can be protected in a variety of ways depending on how they are to be used.

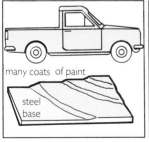

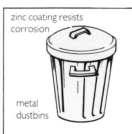

12 TIMBER

Wood is a very versatile material. It is strong for its weight, tough, long-lasting, easy to work with, and attractive, especially when polished. It is also a good insulator of heat and sound.

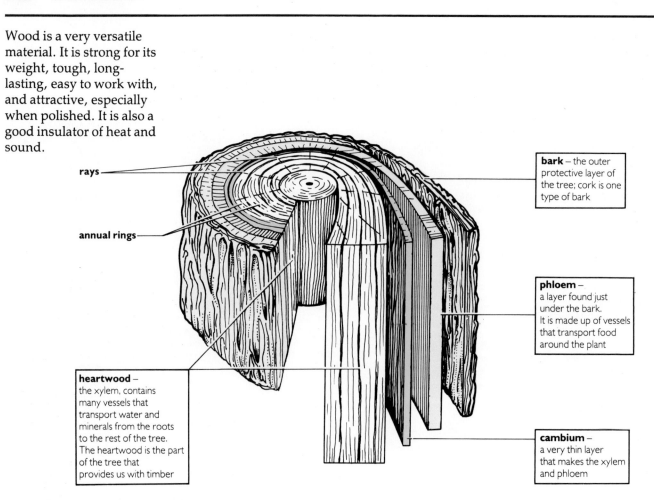

rays

annual rings

bark – the outer protective layer of the tree; cork is one type of bark

phloem – a layer found just under the bark. It is made up of vessels that transport food around the plant

heartwood – the xylem, contains many vessels that transport water and minerals from the roots to the rest of the tree. The heartwood is the part of the tree that provides us with timber

cambium – a very thin layer that makes the xylem and phloem

Since 1900 the annual timber harvest has hardly increased even though the demand for timber has increased dramatically. What has changed is the efficiency with which wood is converted to useful products. Increased efficiency in the sawmills and the development of manufactured wood products such as plywood account for the change (see page 179).

Producing timber

In the sawmill the sawyer must convert each tree trunk into the maximum amount of sawn timber. This is then graded for quality according to its appearance and use. It may then be finished by planing and shaping. Timber can provide the framework for houses, as well as for roofing timbers and floor boards. It can be used in all kinds of furniture and consumer goods. Low quality timber can be used to make composite wood, or be given a veneer to improve its appearance.

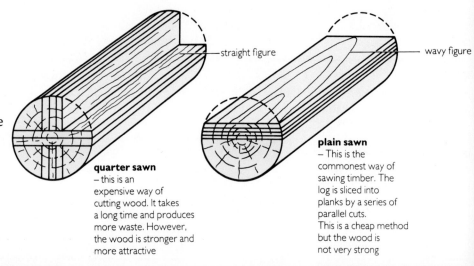

straight figure

wavy figure

quarter sawn – this is an expensive way of cutting wood. It takes a long time and produces more waste. However, the wood is stronger and more attractive

plain sawn – This is the commonest way of sawing timber. The log is sliced into planks by a series of parallel cuts. This is a cheap method but the wood is not very strong

Grain and figure

The *grain* is determined by the direction and arrangement of the fibres in the heartwood. The *figure* or pattern in the wood depends on the presence of the annual rings and rays, and the way in which the timber is sawn. Hardwoods usually have a much better figure than softwoods. Knots are caused where branches leave the main trunk of the tree.

Seasoning

Before it can be used timber must be dried or *seasoned*. If this is not done the timber will warp and split. During seasoning the amount of water in the wood must be reduced to below 20 %. Timber may be seasoned naturally in the open air, or artificially in drying kilns. Preservatives may be added to the timber after seasoning.

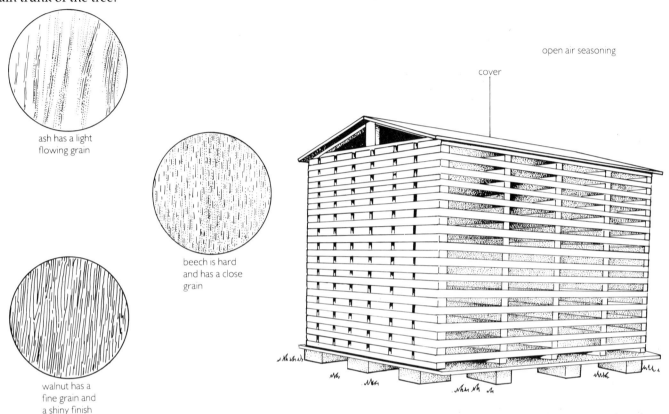

ash has a light flowing grain

beech is hard and has a close grain

walnut has a fine grain and a shiny finish

open air seasoning

cover

Chemicals from wood

Much of the wood in a tree is not used by the building trade. The stump and branches are often used to produce useful and valuable chemicals. The main way of doing this is by *distillation*, when the wood is heated strongly without air. As it is heated the wood breaks down, releasing gases and making *charcoal*. This can be used by artists for drawing, by chemists for purifying chemicals, smelting metals, or even for barbecues! It is used in many countries as a fuel. The hot gases released are cooled to produce a mixture of liquids that includes:

wood alcohol (methanol) which is an important industrial solvent;

oils which are used to make many types of disinfectant;

creosote which is used to stop wood being attacked by insects and fungus;

gums which can be used to make other chemicals such as turpentine.

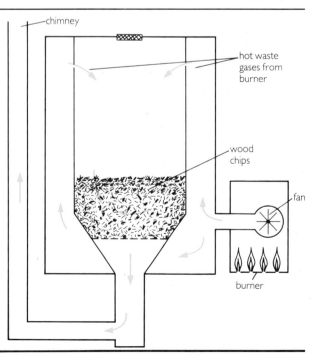

chimney

hot waste gases from burner

wood chips

fan

burner

Wood pulp

This is wood that has been broken down into very small pieces. Wood pulp is a major raw material from which we make paper, cardboard, rayon and cellulose. Paper and cardboard are made at paper-mills. The best trees for making wood pulp are softwoods, and most of the pulp used in the United Kingdom is imported. The fibres of cellulose that are joined together in wood are separated to form a felt-like pulp.

Mechanical pulp

In this method short logs are fed between a series of grinding rollers. Water is used to cool the rollers. The wet pulp is then dried. This type of pulp is cheap but coarse. It is used mainly for making newspapers, wallpaper and cardboard.

Chemical pulp

The logs are cut into small chips and then heated in a large pressure cooker with various chemicals to produce a strong but expensive pulp. This can be bleached to produce a very white paper used to make art paper and printing paper. The paper of this book is made from chemical pulp.

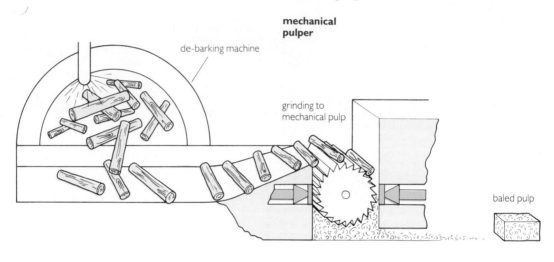

de-barking machine

mechanical pulper

grinding to mechanical pulp

baled pulp

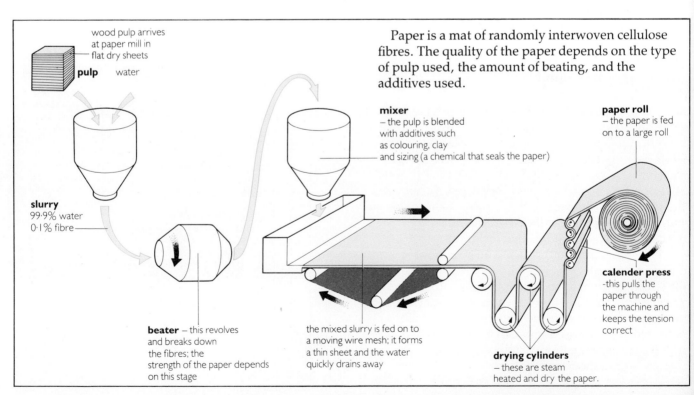

wood pulp arrives at paper mill in flat dry sheets

pulp   water

Paper is a mat of randomly interwoven cellulose fibres. The quality of the paper depends on the type of pulp used, the amount of beating, and the additives used.

slurry
99·9% water
0·1% fibre

mixer
– the pulp is blended with additives such as colouring, clay and sizing (a chemical that seals the paper)

paper roll
– the paper is fed on to a large roll

beater – this revolves and breaks down the fibres; the strength of the paper depends on this stage

the mixed slurry is fed on to a moving wire mesh; it forms a thin sheet and the water quickly drains away

drying cylinders
– these are steam heated and dry the paper.

calender press
-this pulls the paper through the machine and keeps the tension correct

Manufactured composite boards

Many types of board are used in the building and furniture industries. Some of these are made from wood waste and, therefore, are cheaper than natural wood. Other boards have advantages over natural wood.

Veneers

These are very thin sheets of wood that are sliced from a log. Cheap veneers are used to make plywood, matches and matchboxes. Expensive veneers are made from woods with fine figures such as walnut, teak, rosewood or mahogany. These veneers are used to cover cheaper wood to give it an improved appearance.

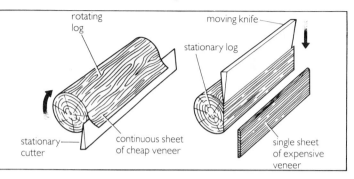

Plywood

This is made from an odd number of veneers glued together. The sheets of veneer are glued together so that the grain of one sheet is at right angles to the grain of the next. This makes plywood much stronger than natural wood of the same thickness. An odd number of veneers is used so that the grain of the outer faces runs in the same direction. Plywood is often used in modern furniture because of its strength.

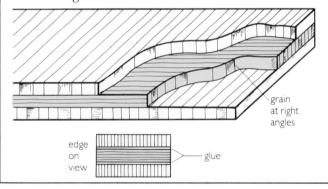

Hardboard

This is made from small wooden chips heated to a high temperature so they form a mass of fibres. These are then put in a heated press to produce a thin board with a very hard water-resistant finish. Hardboard is used to make doors and cupboards.

Chipboard

Logs are broken down into fine chips which are then glued together by a glue or resin. The mixture of chips and resin is rolled into sheets, allowed to dry then cut to size. Chipboard may be faced with a veneer to improve its appearance. Chipboard is often used in modern furniture.

Blockboard

This is made from two sheets of veneer that are separated by a core of strips of softwood. This produces a strong board that is cheaper than plywood but is still strong. Blockboard is often used for making doors.

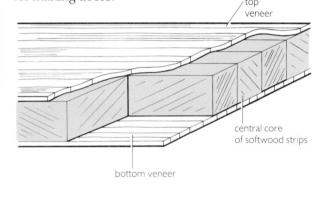

Softboard

This is made from small chips of wood that are heated to make a mass of fibres. This is then passed between two rollers and is squeezed lightly. Softboard has very good properties of insulation against heat and sound. It is also used for notice boards.

Glass

Glass is a very common and cheap material. Sand which is plentiful, and therefore cheap, is the main ingredient.

Glass can be used to make a wide variety of consumer items, such as light bulbs, windows, car windscreens, heatproof oven dishes and cut-glass decanters.

Making glass

Glass is made by heating the four basic ingredients in a large furnace. The molten glass is removed from the furnace and treated in various ways.

Manufacture of float glass

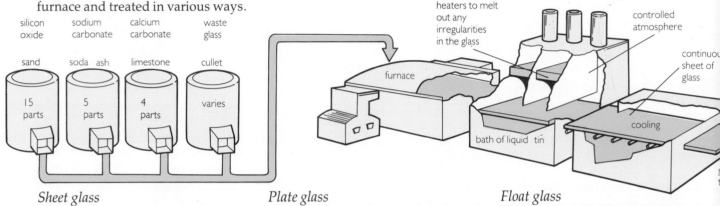

silicon oxide — sand — 15 parts

sodium carbonate — soda ash — 5 parts

calcium carbonate — limestone — 4 parts

waste glass — cullet — varies

furnace

heaters to melt out any irregularities in the glass

controlled atmosphere

continuous sheet of glass

cooling

bath of liquid tin

Sheet glass

This is the cheapest form of flat glass. The glass is pulled vertically out of the furnace and passed through rollers. It often has flaws in it that cause distortions.

Plate glass

This is expensive because it is free of any distortions. It is drawn out of the furnace horizontally and is then smoothed by grinding and polishing.

Float glass

This combines the best qualities of sheet and plate glass. The glass is drawn out of the furnace over a bed of molten tin. Heaters above the tin melt any irregularities that might cause distortions. Float glass needs no polishing and is much cheaper than plate glass.

Moulded glass

Molten glass from the furnace is fed straight into a mould. Compressed air automatically blows the glass into the shape of the mould.

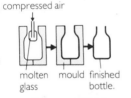

compressed air

molten glass — mould — finished bottle.

Glass blowing

Quality products are still made in traditional ways.

Strengthened glass

Glass can be strengthened in two main ways:

Laminated glass is simply two layers of glass which sandwich a layer of plastic. This glass may crack but will not shatter.

Toughened glass is stronger than normal glass but can break. If it does it forms small pieces which are not too sharp.

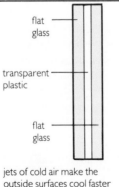

flat glass

transparent plastic

flat glass

jets of cold air make the outside surfaces cool faster and shrink

the inside of the glass is compressed and cools more slowly, becoming much stronger

newly formed hot glass

Fibre glass

Very fine threads of glass can be drawn from molten glass. These can be formed into fibre glass mats which can be used to reinforce plastic. This material is very light and strong, and does not corrode.

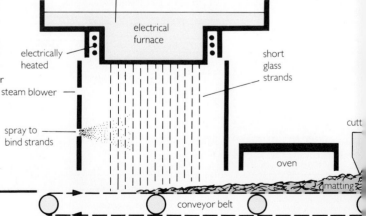

molten glass

electrical furnace

electrically heated

short glass strands

steam blower

spray to bind strands

oven

cutt

conveyor belt

matting

Bricks

Bricks are made from baked clay. When the clay is wet it is plastic and can be easily moulded to the shape of a brick. Bricks normally measure 22 cm by 11 cm by 5·5 cm, which is a convenient size for a man's hand. The colour of bricks used to depend on where the clay came from but these days dyes are used to produce the desired colour. The moulded and dyed clay is dried and fired in a kiln at a high temperature to make the finished brick.

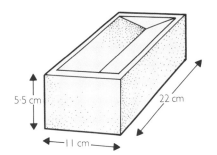

Stone

Natural stone is an expensive material, and its uses tend to be restricted to prestige buildings such as town halls. The commonest natural stone still in common use is probably *slate* which is used for roofing, particularly in some rural areas.

Reconstituted stone is cheaper than natural stone. It is formed by pulverising rocks then using pressure to reform them into blocks. These blocks are commonly used in the building industry because they are cheap. They are very light and larger than bricks so speed up building work. Some types, called breeze blocks, are made from pulverised cinders from coal power stations.

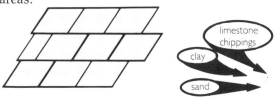

Cement

This grey powder is made from clay, sand and limestone chippings in a rotating kiln. The residue produced is mixed with gypsum (calcium sulphate) and then ground into a powder. Cement is the most important single material used by the building industry.

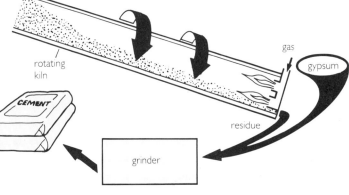

Mortar

Bricks and stones can be stuck together using mortar. This is a mixture of sand, cement and water. As it dries out it sticks the bricks together. An average three-bedroomed house has about 10 000 bricks in it, all stuck together by mortar.

Concrete

This is the main building material of this century. It has been used to replace the traditional materials such as bricks and stones, especially for large buildings. Sand and gravel are used as an aggregate to provide bulk. Normally the ratio is 6 parts of aggregate to 1 part of cement.
The aggregate and cement are mixed thoroughly to produce the semi-liquid concrete. As it dries it sets into a solid form.

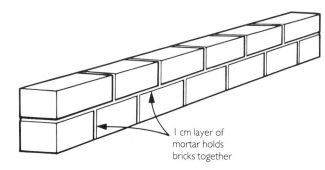

1 cm layer of mortar holds bricks together

Reinforced concrete

Concrete is normally very strong when compressed, but not when under tension.

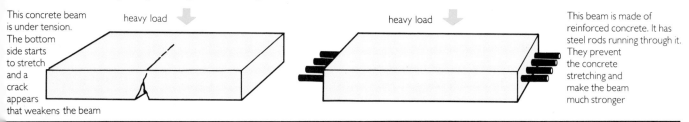

This concrete beam is under tension. The bottom side starts to stretch and a crack appears that weakens the beam

This beam is made of reinforced concrete. It has steel rods running through it. They prevent the concrete stretching and make the beam much stronger

ENERGY

CHAPTER 7

■ WHAT IS IT?

If you asked your friends you would get all sorts of different answers. Some might be more accurate than others but, strangely enough, you would be unlikely to get identical answers from teachers, engineers or technologists. Our understanding of energy is constantly changing and it will probably continue to do so.

What we **can** do is to measure energy. Although we cannot see it or feel it we can experience its effects, e.g. we cannot see electrical energy but we can experience it as sound from loudspeakers, heat from fires and light from bulbs. Energy can take many forms.

The electricity maker's view
The electrical energy released from Fiddlers Ferry Power Station is 2000 MW. This means it can produce 2 000 000 000 watts (W) of power – enough to light over 20 million 100 watt light bulbs at any one time! The number of megawatts (MW) a power station can produce is a measure of its ability to provide industry, offices, shops and homes with electrical energy. The latest nuclear power stations are designed to give an output of about 1200 MW. Many smaller power stations are being replaced by a few larger ones.

The electricity consumer's view
Our use of electricity is measured in units called kilowatt hours (kWh) by an electricity meter. If a machine uses 1000 watts over a period of one hour it will use up 1 kWh of electricity. Domestic consumers pay a set price for the electricity they use. This price is set by the local Electricity Board.

The eater's view
The amount of energy in food can be estimated by measuring the amount of heat that is given out when the food is burnt. This amount of heat is measured in kilojoules (kJ) by scientists, but dieticians and nutritionists use an older measure called the Calorie.

The technologist's view
This view is about using energy more efficiently. In other words, getting more work out of a machine for the same amount of energy put in. For example, as petrol prices increase, engineers design cars to give more miles per gallon.

The traveller's view
All forms of transport use energy. Most use some sort of fuel which can be thought of as a convenient stored form of energy – usually chemical.

The poet's view
> Energy is the only life and is from the body;
> and Reason is the bound or outward circumference of
>   Energy.
> Energy is the Eternal Delight.

William Blake

It is an impossible task to define what energy is. Without doubt there would be no life without it. Whatever others say, Blake is right – energy is the giver of life.

So what is energy?

This is a question with lots of answers. We put it in our cars as *petrol*, we burn it as *coal*, we eat it in our *food*, we use it as *electricity* to run our T.V.'s, we keep warm by it as *heat*, we use it to *light* our homes, we listen to it as *sound*. We experience its effect when something hits us. We can use its effects to do the things we want to do.

2 ENERGY CONVERSIONS

As you have seen, it is very difficult to give a good definition of energy but, in general, things have energy if they can do work. There are many different forms of energy:

Heat energy

This is really the effect of the movement energy of molecules – if we heat up a substance we make its molecules move faster. Heat can be used to do work. For example, a car moves when petrol is burnt to produce heat.

Chemical energy

This is the energy stored within chemicals. Food contains chemical energy that is released when it combines with oxygen. Fossil fuels such as coal and oil also contain chemical energy.

Potential energy

This is the energy that something has because of its position. When something is lifted higher it is given more energy. This is sometimes called *gravitational energy*. The energy will be released when it falls down. Another type of potential energy is the energy that is stored in pressed springs or stretched elastic.

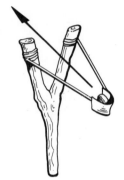

Kinetic energy

This is sometimes called *movement energy*. It is the energy that something has because it is moving. The faster it moves, the more kinetic energy it has.
The kinetic energy of the wind is captured by a windmill.

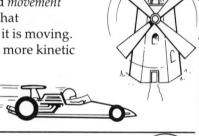

Electrical energy

The energy of an electric current is one of the most convenient and easily used forms of energy that we have.

Sound energy

The energy carried by sound waves is used to transmit messages, e.g. singing.

Nuclear energy

This energy is stored inside the nucleus (centre) of every atom. The Sun, nuclear power stations and nuclear weapons all use nuclear energy.

Light energy

This is the energy carried by light waves. It is one of the most important forms of energy because it is used by plants to make food in photosynethesis (page 110). Without this there would be no life on the Earth. Radio waves and X-rays are a similar form of energy.

While we cannot measure energy directly, we can measure the work that it does. Scientists measure work, and energy, in units called *joules* (J). The joule is a very small unit – a burning match releases about 2000 J. It is often more convenient to use larger units:

    1000 joules = 1 kilojoule = 1 kJ
    1 million joules = 1 000 000 J = 1 megajoule = 1 MJ

Power is the amount of work done in a given time and this is measured in watts (W), kilowatts (kW) or megawatts (MW)

Energy cannot be created or destroyed but can be converted from one form to another. We can use these conversions to change energy into a more useful form. Unfortunately these conversions are never 100% efficient; whenever we change energy from one form to another we also produce heat – a sort of heat tax on the conversion.

Touch an ordinary light bulb – you can feel the heat tax from the conversion!

A car converts the chemical energy in petrol into movement energy, but 75% of the energy is wasted as heat. This heat tax can be reduced by using a more efficient engine, e.g. diesel engines where only 60% of the energy is wasted.

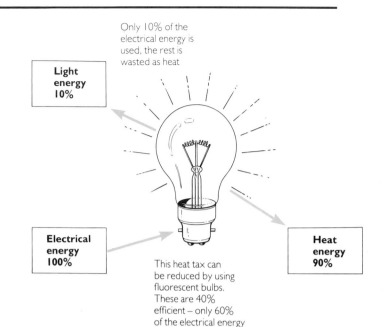

Only 10% of the electrical energy is used, the rest is wasted as heat

Light energy 10%

Electrical energy 100%

Heat energy 90%

This heat tax can be reduced by using fluorescent bulbs. These are 40% efficient – only 60% of the electrical energy is wasted as heat

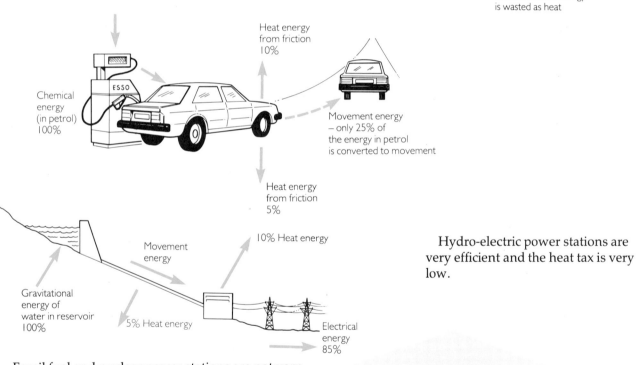

Heat energy from friction 10%

Chemical energy (in petrol) 100%

Movement energy – only 25% of the energy in petrol is converted to movement

Heat energy from friction 5%

Gravitational energy of water in reservoir 100%

Movement energy

10% Heat energy

5% Heat energy

Electrical energy 85%

Hydro-electric power stations are very efficient and the heat tax is very low.

Fossil fuel and nuclear power stations are not very efficient. This is because the energy in the coal or uranium has to be converted three times, firstly to heat, then to movement, then to electrical energy. Each conversion has a heat tax.

70% Heat energy

Heat energy (in boiler or reactor)

Movement energy (in generator)

Nuclear energy in Uranium 100%   or   Chemical energy in coal, oil or gas 100%

Electrical energy 30% [only 30% of the energy in the fuel has been converted to electricty.

The heat tax is high because there are 3 conversions

3 WHERE DOES ENERGY COME FROM?

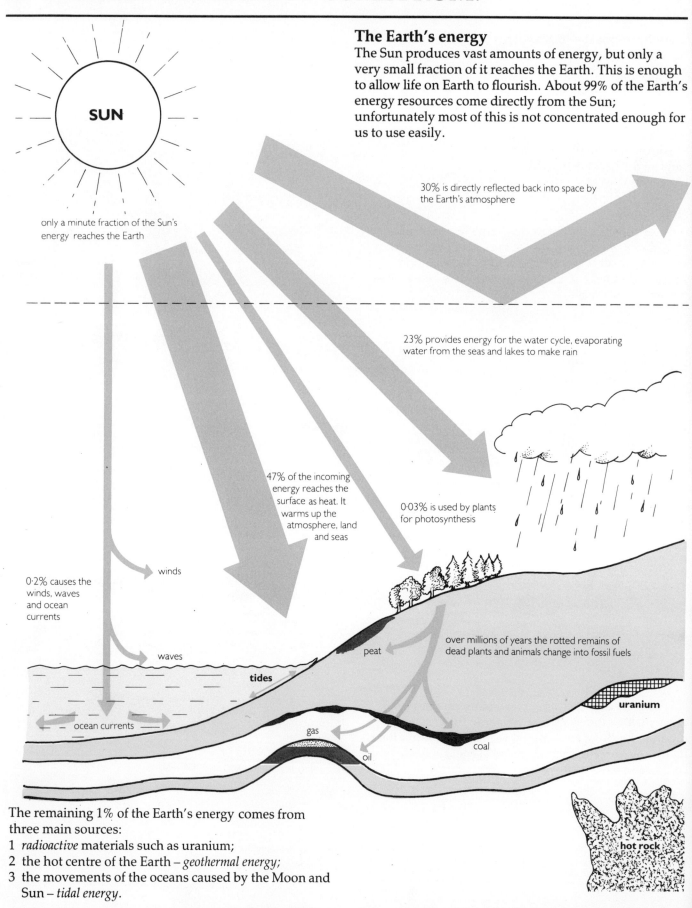

The Earth's energy

The Sun produces vast amounts of energy, but only a very small fraction of it reaches the Earth. This is enough to allow life on Earth to flourish. About 99% of the Earth's energy resources come directly from the Sun; unfortunately most of this is not concentrated enough for us to use easily.

SUN

only a minute fraction of the Sun's energy reaches the Earth

30% is directly reflected back into space by the Earth's atmosphere

23% provides energy for the water cycle, evaporating water from the seas and lakes to make rain

47% of the incoming energy reaches the surface as heat. It warms up the atmosphere, land and seas

0.03% is used by plants for photosynthesis

0.2% causes the winds, waves and ocean currents

winds

waves

over millions of years the rotted remains of dead plants and animals change into fossil fuels

peat

uranium

tides

ocean currents

gas

oil

coal

hot rock

The remaining 1% of the Earth's energy comes from three main sources:

1 *radioactive* materials such as uranium;
2 the hot centre of the Earth – *geothermal energy;*
3 the movements of the oceans caused by the Moon and Sun – *tidal energy*.

Commercial sources of energy
There are only a few commercial methods of providing energy in use at the present time.

Chemical power
Most of the world's energy comes from wood and the fossil fuels peat, coal, oil and gas. They are stores of chemical energy first produced by the photosynthesis of plants using the Sun's energy. Most fossil fuels have taken about 500 million years to build up. We are likely to use them all up in about 400 years. Fossil fuels are still being formed today, but far too slowly to be of any use to us. Every day we use up over 1000 years' production of fossil fuels. It is worth remembering that wood is the main source of energy for the vast majority of the people on the Earth.

Tidal power
The action of the Sun and Moon on the oceans causes regular tides. Energy can be removed from these tides by using special turbines in dams. There are two small pilot stations at La Rance in France and Murmansk in the Soviet Union.

Geothermal power
Hot water springs and geysers have been used in Iceland, Italy, New Zealand and the USA to supply heat energy and electrical energy.

Nuclear power
At present the most common nuclear fuel in use is enriched uranium. Energy is extracted from uranium by breaking its nucleus, a process called *fission*. This releases vast amounts of heat energy. There is probably less than 40 years' supply of uranium left in the Earth.

Hydro-electric power (HEP)
Energy from the Sun evaporates water from the surface of the sea and water vapour rises into the atmosphere. When it returns as rain over hills, the water can be trapped in reservoirs and used to provide electrical energy. HEP is very clean and efficient.

The demand for energy

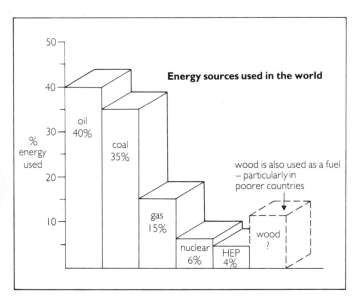

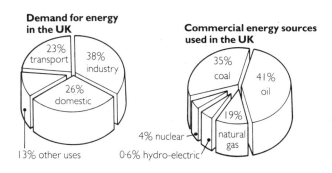

Renewable or non-renewable?
These are the sources of energy we use today. We cannot use all of them forever – fossil fuels and uranium will eventually run out, HEP dams will silt up and the Earth's rocks will cool. Strictly speaking only tidal energy and solar power are really renewable. In the future we must develop new sources of energy.

Electricity can be produced from fossil fuels – peat, coal, oil and gas, or nuclear fuels. Chemical energy in the fuel is converted to heat energy which is used to produce steam.

Fossil fuels

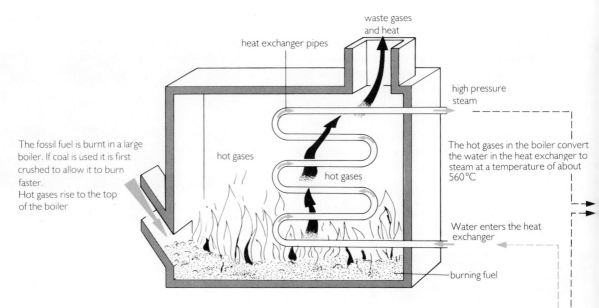

waste gases and heat

heat exchanger pipes

high pressure steam

The fossil fuel is burnt in a large boiler. If coal is used it is first crushed to allow it to burn faster.
Hot gases rise to the top of the boiler

hot gases

hot gases

The hot gases in the boiler convert the water in the heat exchanger to steam at a temperature of about 560°C

Water enters the heat exchanger

burning fuel

Nuclear power
Electricity can be produced from the breakdown of large atoms such as uranium or plutonium. When the nuclei of these atoms are split, large amounts of heat are released. This heat is then used to convert water to steam.

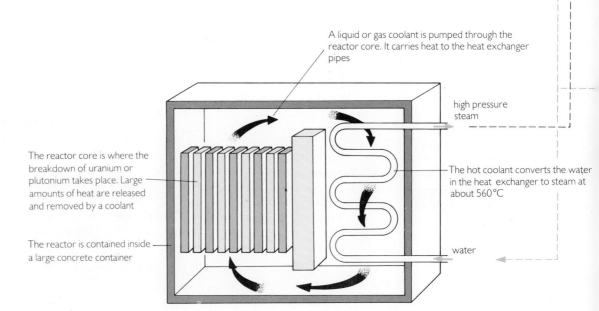

A liquid or gas coolant is pumped through the reactor core. It carries heat to the heat exchanger pipes

high pressure steam

The reactor core is where the breakdown of uranium or plutonium takes place. Large amounts of heat are released and removed by a coolant

The reactor is contained inside a large concrete container

The hot coolant converts the water in the heat exchanger to steam at about 560°C

water

A power station is only about 30% efficient. This means that most of the energy in the fuel is wasted. The energy conversion can be written like this:

chemical energy in the fossil fuel
or
nuclear energy in the uranium or plutonium ⟶ **heat energy** in the steam ⟶ **movement energy** in the turbine and generator ⟶ **electrical energy**

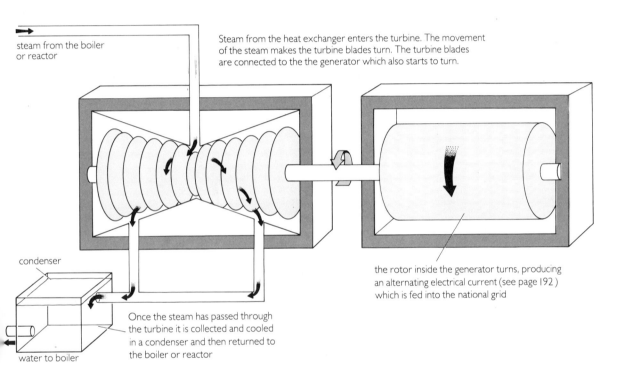

steam from the boiler or reactor

Steam from the heat exchanger enters the turbine. The movement of the steam makes the turbine blades turn. The turbine blades are connected to the the generator which also starts to turn.

condenser

the rotor inside the generator turns, producing an alternating electrical current (see page 192) which is fed into the national grid

Once the steam has passed through the turbine it is collected and cooled in a condenser and then returned to the boiler or reactor

water to boiler

Hydro-electric power
If water is trapped in mountainous areas it can be used to produce electricity. The water is used to turn a turbine directly, and this is connected to a generator in the normal way (see page 199). The energy conversions are:

potential energy of the water ⟶ **movement energy** of turbine and generator ⟶ **electrical energy**

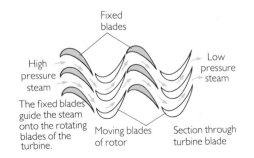

Fixed blades

High pressure steam

Low pressure steam

The fixed blades guide the steam onto the rotating blades of the turbine.

Moving blades of rotor

Section through turbine blade

5 SUPPLYING ELECTRICITY

Electricity is probably the most convenient form of energy to use. It can be switched on and off easily and is very versatile. When you switch on a light the electricity that moves through a wire consists of billions of electrons moving through the wire. These electrons drift along slowly, between 2 and 5 cm every second, but the electrical energy is passed as a wave at the speed of light (see page 238).

An electrical current is a measure of the number of electrons that pass a given point in a circuit in one second. The current is called *direct* if all the electrons drift in the same direction all the time. The current is called *alternating* if it reverses its direction regularly.

The generators at the power station produce an alternating current (AC) which can be transmitted further than a direct current (DC).

Electrical transmission

The generator at the power station usually produces electricity at about 25 kV (25 000 volts). Electrical power is calculated by multiplying the voltage and current together.

A generator producing 1 MW (1 megawatt = 1 000 000 watts) could transmit electricity along a power line in two ways:

> **electrical power** (watts) = **voltage** (volts) × **current** (amps)

high voltage and low current **or**
e.g. 1 000 000 = 100 000 × 10
       watts   volts   amps

High voltages are dangerous and the conductor must be well insulated.

low voltage and high current
e.g. 1 000 000 = 100 × 10 000
       watts   volts amps

High currents produce heat in conductors.

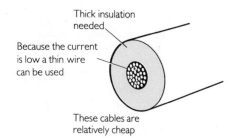

Thick insulation needed

Because the current is low a thin wire can be used

These cables are relatively cheap

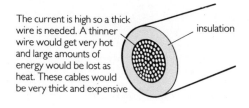

The current is high so a thick wire is needed. A thinner wire would get very hot and large amounts of energy would be lost as heat. These cables would be very thick and expensive

insulation

We use high voltage and low current because it reduces the energy loss during transmission.

The national grid
This includes the supergrid and the local area board grids.

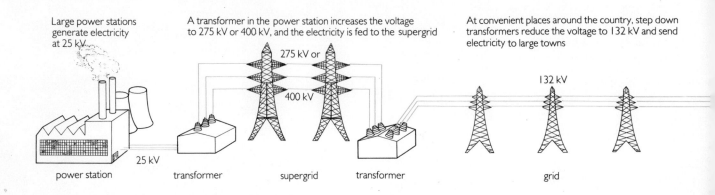

Large power stations generate electricity at 25 kV

A transformer in the power station increases the voltage to 275 kV or 400 kV, and the electricity is fed to the supergrid

At convenient places around the country, step down transformers reduce the voltage to 132 kV and send electricity to large towns

275 kV or 400 kV

132 kV

25 kV

power station   transformer   supergrid   transformer   grid

The CEGB

The Central Electricity Generating Board or the CEGB as it is generally called, produces electricity, and manages all the power stations in England and Wales. Scotland's electricity is produced by the North of Scotland Hydro-electricity Board and the South of Scotland Electricity Board.

Modern fossil fuel and nuclear power stations cannot be switched on and off quickly because they take a long time to reach their peak load or maximum working capacity. Electricity cannot be stored, it must be produced on demand. The job of the CEGB is to balance the supply and demand for electricity by switching electricity from one part of the country to another. It does this by means of a network of transmission lines called the supergrid. This supplies electricity at 400 kV or 275 kV to all parts of England and Wales. It also connects with a similar system in Scotland and through a channel link with the French system. The CEGB controls the nation's supplies of electricity.

The area electricity boards

These buy their electricity from the CEGB and distribute it along their own grids. While most of the supergrid system is transmitted on overhead cables, the local supply, especially in urban areas, is usually underground. The area boards supply and fix the price of electricity, send out bills and run electricity showrooms.

Under- or overground?

The CEGB supergrid is very noticeable. The pylons may be over 60 m tall and they cover over 8000 km. There are also over 24 000 km of other overhead cables carrying electricity. In areas of great beauty these cables may be put underground and there are about 2400 km of underground cable in use. Unfortunately these cables are about twenty times more expensive than overhead cables. An overhead cable is safely out of the way and is insulated and cooled by the air around it. An

The Supergrid.

cross-channel cable

underground cable must be insulated much more and must be cooled by water in special pipes. This is very expensive.

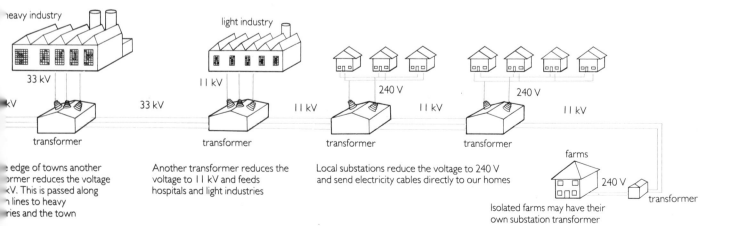

heavy industry

light industry

33 kV

11 kV

240 V

240 V

33 kV   33 kV   11 kV   11 kV   11 kV

transformer   transformer   transformer   transformer

farms

240 V

transformer

...e edge of towns another ...rmer reduces the voltage ...kV. This is passed along ...n lines to heavy ...ries and the town

Another transformer reduces the voltage to 11 kV and feeds hospitals and light industries

Local substations reduce the voltage to 240 V and send electricity cables directly to our homes

Isolated farms may have their own substation transformer

6 NUCLEAR TECHNOLOGY

Electricity is produced by over 150 power stations in the UK. There are 21 nuclear power stations in operation, or being built, and these will be able to produce over 13 000 MW of electricity. These power stations are operated by the CEGB and the Scottish electricity boards. The UK Atomic Energy Authority and British Nuclear Fuels Ltd operate 4 nuclear reactors that also generate some electricity.

Nuclear fission

There are at least nine different types of nuclear reactor, but they all rely on the splitting of atoms of uranium-235 (nuclear fisson). If the nucleus of a uranium-235 atom is hit by a neutron, it breaks into fragments, releasing energy and more neutrons.

* Reprocessing works
△ Fast Breeder
● Magnox
○ AGR
□ PWR?
✛ SGHWR

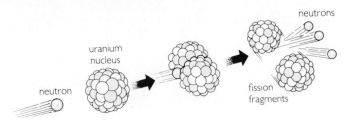

These new neutrons can hit more uranium-235 atoms, causing them to split. This is the start of a *chain reaction*. The fission fragments move apart at great speed creating heat that is removed and used to convert water to high-pressure steam.

Slow-moving neutrons are more likely to split a uranium atom than fast-moving neutrons. Nuclear reactors slow down the neutrons by using *moderators* such as graphite or water. The chain reaction is controlled by *control rods* of boron which absorb spare neutrons, preventing them from splitting other uranium atoms. The number of atoms split is controlled by the position of these control rods.

The general design principles of a nuclear reactor are shown in the diagram.

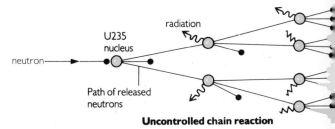

Uncontrolled chain reaction

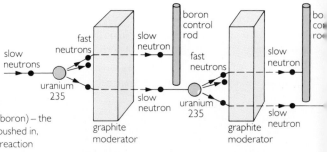

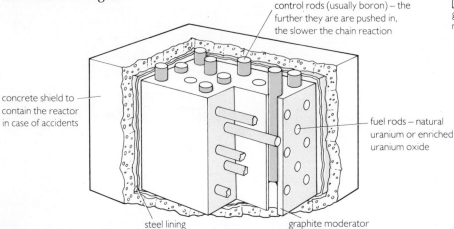

control rods (usually boron) – the further they are are pushed in, the slower the chain reaction

concrete shield to contain the reactor in case of accidents

fuel rods – natural uranium or enriched uranium oxide

steel lining

graphite moderator

There are many types of nuclear reactor. The designer of a nuclear reactor has many choices. The fuel can be natural uranium, or enriched uranium where the amount of the isotope U^{235} has been artificially increased. The moderator can be water, heavy water or graphite, and the coolant can be a gas or water. Different reactors use different combinations of these materials.

The four reactors shown here have all been used for commercial production of energy.

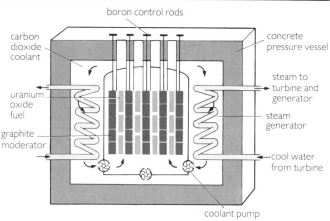

Advanced gas-cooled reactor (AGR)
British design. Uses enriched uranium oxide fuel. The moderator is graphite and carbon dioxide is used to transfer the heat to a steam generator. There will eventually be 8 AGRs with a capacity of about 9000 MW. These reactors are designed to be about 40% efficient although they have not achieved this level in practice. They are complicated reactors and there have been considerable delays in their construction.

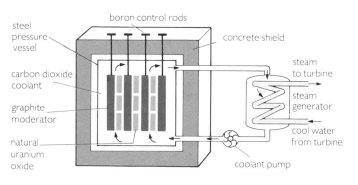

Basic gas-cooled reactor (Magnox)
British design. Uses natural uranium fuel. The moderator is graphite and carbon dioxide gas is used as the coolant. There are 11 Magnox reactors in the UK, providing about 4000 MW of power. These reactors are about 30% efficient, and have been operating since 1956.

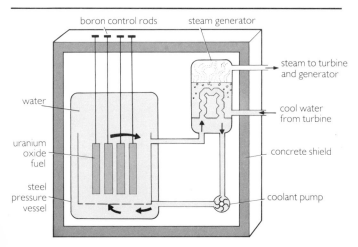

Pressurised water reactor (PWR)
United States design. Uses enriched uranium oxide fuel. Ordinary water is used as the moderator **and** the coolant. This type of reactor went badly wrong in the Three Mile Island accident in the United States in 1979. The CEGB wish to build and operate these reactors in Britain. They are about 30% efficient. Their construction and operation in other parts of the world has caused problems for their operators and owners.

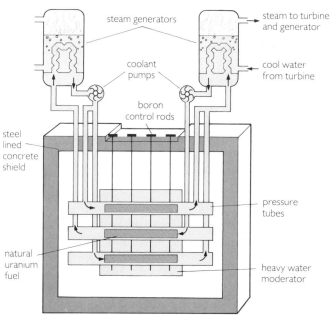

Heavy water reactors (HWR, e.g. CANDU)
Canadian design. Heavy water contains an artificially high concentration of *deuterium* – an isotope of hydrogen. This is a better moderator than ordinary water, and allows ordinary uranium to be used as fuel. The heavy water also acts as the coolant. The CANDU is the most efficient nuclear reactor in commercial use today. A reactor of modified design has been built in Britain at Winfrith.

7 FUTURE REACTORS

The fast breeder reactor

Natural uranium is made up of 99·3% uranium-238 and 0·7% uranium-235. Only the uranium-235 can split to release energy. Magnox and CANDU reactors use natural uranium fuel, but most other reactors use a fuel that has been artificially enriched – by increasing the proportion of uranium-235. However, even the richest nuclear fuel contains a large amount of uranium-238. Slow neutrons sometimes hit a uranium-238 atom, converting it to another material called plutonium-239.

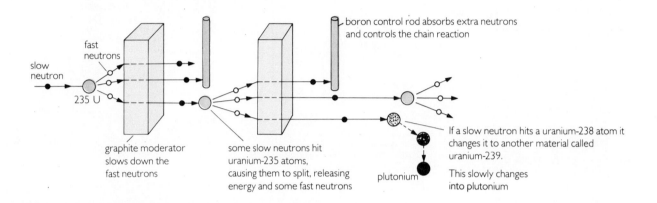

Plutonium-239 from the UKAEA reactors at Calder Hall and Chapelcross is used in the production of the UK's atomic weapons. Plutonium-239 from CEGB reactors will be used as fuel for fast breeder reactors.

During the operation of a normal reactor, the amount of uranium-235 gradually decreases and the concentration of plutonium-239 increases. Eventually the fuel rods must be changed. The used fuel is cooled and three main products are separated:

1 unused uranium (97%) which is kept for use in fast breeder reactors;
2 plutonium (1%) which is the fuel of fast breeder reactors;
3 fission products (2%) which are highly radioactive nuclear wastes.

Fast breeder reactors use a very concentrated fuel, usually a mixture of plutonium-239 and uranium-235. These reactors have no moderators and the neutrons move around at high speed. Because there is no moderator, the reactor core is very small (about 1 cubic metre) and heat is produced extremely quickly. A very efficient coolant is needed such as molten sodium which is used to take this heat to the steam generator.

A layer of uranium-238 is placed around the reactor core and this is slowly converted into more plutonium as it absorbs escaping neutrons. This means the reactor can make more fuel for another fast breeder reactor. It takes about 20 years to get enough plutonium-239 in this way to start another reactor.

Fast breeders are very efficient and a small one has been in operation at Dounreay in the north of Scotland since 1959.

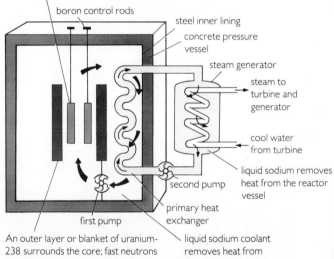

Nuclear fusion

Nuclear fission is the splitting up of atoms, while nuclear fusion is the joining together of small atoms to form a larger atom. Most of the Sun's heat comes from a massive number of fusion reactions that take place at its centre. Researchers are trying to copy this fusion reaction by joining two isotopes of hydrogen together to form a larger atom of helium.

nucleus of **deuterium** (hydrogen-2)

nucleus of **tritium** (hydrogen-3)

fusion – large amount of energy is released

one high energy neutron is released

nucleus of helium atom is produced

Deuterium is plentiful and occurs naturally in water. One cubic metre of water would provide enough deuterium to produce as much energy as 150 tonnes of oil, if fusion power was developed. Tritium is rarer but can be easily produced from lithium which is quite common.

Fusion is likely to be very difficult to achieve because the atoms repel each other and prevent the very close contact that is needed. In order to overcome this the atoms must approach each other at very high speed. One way of doing this is to heat the mixture of deuterium and tritium to a temperature of at least 100 million °C (6 times the temperature at the centre of the Sun). At this temperature the electrons of the atoms fly off and the gases become a *plasma* (ionised gases).

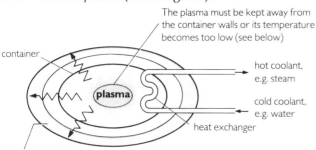

The plasma must be kept away from the container walls or its temperature becomes too low (see below)

container

plasma

hot coolant, e.g. steam

cold coolant, e.g. water

heat exchanger

Neutrons released from the plasma pass out of the container. If they hit a lithium atom they produce a new chemical – tritium, which will be used in later fusion reactions

A working fusion reactor will have a container to hold the plasma. This container will be surrounded by a blanket of lithium. A successful fusion reactor will have to:

1 heat the plasma to a temperature of about 100 million °C;

2 keep the plasma well away from the container wall for more than a second in order to allow enough fusions to take place;

3 remove the heat rapidly.

In theory the potential of fusion reactors is enormous, but they are a long way from being a reality. There are two main lines of research.

Laser confinement

These will aim a series of laser beams at a small pellet of fuel positioned at the centre of the container. The lasers will provide the necessary heat and will also hold the plasma in the centre of the vessel.

Tokamaks

These will keep the plasma in the centre of the container.

8 SOLAR ENERGY

The Earth receives a vast amount of energy from the Sun, more than ten thousand times the total world demand. It is a source of energy that is always being renewed. It is free and clean, producing no pollution. It seems an ideal solution to our energy problems. Unfortunately it's not as simple as that. We need most energy precisely when the energy from the Sun is at its lowest, in the winter. The energy from the Sun is spread out and there are problems in collecting, storing and distributing it. However, it may become more practicable as a source of energy in the future. There are various ways of harnessing the Sun's energy.

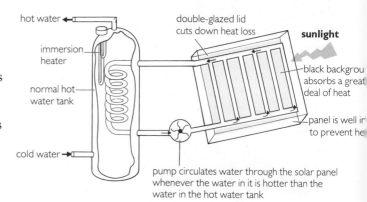

hot water

immersion heater

normal hot water tank

cold water

double-glazed lid cuts down heat loss

sunlight

black backgrou absorbs a great deal of heat

panel is well ir to prevent he

pump circulates water through the solar panel whenever the water in it is hotter than the water in the hot water tank

Direct use
The most common use of the Sun's energy is to heat water in a solar panel.

A more effective way of using the Sun's heat is to use curved mirrors to focus the sunlight on to a pipe carrying water. This concentrates the light and heat on to a much smaller area. These collectors must be turned to face towards the Sun. This method is used on a large scale at Odeillo in the French Pyrenees. Hundreds of computer-controlled mirrors follow the Sun and reflect the light on to a giant collector. A similar system is used in the USA to generate electricity.

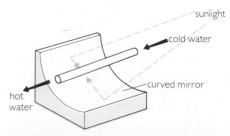

sunlight

cold water

hot water

curved mirror

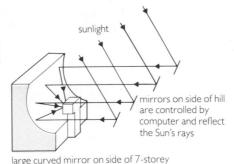

sunlight

mirrors on side of hill are controlled by computer and reflect the Sun's rays

large curved mirror on side of 7-storey building, reflects light into furnace

Solar cells
These are devices that convert sunlight directly to electricity. Their main use has been where other sources are not available, such as space satellites and navigational buoys. The amount of electricity produced by each cell is tiny and many thousands are needed to produce worthwhile amounts of electricity. At the moment these cells are only about 20% efficient but a great deal of research is going on to try and improve their efficiency.

Plans have been put forward to cover 26 000 km² of North American deserts with solar cells. These would be able to provide enough electricity for the whole of the USA. Another suggestion has been to build a series of satellites in orbit 32 000 km above the Earth. These would have huge panels of solar cells and would convert the electricity into microwaves that could be beamed down to aerials on the Earth. At the moment both these ideas are interesting but not really practicable.

solar panel (8 km × 8 km)

microwave beam

transmitter

32 000 km (satellite stays in same position)

receiving aerial (70 km²)

Hydro-electric power (HEP)

About 22% of the incoming energy from the Sun is used to evaporate water from the oceans, driving the water cycle and causing our weather. The evaporated water will eventually fall as rain. Some of the rain will form rivers that can be dammed. The trapped water can be passed through turbines to produce electricity.

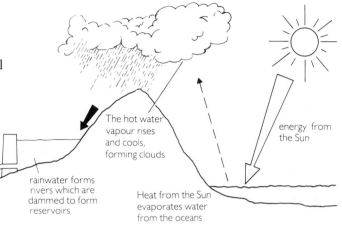

The water turns turbines in the power house. These turn generators, producing electricity. The water is then released into rivers

The hot water vapour rises and cools, forming clouds

energy from the Sun

rainwater forms rivers which are dammed to form reservoirs

Heat from the Sun evaporates water from the oceans

Pipeline takes water to a powerhouse

HEP is one of the cleanest sources of energy. There is nothing to burn so there is no pollution. The movement of the water is converted directly into electricity. It is also cheap. Once the dam and power station have been built there is little cost, apart from maintenance. Problems arise when valleys are flooded to provide the water for HEP schemes. Many large schemes, particularly in the third world (e.g. Brazil), have not been very successful. The UK has many hydro-electric power stations, particularly in the north of Scotland, and about 70% of the possible sites have been used. The total power capacity of hydro-electric stations in this country is about 2000 MW, roughly the same as one modern coal power station. They provide about 1% of the electricity we use. In the future it may well be worthwhile building small-scale schemes for local use.

HEP stations in Great Britain.

Ocean thermal energy converter (OTEC)

In the tropics the Sun heats the surface water to a temperature of about 26°C. Water at a depth of 600 m is much cooler, about 8°C.

This temperature difference can be used to boil and cool ammonia.

OTECs can only work in warm tropical water and they may well affect the environment. Pilot schemes are in operation in Japan and the USA.

2 Gas turns a turbine connected to a generator, producing electricity. A small amount of electricity is used to drive the pumps, the rest will be taken away by cable, or used to produce hydrogen, by electrolysis from sea water (see page 200)

I Evaporator – the hot water heats liquid ammonia and evaporates it into a gas

3 Condenser – the cold water cools the ammonia gas and turns it back to a liquid

warm water pump

4 pump forces the liquid ammonia from the condenser to the evaporator

cold water pump

hot water inlet (26°C)

hot water output (25°C)

cold water outlet (8°C)

cold water inlet (7°C)

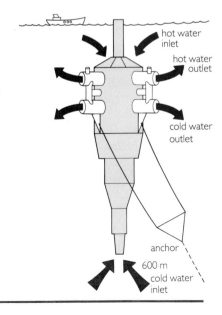

hot water inlet

hot water outlet

cold water outlet

anchor

600 m cold water inlet

Wind power

Wind is a form of solar energy. More heat from the Sun reaches the equator than the poles. This is because the Sun's rays hit the Earth directly at the equator but hit the poles at an angle, so the heat is spread out over a greater area. Hot air rises at the equator and drifts towards the poles, forming the winds (see page 18).

Energy from the wind has been used for many years, but it is only recently that large-scale windmills have been designed to produce electricity. This type of windmill is called an *aerogenerator*. The largest aerogenerator in the world is the 2 MW aerogenerator in North Carolina, USA. This has blades that are 60 m across. In the UK the CEGB has built a small aerogenerator in mid-Wales. This has blades that are 24 m across. This aerogenerator turns whenever the wind speed is greater than 6 knots, and produces 200 kW of electricity with a wind speed of 25 knots. This is enough to supply electricity to a small village. Large-scale aerogenerators are extremely large

and must be spread out at intervals of about 1 km. The windiest parts of the UK are also usually the most beautiful parts and many people would object to large numbers of aerogenerators being built there.

It has been suggested that it would be possible to site clusters of windmills in shallow areas off our coast. This has two advantages: there would be less damage to the environment and wind speeds at sea are higher than on land. It seems likely that the UK could obtain about 2% of its electricity needs from such a scheme. Once the windmills had been installed there would be no fuel costs and no pollution. However, it seems more likely that the future of aerogenerators in the UK is for small schemes supplying isolated communities.

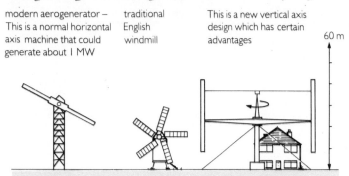

modern aerogenerator – This is a normal horizontal axis machine that could generate about 1 MW

traditional English windmill

This is a new vertical axis design which has certain advantages

60 m

Wave power

Waves are caused by winds blowing over the surface of large areas of water. They are a concentrated form of energy and there is a great deal of research into ways of using this energy. The north west of Scotland is one of the world's best sites for harnessing wave power. There are two basic designs of wave power machines. The most famous design is the bobbing duck. Waves make the front of the machine bob up and down while a balancing float remains still. This movement is used to produce electricity which is sent ashore along an underwater cable, or is used to release hydrogen from water. Other devices have fewer moving parts and the waves are used to force air through turbines, producing electricity.

It has been estimated that it might be possible for Britain to get over 120 000 MW of electricity from the seas around our shores. However, there are many problems to overcome and wave power is unlikely to replace our present energy sources for a long time to come. One interesting proposal is to build huge floating factories that would use the energy from waves to extract important minerals, such as uranium, from seawater.

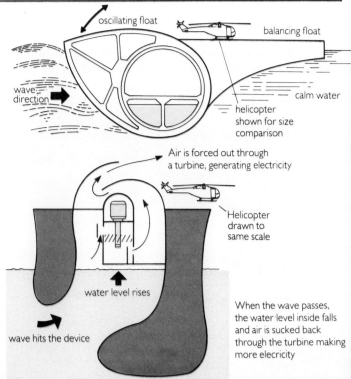

oscillating float

balancing float

wave direction

calm water

helicopter shown for size comparison

Air is forced out through a turbine, generating electricity

Helicopter drawn to same scale

water level rises

wave hits the device

When the wave passes, the water level inside falls and air is sucked back through the turbine making more elecricity

Tidal power

The Moon and Sun cause huge movements of water in the Earth's oceans – these movements are called tides (see page 11). If these tides are used to fill reservoirs, the trapped water can be used to drive turbines and produce electricity.

Two small tidal power stations are in operation, one in Murmansk, in the USSR and one at La Rance in Northern France. The effect of tides is increased if the water is funnelled into a narrow estuary. One of the best tidal power station sites in the world is in Britain – the Severn estuary.

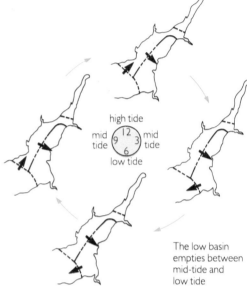

The high basin fills between mid-tide and high tide

high tide
mid tide — mid tide
low tide

The low basin empties between mid-tide and low tide

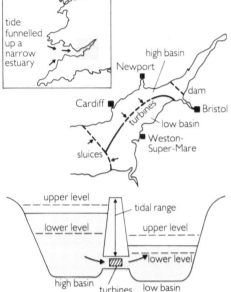

La Rance is a one-basin scheme. A two-basin scheme in the Severn estuary would allow electricity to be generated 24 hours a day.

There is always a difference in the water levels between the two basins, so the turbines keep operating. A tidal power station in the Severn estuary would take 20 years to build and would be very expensive. However, it would produce at least 10% of our electricity, with no fuel costs. There are problems – it would be a vast engineering project, it would silt up slowly and there would be a severe environmental impact.

Geothermal power

Geothermal power stations make use of the heat of the Earth. In some parts of the world there is a great deal of volcanic action and hot water and steam reaches the surface. Italy, New Zealand and the USA have all built geothermal power stations that use this steam to turn turbines and generate electricity. There are no such areas in the UK. However, if holes are drilled down several kilometres hot rocks are found. It has been suggested that it might be possible to send cold water down tubes to these hot rocks where it would be turned to steam. This would then return to the surface and could be used to generate electricity. It is likely that this method will be of more use in the UK for providing hot water for district heating because the cost of drilling is high and the amount of steam produced is low.

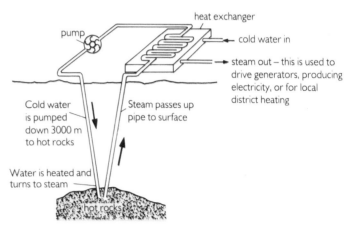

heat exchanger
pump
cold water in
steam out – this is used to drive generators, producing electricity, or for local district heating
Cold water is pumped down 3000 m to hot rocks
Steam passes up pipe to surface
Water is heated and turns to steam
hot rocks

10 BIOMASS

In a single week the Earth receives solar energy that is equivalent to all the known reserves of coal, oil and gas. Only a minute fraction of this solar energy (0·03%) is trapped by plants and yet every year the total amount used by plants is ten times the world's consumption of energy.

Plants fix this solar energy by a process called *photosynthesis*. The plant takes in water and carbon dioxide and uses light energy to convert this into chemical energy. The chemical energy is then used to keep the plant alive and allow it to grow.

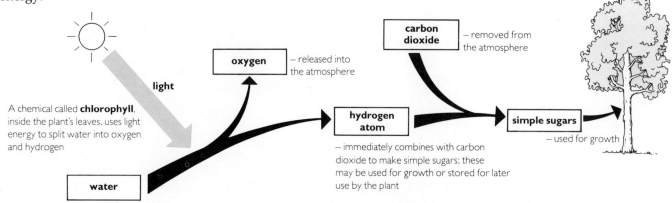

light

oxygen — released into the atmosphere

carbon dioxide — removed from the atmosphere

A chemical called **chlorophyll**, inside the plant's leaves, uses light energy to split water into oxygen and hydrogen

water

hydrogen atom

— immediately combines with carbon dioxide to make simple sugars; these may be used for growth or stored for later use by the plant

simple sugars — used for growth

The plants and their trapped chemical energy may be eaten. In this way the energy is passed on to animals. The term biomass is used to refer to anything organic that depends on the activity of plants and photosynthesis. It includes all plants, animals, their waste products, our food, our waste and of course, us!

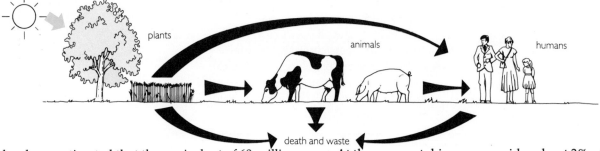

plants

animals

humans

death and waste

It has been estimated that the equivalent of 60 million tonnes of coal are thrown away each year in the form of biological waste. Most of this comes from farms, forests and industry. We could use this waste as a source of energy.

At the moment, biomass provides about 3% of the world's energy needs, mainly through burning firewood. It does not contribute as much as coal, oil, gas or nuclear fuel to our energy sources – but it is renewable. There are many ways of increasing our use of biomass as a source of energy.

Bioreactors

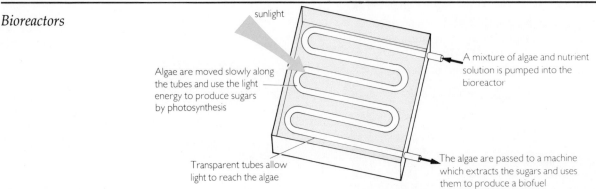

sunlight

Algae are moved slowly along the tubes and use the light energy to produce sugars by photosynthesis

A mixture of algae and nutrient solution is pumped into the bioreactor

Transparent tubes allow light to reach the algae

The algae are passed to a machine which extracts the sugars and uses them to produce a biofuel

These would use algae, the simplest type of plant, to trap the energy of the Sun.

Scientists are trying to copy one of the stages of photosynthesis by using light energy to split the water molecule to produce oxygen and hydrogen. The hydrogen would then be used as a useful energy source – it has been called 'the fuel of the future'.

Burning refuse

In Britain we throw away about 20 million tonnes of household rubbish every year. Much of this is biomass and is about the same, in energy terms, as 6 million tonnes of coal. Amsterdam, Frankfurt and Paris all have power stations that burn household rubbish and produce electricity. The Paris power station produces 10% of the city's electricity.

Biogas

This is gas that has been produced from waste biomass. It is usually a mixture of methane and carbon dioxide. Methane is the main part of *natural gas*. The device for producing the gas from waste is called a *digester*. In 1978 the Chinese had over 7 million digesters producing methane which was used as a fuel.

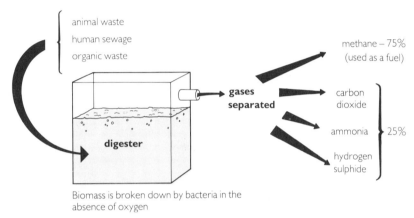

animal waste
human sewage
organic waste

digester

gases separated

methane – 75% (used as a fuel)

carbon dioxide

ammonia ⟩ 25%

hydrogen sulphide

Biomass is broken down by bacteria in the absence of oxygen

Biofuels

Many plants, such as maize, cassava and sugar cane are rich in sugars. It is possible to refine these plants and produce alcohol. This is a valuable concentrated source of energy. Brazil has been trying to reduce its oil imports by growing these plants and using the alcohol as a petrol substitute. By the year 2000 Brazil hopes to be growing all its fuel.

Some plants such as the gopher plant grow well in desert regions. These plants are often rich in hydrocarbons. It would be possible to farm these unproductive areas with such plants, which could be processed.

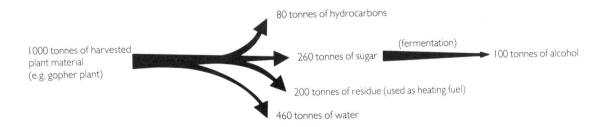

1000 tonnes of harvested plant material (e.g. gopher plant)

80 tonnes of hydrocarbons

260 tonnes of sugar

(fermentation)

100 tonnes of alcohol

200 tonnes of residue (used as heating fuel)

460 tonnes of water

It is also possible to use fast-growing trees such as willow and poplar. These could be harvested every year to provide wood which would be used as a fuel. However, as with all methods of using solar energy large areas of land would be needed. This land would be in competition with farms growing crops for food. If non-productive land could be used, biomass sources could provide a significant amount of the world's energy needs. An estimate suggests that in the next 20 years it could provide 10% of Europe's energy demand.

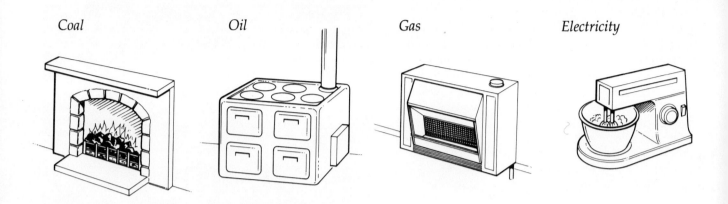

Coal   Oil   Gas   Electricity

These are the four major fuels used in our homes, although in some parts of the UK wood and peat are commonly used.

Domestic uses of energy

	Space heating and hot water	Cooking	Domestic appliances
Electricity	Storage heaters Immersion heaters Fan heaters	Electric cookers Food mixers Microwave ovens	Washing machines Televisions Radios Irons Fridges
Gas	Gas fires Gas boilers	Gas cookers	Some fridges
Solid fuel	Open fires Boilers	AGA/Rayburn types of cooker	—
Oil	Oil burning boilers	AGA/Rayburn types of cooker	—

Gas

Natural gas has become one of the most popular domestic fuels. It is a clean fuel which burns efficiently and does not pollute the air. Most of the natural gas we use comes from large gas fields under the North Sea. It is piped ashore and distributed throughout the country. The gas is almost pure methane. When this burns it produces heat and gives off carbon dioxide and water vapour.

The amount of gas used in the home is measured by a gas meter. When a gas fire or oven is turned on, gas is drawn in through the gas meter. As it passes through the meter a series of dials are turned and show how much gas has been used.

Oil

We only use oil for central heating and supplying hot water. It was once a cheap fuel, but the oil crisis of the early 1970s caused the price to increase. Central heating oil comes from the light gas oil fraction of crude oil. It is supplied to the domestic user by tankers and is stored in large tanks before being used.

Solid fuel

The use of coal as a source of heat caused a great deal of air pollution in urban areas. In 1956 the Clean Air Act was passed by parliament. This introduced *smoke control zones*, where only smokeless fuels could be burnt. Modern solid fuels can be grouped into two main classes: natural and manufactured fuels.

Natural fuels These fuels are mined then washed.		Manufactured fuels These are coals which have been specially treated. Most are smokeless fuels that can be used in smoke control zones.	
Housecoal – lights easily and burns well. It cannot be used in smoke control zones.	**Anthracite** – a dense type of coal which is naturally smokeless and burns slowly.	**Sunbrite** – the commonest manufactured fuel. It burns slowly and does not produce smoke.	**Coalite** – a manufactured coal that is baked in ovens to make it smokeless.

Central heating

More and more homes have central heating installed as their major form of space and water heating. Any of the fuels mentioned on these pages can be used to heat the water in the boiler.

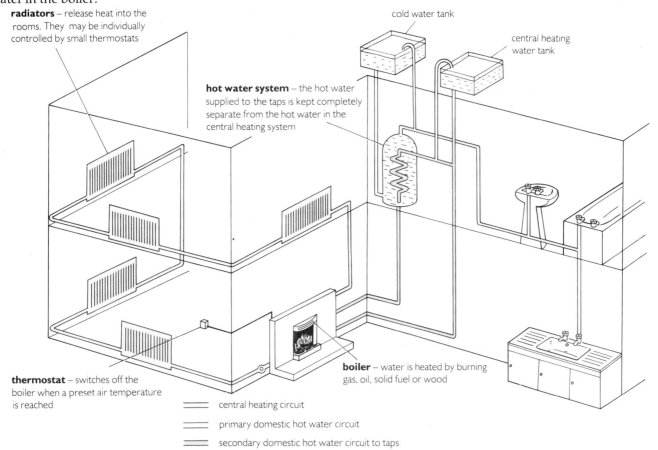

radiators – release heat into the rooms. They may be individually controlled by small thermostats

cold water tank

central heating water tank

hot water system – the hot water supplied to the taps is kept completely separate from the hot water in the central heating system

boiler – water is heated by burning gas, oil, solid fuel or wood

thermostat – switches off the boiler when a preset air temperature is reached

central heating circuit

primary domestic hot water circuit

secondary domestic hot water circuit to taps

12 ENERGY IN THE HOME

Electricity is the most convenient and versatile form of energy we use in our homes.

mains fuse – cuts off the supply if too much electricity is being used in the home. It cannot be replaced by the householder

electricity meter – records the amount of electricity used in the home. The units used are kilowatt hours (kWh)

consumer unit – has a mains switch which can be used to cut off all electricity in the house. It also contains circuit breakers or fuses which protect different electrical circuits in the house.

wires to the house circuits

Electricity enters the home through a thick mains service cable. In the UK, this supply is at 240 volts

earth wire – connected to a water pipe or a metal ground spike, which increases the safety of the electricity circuits

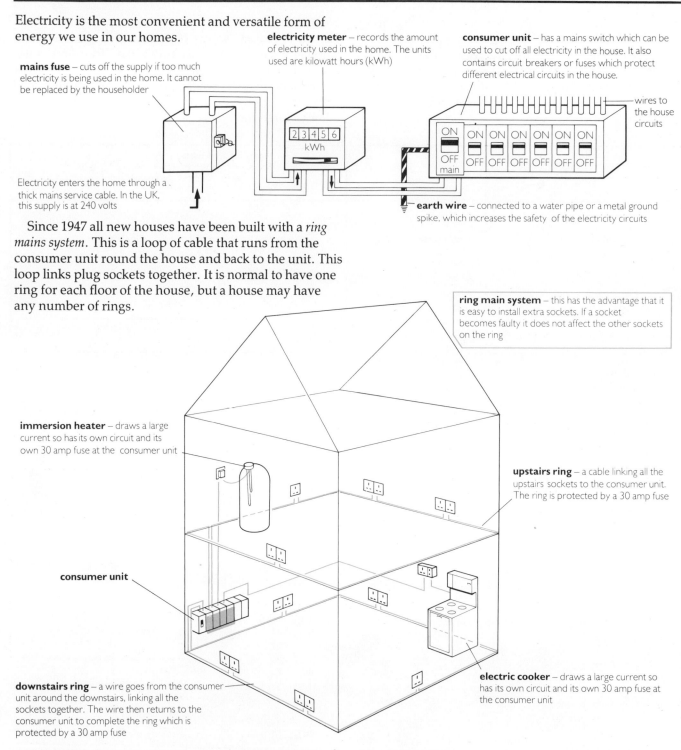

Since 1947 all new houses have been built with a *ring mains system*. This is a loop of cable that runs from the consumer unit round the house and back to the unit. This loop links plug sockets together. It is normal to have one ring for each floor of the house, but a house may have any number of rings.

ring main system – this has the advantage that it is easy to install extra sockets. If a socket becomes faulty it does not affect the other sockets on the ring

immersion heater – draws a large current so has its own circuit and its own 30 amp fuse at the consumer unit

upstairs ring – a cable linking all the upstairs sockets to the consumer unit. The ring is protected by a 30 amp fuse

consumer unit

downstairs ring – a wire goes from the consumer unit around the downstairs, linking all the sockets together. The wire then returns to the consumer unit to complete the ring which is protected by a 30 amp fuse

electric cooker – draws a large current so has its own circuit and its own 30 amp fuse at the consumer unit

Each ring main has a 30 amp fuse on the consumer unit. This fuse will melt and break if the total current being used on that ring is greater than 30 amps. This is called *overloading* the circuit. It is possible to work out if you are likely to overload a ring. Each electrical appliance is marked with a power rating or wattage. In Britain the voltage is 240 volts.

The current that an appliance will use is calculated:

$$\text{current} = \frac{\text{wattage}}{\text{voltage}}$$

A 3 kW electric fire will use $\dfrac{3000}{240} = 12 \cdot 5$ amps

If you tried to plug in three of these fires on one ring you would need 37·5 amps, and this would blow the fuse for this circuit in the consumer unit.

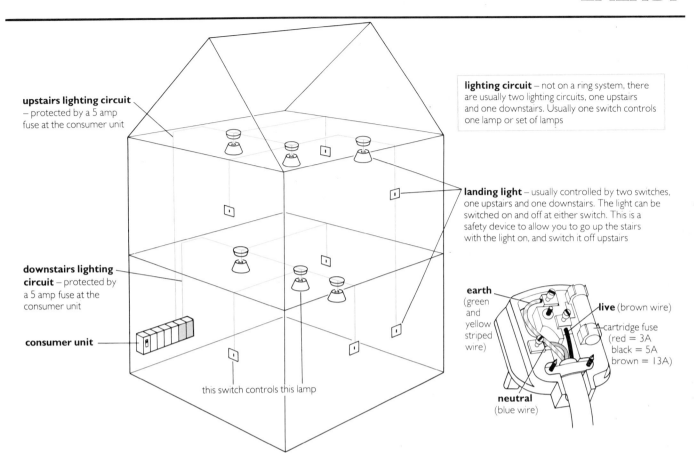

upstairs lighting circuit – protected by a 5 amp fuse at the consumer unit

downstairs lighting circuit – protected by a 5 amp fuse at the consumer unit

consumer unit

this switch controls this lamp

lighting circuit – not on a ring system, there are usually two lighting circuits, one upstairs and one downstairs. Usually one switch controls one lamp or set of lamps

landing light – usually controlled by two switches, one upstairs and one downstairs. The light can be switched on and off at either switch. This is a safety device to allow you to go up the stairs with the light on, and switch it off upstairs

earth (green and yellow striped wire)

live (brown wire)

cartridge fuse (red = 3A, black = 5A, brown = 13A)

neutral (blue wire)

Plugs

Houses that are fitted with a ring main have 13 amp 'square' pin plugs. These contain fuses, the value of the fuse depending on the electrical appliance.

The purpose of the earth wire is to make sure that if a fault occurs the appliance does not become live, and give you an electric shock. The current will flow to the earth and the fuse in the plug will melt and break. Some modern electrical appliances are supplied with a cable that does not have an earth wire. These appliances are said to be *double insulated* because they have special insulation.

Plug fuses	Load (wattage)	Typical appliances
3 amp	up to 700 watts	TV, stereo, radio lamps, mixers, hair driers
5 amp	700–1400 watts	refrigerator, iron, small electric fires
13 amp	1400–3000 watts	large electric fires, electric kettles

Fuses

There are two types of fuses – the rewireable fuse which is often found in the consumer unit, and the cartridge fuse which is used in 13 amp plugs, and some consumer units.

cartridge fuse

metal contact

colour coded to indicate rating of fuse

fuse wire

brass connector

porcelain

insulator

A fuse is a deliberate weak spot in an electrical circuit. It is designed to fail (blow) if a circuit is overloaded.

It is important to use the correct fuse. For example, a stereo system rated at 600 watts will use

$$\frac{600 \text{ watts}}{240 \text{ volts}} = 2.5 \text{ amps}.$$

If a fault occurs, resulting in a higher current, a 3 amp fuse would blow, protecting the equipment from damage. If a 3 amp fuse was fitted it might not blow and the ampliance could be damaged.

Most modern consumer units now use *circuit breakers* instead of fuses. These automatically break a circuit if it is overloaded. They are more convenient to use.

13 CONSERVATION IN THE HOME

Domestic houses use up about 30% of all the energy used in the UK. Most of this energy is used to heat water and the house. Unfortunately a large amount of it is lost by conduction, convection and radiation. In a house with no insulation the heat can escape in many ways. A large amount of energy is being lost that could be usefully used.

25% can escape through the roof

10% can escape through the windows

35% can escape through the walls

15% can escape as draughts through various gaps

15% can escape through the floor

On a cold winter's day the average uninsulated house can lose up to 35 kW of heat every hour. This is the equivalent of twelve 3 kW fan heaters. Energy is not cheap and looking for ways of using less energy is as important as finding new sources of energy.

Insulation

Draught-proofing
This is one of the cheapest ways of reducing heat loss and is very cost-effective. Draught excluders fill in small gaps, usually between doors and windows and their frames. The cheapest form is simply a layer of foam with an adhesive backing.

Double glazing
Some heat is lost through windows. A double-glazed window has two panes of glass and a layer of air in between. Air is a good insulator that reduces the heat lost by conduction through the glass. A vacuum is an even better insulator and some expensive double-glazed windows have a vacuum in between the glass. Double glazing will also reduce condensation and noise. In some countries windows of new houses must be triple glazed.

Wall insulation
Modern houses are built using a double layer of bricks with a cavity in between them. The cavity reduces heat loss by conduction but still allows some heat to leave the house. It is possible to fill the cavity with foam or glass fibre which further reduces convection and conduction. Care must be taken not to use a material that allows water to rise up, causing damp.

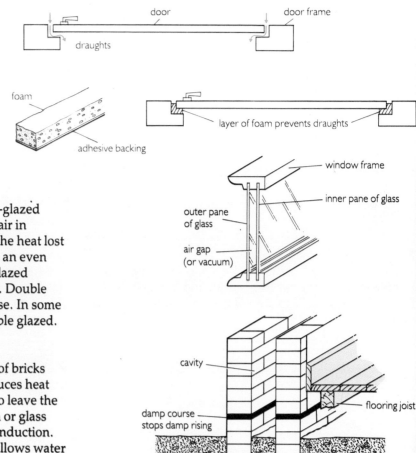

door

door frame

draughts

foam

adhesive backing

layer of foam prevents draughts

window frame

inner pane of glass

outer pane of glass

air gap (or vacuum)

cavity

flooring joist

damp course stops damp rising

Roof insulation

Heat from the house rises and eventually reaches the roof space. A layer of glass fibre between the ceiling joists dramatically reduces the amount of heat lost in this way. The glass fibre traps a layer of air – a poor conductor of heat. The thicker the layer of glass fibre, the more heat is saved.

Lagging

Heat can be lost very easily from the hot water tank and hot water pipes. We can reduce the heat loss from these if we insulate them – this is called lagging. Cold water tanks are also lagged – to keep them warm in winter and prevent the water from freezing. When a roof is insulated it is important *not* to insulate the space underneath the cold water tank. Heat rising through this space warms the water in the cold tank and also helps to stop it freezing.

When you decide to insulate a house it is important to choose the best method for that house. This can be done by calculating the *pay-back time* for each method. The pay-back time is the time taken to pay for the insulation from the savings achieved. For example, if it costs £20 to buy draught-proofing for a house, and you save £40 a year on your heating bill, then the pay-back time is $\frac{20}{40}$ years, or 6 months. As fuel costs increase, the pay-back times will decrease because the amount of money saved each year will increase.

Method of insulation	Reduction in heat loss	Pay-back time
Roof insulation	80%	1 year
Cavity wall insulation	60–70%	3 years
Double glazing	50%	30-40 years
Draught-proofing	50–60%	6 months

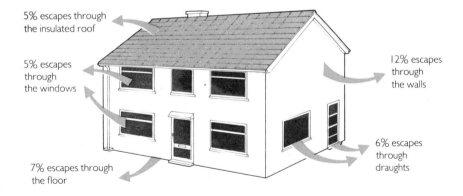

5% escapes through the insulated roof

5% escapes through the windows

7% escapes through the floor

12% escapes through the walls

6% escapes through draughts

Draught-proofing and roof-insulation are the first methods to use in a house along with lagging the hot-water system. Double glazing should only be considered if all the other forms of insulation have been done, or if the windows need replacing because they are rotten. This is the same house as on the opposite page but it is well insulated. This house saves 65% of the heat that is lost by the uninsulated house.

A completely sealed house will be very well insulated but have no way of regularly changing the air. It will get very stuffy and condensation or dampness problems are likely.

14 STORING ENERGY

Electricity is one of the most convenient forms of energy that we use. However, the demand for electricity varies throughout the day – we use a lot of electricity in the morning and early evening and very little after midnight. This causes problems for the CEGB. Modern power stations, whether they are coal or nuclear powered, must operate at peak capacity, 24 hours a day, if they are to be as efficient as possible. These power stations cannot be started up quickly – some take up to 14 days to reach peak output after being switched on. Alternative power stations have a variable output – aerogenerators cannot produce electricity when the wind isn't blowing. This means that the CEGB must have some means of storing electricity. Unfortunately it cannot be stored directly, but must be converted into a form that can be stored and then reconverted to electricity when the demand is high.

Pumped storage

This is the most common method of storing electricity from the national grid. It is a modified hydro-electric power scheme. Water is pumped between two reservoirs situated at different heights. During the night, when there is little demand for electricity, water is pumped to the top reservoir. During the day, at times of high demand, the water is allowed to return to the lower reservoir, turning turbines and generating electricity as it does so. The largest pumped storage scheme in Europe is at Dinorwic, in North Wales. There are other similar schemes in Scotland.

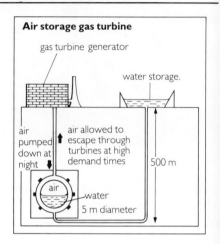

Air storage gas turbine

gas turbine generator

water storage.

air pumped down at night

air allowed to escape through turbines at high demand times

500 m

air

water

5 m diameter

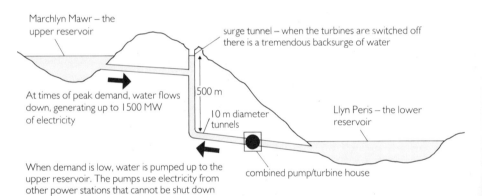

Marchlyn Mawr – the upper reservoir

surge tunnel – when the turbines are switched off there is a tremendous backsurge of water

At times of peak demand, water flows down, generating up to 1500 MW of electricity

500 m

10 m diameter tunnels

Llyn Peris – the lower reservoir

When demand is low, water is pumped up to the upper reservoir. The pumps use electricity from other power stations that cannot be shut down

combined pump/turbine house

UPPER RESERVOIR

DINORWIC QUARRY

LOWER RESERVOIR

LLANBERIS

Hydrogen storage

Electricity can be used to produce hydrogen from water. When an electrical current is passed through water, the gases hydrogen and oxygen are released by a process called *electrolysis*.

The hydrogen gas can be used as a fuel in gas or liquid form. Hydrogen is easily stored and when it is burned in air it produces water and so does not cause pollution. Hydrogen is already being used in experimental cars and lorries as a replacement for petrol. The CEGB is examining this idea very closely because it would be possible to use the electricity from wave machines, OTECs or aerogenerators to produce hydrogen from sea water. This would be easier to collect and transport by ship rather than sending electricity ashore through underwater cables.

Fuel cells

These reverse electrolysis. The chemical energy in hydrogen and oxygen can be directly converted to electrical energy in a fuel cell.

More advanced fuel cells can use alcohol or natural gas as a source of hydrogen, and air as the source of oxygen.

Fuel cells are very efficient, with up to 90% of the energy in the fuel being converted to electricity. The only by-products of the energy conversion are heat and warm water, so there is no pollution.

Fuel cells are capable of producing large amounts of power. Unfortunately at present they are expensive and quite bulky. A large fuel cell power station is being built in New York. It will take oxygen from the air and use various types of fuel as its source of hydrogen. The electricity produced will be fed into the city's grid, and the waste heat will be used to pre-heat the fuel.

Small fuel cells are used in the United States Space shuttle and the Soviet space-laboratory.

Batteries

These store chemical energy which can be released as electrical energy when the battery is used.

Simple batteries The best example is a torch battery. The electrolyte attacks the zinc and the chemical energy is converted to electrical energy. Electrons leave the zinc and pass round the circuit.

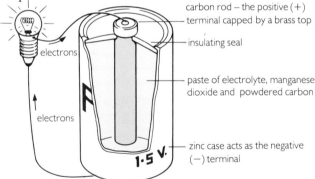

carbon rod – the positive (+) terminal capped by a brass top

insulating seal

paste of electrolyte, manganese dioxide and powdered carbon

zinc case acts as the negative (−) terminal

1·5 V.

Some batteries have different terminals and electrolytes. These are called long-life batteries because they last longer. Simple batteries cannot be recharged after they have been used.

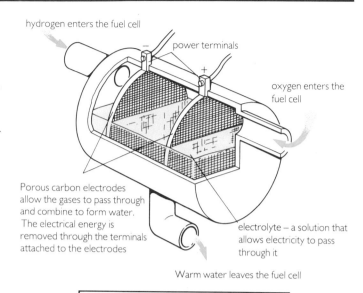

hydrogen enters the fuel cell

power terminals

oxygen enters the fuel cell

Porous carbon electrodes allow the gases to pass through and combine to form water. The electrical energy is removed through the terminals attached to the electrodes

electrolyte – a solution that allows electricity to pass through it

Warm water leaves the fuel cell

hydrogen + oxygen = water + electrical energy

Rechargeable batteries The best example is the car battery. These are also called *accumulators*. The chemical reactions can be reversed and electrical energy can be used to recharge them.

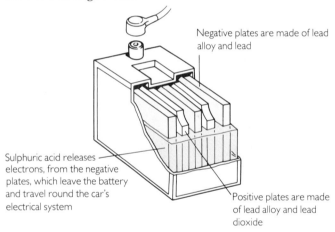

Negative plates are made of lead alloy and lead

Sulphuric acid releases electrons, from the negative plates, which leave the battery and travel round the car's electrical system

Positive plates are made of lead alloy and lead dioxide

When all the chemical energy has been released the battery is said to be flat and it must then be recharged by using electricity to reverse the chemical reactions.

Small rechargeable batteries have been developed for portable electrical machines. These have a negative plate made of nickel and a positive plate made of cadmium. The plates are surrounded by an electrolyte of potassium hydroxide. These are often called *nickel–cadmium* (Nicad) batteries.

Electric cars

It is often suggested that electric cars could eventually replace petrol cars. This depends entirely on the development of new advanced types of batteries. Normal lead–acid batteries do not store enough energy, are too heavy and restrict the top speed and range of the car.

15 POLLUTION

The production of power often produces pollutants.

Fossil fuels

Acid rain

Fossil fuels release the gases sulphur dioxide and nitrogen dioxide when they are burnt. These gases rise up chimneys and escape into the atmosphere where they dissolve in water to form dilute sulphuric and nitric acids. These acids form *acid rain*.

Fish are dying in the lakes of North America, Scandinavia and Scotland. Trees in Northern and Central Europe are dying. Statues in European cities are corroding. All these effects are caused by acid rain. Normal rain has a pH of about 5·6, while acid rain has a pH or 4·0 or less. The most acid rain that has fallen had a pH of 2·4 – much more acidic than vinegar!

The main effect of acid rain on soil is to release metal ions such as magnesium, calcium and aluminium from the soil. Magnesium and calcium ions are washed away and cannot be used by the trees for normal growth. The released aluminium ions are toxic and damage plant roots, allowing germs to enter and attack the plant. Aluminium ions get carried down to lakes where they affect the gills of fish and kill them.

Building high chimneys, which release the gases up to 200 m into the air reduces the effects locally, but exports the pollution to other areas. The prevailing winds of Europe come from the south west and carry most of the acids towards Scandinavia, in particular to Sweden and southern Norway.

The source of acid rain falling on Scandinavia

26% from unknown sources

There are ways of avoiding acid rain, but these are all expensive.

Low sulphur fuels   Oil refineries can produce oil that is low in sulphur, and most coals can be cleaned before they are burnt. Unfortunately, this is expensive and the soft coals like lignite cannot be cleaned.

Adding limestone   If calcium carbonate is added to the fossil fuel as it is being burnt, the amounts of acid gases released can be cut by 80%.

Scrubbing   If the waste gases from the burnt fuel are passed through an alkaline solution, 95% of the acid gases can be removed.

The problem of acid rain is a political and economic one. The technology exists to solve it.

Carbon dioxide (CO₂)

This is another gas that is released when fossil fuels are burnt. As we burn more and more coal, oil and gas we release more and more CO_2 into the atmosphere. Many scientists are worried that this will cause what they call a *greenhouse effect*. The carbon dioxide allows the incoming solar energy to pass through the atmosphere, but slows down the escape of heat from the Earth's surface. It is possible that increased levels of carbon dioxide in the atmosphere could cause an increase in the average temperature of the Earth. This could have severe effects, possibly causing the north and south ice caps to melt and, therefore, raising the levels of the oceans. However, not everyone agrees that this is a problem.

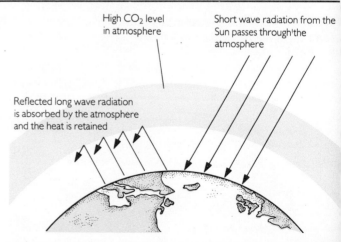

High CO_2 level in atmosphere

Short wave radiation from the Sun passes through the atmosphere

Reflected long wave radiation is absorbed by the atmosphere and the heat is retained

Nuclear fuel

Nuclear reactors also produce waste, most of which is radioactive. During the day-to-day running of a nuclear reactor a large amount of radioactivity is produced, some of which is released from the power station as low-level waste. This slightly radioactive waste includes –

waste gases: radioactive gases such as argon, krypton-85 and iodine-129 are released in small amounts;

waste liquids: radioactive liquids from cooling ponds and safety showers are diluted and released into rivers, lakes or the sea;

waste solids: these include contaminated clothing and cleaning materials. They are buried and covered with 1 m of topsoil.

Uranium fuel is used in reactors for several years, but eventually has to be replaced. This used fuel contains about 97% uranium, 1% plutonium and 2–3% fission products (see page 196). The uranium and plutonium is valuable and can be reused so the spent fuel is *reprocessed*. At the reprocessing plant the outer casing of the fuel rods is removed and the used fuel is dissolved in concentrated nitric acid. The radioactive casings are called *medium-level waste*. Most of this is stored in cooling ponds at the reprocessing works at Sellafield (Windscale), but some is cased in concrete and dumped at sea. The dissolved fuel is treated to remove the uranium and plutonium which is used in other reactors. The remaining fission products are extremely radioactive and are called *high-level wastes*. Some of these high-level wastes have very long half-lives (see page 156).

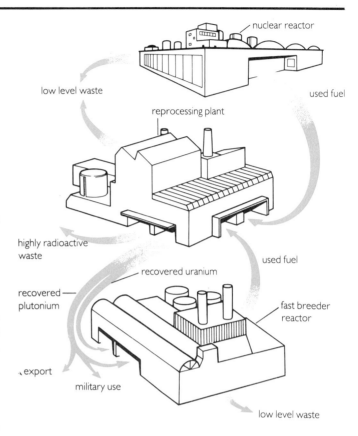

Waste	Half-life (years)
Strontium -90	29
Caesium -137	30
Americium -241	458
Plutonium -239	24 000
Neptunium -237	2 200 000
Iodine -129	17 000 000

The medium-level wastes that are stored at Sellafield reprocessing plant will eventually be removed to a special dump. The waste will be sealed in concrete inside corrosion-resistant drums and stored in concrete-lined tunnels in suitable rocks.

High-level waste is highly radioactive and extremely dangerous. It is hoped that this liquid waste will be turned into an artificial glass or rock which can be stored in special dumps similar to those proposed for medium-level wastes.

Many people are concerned about the release and storage of all these radioactive wastes. The reprocessing plant at Sellafield releases about half a million litres of radioactive cooling water into the Irish Sea every year, with the result that it has been called the most radioactive sea in the world. The UK was responsible for 90% of all

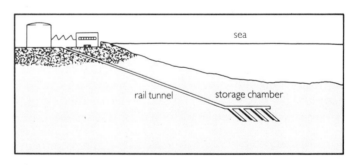

the radioactive waste that was dumped at sea in 1983, and it is likely that worldwide concern over this will eventually ban this sort of dumping.

Scientists are also concerned about the storage of high-level wastes containing radioactive chemicals with very long half-lives.

Heat

All power stations, whether they are fossil fuel, or nuclear powered, need huge amounts of cooling water. This is removed from rivers, lakes or the sea, and warm water is returned in its place. This release of heat has been called thermal pollution. It reduces the amount of oxygen in the water, and may have severe effects on the animals and plants living in the immediate area. This heat could be used for heating local houses and offices, (see page 214).

16 FUTURE DEVELOPMENTS

Fluidised bed boilers

It is possible to reduce the heat tax (see page 187) of a coal power station from 70% to 50% by using a fluidised bed boiler. This works by putting crushed coal straight into a churning red-hot bed of sand. The sand is kept moving by jets of air from beneath. The coal burns very efficiently in this hot sand. Water-pipes pass through the bed and the heat changes the water to steam. The cold water in the pipes is pre-heated in the top part of the boiler by the hot waste gases; this increases the efficiency of the station.

Pollution can be reduced in this type of power station if crushed limestone is mixed in with the sand and coal. The limestone traps 95% of the sulphur dioxide produced when coal burns, preventing it from entering the atmosphere.

Fluidised bed boilers can be used to burn low-grade coal, domestic and industrial waste.

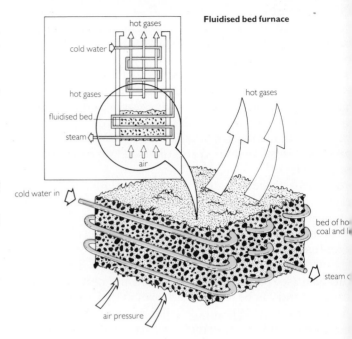

Fluidised bed furnace

Combined heat and power stations (CHP)

Most of the heat produced by a power station is lost to the atmosphere, or to rivers, lakes or the sea. In a CHP station the hot water produced is supplied to local houses and offices through insulated pipes. It is then connected to central heating systems and used for space heating or heating water. Only 15% of the energy of the fuel that is used at the CHP is lost as heat to the air.

These CHP stations are used in over 25 countries and Denmark supplies over 50% of its heating need from this type of station. A CHP station is operated by the Midlands Electricity Board in Hereford.

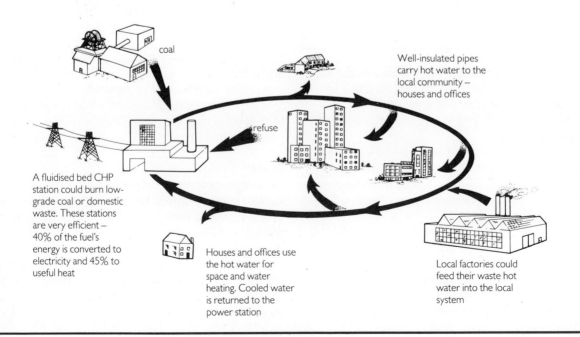

Well-insulated pipes carry hot water to the local community – houses and offices

A fluidised bed CHP station could burn low-grade coal or domestic waste. These stations are very efficient – 40% of the fuel's energy is converted to electricity and 45% to useful heat

Houses and offices use the hot water for space and water heating. Cooled water is returned to the power station

Local factories could feed their waste hot water into the local system

Magnetohydrodynamic (MHD) generators

In 1832 Michael Faraday connected two copper wires to a sensitive meter, then lowered them into the River Thames. He found a weak electrical current. As the river flowed through the Earth's magnetic field it was generating a weak electrical current. This method of generating electricity is being used in Moscow and the USA.

Coal is burnt at a very high temperature and the hot gases produced are blown at supersonic speeds through a tunnel. The sides of the tunnel are made up of very powerful magnets, Cooled electrodes tap the direct current from the gas. The gases leaving the MHD generator are still hot enough to turn water to steam which can generate even more electricity. MHD generators are about 55% efficient. More than half the energy in the fuel is converted to electricity.

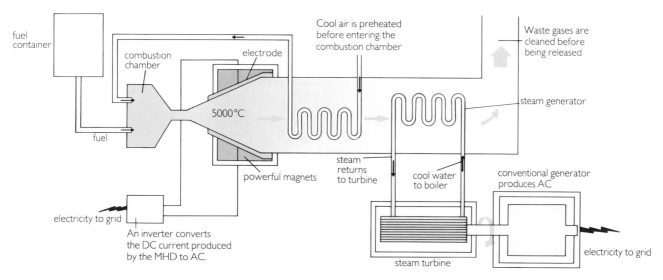

Heat pumps

Energy can be used to cool things down. In a refrigerator energy is used to pump a liquid with a low boiling point, e.g. freon or ammonia, through a series of pipes.

A similar method can be used to heat a building by removing heat from outside and transferring it inside. A machine that can do this is called a *heat pump*.

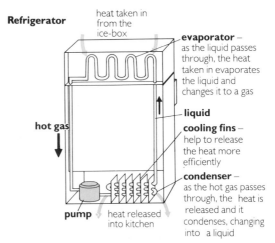

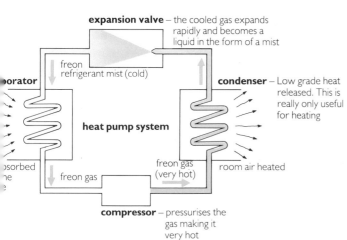

Heat pumps can absorb heat from water, from the ground or from the air, and they will do this even if the temperature outside is as low as −7°C. The only energy they need is electricity to drive the compressor, which converts the gas into a liquid that takes in heat, and pumps it round the system. They are extremely efficient and can provide about three times as much heat as an electric fire using the same amount of current.

In hot summers a heat pump can be used in reverse to cool the air in the house. An OTEC (see page 199) is simply an extremely large heat pump that generates electricity.

MACHINES

THE MULTI-MOVEMENT TABBY SILENCER

This apparatus can be operated from the bedroom window and is guaranteed to reach any part of the back yard

WHAT IS A MACHINE?

Many mechanical machines are collections of parts that can transmit or change forces in order to do work.

Machines help us to use forces more easily. They come in all shapes and sizes and can be very simple or quite complicated.

> **A MACHINE IS ANY DEVICE THAT CAN TRANSMIT OR CONVERT ENERGY.**

Levers

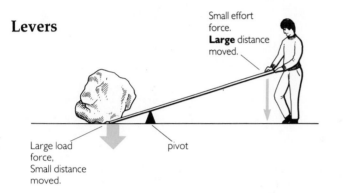

Small effort force. **Large** distance moved.

Large load force, Small distance moved.

pivot

The muscles and bones of our bodies are a lever system. When our arm picks up a heavy object the muscles produce a larger *effort force* than the object's *load force*. The object will move much further than the muscle because the muscle and bone system magnifies the distance.

A pair of scissors magnifies a small effort force and produces a large load force. The effort force moves through a larger distance than the load force.

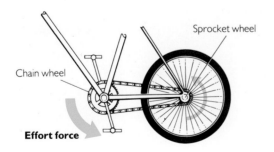

Chain wheel

Sprocket wheel

Effort force

Levers are very simple machines.

When a crowbar is used to move heavy objects a small *effort force* can move a large *load force*. This is because the man is producing the effort force a longer distance from the pivot. The crowbar *magnifies* the force.

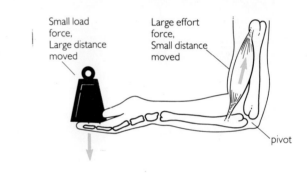

Small load force, Large distance moved

Large effort force, Small distance moved

pivot

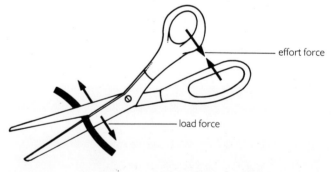

effort force

load force

Gears

Gears are a kind of continuous lever that can either increase a force or a distance. The chain wheel and rear sprocket of a bicycle are joined by a chain and they all act as one gear system. The larger chain wheel moves slowly but with more force than the smaller rear sprocket wheel. The rear wheel of the bike is attached to the sprocket wheel so this also moves faster but with less force than the chain wheel. The bicycle is a distance magnifying machine.

Pulleys

These are very useful machines that can be used to lift or pull heavy objects. A large load can be lifted by using a small effort force that moves through a larger distance. It is easier to lift a heavy load if the lifting rope passes through two or more pulleys. As you add more pulleys to a system, the effort needed to lift the load becomes less, but the distance this effort force must move through gets bigger.

In the diagram, if the object is to be lifted through one metre, each of the sections of rope must be shortened by one metre. This means that the complete rope must be pulled over the top pulley by four metres. The effort force required to do this is far less than the load force.

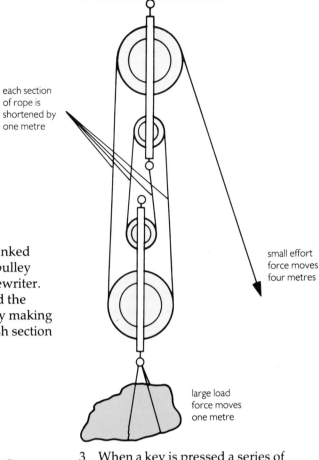

each section of rope is shortened by one metre

small effort force moves four metres

large load force moves one metre

The typewriter

This is an example of a complex machine that is in everyday use. It uses many gears, pulleys and levers.

1 The carriage return lever is connected to a set of simple gears. When the lever is pushed, the gears are turned and the paper roller moves feeding paper into the typewriter.

2 The typewriter has an inked ribbon that is pulled by a pulley across the front of the typewriter. Every time a key is pressed the ribbon pulley turns slightly making sure the typebar hits a fresh section of ribbon.

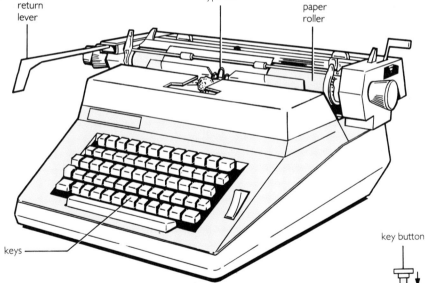

carriage return lever

type bar

paper roller

keys

3 When a key is pressed a series of levers move, and the typebar is thrown forwards violently, pressing the ribbon against the paper and leaving a printed letter behind.

pivot

typeslug

typebar

key button

key lever

typebar linkage

No machine, however simple or complex, can be 100% efficient since some friction is always present. The work done by a machine is always *less* than the work put into the machine. The efficiency of a machine can be calculated by this formula:

$$\text{efficiency} = \frac{\text{work done by the machine}}{\text{work put into the machine}}$$

2 CAR ENGINES

An engine is a machine that is designed to convert energy into useful mechanical work. Heat engines convert the chemical energy of a fuel into movement (kinetic) energy. The fuel is usually burnt at a very high temperature producing heat which is converted into large amounts of kinetic energy to turn the engine and drive the vehicle along.

The four-stroke petrol engine

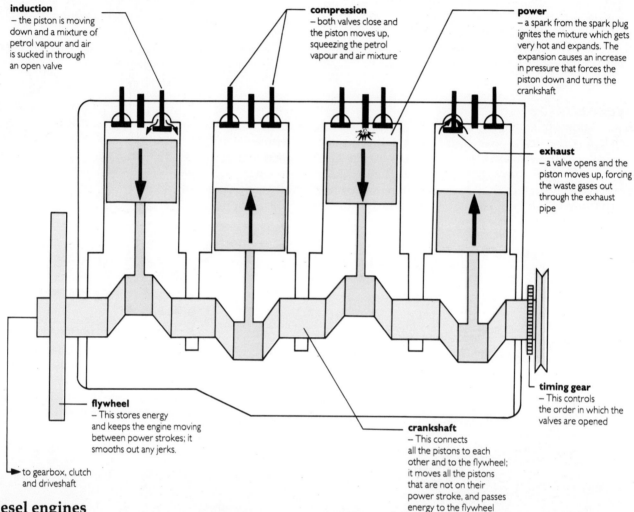

induction
– the piston is moving down and a mixture of petrol vapour and air is sucked in through an open valve

compression
– both valves close and the piston moves up, squeezing the petrol vapour and air mixture

power
– a spark from the spark plug ignites the mixture which gets very hot and expands. The expansion causes an increase in pressure that forces the piston down and turns the crankshaft

exhaust
– a valve opens and the piston moves up, forcing the waste gases out through the exhaust pipe

timing gear
– This controls the order in which the valves are opened

flywheel
– This stores energy and keeps the engine moving between power strokes; it smooths out any jerks.

crankshaft
– This connects all the pistons to each other and to the flywheel; it moves all the pistons that are not on their power stroke, and passes energy to the flywheel

to gearbox, clutch and driveshaft

Diesel engines

Diesel fuelled engines are similar to petrol fuelled engines, but there are some important differences. Diesel engines have injectors instead of spark plugs. The diesel fuel is injected directly into the cylinder at the same time as air enters through the valves. The air is squeezed much more than in a petrol engine and it gets so hot that the diesel oil explodes the moment it is injected into the cylinder.

Diesel engines used to be much bigger and noisier than petrol engines and so were usually found only in commercial vehicles. Recent developments have made them much quieter and smaller and they are now found in many private cars. These engines are much more efficient than petrol engines and usually use much less fuel.

Diesel engines are about 40% efficient while petrol engines are only about 25% efficient, so most of the fuel in both engines is wasted. The rest of the energy in the fuel will eventually become heat which is removed by the cooling system.

Diesel oil (DERV) is easier to produce than petrol and it does not have to be blended at the refinery, so it is cheaper to make than petrol. However, because the demand for it is less, and taxes are high, it is almost as expensive as petrol to buy.

Road transport in the United Kingdom

When the internal combustion engine was developed, roads became, for the first time, competitive with the canals and railways for moving freight and passengers. Road transport had the great advantage of door-to-door transport and greater flexibility. These advantages led to the very rapid growth of all forms of road transport at the expense of the other transport systems. This sudden expansion caused many problems because most of the existing roads were not designed for cars and lorries. Most of our present day roads are old. They were originally designed for horse traffic going from town centre to town centre.

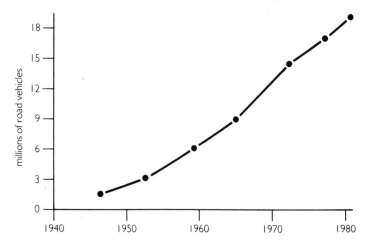

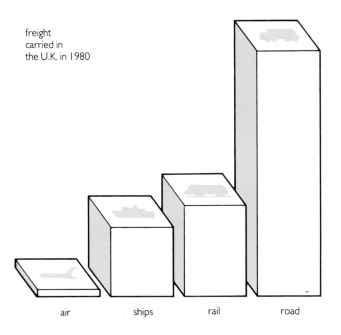

freight carried in the U.K. in 1980

Heavy road traffic has caused congestion especially in towns where many roads meet. This traffic has caused damage to buildings and brought about accidents and pollution in the form of lead, carbon monoxide and noise.

Road improvements

Roads have been straightened and widened to make travel faster and easier. By-passes and ring roads allow vehicles to travel round the congested town centres. However, these improvements are very expensive, especially near towns where the price of land is high and houses have to be demolished. These types of improvement frequently increase the congestion on the stretches that are still unimproved.

The motorway system

Motorways were designed to speed up travel without the problems of by-passes and ring roads. They are fast direct routes between large cities which reduce the travelling time greatly.

Motorways have reduced congestion on the older roads they replaced and vehicles on these minor routes now move faster. They are safer than normal roads because they have no sharp bends or on-coming traffic. However, they are expensive to build and take up a large amount of land. They are difficult to cross and there are only certain points at which traffic can join or leave the motorway. Many people think they are boring to use and that they increase traffic congestion at the ends of the motorway. Because of this many people object to the building of new motorways and there are many arguments for and against them at public inquiries.

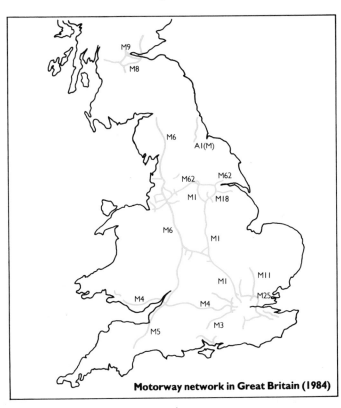

Motorway network in Great Britain (1984)

3 JETS AND ROCKETS

Rockets

Firework rockets are made up of a form of gunpowder in a tube closed at the front end. When the rocket is fired, the gunpowder burns fiercely producing hot gases which escape through a nozzle at the rear end. As this hot gas is pushed out, the rocket is pushed in the opposite direction.

Modern *missiles* also use solid fuel. They can be ignited and blasted off very rapidly, unlike liquid fuel rockets which have to be prepared for blast off. Most space rockets use liquid hydrogen as fuel; liquid oxygen is also carried. Both liquids are forced into a combustion chamber where the hydrogen burns violently in the oxygen. This produces very hot gases which are forced out of the rear of the rocket through a nozzle. The rocket is pushed in the opposite direction.

Jets

Jet engines also push out large amounts of hot waste gas and, therefore, are pushed forwards. They use a type of paraffin as their fuel, together with oxygen from the air. This means they cannot be used in space. On the ground, the jet is started electrically to get the compressor fans moving. A jet engine has similar stages to a petrol engine: induction, compression, power and exhaust, but the stages happen in a continuous stream.

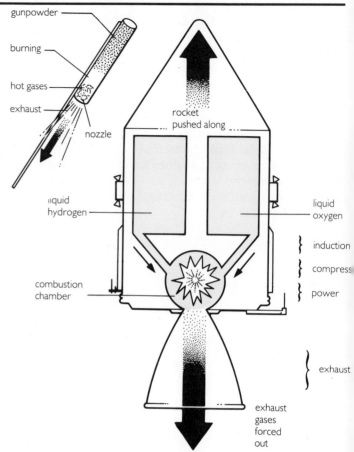

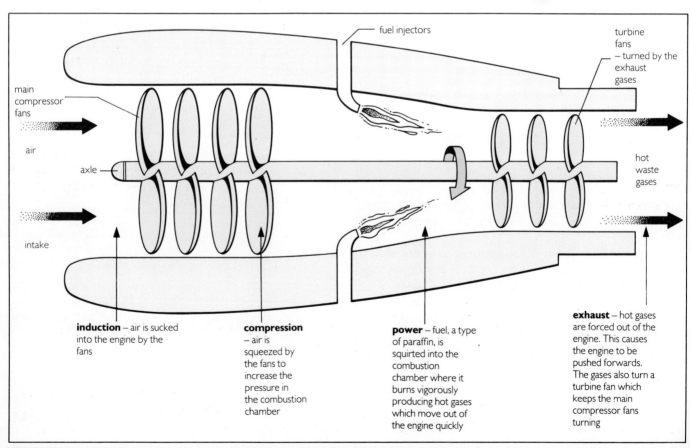

induction – air is sucked into the engine by the fans

compression – air is squeezed by the fans to increase the pressure in the combustion chamber

power – fuel, a type of paraffin, is squirted into the combustion chamber where it burns vigorously producing hot gases which move out of the engine quickly

exhaust – hot gases are forced out of the engine. This causes the engine to be pushed forwards. The gases also turn a turbine fan which keeps the main compressor fans turning

Flight

An aeroplane is pushed forwards by an engine. Air flows over and under the wings. Because of the *shape* of the wing, air passing over the top surface has to travel further than air passing under the wing.

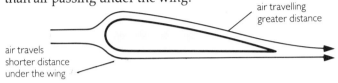

air travelling greater distance

air travels shorter distance under the wing

This causes the air above the wing to move faster and it becomes less dense, exerting less pressure than the air under the wing. The wing will lift into the area of reduced pressure.

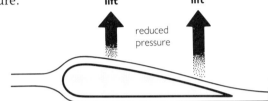

lift   **lift**

reduced pressure

If the front of the wing is lifted the air under the wing will become compressed by the wing and will exert more pressure.

wing tilted

air under wing becomes compressed

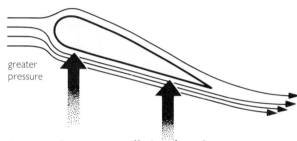

greater pressure

This increased pressure will give the wing even more lift and it will rise more steeply. If the wing is lifted too far, the air flow becomes disturbed and the plane will start to *stall* (fall).

Airports

Britain has five major airports, two serving London (Gatwick and Heathrow), Birmingham, Manchester and Prestwick which serves Glasgow and Edinburgh. There are other regional and minor airports scattered over the British Isles. The movement of aircraft over Britain is regulated by Air Traffic Control. This makes sure that an aircraft is flying along the correct air route and is safely separated from all other aircraft.

As more people use aircraft to fly to different parts of the world there is a need for more large international airports. However, these major airports can have a great effect on the surrounding area.

1   Aircraft noise can be a nuisance over a wide area around the airport and under the main air routes.
2   Airports attract large numbers of people and, therefore, heavy road traffic.
3   Industrial development is attracted to the area providing more jobs for the local community.
4   Airports take up large areas of land which may have been used for agricultural use.

The arguments for and against developing an airport are complicated and give rise to many objections and arguments at a public inquiry.

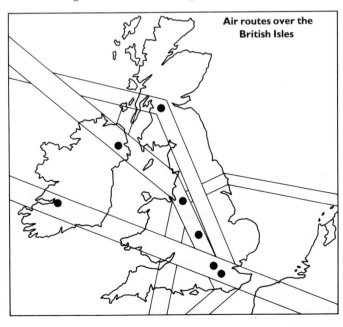

Air routes over the British Isles

4 STEAM ENGINES

A petrol engine is an example of an *internal combustion engine*; the fuel is burnt **inside** the working cylinder. The steam engine is an example of an *external combustion engine* because the fuel is burnt **outside** the working cylinder.

A steam engine is a machine that converts heat energy to mechanical energy. Water is heated and converted to mechanical energy. Water is heated and converted to steam which is then used to move a piston inside a cylinder. The steam engine was the major source of power during the industrial revolution and can still be useful today because it develops full power at low engine speeds.

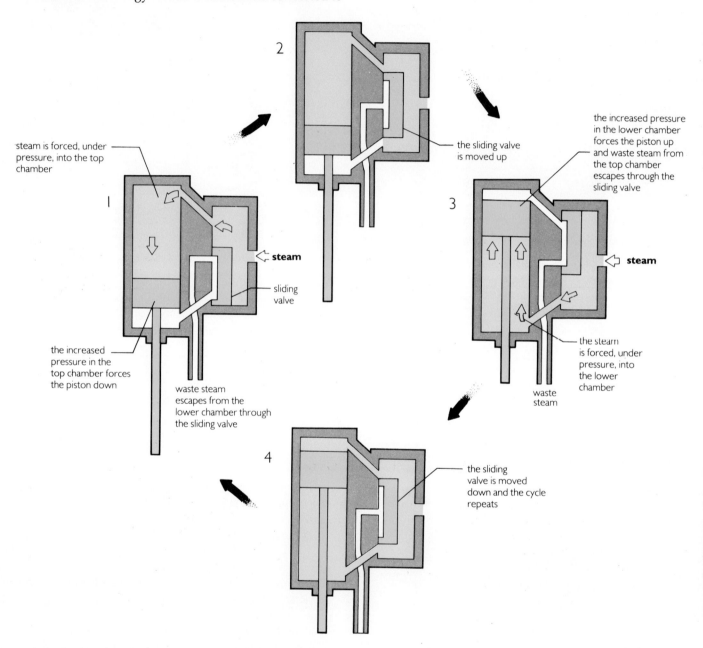

steam is forced, under pressure, into the top chamber

the increased pressure in the top chamber forces the piston down

waste steam escapes from the lower chamber through the sliding valve

steam

sliding valve

the sliding valve is moved up

the increased pressure in the lower chamber forces the piston up and waste steam from the top chamber escapes through the sliding valve

steam

the steam is forced, under pressure, into the lower chamber

waste steam

the sliding valve is moved down and the cycle repeats

Both the downstroke and the upstroke of the piston produce power. A crankshaft may be used to convert the up and down movement of the piston into a turning movement. If the steam engine has more than one cylinder then the crankshaft will connect all the pistons together and smooth out any jerks.

Rail transport

Until 1948, steam engines provided the power to pull our trains. Nowadays, they are pulled by diesel or electric engines. The rail network has been cut regularly since 1948 to its present size (in 1982) of about 18000 km (11000 miles). This reduction in size has come about because passengers and freight hauliers prefer road travel. Unfortunately rail transport cannot offer the convenience of door-to-door travel. However, rail transport does have many advantages over road transport.

1 Railways cause much less air and noise pollution.
2 Rail systems take up less room than road systems and trains are capable of carrying much more than road vehicles.
3 Trains are more efficient than road vehicles in their use of fuel.
4 Rail transport is far safer than road transport.

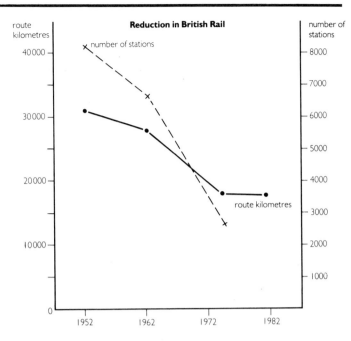

The high speed train

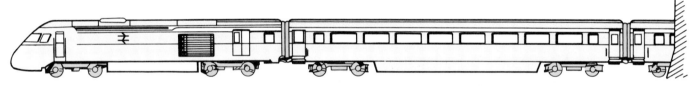

The Rail Network

Some main lines have been electrified, and there are now over 3600 km (2200 miles) of electrified railway in Britain, some 20% of the total British Rail network. Most of the main passenger and commuter lines into London are now electrified. British Rail has also introduced new *high speed trains* which are made up of two streamlined units at either end of the train. These trains are very light and powerful with a top speed of 200 km/h (125 mph). As more and more lines become electrified the rail system becomes more efficient, because electric trains are faster and cheaper to operate. However, the smaller less efficient and less profitable branch lines are threatened with closure to allow the concentration of materials, resources and money on the more profitable Inter City lines.

Government grants are paid to keep open about 250 passenger services which are considered to be socially necessary but would otherwise be closed. A regular, but small number of passengers is not enough to prevent lines being closed. Some closed lines are converted into nature trails, long distance footpaths, bicycle routes or are taken over by railway preservation societies who operate steam trains on them.

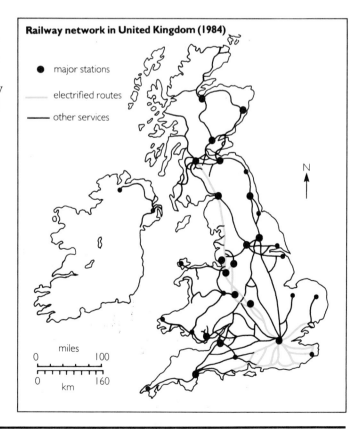

If a magnet is hung on a piece of string it will swing and eventually point north and south. This is how a compass works. The end that points to the Earth's north pole is called the north-seeking pole, or more commonly, the *north pole* of the magnet. The other end is called the *south pole* of the magnet.

If a second magnet is brought close to the first hanging magnet, the north poles will move apart. This will also happen if the south poles are brought together.

If the north pole of the second magnet is brought near the south pole of the first magnet then they will move towards each other.

> **like poles repel each other**
> **unlike poles attract each other**

The Earth acts as though it had a very large bar magnet inside it, tilted slightly to one side. The south pole of this imaginary magnet lies to the west of the north pole at a point called the *magnetic north pole*.

Compasses point to the magnetic north pole and not to the true north. Map readers and navigators must take this into account when they are planning a journey.

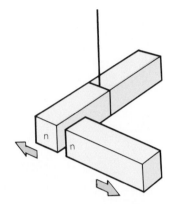

If a magnetic compass is placed near a wire carrying a current, then the compass needle will move. The needle of a compass is a weak magnet that has a magnetic field. An electric current is a flow of electrons along a conductor, from a negative terminal to a positive terminal. This current produces a weak magnetic field that interacts with the magnetic field of the compass needle, causing the needle to move.

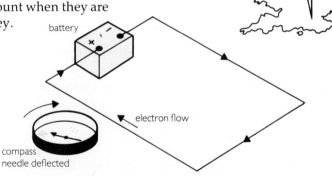

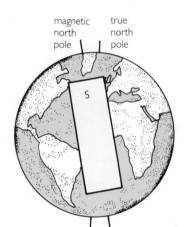

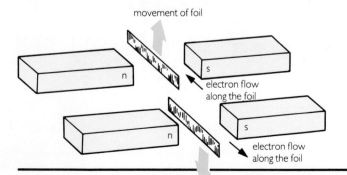

If a current is passed along a piece of thin aluminium foil held between two magnets, the foil will move. This is because the current moving in the foil will produce a weak magnetic field that interacts with the magnetic field of the magnets. The direction in which the foil moves depends on the direction of the current. Two magnetic fields are always needed before any movement takes place. This is the basis of all electric motors.

The electric motor

A coil of wire is placed in a magnetic field between the poles of a magnet. The coil starts to turn when a current passes through it. The current in the two sides of the coil moves in a different direction, so the two sides of the coil move up and down out of the magnetic field. The coil would normally stop turning when it was at right angles to the magnets, but a split ring (*commutator*) reverses the current in the coil and it continues turning (see diagrams).

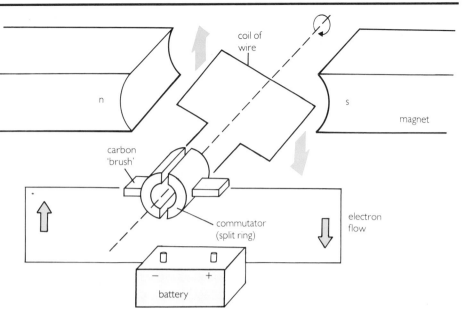

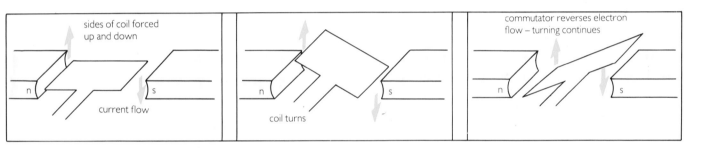

An electric motor should really be called an electric machine because it can be used either as a motor or a generator (*dynamo*). If an electric current passes into the coil it will become a motor and the coils will rotate on an axle. If the electricity is turned off, and the axle is rotated (like the dynamo on a bike), the machine becomes a generator and will produce an electrical current in the turning coil.

Motors don't have to rotate. It is possible to build a flat or *linear motor*. This will produce movement in a straight line. A linear motor can be produced so that the moving part floats in the magnetic field above the magnets. These motors are being developed as high-powered, high-speed motors for fast vehicles such as trains. However, they need a special track which is extremely expensive, and this may limit their use to special areas such as airport terminals. Japan and West Germany have experimental trains which use these motors and travel at speeds of up to 400 km/h (250 mph).

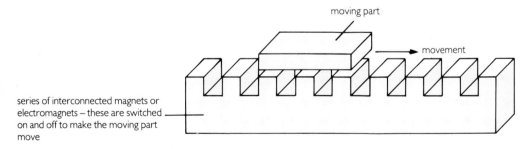

Electromagnets

A coiled wire carrying an electric current will act as if it was a magnet. It has a north and south pole and attracts magnetic materials. The poles will change over if the direction of the current is changed.

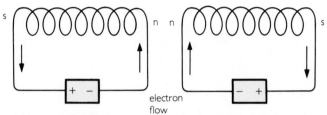

electron flow

If a bar of iron is placed inside the coil it will become magnetic when the current is flowing. This is called an *electromagnet*. The electromagnet can be made stronger by increasing the number of turns of the wire in the coil or by increasing the current flowing in the wire. The magnetic effect stops when the current stops flowing.

Electromagnets are very useful because their magnetism can be switched on or off. They are used in many machines. In scrap yards and steel works a large strong electromagnet is used to move scrap iron and steel. The scrap is attracted to the electromagnet when the current flows. The scrap can be dropped by switching off the current.

The electric bell

When a door bell push is pressed a current flows through the coils and turns them into electromagnets. They attract the armature and the hammer strikes the bell. When the armature moves, the circuit is broken at the fixed contact and the current stops flowing. The coils stop acting as electromagnets and the spring returns the hammer to its original position. This makes the circuit complete once more and the armature is again attracted towards the electromagnets. This cycle of events repeats until the door bell push is released.

Relays

A relay is an electromagnetic switch which can control another electrical circuit. When a current flows in the coil it becomes an electromagnet and attracts an *armature*. The armature works on a pivot and closes the contacts.

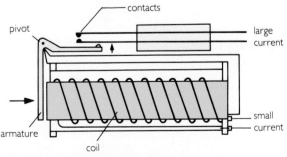

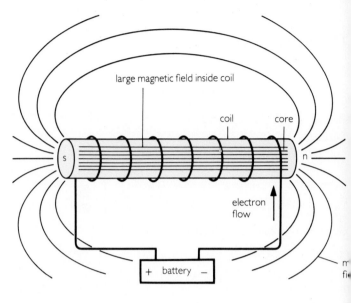

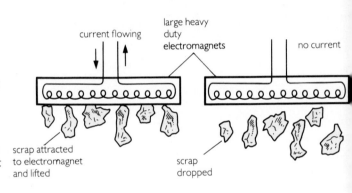

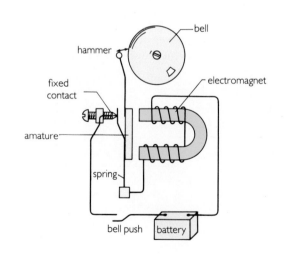

The small current in the relay can be used to control a much larger current in another circuit. This is useful in telephone exchanges, controlling lifts and the ignition circuits of cars.

Electromagnets are used in many other machines such as microphones, loudspeakers, radios, televisions and telephones (see page 240).

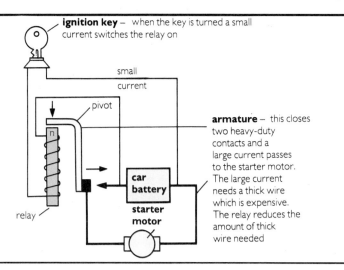

ignition key – when the key is turned a small current switches the relay on

small current

pivot

armature – this closes two heavy-duty contacts and a large current passes to the starter motor. The large current needs a thick wire which is expensive. The relay reduces the amount of thick wire needed

relay

car battery

starter motor

Using magnets to make electricity

If a magnet is moved into, or out of, a coil of wire it will make an electric current flow in the wire. This will only happen while the magnet is moving. The strength of the current produced depends on how strong the magnet is, how fast it is moving, and how many turns of wire there are in the coil. As the magnet approaches the coil the magnetic field in the coil will get stronger, and as it moves away the magnetic field in the coil will get weaker. The current is produced because a changing magnetic field is passing over the coil. This is the principle behind the dynamo or generator (page 227).

Transformers

Transformers are machines which change voltage. They always operate on an alternating current such as the mains electrical supply. A transformer contains an iron core and two coils of wire called the *primary coil* and the *secondary coil*.

When the primary coil is connected to an alternating current it will act like an electromagnet, switching on and off very rapidly. In this way it produces a changing magnetic field which passes over the secondary coil and produces a current.

If the secondary coil has **more** turns of wire than the primary coil it is called a *step-up* transformer. The voltage produced in the secondary

coil is higher than the voltage entering the transformer, but the current is lower. If the secondary coil has **fewer** turns of wire than the

primary coil it is called a *step-down* transfomer. This produces a lower voltage but higher current than that entering the transfomer.

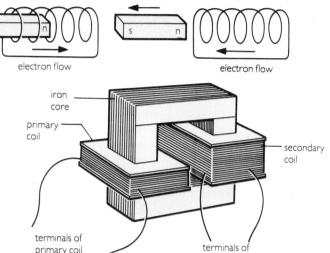

electron flow

electron flow

iron core

primary coil

secondary coil

terminals of primary coil

terminals of secondary coil

Step-up transfomers are used to raise the voltage and lower the current in the national grid (see page 192). This reduces the amount of electricity wasted because high currents would heat up the electricity cables.

Step-down transfomers are used to get low voltages from the mains supply, in order to use hi-fi equipment, microcomputers, washing machines, televisions, door bells, etc.

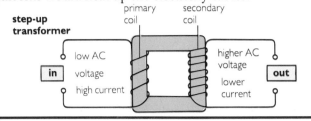

step-up transformer

primary coil

secondary coil

in

low AC voltage

high current

higher AC voltage

lower current

out

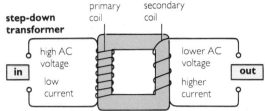

step-down transformer

primary coil

secondary coil

in

high AC voltage

low current

lower AC voltage

higher current

out

7 LIGHT MACHINES

Light is a form of energy we can see. Light travels in straight lines at very high speeds (about 300 million metres a second). Light bounces off shiny surfaces and bends as it passes through substances. This bouncing is called *reflection*, and the bending is called *refraction*.

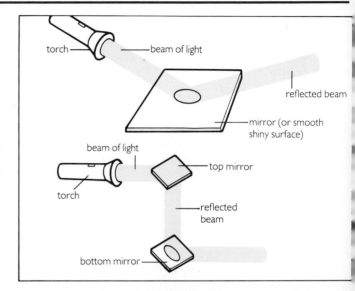

Reflection

If a ray of light hits a mirror or other shiny surface, it will be reflected. The angle the light makes when it leaves the surface is the same as the angle it makes when it arrives – just like a billiard ball bouncing off the side of the table. This can be useful – *periscopes* use two mirrors, one above the other. They are used in submarines so sailors below the surface can see what is happening above the surface. They can also be used to see above crowds on special occasions. Most mirrors are flat. Curved mirrors also reflect light but make things appear smaller or larger.

Concave mirrors   These are bowl shaped with the shiny surface on the inside. They are sometimes called *converging* mirrors because they make the reflected light rays come together, or converge. If an object is placed close to a concave mirror, the image in the mirror will appear to be larger than the object really is. They are used in shaving mirrors and make-up mirrors to make the face look larger. If a concave mirror is used to look at a distant object, the object will appear very small and upside-down.

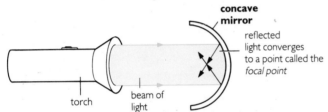

Convex mirrors   These curve outwards. They are sometimes called *diverging* mirrors because they make the reflected light rays spread out, or diverge. An object placed in front of a convex mirror gives an image that is small. These mirrors give a very wide view and are used as rear view mirrors in cars, staircase mirrors on double decker buses and in supermarkets to help detect shoplifters.

You can use a shiny spoon to see the different effects of concave and convex mirrors. Look in the concave part. What do you see? Now turn it over. What do you see now?

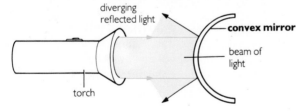

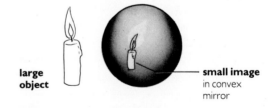

Refraction

Light travels through space at 300 million metres a second. When it enters a transparent material at an angle it slows down and the ray of light bends. As it leaves the material it will speed up and bend once more. This bending is called refraction.

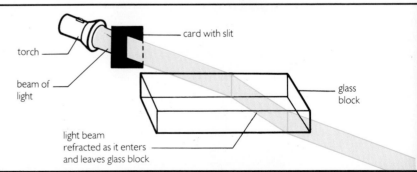

The spectrum

Because colours are refracted by different amounts, white light is often split up into a range of colours when it passes through transparent materials. This is best shown by a prism. The range of colours produced is called the *spectrum*. A prism can also be used to reflect light, especially in instruments such as cameras and binoculars (see page 232).

prism

ray of white light

red
orange
yellow
green
blue
indigo
violet

Lenses

Lenses are designed to bend (refract) light to form images of things placed in front of them. A lens which is thicker at the centre than at the edges is called *convex* and acts as a **converging lens**. A lens which is thinner at the centre than at the edges is called *concave* and acts as a **diverging lens**.

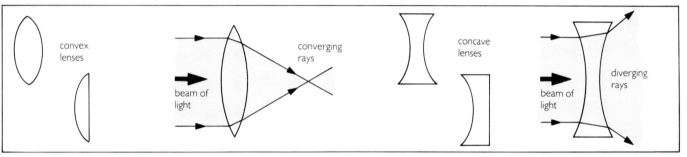

convex lenses

beam of light

converging rays

concave lenses

beam of light

diverging rays

The thicker the lens, the more the light is refracted. Thick lenses are frequently called 'strong' lenses, while thin ones are called 'weak'.

The images that a lens produces can be larger than, smaller than, or the same size as the actual object.

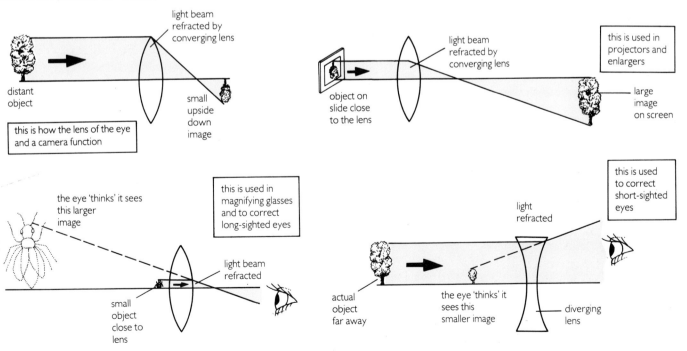

light beam refracted by converging lens

distant object

small upside down image

this is how the lens of the eye and a camera function

light beam refracted by converging lens

object on slide close to the lens

this is used in projectors and enlargers

large image on screen

the eye 'thinks' it sees this larger image

this is used in magnifying glasses and to correct long-sighted eyes

light beam refracted

small object close to lens

this is used to correct short-sighted eyes

light refracted

actual object far away

the eye 'thinks' it sees this smaller image

diverging lens

8 MAGNIFIERS

Telescopes

The astronomer's refracting telescope is the simplest type. It is made up of two lenses, usually a large weak convex lens (called the *objective*) and a smaller stronger lens (called the *eyepiece*). This telescope produces a magnified image that is upside down. If the eyepiece is replaced with a concave lens, the image will be the right way up and the telescope can be used to look at things on the Earth.

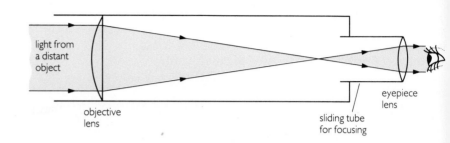

light from a distant object

objective lens

eyepiece lens

sliding tube for focusing

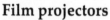

prism

light path

Some telescopes use a large concave mirror to collect the light instead of an objective lens. These are called reflecting telescopes. Large mirrors are much easier to make than large lenses, and they are easier to polish perfectly smooth. The light from a distant object is reflected off the large curved mirror on to a small flat mirror, which turns the light on to the side eyepiece. This arrangement makes it easier to use. Most large optical telescopes are of this type.

Film projectors

Light rays from a powerful lamp are reflected back off a concave mirror along their own path. A *condenser*, made up of two convex lenses makes the light rays converge on to the slide. Light passing through this film is focused by another convex projection lens on to a screen. The image that appears on this screen will be greatly magnified and upside down. Film is put into the projector upside down so that the image on the screen will appear the right way up.

Binoculars are made up of two refracting telescopes mounted side by side, one for each eye. They are joined together so that they both focus together. Most good binoculars tend to be much shorter and easier to handle than a normal telescope. They also turn the magnified image so it appears the right way up.

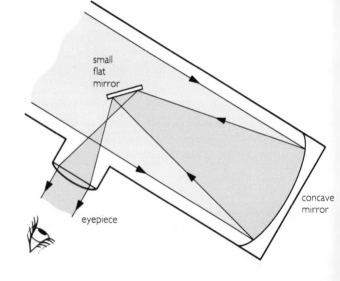

small flat mirror

eyepiece

concave mirror

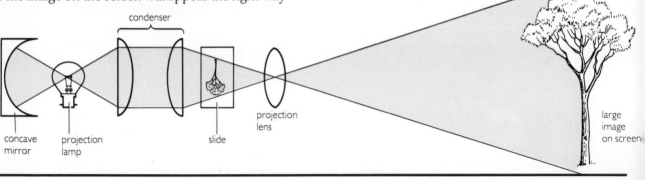

condenser

concave mirror

projection lamp

slide

projection lens

large image on screen

Microscopes

A microscope uses lenses to magnify very small objects. A simple microscope has two strong converging lenses in a tube. These are called the objective and eyepiece lenses. Light is shone through the specimen and passes through the objective lens. This acts like a small projector and produces an enlarged image inside the tube. The eyepiece lens acts like a magnifying glass and increases the size of this image. The final, much magnified image is upside down, but this is usually not important.

The final image produced by a good light microscope can be up to 1000 times larger than the real size of the specimen. To get larger images than this, a different instrument, the *electron microscope*, has to be used.

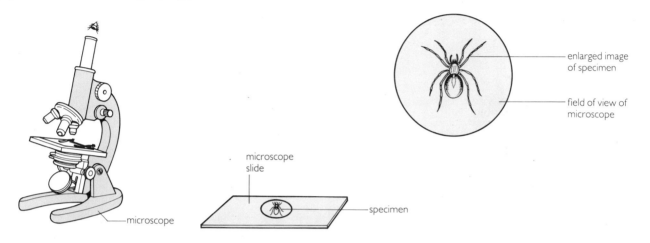

enlarged image of specimen

field of view of microscope

microscope

microscope slide

specimen

Cameras

A camera is made up of a converging lens, a light-tight box and a light-sensitive film. The convex lens produces a small upside down image on the film. This causes a rapid chemical change in the film, which can later be developed into a photograph. The amount of light reaching the film can be controlled either by a shutter which briefly opens letting light in or by an adjustable ring of sliding metal or plastic plates, called a diaphragm. The diaphragm alters the size of the hole or aperture through which the light rays pass. The image can be focused on the film by moving the lens backwards or forwards.

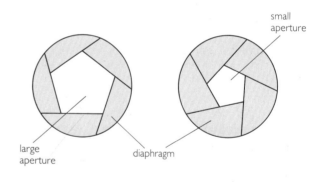

small aperture

large aperture

diaphragm

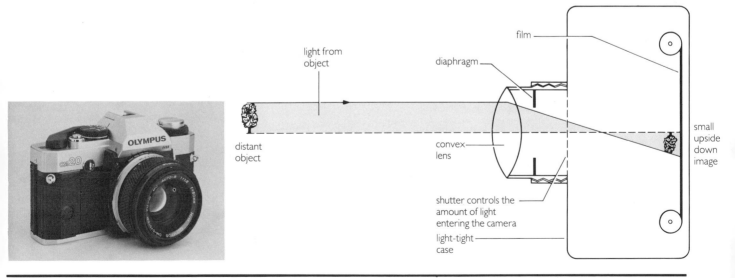

light from object

film

diaphragm

distant object

convex lens

shutter controls the amount of light entering the camera

light-tight case

small upside down image

9 LASERS

The word laser is short for: **L**ight **A**mplification by **S**timulated **E**mission of **R**adiation.

An atom is made up of a nucleus surrounded by electrons which move around it. Sometimes the energy in an atom can be increased by moving an electron further away from the nucleus. If the energy in an atom increases in this way it is called an 'excited atom'. Eventually the electron will move back to its original orbit, and the extra energy in the atom will be released, usually in the form of light.

The *ruby laser* is a thin artificial ruby rod that is surrounded by flash lamps. The ruby has a silvered mirror at one end and a semi-transparent mirror at the other end. The whole apparatus is cooled by a liquid or a gas.

cooling gas in

flash lamp

ruby rod

transparent tube

cooling gas out

Light from the flash lamps will hit some of the atoms in the ruby rod. This excites the atoms. The next time the lamps flash, some light may hit an atom that has already been excited. This makes the atom release the extra energy, in the form of light, and return to normal.

Most of the light energy released by the excited atoms will escape sideways, but some will start to move along the length of the ruby rod. If this hits an excited atom, even more light will be released. The light wave bounces off the mirrors at the end of the rod and makes a great number of round trips, picking up more energy each time. Some of the intense light eventually shoots out through the semi-transparent mirror to form the *laser beam*.

mirror

light escaping

semi-transparent mirror

laser beam

atoms in the rod

ruby rod

The commonest lasers in use today use tubes filled with various gases. These *gas lasers* work in a similar way to the ruby laser.

Using lasers

A laser beam can be focused just like a normal light wave. Laser beams can contain tremendous amounts of energy and when focused on to a small area they can become powerful cutting and welding tools. They are often used in medicine for welding torn retinas on to the back of the eye, and for destroying or removing cancer cells without affecting normal healthy cells. **You should never look directly into a laser.**

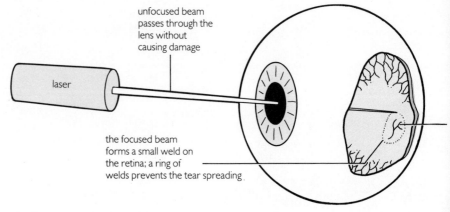

unfocused beam passes through the lens without causing damage

laser

the focused beam forms a small weld on the retina; a ring of welds prevents the tear spreading

Because laser beams are thin and travel at the speed of light they can be used as highly accurate measuring tools. They are frequently used in survey work and have been bounced off the Moon in order to measure accurately the distances between the Earth and the Moon (in 1970 this was calculated to an accuracy of 15 cm!).

Lasers are regularly used to track orbiting satellites. When a satellite passes overhead, the laser beam is flashed into space to intercept it, and the reflected beam is picked up by a receiver which calculates the satellite's position accurately. The thin laser beam can be used to get information off special laser discs (see page 253).

Lasers can be used to store vast amounts of information in special computers, but a more interesting use is in the communications business. A laser can be used to carry information in exactly the same way as a radio wave (see page 242) but a single laser beam could carry the equivalent of millions of radio programmes. Unfortunately, most lasers can be stopped by fog, mist or clouds. This means that lasers used for communication on the Earth will have to operate inside tubes or pipes that are called *fibre optics*.

A fibre optic is a glass fibre or plastic tube that is fitted inside a sheath. A laser beam passing down the fibre optic will be totally reflected off the sides and pass down the tube. This is known as *total internal reflection*. This means that the fibre optic can be flexible, allowing light to pass round corners. Lasers can be used in long lengths of fibre optics to carry radio, TV and telephone messages around the country. Fibre optics can also be used with normal light beams to illuminate awkward places or to allow people to see and photograph inaccessible places such as the inside of our bodies.

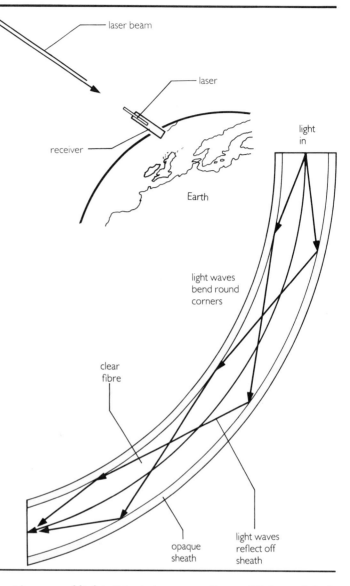

Holography

Lasers can be used to take three-dimensional pictures. The method is called holography, and the picture is called a *hologram*. A laser beam is shone on the object to be photographed. The reflected light is combined with light from another laser and shone on to a photographic plate which becomes the hologram. If this hologram is looked at in normal light, it just shows a pattern of light and dark bands. However, if a laser beam is shone through the hologram a three dimensional image is seen. The picture appears to have depth and if you move your head from side to side you will see the different sides of the image. Holograms make it possible to store many pictues on one photographic plate.

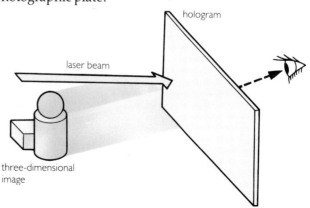

COMMUNICATIONS

CHAPTER 9

THE ELECTROMAGNETIC SPECTRUM

X-rays, light and radio waves are all examples of *electromagnetic waves* – a form of energy that is produced when electrons vibrate. These waves move from side to side and up and down, just like waves on the surface of the sea. They are examples of transverse waves. If you take a long spring and give one end a quick shake you will be able to see a transverse wave.

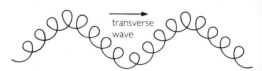

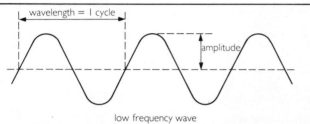

A radio wave that vibrates one million times a second will travel 300 million metres in one second. The wave will travel 300 m during each vibration – this is its wavelength. The frequency and wavelength of all waves are related:

$$\text{frequency} = \frac{\text{speed}}{\text{wavelength}}$$

Electromagnetic waves travel at the speed of light, about 300 million metres a second. The number of times a wave vibrates every second is called the *frequency* – measured in *hertz*. The distance a wave travels during a single vibration is called the *wavelength*.

X-rays, light waves and radio waves are only a part of the complete electromagnetic spectrum. The waves that make up this spectrum have different wavelengths and frequencies. Because of this, they have different properties.

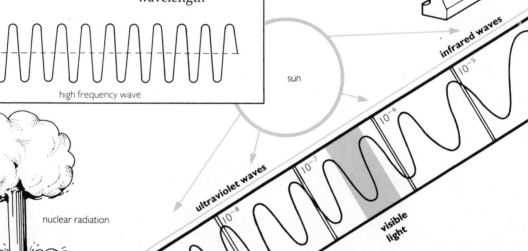

electric heaters

infrared waves

sun

ultraviolet waves

visible light

nuclear radiation

gamma rays

X-ray waves

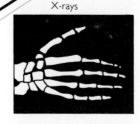

X-rays

Visible light

This is the part of the electromagnetic spectrum that the eye can see. White light is really a mixture of several colours. These colours can be separated by passing the light through a prism. We see a rainbow when raindrops act like tiny prisms. The light is separated into bands of colour ranging from red to violet. Red light has the longest wavelength, while violet light has the shortest wavelength.

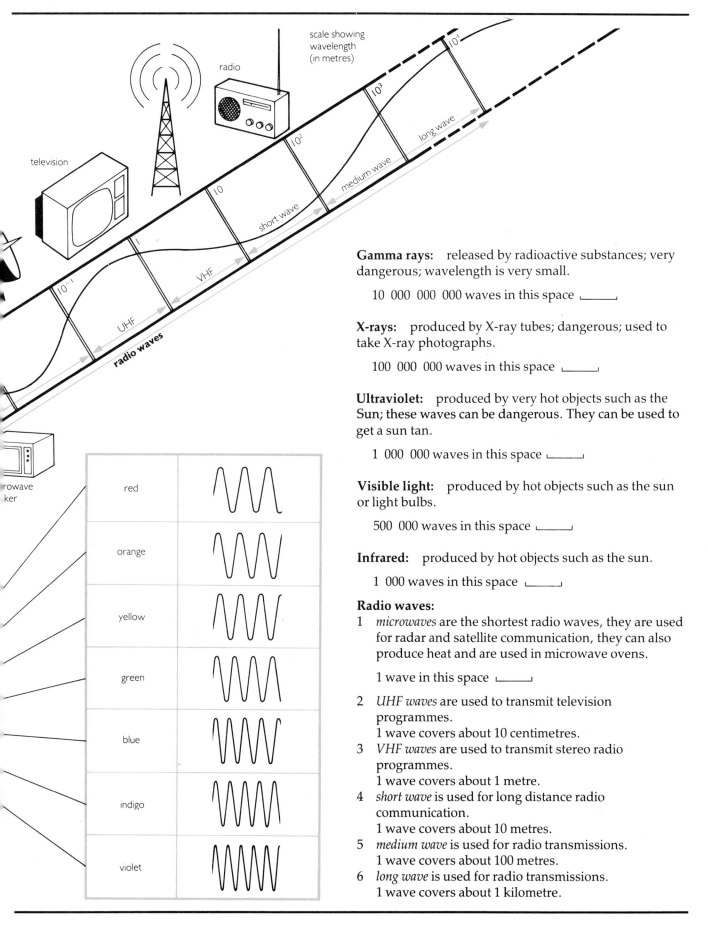

scale showing wavelength (in metres)

radio

television

10^3

10^2

10

long wave

medium wave

short wave

VHF

UHF

10^{-1}

radio waves

microwave ker

red	
orange	
yellow	
green	
blue	
indigo	
violet	

Gamma rays: released by radioactive substances; very dangerous; wavelength is very small.

10 000 000 000 waves in this space ⌐————⌐

X-rays: produced by X-ray tubes; dangerous; used to take X-ray photographs.

100 000 000 waves in this space ⌐————⌐

Ultraviolet: produced by very hot objects such as the Sun; these waves can be dangerous. They can be used to get a sun tan.

1 000 000 waves in this space ⌐————⌐

Visible light: produced by hot objects such as the sun or light bulbs.

500 000 waves in this space ⌐————⌐

Infrared: produced by hot objects such as the sun.

1 000 waves in this space ⌐————⌐

Radio waves:

1   *microwaves* are the shortest radio waves, they are used for radar and satellite communication, they can also produce heat and are used in microwave ovens.

1 wave in this space ⌐————⌐

2   *UHF waves* are used to transmit television programmes.
1 wave covers about 10 centimetres.

3   *VHF waves* are used to transmit stereo radio programmes.
1 wave covers about 1 metre.

4   *short wave* is used for long distance radio communication.
1 wave covers about 10 metres.

5   *medium wave* is used for radio transmissions.
1 wave covers about 100 metres.

6   *long wave* is used for radio transmissions.
1 wave covers about 1 kilometre.

2 CHANGING SOUNDS

Sound waves are a form of energy that are caused by vibrations. Your voice is produced by the vocal cords in your throat. When you speak, these move and make the air around them vibrate. Sound waves are produced, which spread out from your mouth. If someone is

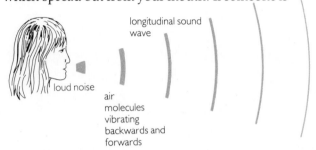

listening to you their ears will detect sound waves. Sound waves gradually lose their energy and become weaker as they travel away from the speaker.

As the sound waves travel they make the air molecules vibrate backwards and forwards. The molecules themselves do not travel. This type of wave is called a *longitudinal wave*. You can see longitudinal waves by taking a long spring and giving it a quick shake along its length.

Sound waves can travel through solids, liquids and gases, but not through a vacuum.

A microphone and a loudspeaker can be used to make sounds travel over greater distances.

Microphones

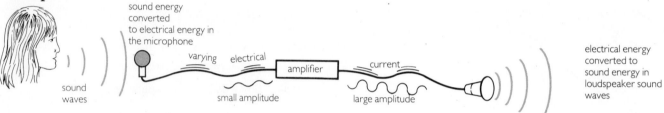

These are machines that convert sound energy into electrical energy. There are many different types, but all microphones contain a disc called a *diaphragm*. When sound waves reach the microphone the air vibrations hit the diaphragm and make it vibrate in sympathy. The vibrating diaphragm will produce, or alter, an electric current which varies in strength in time with its movements.

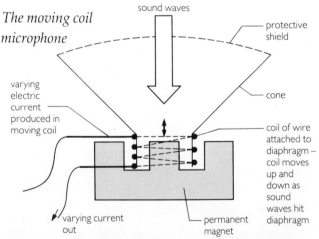

The diaphragm is attached to a very light coil hanging between the poles of a permanent magnet. Sound waves hitting the diaphragm make it vibrate. This moves the coil up and down, and an electric current is produced in the wires of the coil (see page 226). The more the diaphragm moves, the greater the electric current produced. The electric current varies in strength according to the strength of the sound waves hitting the diaphragm. This changing current then passes along a wire away from the microphone.

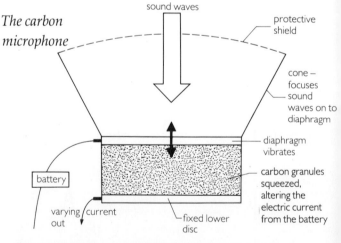

A battery supplies an electric current to this type of microphone. The diaphragm is a small metal disc. A layer of carbon granules is sandwiched between the diaphragm and a fixed lower disc. When sound waves reach the diaphragm it starts to vibrate in sympathy. The carbon granules are squeezed together then loosened. More electric current will pass from the diaphragm to the lower disc when the granules are squeezed. So the current passing through the microphone changes strength in time with the movements of the diaphragm. This changing current passes along wires away from the microphone.

Loudspeakers

A microphone is of little use on its own. The changing electrical currents may be stored, for example on record or tape, but eventually they must be changed back to sound waves. A machine that converts electrical energy into sound energy is called a *loudspeaker*.

There are many different types of loudspeaker, but the commonest is the *moving coil loudspeaker*. This is really a moving coil microphone working in reverse.

Wires from a microphone, record player or tape recorder are connected to a small coil. This hangs loosely between the poles of a permanent magnet. When an electrical current flows in this coil it is pushed away from the magnet. The amount the coil is pushed away, and how often this happens, is controlled by the current that flows in the coil. The coil will vibrate in time and in strength with the vibrations produced in the original microphone. The coil is attached to a large diaphragm or cone. When the coil vibrates the cone does too. It pushes and pulls the surrounding air, sending out sound waves from the loudspeaker.

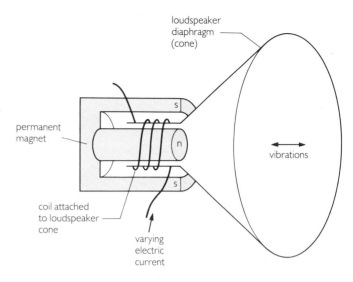

Earpieces

These are small loudspeakers that are designed to be placed near the ear. Varying electric currents from a microphone, cassette or radio enter the earpiece and pass round the coils of an electromagnet. This attracts a thin metal diaphragm. The movement of the diaphragm will change with the current. The changing vibrations move the air in front of the diaphragm and weak sound waves are produced.

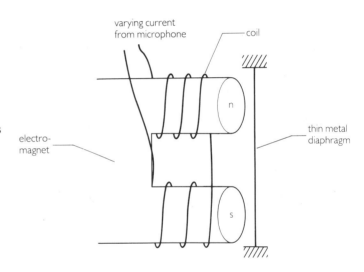

The telephone

Each telephone contains a carbon microphone and an earpiece.

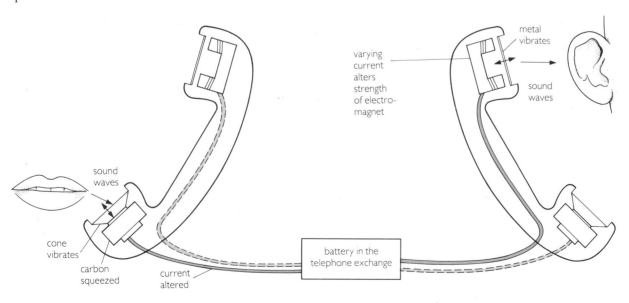

3 RADIO

A radio station produces a signal which is in the form of an alternating current. If this current is put into an aerial it will produce a series of electromagnetic waves that spread out rapidly. The electromagnetic waves will vibrate in time with the changes in the alternating current.

Each radio station has its own particular wavelength. This is the *carrier wave*. It can be altered or *modulated* to carry music or speech. There are two ways this is done in the UK, by amplitude modulation (AM) or frequency modulation (FM).

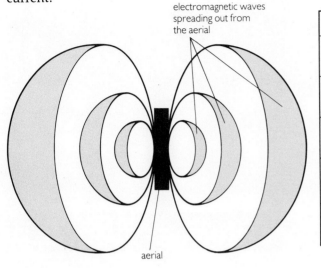

electromagnetic waves spreading out from the aerial

aerial

radio station	frequency	wavelength
Radio 1	MW/LW 1089 kHz VHF 89·1 MHz	275 m 3·37 m
Radio 2	MW/LW 693 kHz VHF 89·1 MHz	433 m 3·37 m
Radio 3	MW/LW 1215 KHz VHF 91·3 MHz	247 m 3·28 m
Radio 4	MW/LW 200 kHz VHF 93·5 MHz	1500 m 3·21 m
Radio Luxemburg	MW/LW 1442 kHz	208 m

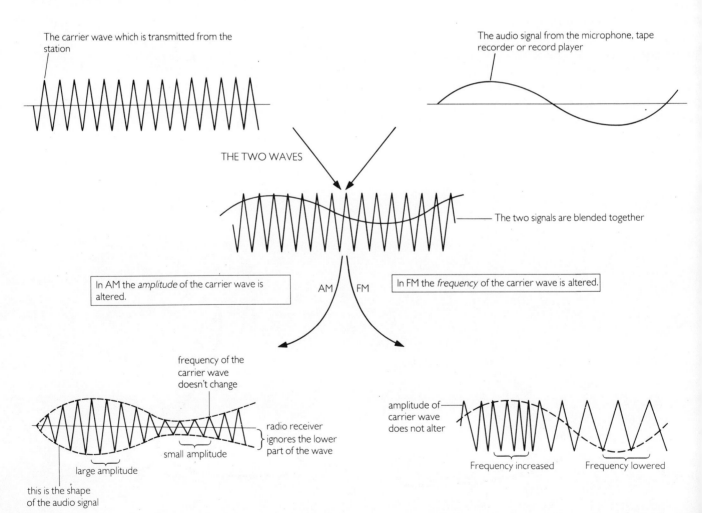

The carrier wave which is transmitted from the station

The audio signal from the microphone, tape recorder or record player

THE TWO WAVES

The two signals are blended together

In AM the *amplitude* of the carrier wave is altered.

AM FM

In FM the *frequency* of the carrier wave is altered.

frequency of the carrier wave doesn't change

radio receiver ignores the lower part of the wave

large amplitude

small amplitude

this is the shape of the audio signal

amplitude of carrier wave does not alter

Frequency increased   Frequency lowered

Radio waves

Radio waves spread out from the station's transmitting aerial in all directions. The distance that each wave travels depends on its wavelength. Long waves and medium waves are bent slightly by the ionosphere and can travel about 800 km before they are too weak to pick up. Short waves are reflected back off the ionosphere – they can travel much further. VHF and UHF waves are neither bent nor reflected by the ionosphere so they cannot travel beyond the horizon.

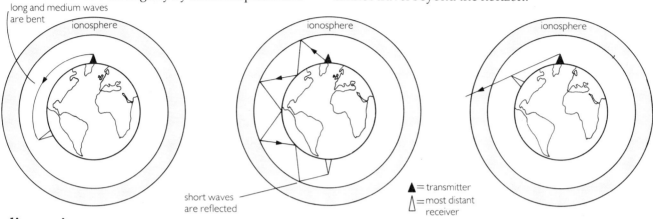

long and medium waves are bent

ionosphere

short waves are reflected

ionosphere

ionosphere

▲ = transmitter
◁ = most distant receiver

Radio receivers

Every radio has an aerial which can detect the electromagnetic wave transmitted by a radio station. An electric current is produced in the aerial which changes in time with the electromagnetic wave. This weak electric current is amplified in the radio.

The air is full of radio waves from many sources – TV stations, the police and army as well as radio stations. A radio aerial will pick up all these waves. Each radio set can be tuned to select which waves it will amplify. Citizen band users and radio hams use radio transmitters for pleasure.

Parts of the radio

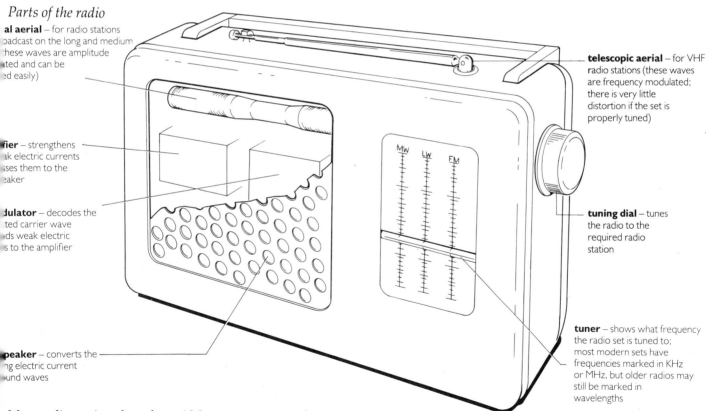

...al aerial – for radio stations
...oadcast on the long and medium
...hese waves are amplitude
...ted and can be
...ed easily)

...fier – strengthens
...ak electric currents
...sses them to the
...eaker

...dulator – decodes the
...ted carrier wave
...ds weak electric
...s to the amplifier

...peaker – converts the
...ng electric current
...und waves

telescopic aerial – for VHF radio stations (these waves are frequency modulated; there is very little distortion if the set is properly tuned)

tuning dial – tunes the radio to the required radio station

tuner – shows what frequency the radio set is tuned to; most modern sets have frequencies marked in KHz or MHz, but older radios may still be marked in wavelengths

MW LW FM

Most radio stations broadcast AM programmes on the long or medium waves and the same FM programme on VHF. This gives a high quality signal to people who have VHF radios. It also allows people with older, or cheaper, AM sets to receive the programme. Radio stations can transmit two different programmes at the same time, on different frequencies.

4 TELEVISION

Look at this enlargement from a newspaper picture. It is made up of a large number of black dots. Each dot is a different size. The dots are very small in the light parts of the picture. In the darkest parts the dots are large and they touch. Shades of grey are made up of dots of medium size. At normal viewing distances the dots make up a lifelike picture. These dots are called *elements* of the picture.

A television picture is produced in a similar way. The dots on a black and white television are all of the same size, but each one will vary from black, through many shades of grey, to white. They are over 100 000 elements on a British TV screen, and each one will vary in brightness. At normal viewing distances these elements blend together to give a single image.

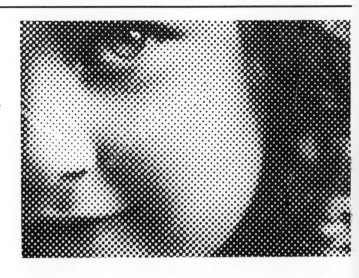

The TV camera

This translates the light from a scene into a series of electrical impulses. These are amplified and sent to a transmitter. Electromagnetic waves then carry the electrical form of the picture to the television set.

In the TV camera an image is focused on a small plate made up of many squares. These are arranged in 625 lines, and each line will have up to 200 000 squares. Each square is photosensitive and will gain a positive electric charge when light falls on it. A square illuminated with bright light will gain a large charge, while a darker square will gain a small charge.

An electron gun produces a fine beam of electrons that zigzags across the screen, line by line, 25 times a second. This movement is known as *scanning*. The electron beam scans each photosensitive square in turn and the different electric charges on each square cause a varying electric current to pass to an amplifier. This changing electric current represents the brightness of each square on the screen.

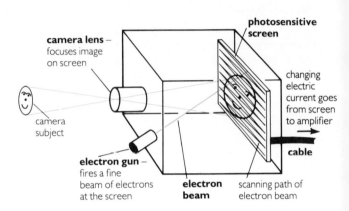

camera lens – focuses image on screen

photosensitive screen

changing electric current goes from screen to amplifier

cable

camera subject

electron gun – fires a fine beam of electrons at the screen

electron beam

scanning path of electron beam

The TV set

The picture tube in a TV set is a *cathode ray tube*. This has an electron gun that produces a narrow beam of electrons. This beam scans the screen exactly in time with the electron beam in the TV camera. The TV set receives electromagnetic waves from the television station and converts them back to a changing electric current. This current is sent to the electron gun in the tube. The intensity of the beam is controlled by this current. A large current produces an intense beam, a small current produces a weak beam.

The screen is coated with thousands of phosphor dots. These dots can convert the energy in the electron beam into light, and the brightness of the light produced will depend on the intensity of the beam. The dots are arranged in 625 lines across the screen, and these are scanned 25 times a second. This is fast enough to give an impression of a continuously moving picture on the screen.

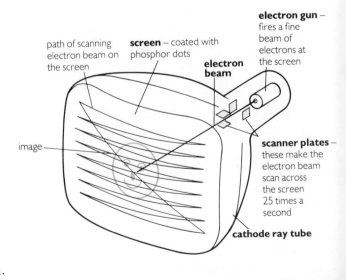

path of scanning electron beam on the screen

screen – coated with phosphor dots

electron beam

electron gun – fires a fine beam of electrons at the screen

image

scanner plates – these make the electron beam scan across the screen 25 times a second

cathode ray tube

Colour television

A colour television system is basically a black and white system with extra signals. These give information about the colour of a scene. It is possible, by using only three colours, red, green and blue, to make any other colour.

The colour TV camera splits light into red, green and blue parts. This is done by using special mirrors that reflect light of a particular colour. The camera has three photosensitive screens, one for each of the colours.

The screens are scanned at exactly the same time. Three signals are produced and these are sent to the colour television.

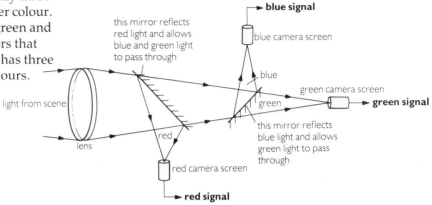

The colour television has three electron guns, one for each colour. These scan the TV screen at exactly the same time. The screen is covered with three types of phosphor dots, arranged in groups of three. One type will glow red, one green and the other blue when the electron beam hits them. A thin metal screen, called a *shadow mask* is placed between the guns and the screen. This mask makes sure that the beam from the red electron gun can only hit the red phosphor dots, the green beam can hit only green dots and the blue beam can hit only the blue

phosphor dots. The colour seen at any one group of dots will depend on which dots are glowing, and how brightly.

The Sony Trinitron screen is slightly different. It is coated with three types of phosphor stripes. A metal grill is used instead of a shadow mask. It is possible to combine the three guns into one with this sytem and the TV can be very small. This screen is used in portable TV sets, but is not quite as successful in larger televisions.

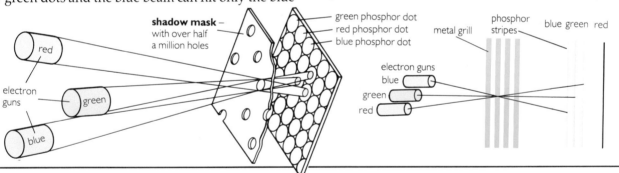

The flat screen television set

Television sets, even portable ones, are fairly large. This is because the tube has to be reasonably long. In flat screen TVs the tube is turned through 90 degrees. The electron beam is then fired parallel to the screen. This allows the set to be very thin, possibly less than an inch thick. Television sets like this would be thin enough to hang on the wall like a picture.

Another flat screen system being developed uses liquid crystal displays – like those in a digital watch.

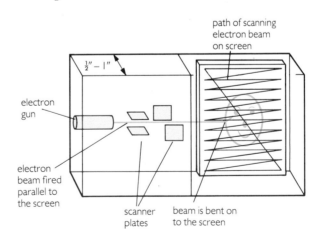

TELEVISION

Closed circuit television

If a television set is directly connected to a camera it forms a *closed circuit system*. The television set will show whatever the camera is pointing at. There is no need to convert the camera's signal into UHF waves. This allows the camera to be used wherever it would be awkward or dangerous to have a human observer.

Closed circuit television can be used to assist in traffic control, for security purposes and in teaching. This system can also be used for displaying information that is frequently updated, such as timetables at airports and railway stations.

It can also be used to produce programmes on a video recorder.

Cable television

In this system a signal is brought into the TV set by means of a cable rather than via an aerial on the roof. The signal either comes directly from a local cable television station or from a large neighbourhood aerial on a nearby high point.

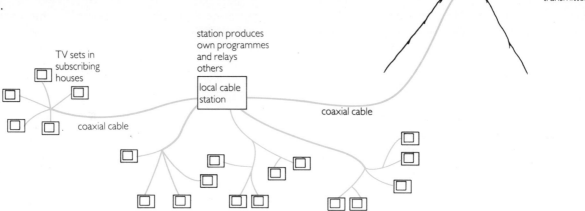

Cable television systems can be thought of as closed circuit television on a much larger scale. The cables usually only extend a short distance from the central point. For this reason they are ideally suited for relaying local television programmes. Cable television suffers less from interference than normal television because the cable can be electrically shielded.

If the cable is *coaxial* and screened with a metal sheath, it can carry vast amounts of information. Cable television systems in the USA can carry over 40 different channels.

When cable television is set up on a national network in the UK it will be possible to have the normal ITV and BBC programmes as well as special programmes. These might include special channels for Wales, Scotland and Northern Ireland; a school channel; a sport channel; an Open University channel; a channel televising parliament and local television stations. Coaxial cable would allow a two-way system and people who wanted to could order goods from shops and even work at home.

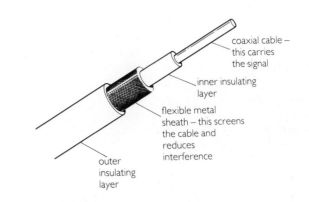

The amount of information that could be sent down a cable would be increased even more if fibre optics were used instead of coaxial cable (see page 235). This would allow two-way linking of TV sets to send messages from one house to another. It would also allow the development of a national personal computer network.

Satellite television

Because UHF television carrying waves can only travel in straight lines, a TV transmitter can only cover an area about 80 km in radius. TV companies have to build large expensive booster transmitter aerials at regular intervals all over the country and this still does not guarantee television for everyone.

One way of getting good TV reception in awkward areas is to use a large receiver aerial and use cable to provide a signal to the area. Another way is to use a communications satellite to relay the TV signal. The transmitter beams the signal up to the satellite which relays the signal down over a very large area. One television satellite could cover most of Europe.

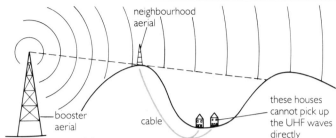

The signal from the satellite is sent via microwaves. A special dish is pointed at the satellite which reflects the microwaves on to the central aerial. Dish aerials can only be aimed at one satellite at a time. New flat aerials have been developed which can be electronically altered to receive information from different satellites.

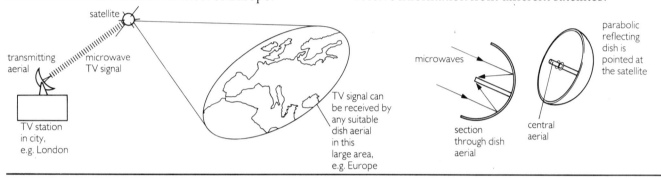

Teletext

Part of the signal from a television station is ignored by a normal television set. These signals are used to provide an information service called *Teletext*. The BBC version is called *Ceefax* and the ITV version, *Oracle*. They can only be picked up by special receivers that are attached to, or built into, ordinary television sets. The system displays many screenfuls of useful information about news, the weather, sport and financial information as well as games, puzzles and timetables.

The information can be rapidly updated, even while the screen is being watched. It is possible to print a teletext page over a normal television programme. This allows the television companies to put sub-titles on the teletext pages for deaf people to use. Teletext pages can also be used to transmit computer programs and data.

Viewdata

This is an information service that is similar to teletext. It sends the information along the telephone system. The television set has to be connected to the telephone system using a decoder called a *modem*.

Viewdata can supply many more screenfuls of information than teletext, but they cannot be updated so easily. The information that is needed is chosen using a push button keypad. If you are viewing a viewdata screen you will also be paying for the use of the telephone. *Prestel* is the commercial version produced by British Telecom.

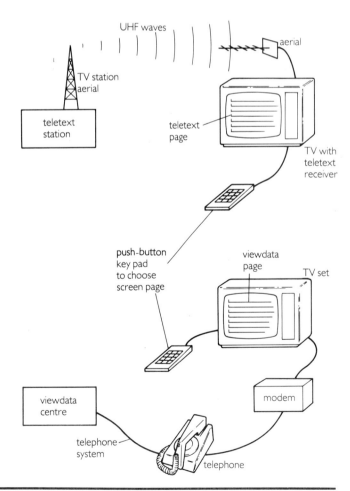

5 TELECOMMUNICATIONS

High frequency waves for radio and television can only travel in straight lines. This means that their range is limited to the horizon. This is no problem for local radio stations, which only serve a small area. However, it does cause problems for national radio and TV stations. One way round the problem is to have very high transmitting aerials, which increase the range. Another way is to have booster aerials (about 80 km apart) linked to the main transmitter by relay stations. The relay stations are linked by microwaves.

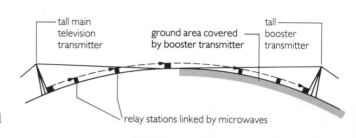

Many telephone links in this country are made along microwaves. Telephone relay stations must be in line of sight of each other because microwaves travel in straight lines. It is obviously not possible to use this method for sending information across large oceans such as the Atlantic. Links between America and Europe have been made via undersea cables and by bouncing short waves off the ionosphere. A modern way is to use communication satellites. These can relay microwaves across the ocean to create television, radio or telephone links.

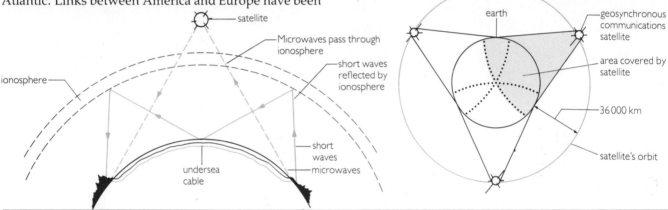

If the satellite is launched into an orbit that is about 36 000 km out, it will take 24 hours to circle the earth. This means it will stay over the same place. This type of satellite is called a *geosynchronous satellite*. These communications satellites can be launched into orbit by a normal rocket such as the European *Ariane rocket* (see page 222). They can also be launched using the American *Space-Shuttle* which is re-usable.

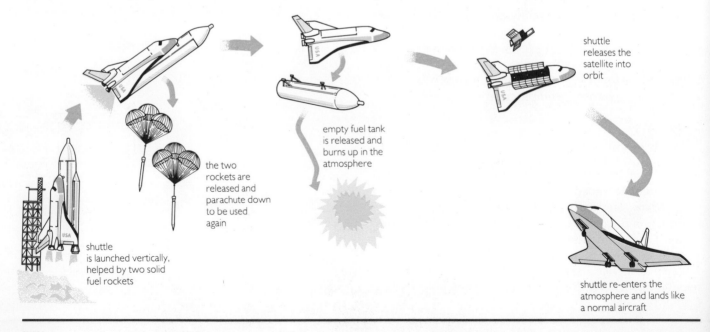

Telex

This is a system that is similar to the telephone system, but uses teleprinters at each end. The operator types in the message which is then coded. Each letter has its own code, made up of dots.

C = • • • •   I = • • ••   O = •• • ••   T = • • • ••
E = • •• • •   L = • • • •   R = • • • •   U = • • •• •
F = • •• • •   N = • •• ••   S = • • • •

The coded message is then fed into the teleprinter where it is converted to electrical pulses. Each dot becomes a pulse of electricity that is fed down the telex cable. The receiving machine types out the message on to paper and rings a bell to attract the operator's attention. These teleprinters are connected through automatic exchanges and each machine has its own telex number. Telex messages are fast (printed at 13 letters per second), cheap and produce a permanent record. They are used a great deal in business.

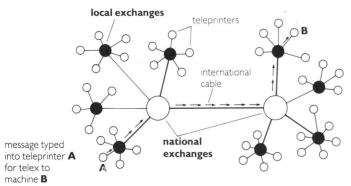

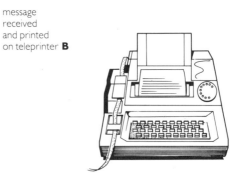

message received and printed on teleprinter **B**

Fax

This is short for *facsimile transmission*, a method of sending pictures around the world rapidly. It is widely used in business and newspapers. A machine scans a document or picture and converts the image into electrical impulses. These are sent through the telephone system or by radio to a receiver. The receiver converts the electrical impulses back to an identical copy of the original picture or document.

The transmitter

The picture to be copied is placed on a revolving drum. A light is focused on the picture and the reflected light goes to a photocell. The white parts of the picture reflect most light and the black parts reflect the least. The photocell converts the light into a changing electric current which depends on the amount of light it receives. This currrent modulates (see page 242) a carrier wave that is sent to the receiver.

The receiver

This decodes the signal and transfers the image on to paper on a revolving drum. This can be done using photographic paper to produce a high quality copy for newspaper use. Special sensitive paper can be used for lower quality work such as sending letters by fax. This is a fast and safe way of sending important business letters.

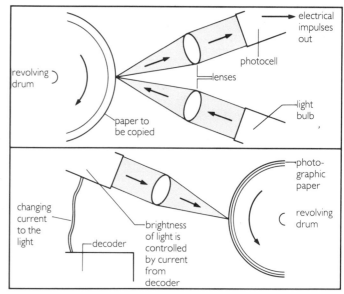

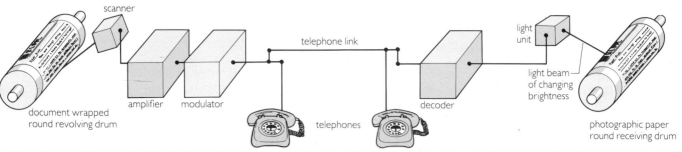

6 RECORDING

A tape recorder is a machine that stores sound on a magnetic tape. Magnetic tape is a plastic tape with a thin coating of metal oxide (or sometimes pure metal) particles attached. Each centimetre of tape will contain millions of these small particles, and each particle acts like a small magnet.

A tape recorder has two reels, the supply reel and the take-up reel. Tape passes from the supply reel to the take-up reel during recording and playback. A recording head and playback head allow sounds to be recorded and replayed. An erase head removes unwanted recordings. In cheaper tape recorders the recording head and playback heads are combined.

Recording

A microphone converts the energy in sound waves into changing electrical currents. These are sent to the recording head of the tape recorder. This is an electromagnet, a small coil wrapped round a circular iron core. The core has a very small slit at the front. When an electric current passes round the coil the strength of the electromagnet will alter. This will make a changing magnetic field across the slit which will magnetise the particles in the tape. The particles will form a pattern which will imitate the strength and frequency of the sound waves that entered the microphone.

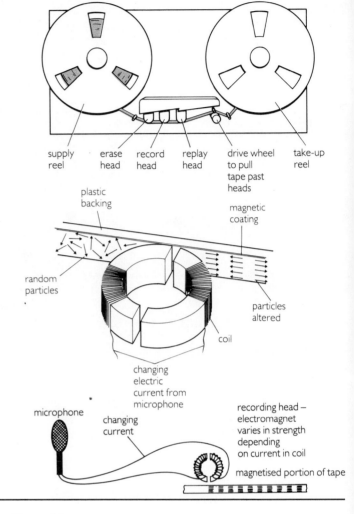

Playback

The recorded tape is pulled at the same speed past a playback head which is similar to a recording head. In many cheaper tape recorders one head is used for recording and playing back. The changing magnetic patterns on the tape set up an identical pattern of electric current in the coil. These changing currents are amplified

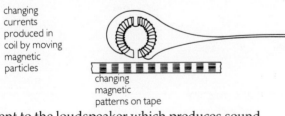

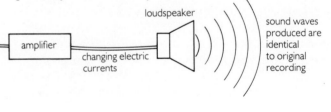

and sent to the loudspeaker which produces sound waves that are almost identical to the original sounds.

The quality of the played back recording depends on three factors:

1　the quality of the recorder, particularly the three heads;
2　the type of magnetic tape used;
3　the speed of the tape during recording and playback.

Type of tape

The cheapest tapes are the *ferric* or *low noise* tapes which have a coating of iron oxide. *Chrome* tapes have a chromium dioxide coating and give a better sound. *Metal* tapes have a coating of pure iron particles and give the best sound. They are expensive and the extra quality is probably not needed by most users.

Speed of tape

The sound quality gets better as the tape speed increases. Recording studios usually record at 76 cm per second. This gives a very high quality but uses a lot of tape. Domestic recorders use speeds of 9·50 or 4·75 cm per second which gives fair quality and is reasonably economical.

Cassette recorders

Until 1963 most tape recorders were of the reel-to-reel type. These give very good quality but can be inconvenient to use. The tape must be carefully threaded round all the heads and must be rewound before it can be removed. In 1963 Phillips introduced the tape cassette and it has since become an internationally accepted standard. The tape is wound on two hubs inside a plastic case. It is threaded round two rollers fitted to the case. There are three large slots at the front of the case which take the erase head, record and playback head and the drive wheel that moves the tape. When the cassette is placed in the recorder the heads are moved through the slots and into contact with the tape.

Cassettes have the following advantages.

1. They do not need to be threaded, so the tape recorder is easier to use.
2. They can be stopped and removed without the need to rewind the tape.
3. The tape is protected in the plastic case – dust and rough handling do not cause damage.
4. They are small and compact and take up less room.
5. They are much cheaper than reel-to-reel tapes.

Cassette tape is very thin and travels at only 4·75 cm a second. At this slow speed the quality of the recorded sound can be badly affected by a background hiss. This can be reduced by using more expensive tapes, or by

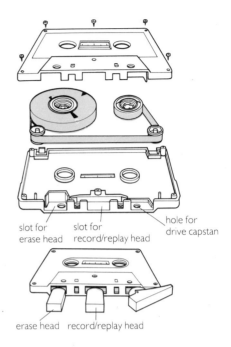

slot for erase head   slot for record/replay head   hole for drive capstan

erase head   record/replay head

using electronic noise reduction. The commonest noise-reducing system is *Dolby*. This detects quiet parts of the recording and artificially boosts them. When the tape is played back, the Dolby system reduces this boosting to its normal quiet level. The hiss on the tape is also reduced and becomes less noticeable.

Stereo sound

At a live performance the music or sound reaching the left ear is slightly different from that reaching the right ear. These differences allow us to detect where each sound comes from. Stereo sound recreates this effect from a recording on tape or record. Two microphones are used during the recording. Each microphone records a slightly different sound which is recorded and played back separately through different channels.

live performance

sound of guitar is loudest in left ear

sound of drums is loudest in right ear

stereo recording

left microphone picks up loud guitar

right microphone picks up loud drums

stereo recording head

left channel   right channel

left channel on tape   right channel on tape

stereo playback

loud guitar soft drum

loud drum soft guitar

stereo playback head

left ear hears guitar loudly

right ear hears drum loudly

Video tape recorders

These are tape recorders that store information about light and sound. They can record directly from a camera or by picking up UHF waves from a television station. A changing electric current is sent to a tilted head. Very wide tape is used and the information is stored on the tape in diagonal tracks. Each track contains enough information to produce half a television screenful of information. The tape head rotates in order to get more information on the magnetic tape.

supply spool   recording/ playback head   take up spool

wide magnetic tape

information about next half screen   information about half screen

RECORDING

A record has a single spiral groove on each side. This groove contains information that can be used to produce music or other sounds.

Recording

In a recording studio the music is first recorded using a professional tape recorder. The tape is then played back through a record cutter that scratches a groove into a plastic *master* disc. This disc is used to make a steel *negative* that is used to press the finished record.

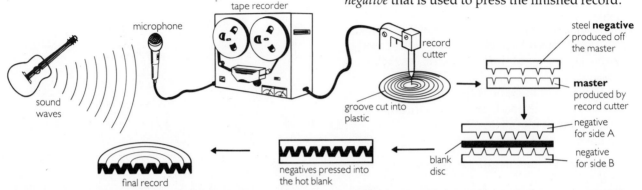

tape recorder

microphone

sound waves

record cutter

groove cut into plastic

steel **negative** produced off the master

master produced by record cutter

negative for side A

negative for side B

blank disc

negatives pressed into the hot blank

final record

Records

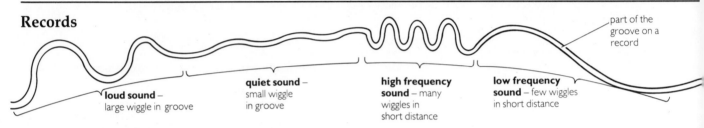

part of the groove on a record

loud sound – large wiggle in groove

quiet sound – small wiggle in groove

high frequency sound – many wiggles in short distance

low frequency sound – few wiggles in short distance

The groove in the record contains information about the sounds recorded. A loud sound has a wide wiggle in the groove, while a quiet sound with a small amplitude has a narrower wiggle. A high frequency noise, such as a whistle, has many wiggles in a short distance. A low frequency noise, like a base drum, has fewer wiggles in a short distance. The shape of the groove directly represents the shape of the sound waves recorded there.

Some records are recorded in mono, and these have simple grooves. The left-hand side of the groove is identical in shape to the right-hand side. Most records are recorded in stereo and the groove must have two separate pieces of information – the sound to come out of the left speaker and the sound to come out of the right speaker. These pieces of information are carried on the left-hand and right-hand sides of the groove, respectively. Stereo records have grooves that have different sides.

section through disc

left hand side – carries information about the sounds to go to the left loudspeaker

right hand side – carries information about the sounds to go to the right loudspeaker

Record player

This reproduces the sound that has been recorded in the groove of the record. A needle, or *stylus*, is placed at the start of the groove and the record revolves. The stylus follows the path of the groove as the record turns. The wiggles in the groove make the stylus vibrate. The vibrations are then converted into weak electric currents which change as the wiggles alter. Most record players use a moving magnet cartridge. The stylus is attached to a weak magnet, suspended between some coils. As the

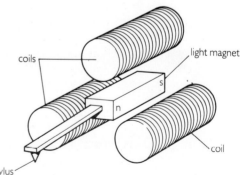

coils

light magnet

s

n

stylus

coil

stylus moves, so does the magnet and an electrical current is produced in the coils. The size of this current depends on how much the stylus moves. The electric current is amplified and sent to the loudspeaker.

Stereo records

The two sides of the groove are different. The left-hand side carries information for the left speaker. The right-hand side carries information for the right loudspeaker. Because the sides are angled at 90° to each other they cause the stylus to move in different directions.

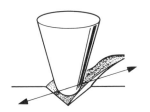

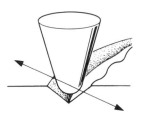

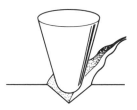

left side – if the left side is wiggly and the right side is smooth the stylus moves in the direction of the arrow. This information goes to the left speaker only.

right side – if the right side is wiggly and the left side is smooth the stylus moves in the direction of the arrow. Information goes to the right speaker only.

both sides – in practice, both sides are wiggly. In stereo records they are also different in a complex way and different information goes to each speaker.

Digital recording

Another method of recording sound is to measure the frequency and amplitude of the sound wave at fixed small intervals of time. These are then coded as a number which can be stored or transmitted electronically. The sampling of the sound has to be done so often that it cannot be used for normal tape recorders or records. It is possible though to design special tape recorders or record players which use this method.

The digital code has to be decoded before it is sent to the loudspeakers. The great advantage of digital recording is that is is possible to produce an extremely high quality recording with little if any interference. Digital records will not wear out, even after years of use. Video discs are digital records.

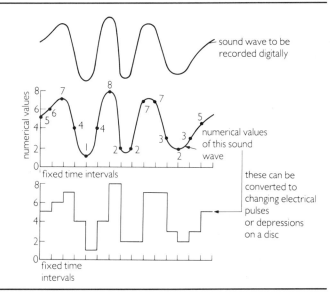

sound wave to be recorded digitally

numerical values of this sound wave

these can be converted to changing electrical pulses or depressions on a disc

Video discs

A video disc stores information about sound and pictures. The only way to store this information accurately on a disc is to use a digital method. The disc is made of a plastic that is coated with a highly reflective metal surface. The information is recorded in the form of a spiral track like an ordinary disc. Instead of a groove there is a series of depressions of different lengths spaced along the track. The spacing and lengths of the depressions contain digital information about the sound and colours of the picture. The record turns 25 times a second so a stylus cannot be used. A small helium-neon laser (see page 235) shines a small, powerful spot of light on to the disc. The reflection will change, depending on the pattern of depressions. The reflection is picked up by a detector and the information decoded into a changing electric current which is sent to the TV screen. Each revolution of the disc provides one complete screenful of information. Video discs are the same size as LP records. The same system is used to play small, sound only, digital discs.

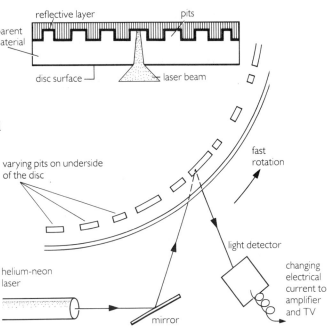

reflective layer

pits

transparent disc material

disc surface

laser beam

varying pits on underside of the disc

fast rotation

light detector

changing electrical current to amplifier and TV

helium-neon laser

mirror

7 COMPUTERS

These are machines that can do arithmetic very quickly. However, the majority of computers are used to sort, file and analyse information rapidly. This is called *data processing*. Some computers are used to control scientific and industrial machines. Others are used to play games. There are three main types of computers.

Mainframe computers

These take up a large amount of space because they need constant temperature and humidity in order to work. They are the most powerful computers because they can store and analyse vast amounts of information very quickly. A modern mainframe computer can carry out billions of instructions every second. They work so fast they appear to do more than one job at the same time. They are extremely expensive and are used by governments, large businesses and universities.

Minicomputers

These are smaller than mainframe computers. They are usually used to do one job. They cannot store as much information as a mainframe and they work more slowly. They are used by government departments, small businesses and in education.

Microcomputers

These are the smallest computers. They are found in small businesses, schools and homes. They are not as powerful as the other types, but they are very cheap and versatile. They can be used to control machines and may be connected to television sets.

How computers work

A computer does its work by sending pulses of electricity to its various parts. These pulses are produced and controlled by electronic components. Early computers, in the 1940s, used valves but these caused overheating

A computer converts all information into a numerical code. There are only two signals in the code, a pulse of electricity or no pulse of electricity. This code is called a *binary system*. The pulses travel around the circuits on the

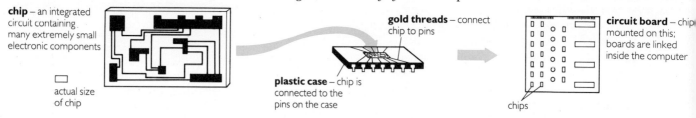

chip – an integrated circuit containing many extremely small electronic components

actual size of chip

gold threads – connect chip to pins

plastic case – chip is connected to the pins on the case

circuit board – chips mounted on this; boards are linked inside the computer

chips

problems. These were replaced in the 1950s by computers which used transistors. More recently, computers use *integrated circuits* or *chips*. An integrated circuit is a tiny chip of silicon which has thousands of tiny transistors engraved on it.

chips, and where the pulses go is controlled by transistor switches called *gates*. There are many different forms of gate which send out pulses under different circumstances.

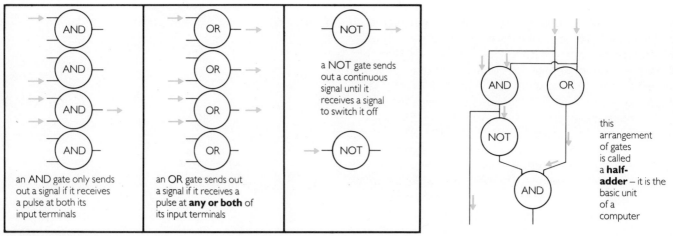

an AND gate only sends out a signal if it receives a pulse at both its input terminals

an OR gate sends out a signal if it receives a pulse at **any or both** of its input terminals

a NOT gate sends out a continuous signal until it receives a signal to switch it off

this arrangement of gates is called a **half-adder** – it is the basic unit of a computer

These different types of gates are arranged in circuits and produce patterns of signals. These patterns can be used to add, subtract, multiply, divide, compare and store information and do all the other work of the computer.

Outline of a computer system

Information that is put into the computer is called *input*. Information that comes out of the computer is called *output*. There are many different ways of inputting and outputting information.

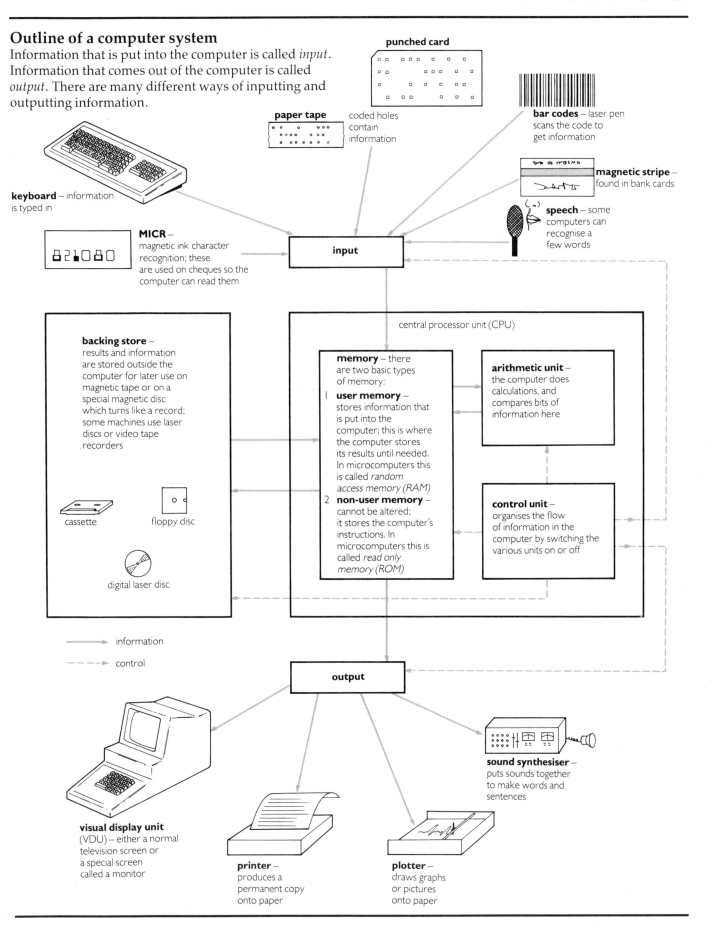

punched card

coded holes contain information

paper tape

bar codes – laser pen scans the code to get information

magnetic stripe – found in bank cards

keyboard – information is typed in

speech – some computers can recognise a few words

MICR – magnetic ink character recognition; these are used on cheques so the computer can read them

input

central processor unit (CPU)

backing store – results and information are stored outside the computer for later use on magnetic tape or on a special magnetic disc which turns like a record; some machines use laser discs or video tape recorders

memory – there are two basic types of memory:

1 **user memory** – stores information that is put into the computer; this is where the computer stores its results until needed. In microcomputers this is called *random access memory (RAM)*

2 **non-user memory** – cannot be altered; it stores the computer's instructions. In microcomputers this is called *read only memory (ROM)*

arithmetic unit – the computer does calculations, and compares bits of information here

control unit – organises the flow of information in the computer by switching the various units on or off

cassette

floppy disc

digital laser disc

→ information

- - → control

output

visual display unit (VDU) – either a normal television screen or a special screen called a monitor

printer – produces a permanent copy onto paper

plotter – draws graphs or pictures onto paper

sound synthesiser – puts sounds together to make words and sentences

COMPUTERS

Databanks

When a computer is switched off it loses all the information stored in its random access memory (RAM). It would be tedious to have to input all this information by hand next time the computer was switched on. To get round this problem the computer uses an external memory or *backing store*. Different computers use different types of backing store.

Magnetic tape

Mainframe computers use large, fast reel-to-reel tape recorders. These move rapidly to record or playback. Small microcomputers often use an ordinary cassette recorder to store information, or *data*, on tape. In both systems the data is stored in the form of pulses.

Magnetic discs

These are a better method of storing data. The disc is usually made of plastic coated with a magnetic surface. The disc rotates quickly and a record or playback head floats across the disc. Large computers use hard discs stacked one on top of the other. Small microcomputers use smaller ones called *floppy discs*.

Laser discs

These are digitally recorded and very similar to video discs (see page 253). They can store vast amounts of information – one 30 cm disc could store two complete Encyclopaedia Britannica (about 80 million words).

Punched card and tape

The information is stored as a pattern of holes in the paper. This method is not used very often these days and it is being phased out.

If a computer has a very large backing store full of data it is called a *databank*. A large databank can be stored on magnetic discs or laser discs. These take up a very small amount of space. The contents of a large library could be put on to a computer databank and would fit into a small suitcase. If a piece of information is in the databank the computer can search for it and find it in seconds. The databank can be many kilometres away from the computer if necessary.

Large databanks are very useful in scientific and medical research. However, it is possible to misuse the information held in databanks, especially those that contain personal information. The use of databanks is often controlled by law.

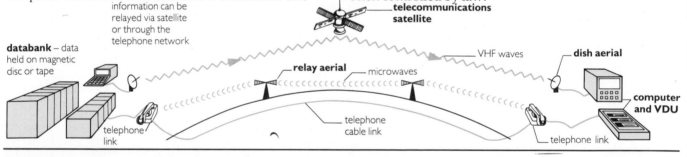

information can be relayed via satellite or through the telephone network

telecommunications satellite

databank – data held on magnetic disc or tape

relay aerial   microwaves   VHF waves

dish aerial

computer and VDU

telephone link

telephone cable link

telephone link

Microprocessors

A microprocessor is an integrated circuit that contains all the parts of a computer. Because they are so small they can be put into many household items. The computer on a microprocessor usually does just one job. Microprocessors are becoming much cheaper and far more commonplace.

sewing machine – some use micros for embroidery stitching

modern washing machine – uses a micro to select the washing programme

cameras – some expensive makes use a microprocessor to select shutter speeds

toys – this lorry has a microprocessor inside it and can be programmed to go on a set journey

video games

radios – some use micros to select radio stations

digital watches – some use micros for stop watches

Robots

A robot is a machine that tries to copy one or more human function. Most present day robots are only capable of doing one job, but some are *programmable* and can be 'taught' to do another job.

Robots controlled by microprocessors or by micro-computers can work in areas that are dangerous or harmful to human workers. For example they can work in the high-level radiation areas of nuclear power stations and in the high-temperature areas near furnaces. Robots are also used to do boring repetitive jobs such as welding car bodies on assembly lines.

A worker must programme these robots before they can start. The worker will guide the robot arm through a complete job, and the microprocessor will measure these movements and store them in its memory. When the programme is operating, the microprocessor will enable the arm to repeat the movements exactly. It has to be re-programmed if the job changes.

Managers consider the robot to be useful because it does not need to rest, can work unsocial hours, does not get bored and is fairly cheap. However, they are not as versatile as human workers and they cannot respond

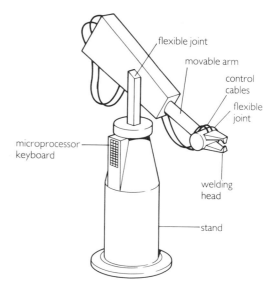

intelligently to unexpected events. Some people think that robots take jobs away from people and are not very reliable. Others think they are a good idea because they do boring jobs and allow us to have more leisure. There is probably an element of truth in both views.

Computers in the home

Computers are becoming much cheaper, much smaller and much more powerful. Eventually they will be found in most homes, just like televisions are today.

Home computers can be used to play games, store information, control the central heating and help to plan your finances. Computers can be linked to databanks and other computers to form a *network*. If this was done on a large scale, possibly through the national telecommunications network, many more possibilities would be opened up.

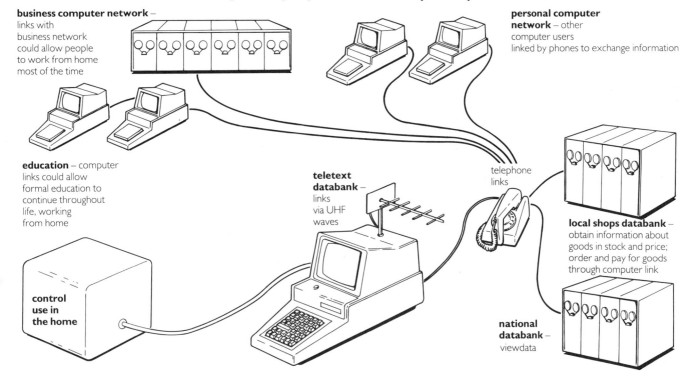

business computer network – links with business network could allow people to work from home most of the time

personal computer network – other computer users linked by phones to exchange information

education – computer links could allow formal education to continue throughout life, working from home

teletext databank – links via UHF waves

telephone links

local shops databank – obtain information about goods in stock and price; order and pay for goods through computer link

control use in the home

national databank – viewdata

INDEX

INDEX

INDEX

ACKNOWLEDGEMENTS

The publishers are grateful to the following sources for permission to reproduce photographs in this book:

A-Z Collection, page 34
Aerofilms Ltd, pages 33, 41, 49, 184
Allsport Photographic/Carl Lewis, page 53
Aqualac Spring Waters, page 43
Architects Journal/Bill Toomey, pages 32, 153
Ardea, page 114
Ashwood/FT/Camera Press, page 180
Billedsentralen/Aage Starløkken, page 148
M. Brigaud/Sodel - EDF, pages 189, 203
The British Tourist Authority, pages 32, 43, 159
Camera Press, pages 148, 164, 223
Central Electricity Generating Board, pages 189, 193, 210
Stefan Chabluk from Argentum transparency, cover
J. Crichton/Camera Press, page 164
Daily Telegraph/Ian Vaughan, page 210
Colin Davey/Camera Press, page 143
G. Ehrmann/Sodel - EDF, page 198
Electricity Council, pages 25, 193, 209
David English, pages 109, 167
Epoque Ltd, page 136
Forestry Commission, page 49
Fraser - Peterhead, page 229
Harry Smith Horticultural Photographic Collection, page 34, 114
Health Education Council, page 74
Heather Angel, page 34
High Commission for New Zealand, page 201
Honeysett, page 133
Hutchinson & Co. Ltd/W. Heath Robinson/Mary Evans Picture Library, page 217
Institute of Dermatology, University of London, page 90
J. Allen Cash Ltd, page 47
Jet Joint Undertaking, page 197
P. R. Lange, page 205

Lucas Chloride, page 211
Metropolitan Police page 147
Mustograph Agency/Barnaby's, pages 49, 183
NASA/Camera Press, pages 6, 7
NASA/Science Photo Library, pages 6, 199
National Archive and Records Services, page 46
National Coal Board, pages 30, 189
National Meteorological Office, pages 20, 23
National Motor Museum, page 185
Natural History Photographic Agency, page 164
M. Nimmo, page 34
Olympus, page 233
Popperfoto, pages 49, 85
RMC Group plc, page 33
J. Sansom, pages 134, 149, 185
Science Photo Library, pages 197, 200, 212
Bill Scott, pages 49, 184
Serda/Sodel - EDF, page 203
Shell, pages 25, 162
Stilton Cheese Association, page 129
St. Mary's Hospital Medical School, page 90
TASS/Camera Press, page 3
Topham, page 47
United Kingdom Atomic Energy Authority, pages 157, 196
University of Dundee, Electronics Laboratory, page 23
C. James Webb, pages 78, 90, 106, 118, 119, 128, 157
Wellcome, pages 61, 85, 117
Percy G. C. Wilding/Barnaby's, page 189
Thomas A. Wilkie, page 164
T. H. Williams/Barnaby's, page 185
Valerie Wilmer/Format, page 237
Fergus Wilson, page 114

The publishers have made every effort to trace copyright holders, but if they have inadvertently overlooked any they will be pleased to make the necessary arrangements at the first opportunity